THE WAKE OF IMAGINATION

By the same author

Poétique du Possible (Editions Beauchesne, Paris, 1984)
Modern Movements in European Philosophy (Manchester University Press, 1986)
Dialogues with Contemporary Continental Thinkers (Manchester University Press, 1984)
Transitions: Narratives in Modern Irish Culture (Wolfhound/ Manchester University Press, 1987)
Myth and Motherland (Field Day, Derry, 1985)
Imagining (Hutchinson, 1988)
Poetics of Imagining (Routledge, 1991)

As editor

The Irish Mind: Exploring Intellectual Traditions (Wolfhound/ Humanities Press, 1984)
Heidegger et la Question de Dieu (Grasset, Paris, 1982)
The Crane Bag Book of Irish Studies I (Blackwater Press, Dublin, 1982)
The Crane Bag Book of Irish Studies II (Wolfhound Press, Dublin, 1987)

THE WAKE OF IMAGINATION

Toward a postmodern culture

RICHARD KEARNEY

London

First published by Century Hutchinson Ltd, 1988
Published in 1994
by Routledge
11 New Fetter Lane, London EC4P 4EE

© 1988 Richard Kearney

Printed and bound in Great Britain by
Redwood Books Ltd, Trowbridge, Wiltshire

British Library Cataloguing in Publication Data

A catalogue record for this book is available from the British Library

ISBN 0–415–11950–2

There expand by now 1001 stories, all told, of the same . . .
But the world, mind, is, was, and will be writing its own
wrunes for ever, man, on all matters that fall under the ban of
our infrarational senses.

(James Joyce, *Finnegans Wake*)

. . . I am the necessary angel of earth,
Since, in my sight, you see the world again.
(Wallace Stevens – on imagination)

For Sarah, my daughter

Contents

Acknowledgements

I wish to thank all those who helped me imagine this text, and particularly the questioning students – undergraduate, post-graduate and extra-mural – at University College Dublin and Boston College.

INTRODUCTION

Imagination Now

1 The civilization of the image

Everywhere we turn today we are surrounded by images. From the home TV or video to the billboard advertisements, election-eering posters and neon signs which festoon the public street or motorway, our Western culture is becoming increasingly a Civilization of the Image.

Even those areas of experience that some might like to think of as still 'unspoilt' are shot through with images. It is virtually impossible today to contemplate a so-called natural setting, without some consumerist media image lurking in the back of one's mind: a beach without an Ambre Solaire body, a meadow without a Cadbury's Flake, a mountain stream without a Marlboro cigarette, a wild seascape without a hairspray or tourism commercial. Our inner unconscious has not been spared either. The psychic world is as colonized as the physical world by the whole image industry. Even the private world of sexual desire has been informed by the streamlined scenarios of TV soap operas like *Dallas* and *Dynasty*: multi-million dollar series which have been broadcast throughout the globe. Nor is there much consolation to be gained from recent statistics which show that since the arrival of multi-channel press-button TV in the US, less than 50 per cent of American children under the age of 15 have ever watched a single programme from start to finish. Such recent trends have prompted some commentators to

suggest that the transition from what McLuhan called the Guten-
berg Galaxy of the print media to the Global Village of telecom-
munications has been so radical as to jeopardize the traditional
equation between education and literacy. The culture of the
Book is being replaced, it would seem, by a culture of the Image.
Some even claim we are entering an era when reading may
become an anachronism, little more than a nostalgic luxury.

The contemporary eye is no longer innocent. What we see is
almost invariably informed by prefabricated images. There is, of
course, a fundamental difference between the image of today
and of former times: now the image *precedes* the reality it is
supposed to represent. Or to put it in another way, reality has
become a pale reflection of the image. This reversal is evident
at a number of levels. In politics, we find presidents and prime
ministers being elected because of the media image they
represent. In the media world, current affairs are brought to us
more and more in the form of sensationalized visual packages or
'pseudo-events' – to such an extent, indeed, that the phenomenon of news making is gradually being substituted for news
reporting. And, at the economic level, it is now a well documented fact that our consumerist society, particularly in its
present post-industrial phase, can sustain material production
only by means of the 'hidden persuaders' of new brand-images
and ever more elaborate advertising campaigns. Even at the
everyday social level, we notice the image taking pride of place
over the real, as in Boorstin's humorous anecdote about the
contemporary suburban housewife who responds to a neigh-
bour's compliment to her child with the boast: 'Yes, he is lovely,
but you should see the photograph.'

Finally, at the level of artistic culture there is a growing
awareness that images have now displaced the 'original' realities
they were traditionally meant to reflect. The real and the
imaginary have become almost impossible to distinguish. This
has given rise to a deep crisis in the contemporary arts. We find
the experimental writings of Borges, Pynchon, Burroughs and
Beckett putting themselves in question, exploring the breakdown of the conventional relationship between fiction and fact.
Similarly, we have films by Godard, Wenders, Lynch and the later

Fellini exposing the complicity between media-manufactured illusions and the so-called 'reality' of our quotidian experience. While in the realm of the plastic arts, the multi-media works of Warhol, Paik or Vautier dramatically erode the difference between art and artifice. Art becomes anti-art. The gap between High Culture and Popular Culture narrows to nothing. The sacrosanct idea of the artistic image as an authentic original (e.g. the Venus de Milo in the Louvre) is effectively debunked by the mass-media image as a technological reproduction. And so we observe that 'art images' increasingly serve as parodies of 'commercial images' (e.g. Warhol's seriographs of Coca-Cola bottles and of Hollywood stars like Liz Taylor or Marilyn Monroe); while 'commercial images' serve as parodies of 'art images' (e.g. perfume ads featuring the Mona Lisa or bath salt ads starring Botticelli's Venus Rising from the Waves).

One of the greatest paradoxes of contemporary culture is that at a time when the image reigns supreme the very notion of a creative human imagination seems under mounting threat. We no longer appear to know who exactly produces or controls the images which condition our consciousness. We are at an impasse where the very rapport between *imagination* and *reality* seems not only inverted but subverted altogether. We cannot be sure which is which. And this very undecidability lends weight to the deepening suspicion that we may well be assisting at a wake of imagination.

The imminent demise of imagination is clearly a postmodern obsession. Postmodernism undermines the modernist belief in the image as an *authentic* expression. The typically postmodern image is one which displays its own artificiality, its own pseudo-status, its own representational depthlessness. Hence the significance of Andy Warhol's brazen boast that if Picasso, the modernist master *par excellence*, could produce four thousand works in a lifetime, he could produce as many in a day. Warhol, the Pope of pop art, rejects the accredited idea of the art work as an original creation in a unique time and space. He proclaims the postmodern message that the image has now become a mechanically reproducible commodity – part of the new 'total communications package' where globally conceived and transmissable styles can be picked up in every place at the same moment and beamed back and forth from continent to continent.[1]*

Postmodern artists are acutely aware of the revolutionary mutations in consciousness brought about by the Graphic Revolution: the discoveries of dry-plate photography, electronic printing, the roll film, the telephone and the phonograph in the second half of the nineteenth century; the first public transmission of both radio voices and motion picture images around 1900; and the rapid expansion of television in America and Western Europe since the forties – a cultural phenomenon so pervasive that by the time multi-channel satellite TV had come into usage in the eighties one finds a situation where almost half a billion people from all over the globe could tune into the 1986 World Cup – including the most isolated Indians from the jungles of Brazil.

The advent of the technological image signalled a momentous shift from an age of production to one of reproduction. In postmodern culture, the relations of industrial production have been subordinated to those of post-industrial communications. Equipped with video recorders, computer screens and printouts, the postmodern mind is becoming daily more oblivious to what Benjamin referred to as the art work's unique and irreplaceable 'aura'. The individual subject is no longer considered the maker or communicator of his own images. There is a growing conviction that the images we possess are reproduced copies of images already there before us. The image which *is* has *already been*. Like every commodity of our mass communications society, the postmodern image has itself become an interchangeable consumer item, a pseudo-imitation which playfully celebrates its pseudonymity, parades its own superficiality and derivitiveness.

In many postmodern works the very distinction between artistic-image and commodity-image has virtually faded. The practice of parody and pastiche, while it frequently intends to subvert the *imaginaire* of contemporary 'late capitalist' society, often ends up being co-opted or assimilated. Even the most

* Superior figures refer to the Notes section beginning on p. 399.

dissident imaginations appear to be swallowed into the 'ideology of the simulacrum' which prevails in our consumer age. Indeed the suspension of subjective inwardness, referential depth, historical time and coherent human expression – four losses listed by Frederic Jameson as symptomatic of postmodernism – is now becoming *de rigeuer* in certain circles.[2] The postmodern artist does not claim to express anything because he does not claim to have anything to express. 'When I look into a mirror', says Warhol of his role as artist, 'I see nothing. People call me a mirror, and if a mirror looks into a mirror what does it see?'[3]

This metaphor of an incessant play between inter-reflecting mirrors is paradigmatic of postmodern culture. And the effects of its logic are by no means confined to the experimental tableau or text. They reverberate throughout the strata of both 'high art' and popular culture generally. Most postmodernist trends would even challenge the validity of this very standard modernist distinction. One commentator offers this representative description:

random music, concrete poetry, computer verse, electronic dance, guerrilla theatre, deliquescent sculpture, autodestructive media, pack-aged nature, psychedelic spectacles, blank canvases, and plain happen-ings; Pop, Op, Funk, Concept, Topographic, and Environmental art proliferate, interpenetrate, even as new kinds of anti-art generate newer styles.[4]

These movements share a basic impulse to *demystify* the preten-sions of high modernism, with its established notions of control-ling author, narrative order and metaphysical profundity. They explode the sacramental status of the humanist imagination and jubilantly proclaim the 'end of art'. The postmodernist dances on the grave of modern idealism. He is as far removed from the Sartrean cult of the self-creating consciousness (*pour soi*) as from the romantic cult of the transcendental *Einbildungskraft*. Post-modern culture jibes at all talk of original creations. It exclaims the omnipresence of self-destructing images which simulate each other in a limitless interplay of mirrors.

Mimesis has returned, it seems; but with a vengeance. No more is it a question of images representing some transcendent reality, as tradition had it. The very notion of such a reality is now unmasked as an illusionist effect. The wheel has turned full circle. But the mirror of the postmodern paradigm reflects neither the outer world of nature nor the inner world of subjectivity; it reflects only itself – a mirror within a mirror within a mirror . . . . Like Lady V's festishized lovemaking by looking glass in Pynchon's novel; like the Beckettian narrator being swallowed up by his endlessly self-multiplying narrators; like Godard's camera filming a camera filming a camera; or like Fellini's TV Dance Spectacular in *Ginger and Fred* doubly reproduced on the mirror-floor of the recording studio and on millions of television screens, the postmodern image is mimesis without origin or end.

2 Changing faces

The story of imagination needs to be told. Like all species under threat of extinction, the imagination requires to be recorded in terms of its genealogy: its conceptual genesis and mutations. Many contemporary commentators are, as noted, speaking of the demise of imagination as we have known it. Some bemoan this cultural phenomenon. Others take a certain delight in its apocalyptic implications. While others again consider it an ineluctable phase of the historical dialectic. But however varied such responses may be, there is a growing belief in certain circles that the very notion of imaginative creativity may soon be a thing of the past. We appear to have entered a postmodern civilization where the image has become less and less the expression of an individual subject and more and more the commodity of an anonymous consumerist technology. Or so a pervasive current of opinion has it. Our task in this work is to assess the reasons for such a persuasion, to trace the historical genesis of the Western concepts of imagination, and to ask, finally, if it is possible for imagination to secure a new lease of life in our rapidly expanding postmodern culture.

The paradigm shifts in the Western understanding of the image are graphically exemplified in the mutations which have

'Christ the Pantocrator'.

Van Gogh, self-portrait

Poster by Martin Sharp

Andy Warhol, Marilyn Monroe seriograph

occurred in the representation of the human face. Three examples from the history of painting will illustrate this – a medieval Icon of Christ as an instance of the premodern imagination; a Van Gogh self-portrait as an instance of the modern; and Martin Sharp's Pop Poster of the Van Gogh portrait as an instance of the postmodern.

The medieval icon *Christ the Pantocrator* is 'anonymous'. The icon-maker who painted it was not encouraged to invest his personality in it. And, by extension, the beholder was not inclined to ask 'who painted it?' or to exclaim 'what superb artistry! what beautiful facial features! what originality of expression and technique!' On the contrary, this typical Christian icon effaces the individual character of the artist (or group of artist-monks) in order to underscore the primacy of divine authority, to profile the sacramental nature of the face depicted – that of the Son of God. This explains, moreover, why such icons were generally *unsigned*, at most being indirectly attributed to one of the great schools of Byzantine or medieval iconography. And it also accounts for the fact that strict rules and formulae were prescribed for the composition of such icons: the aim being to prevent interferences from the human personality of the icon-ographer out of deference to the infinite nature of the divine Creator Himself. Hence the use of standardized goldleaf backgrounds and stylized features to focus the attention of the faithful on the sacred mystery represented rather than on the representation itself. Indeed the common practice of portraying the eyes of Christ as expressionless was an apt symbol of the icon's primary function: to invite the onlooker to travel through the vacant regard of the image towards the suprasensible transcendence of God rather than linger at the surface level of purely human expressions and sensations (e.g. the beguiling, luminous eyes of a mortal face). In other words, the *theocentric* quality of the icon was evident in the fact that every effort was made to eschew worshipping the image itself so as to worship God *through* the image.[5] The makers and beholders of icons were not to follow their own fancies but to harness their imaginations to the sacred visual types laid down by age-old tradition. By requiring the iconographer to observe the ancient Byzantine formulae of representation, the Church authorities effectively discouraged experimentation with more expressive, realist or life-like modes of painting.

The modern practice of self-portraiture, by contrast, lays primary stress on the image as a medium of *human* expression. In this it exemplifies the *anthropocentric* trend of modernity. Van Gogh's expressionist auto-portraits are powerful instances of this aesthetic of subjectivity. There is a basic humanism evident in these paintings; and not only in the vibrant originality of the artist's style and colours, but also in his undaunted will to self-expression – even when there is nothing left to express but his own despair. Here Christ as divine martyr has been replaced by the artist as human martyr. The sacramental prayer has turned into an existential cry. What is most striking about the modern genre of portraiture – from Velasquez' *Las Meninas* and Rembrandt's sombre self-explorations to Van Gogh's self-portraits before his suicide – is a common resolve to dispense with the traditional modes of painting *resemblance* (i.e. as *mimesis* of nature or God) and to treat it instead as an autonomous *expression* of man.

The great paintings of the Italian Renaissance were already pointing in this humanist direction. While such a movement was largely sponsored, at the outset at any rate, by ecclesiastical and royal patronage, its increasing tendency to subvert traditional pieties frequently earned it official censure. Thus, for example, Caravaggio's painting of *St Matthew* as an all too human mortal with wrinkles and rags, caused a scandal when first displayed. And, earlier still, El Greco's innovative version of St Maurice sent King Philip into a fit of rage and won this pointed rebuke from the Inquisitor of Toledo: 'I like neither the angels you paint nor the saints. Instead of making people pray, they make them admire. Beauty inserts itself as an obstacle between our souls and God.' El Greco's defiance of the reproaches made to him by both Church and State prompted Nikos Kazantzakis, one of the most impassioned advocates of the humanist aesthetic in our own century, to write this tribute in his *Report to Greco*:

It was a great moment. A pure righteous conscience stood on one tray of the balance, an empire on the other, and it was you, man's conscience, that tipped the scales. This conscience will be able to stand before the Lord at the Last Judgement and not be judged. It will judge, because human dignity, purity and valour fill even God with terror . . . Art is not submission and rules, but a demon which smashes the moulds. . . . Greco's inner-archangel's breast had thrust him on savage freedom's single hope, this world's most excellent garret . . .[6]

It is not such a giant step from El Greco's mutiny in the sixteenth century to Van Gogh's insanity in the early twentieth. The tormented modern artist stands as an indictment of established society. 'Through the mediation of madness', as Michel Foucault declared in *Madness and Civilization*, 'it is the world that becomes culpable in relation to the work of art.' Convict in his prison or patient in his asylum, the modern artist stares out from his own canvas and back at himself, head shaven, features a blaze of chaotic colours, eyes – so unlike those calm bottomless pools of the medieval Icon of Christ – a turmoil of inconsolable anguish with nothing left to express but itself.

Thirdly, as an example of postmodern visual representation, we take Martin Sharp's Pop Poster of Van Gogh. Here the *theocentric* paradigm of iconography and the *anthropocentric* paradigm of self-portraiture are replaced by the *ex-centric* paradigm of parody. The term 'ex-centricity' is employed here in the sense of Jacques Lacan and his disciples when they speak of the unconscious subject as one that is ex-centric to itself, that does not function as a controlling origin of self-expression. This heterogeneous nature of the subject in postmodern theory and art marks a radical rupture with the humanist notion of autonomous selfhood. Sharp, a former illustrator of the popular magazine *Oz*, and a prominent representative of the Underground Art movement, exhibits a typically postmodern eclecticism in his recent collages called 'artoons'. These are made up of juxtaposed images clipped from reproductions of celebrated museum paintings.[7] In his pop poster of Van Gogh, the contained madness of the original self-portrait has exploded in a psychedelic orgy of multiple reproductions, reversed, superimposed and distorted. From one of the many cut-out reproductions (which features Van Gogh painting his own portrait) extends a yellow comic-strip balloon with these words: 'I have a terrible lucidity at moments, when nature is so glorious in those days I am hardly conscious of myself and the picture comes to me like a dream.' Hagiographic devotion or hallucinogenic fun? Subversion of consumer culture by invoking the great modern martyr Van Gogh? Or burlesque of the whole aesthetic of modern humanism by assimilating Van Gogh to the commodity images of Pop Art? Sharp's work is charged with such ambiguities. Moreover, the repulsive photo-realist eye, which breaks through the centre of the poster like a dehiscent flower disfiguring the axial auto-portrait of Van Gogh, is itself symptomatic of the *undecidable* status of the postmodern image. Does this eye refer to the *original* eye of Van Gogh himself, to that inner eye of his mind which his various self-portraits sought to express? Or does it represent rather a mere 'trick' of hyperrealist technique, betraying the fact that there is nothing *behind* the garish mirror-play of visual 'quotations' featured in the poster?

Our inability to definitively place Sharp's poster parody on the side of 'art' or 'pseudo-art' is itself an indication of its postmodern character. And if the Pop Poster somewhat resembles the medieval Icon as a mode of impersonal mimetism and formalism, it differs fundamentally in that it does not seek to direct the onlooker's attention toward some transcendent being but mischievously exults in its role as a playful item of popular consumption.

As a final amplification of the paradigm shifts in Western concepts of imaging, one might rehearse some of the decisive changes which have occurred in the conception of the *artist*. The premodern cultures of Jerusalem and Athens tended to construe the artist primarily as a *craftsman* who, at best, models his activity on the 'original' activity of a Divine Creator – the biblical *Yotser* or the Platonic *demiourgos*. This theocentric view of the craftsman also prevailed in the medieval period when the work of the icon-maker, painter, scribe or Cathedral designer was generally evaluated in terms of its capacity to obediently serve and imitate the transcendent plan for Creation.

The modern movements of Renaissance, Romantic and Existentialist humanism replaced this theocentric paradigm of the mimetic craftsman with the anthropocentric paradigm of the original *inventor*. Whether drawing from the scientific idiom of experimenter, the colonial idiom of explorer or the technological idiom of industrial engineer, the modern aesthetic promotes the idea of the artist as one who not only emulates but actually replaces God. Thus we find that the legendary sinners of traditional morality – Prometheus, Adam, Lucifer – become the heroes of modern culture. Blake, for example, speaks of Milton writing in fetters when he speaks of God the Father and at liberty when he speaks of Satan. Goethe celebrates Faust's diabolic ambition. Shelley and Melville champion the rebelliousness of Prometheus. Mozart and Kierkegaard are fascinated, despite themselves, by the insatiable energies of Don Juan. And Nietzsche, de Sade, Céline, Lautréamont, Sartre and Genet cultivate the existential virtues of deviants and delinquents. In short, the modern portrait of the artist, as a young person or old, is habitually that of a proud demonic overreacher who negates the given world and resolves to produce a new one out of his or her own imagination.

But this anthropocentric paradigm is itself overturned in postmodern culture. Now the model of the productive inventor is replaced by that of the *bricoleur*: someone who plays around with fragments of meaning which he himself has not created. Here the dominant analogies are frequently borrowed from the post-industrial technology of the computer and communications industry. The artist becomes a 'player' in a game of signs, an 'operator' in an electronic media network. He experiences himself afloat in an anonymous interplay of images which he can, at best, parody, simulate or reproduce. Like a character in a Pynchon novel or Wenders film, the postmodern artist wanders about in a labyrinth of commodified light and noise, endeavouring to piece together bits of dispersed narrative.

The postmodern threat to abolish the humanist imagination coincides with growing talk of the 'demise of man' as a subject of identity. Disseminated into the absolute immanence of sign-play, the imagination ceases to function as a creative centre of meaning. It becomes instead a floating signifier without reference or reason – or to borrow Derrida's idiom, a mass-produced postcard addressed 'to whom it may concern' and wandering aimlessly through a communications network, devoid of 'destiny' or 'destination'. In a recent work, entitled *The Postcard* (1980), Derrida playfully explores our mass-communications culture, quoting at one point a passage from Joyce's *Finnegans Wake* which suggests that the (modern) *penman*, Shaun, has become inseparable from his brother, the (postmodern) *postman*, Shem. And this contemporary 'confusion' of Shem and Shaun – which Derrida identifies as the legacy of Babel, as a decree of 'dichemination' – implies that all modes of expression are now irreparably contaminated by the general erosion of 'original meaning'. This confusion coincides with the expansion of the communications media. A message is now no longer a unique expression sent from an author to a reader. It is invariably bound up in a play of mass-circulation and reduplication. Meaning has become a matter of 'whatever you like . . .'. Derrida's quotations from Joyce are aptly chosen. Beginning his commentary with the enigmatic phrase, 'no my love that's my wake', he punctuates his reading with the telling conundrum, 'Advantages of the Penny Post, When is a Pun not a Pun.' Meanings multiply themselves indefinitely. There is no identifiable origin or end to the Postal network of communications: 'In the beginning was the Post.'[8] The 'post' of postmodernity would thus seem to suggest that the human imagination has now become a post-man disseminating multiple images and signs which he himself has not created and over which he has no real control.

3 Methodological considerations

Some clarifications about the method of this inquiry should be made at the outset. The first point to be stressed is that our approach is predominantly *philosophical*. Thus while it frequently draws from such related disciplines as history, sociology, political economy, theology, and art criticism, the primary focus throughout this study remains philosophical. We propose to investigate some formative *concepts* of imagination as they first emerged in the Greek and biblical traditions and later evolved through the medieval, modern and postmodern periods of our cultural history.

Second, this study is confined to *Western* culture – though admittedly the distinction between Western and world culture has been substantially altered by the globalizing effects of colonization, multi-national technology and the new satellite communications network. In the interests of clarity and coherence, however, we have avoided the temptation to establish parallels or contrasts with, for instance, the Islamic and Sufic categories of imagination (so lucidly commented on by Henri Corbin) or with other related equivalents in Indian and Asian cultures. Such a comparative approach, however desirable for reasons of comprehensiveness, would have taken us too far afield and exceeded our competence. Thus while it might be argued that the Islamic theories of imagination exerted a certain influ- ence on Western understanding (for example, through the medi- eval commentaries of Averroes and Avicenna or certain mystical doctrines), one would have to reply that such an influence remained marginal to the mainstream Western traditions of Greek and Judeo-Christian culture. From the point of view of Western philosophy, the dominant foundational categories of imagination derive from the metaphysical heritage of Plato and Aristotle on the one hand, and the theological heritage of the Bible and its commentaries on the other.

Third, we acknowledge the *pluralist* – or to use a more tech- nical term, polysemantic – nature of the category of 'imagination'. There is no claim to an exhaustive treatment of all the available variants of this term. But we do endeavour, within reasonable limits, to examine some of its most influential versions: the Hebrew *yetser*, the Greek *phantasia* and *eikasia*, the Latin *imag- inatio*, the German *Einbildungskraft* and *Phantasie*, and, of course, the English and French *imagination*. While these different terms carry distinctive cultural and linguistic conno- tations, they share a common reference to the image-making power of man. This is the 'family resemblance' which underlies the diverse terms for imagination.

The human ability to 'image' or 'imagine' something has been understood in two main ways throughout the history of Western thought – 1) as a *representational* faculty which reproduces images of some pre-existing reality, or 2) as a *creative* faculty which produces images which often lay claim to an original status in their own right. These basic notions of imagination have been used – from the ancient Greeks to the modern existentialists – to refer to acts of everyday experience as well as to artistic practice. The pluralist notion of 'family resemblance' enables us to appreciate the equivocal nature of the concept of imagination while also acknowledging certain common features in its different versions and contexts – i.e. as used in ordinary language to describe our fantasies, dreams or conjectures; as used by the artist or art critic to explain the composition of a poem or painting; or as used by the psychologist or epistemologist to analyse the functioning of the human mind.

This pluralist interpretation of imagination recognizes both the continuity and discontinuity of the Western historical understanding of this term from its mythological origins to its postmodern endings. By means of such a model we would hope to avoid two extremes of interpretation: on the one hand, the *nominalist* claim that 'imagination is simply all we choose to call imagination' (i.e. no more than an empty arbitrary term); and, on the other, the *essentialist* claim that the multiple variations all refer to a single timeless essence which remains unaltered by the changing pressures of history or the differing contexts of cultural experience. Imagination is neither an Argus of a thousand glances nor a Cyclops of one eye. Within the very diversity of its terminological and functional variations, imagination lays claim to a certain *analogical* relation of unity through resemblance. Indeed if this were not the case it is hard to see how we could obviate the danger of rendering the term ultimately useless by making it mean anything and everything. In summary, one could identify four main meanings of the term imagination.

1 The ability to evoke absent objects which exist elsewhere, without confusing these absent objects with things present here and now.
2 The construction and/or use of material forms and figures such as paintings, statues, photographs etc. to represent real things in some 'unreal' way.
3 The fictional projection of non-existent things as in dreams or literary narratives.
4 The capacity of human consciousness to become fascinated by illusions, confusing what is real with what is unreal.[9]

This brings us to a fourth consideration – the hermeneutic method utilized in this study. We would not hesitate to call this method *genealogical* – understanding it in the Nietzschean sense of mapping the main shifts and mutations which a concept undergoes as it emerges through history. Every concept tells a story. And this is nowhere more true than in the case of imagination – itself an indispensable condition of all story-telling. To the methodological question: how define imagination? the most effective response is actually to *narrate* the stories of this concept, to recount the history of how it came to be. As the hermeneutic and psychoanalytic models have informed us, each person or community of persons defines its identity by retelling the story of itself. Thus in contrast to the substantialist notion of univocal identity, the notion of *narrative identity* is one which, as Paul Ricoeur argues, admits of historical mutability as an integral part of our self-understanding.[10] In our quest for imagination, we find ourselves accordingly in a hermeneutic circle where the term we are seeking to define can only be defined by means of the search itself. Or to put it another way, we cannot know exactly what imagination *is* until we first narrate the genealogical tales of its becoming, the stories of its genesis. We need to recall what imagination was *then* in order to understand imagination *now*.

Finally, we should add that this genealogical reading of the development of imagination is *paradigmatic*. This means that our analysis proceeds less in terms of a single linear history than in terms of a number of 'paradigm shifts' which signal decisive mutations in the human understanding of imagination during different epochs of Western history. Thus, for example, we will speak of the *mimetic* paradigm of the premodern (i.e. biblical, classical and medieval) imagination; the *productive* paradigm of the modern imagination; and the *parodic* paradigm of the postmodern imagination. Each of these paradigms relates to a general disposition of understanding which governs a specific period and informs the specific way people conceptualize the relationship between imagination and reality. Each historical paradigm privileges some metaphor characterizing the dominant function of imagination at a given time – i.e. the 'mimetic' privileges the referential figure of the *mirror*; the 'productive' the expressive figure of the *lamp*; and the 'parodic' the reflexive figure of a *labyrinth of looking-glasses*. Thus, instead of attempting the encyclopaedic task of providing an exhaustive inventory of every formulation of imagination known to Western culture, we have chosen the more modest proposal of selecting a sample of thinkers who seem to best represent the 'ideal type' (Weber) or 'epistemic structure' (Foucault) which exemplifies the functioning of imagination during a specific epoch.[11] Hence our choice of Plato and Aristotle to represent the premodern paradigm, Kant and Sartre to represent the modern paradigm, and Derrida and the deconstructionists to represent the post-modern paradigm.

This paradigmatic approach will not, however, prevent us from drawing numerous analogies between the philosophical concepts of imagination and corresponding developments in literature or the plastic arts generally. In fact the paradigmatic method actually facilitates this practice of cross-cultural reference, as we shall see most particularly in our concluding chapters on the postmodern imagination. Here the theories of Derrida, Barthes and Foucault, for example, will be seen in relation to parallel movements in literature (Beckett and Pynchon), cinema (Fellini and Wenders), the visual arts (Vautier and Warhol) and other more popular instances of our contemporary culture of parody and pastiche.

4 Hermeneutics and history

The general concern for the fate of postmodern imagination is no doubt informed by the humanist ethos of modern culture. If postmodernity is where we now live, modernity is where we grew up. It could even be argued that the philosophical concept of imagination only fully came into its own in the modern era. Hence our established tendency to read the various biblical, Greek and medieval texts as so many *prefigurations* of the more formalized concept of imagination which came to fruition from the eighteenth century onwards with the rise of German Idealism, Romanticism and Existentialism. It was during this modern period that imagination most centrally assumed a 'local habitation and a name'. And without continuous reference to this period the whole postmodern discourse about the crisis, death and disappearance of imagination would be inconceivable. The premodern and the postmodern, as their prefixes make plain, take their orientation from the modern paradigm.

This is not, of course, to say that the modern is dominant.

Nor is our use of historical paradigms to be taken as a fall back to a kind of *Weltanschauung* historicism, e.g. the view of imagination as some ineluctably developing essence rising to its golden maturity in the modern era and declining rapidly ever since. We reject such determinist models of interpretation, be they materialist, as in what Marx called 'vulgar Marxism', or idealist, as in the progressivist ideology of the Enlightenment or the regressivist ideology of Spenglerism. Our interpretation of the paradigmatic mutations in the Western conception of imagin- ation is based on a flexible hermeneutic which construes history as an open-ended drama of narratives.

While we do attempt to offer some concrete historical details about the three main paradigm shifts of imagination, we do not wish to propose this genealogy as binding in a *chronological* sense. Several premodern writers have proved to be eminently modern; and many modern writers, especially of the late modernist variety, have displayed traits of postmodernism. When, for instance, one looks at Peter Brook's production of Shakespeare's *A Midsummer Night's Dream* one can find evidence of each of the three paradigms of imagination. And one also witnesses an uncanny commingling of modern and post-modern perspectives in the texts of a writer like Nietzsche, who has exerted as much influence on the deconstructionists as on the existentialists. Take, for example, his prophetic-sounding description of *The Land of Culture* in *Thus Spoke Zarathustra*:

You men of the present! And with fifty mirrors around you, flattering and repeating your opalesence, written over with the signs of the past and these signs overdaubed with new signs: thus have you hidden yourself well from all interpretation of signs! . . . You seem to have been baked from colours and scraps of paper glued together. All ages and all peoples gaze motley out of your veils: all customs and beliefs speak motley out of your gestures. . . . Truly, I myself am the fright-ened bird who once saw you naked and without paint; and I flew away when the skeleton made advances to me. . . . You are half open doors at which grave-diggers wait. And this is *your* reality: 'everything is worthy of perishing'.[12]

It would be difficult to find a more apt, if pessimistic, litany of the predominant features of postmodernism – mirror-play, the crisis of interpretation, the logic of the simulacrum, the disappearance of man as creative subject, the cult of pastiche and parody of times past as tokens of a depthless, ahistorical present. And yet this description comes, chronologically speaking, from the pen of a modern rather than postmodern thinker. Moreover, one could recite the obvious point that certain classical and medieval authors were often very modern in attitude while a large number of contemporary authors continue to work from paradigms of former periods. In short, our model of paradigm shifts is invoked in the spirit of a heuristic guideline rather than an historicist dogma.

5 Postmodernism and the avant-garde

It should be noted, from the outset, that one of the main traits of postmodernism is a suspicion of historical chronology. The inclination to divide history into successive periods is often rejected by postmodern commentators as a peculiarly modern obsession – a legacy of the Enlightenment belief in a programme of Universal Progress. This legacy is thought to inform the modernist aesthetic of the Briefly New – the view that every movement in art must be a giant leap forward for mankind, an *avant-garde* innovation which breaks with everything that preceded it and projects utopian models for a transmutation of society. Rejecting such progressivist models, postmodernism has tended – since its deployment as a critical term in architecture, literary theory and philosophy in the sixties and seventies – to construe history as an anthology of diverse styles and traditions. [13] History as continuity becomes history as collage.

Striking evidence of this postmodern attitude is to be found, for example, in architects like Robert Venturi, Charles Jencks and Philip Johnson, who jumble together diverse visual idioms from past traditions. We are presented with a random assortment of stylistic quotations, a sort of polyphonic imitation of yesterday's architecture in a timeless space of today. 'Creating the new', as Venturi has it, 'means choosing from the old.' Postmodernism is to be understood accordingly not simply as that which comes *after* modernism, but as that which parodically reiterates our cultural traditions. And this, of course, includes the whole modernist tradition itself. As Jean-François Lyotard puts it, the postmodern might best be construed as an attempt to *rework* the unconscious legacy of modernity by working it through (*durcharbeiten*) in a radical fashion, exposing and re-examining its unacknowledged assumptions, confronting the crisis of its ending. In a 'Note on the Meaning of *Post*', Lyotard compares the postmodern task of working through the repressed meanings of modernity to the therapeutic activity of anamnetic remembrance conducted by psychoanalysis. He writes,

If we renege on this responsibility, we are certain to condemn ourselves to a simple and undisplaced repetition of the 'modern neurosis', the whole Western schizophrenia and paranoia which have been the source of our well known misfortunes during two centuries. Thus understood, the 'post-' of postmodernism does not signify a movement of *come back*, *flash back* or *feed back*, that is, of repetition, but a process of '*ana-*', analysis, anamnesis, anagogy, anamorphosis, which works out an 'initial forgetting'. [14]

Postmodernism casts a suspecting glance on the modernist cult of creative originality. [15] It puts the basic notion of artistic progress into question. The postmodern mind is one which interrogates, often in a reflexive and retrospective manner, the modernist credo of perpetual *newness*:

Even though the field of the postmodern is very very vast . . . it is based fundamentally upon the perception of the existence of a modern era that dates from the time of the Enlightenment and that has now run its course; and this modern era was predicated on a notion of progress in knowledge, in the arts, in technology, and in human freedom as well, all of which was thought of as leading to a truly emancipated society: a society emancipated from poverty, despotism and ignorance. But all of us can see that development continues to take place without leading to the realization of any of these dreams of emancipation. [16]

Indeed, pushed to its extreme, postmodernism even dismisses the notion of *aesthetic theory* itself as a futile attempt to reimpose some universalist perspective onto the prevailing sense of cultural discontinuity, conjuring up some picture of unity and homogeneity which denies the fragmentary nature of contemporary experience.

The postmodern abandonment of the modern (Enlightenment-Romantic-Modernist) legacy of progressivism also implies, for many critics, the end of the Age of the *Avant-Garde*. The American art critic, Hilton Kramer, announced as much in 1972. And the Australian critic, Robert Hughes, gave wide currency to this view in his influential book and television series, *The Shock of the New*, which appeared in 1980. The basic idea of an *avant-garde* came to prominence in the late nineteenth and early twentieth century when a sense of modernity in European culture was being formulated as a new project for the future: a project often fuelled by a millennarian optimism about the innovative discoveries in engineering and technology. A good example of this was the Eiffel Tower, built for the Paris World's Fair in 1889, the centenary year of the French Revolution. As one commentator has it:

In its height, its structural daring, its then-radical use of industrial materials for the commemorative purposes of the state, it summed up what the ruling classes of Europe considered the promise of technology to be: Faust's Contract, the promise of unlimited power over the world and its wealth. [17]

The *avant-garde* artists were wildly excited by such feats and generally emboldened by the accelerated rate of change in all areas of human experience and discourse. Rimbaud was enjoining writers to jettison old ways of seeing in order to become *absolument moderne*. And Cézanne's related injunction to 'explode perspective' (the basic convention obeyed by painters since the fifteenth century) was followed by a whole succession of *avant-garde* movements: Cubism, Fauvism and Surrealism in France, Dadaism and Expressionism in Germany, Constructivism in Russia, Futurism in Italy and, finally, Abstract Expression and its sequels in the US.

The *avant-garde* aesthetic was mobilized by a sense of almost infinite possibility and change. Thus Picasso and Braque, for example, sought to show that our experience of an object is made up of the different possible views of it (lateral, vertical, horizontal, etc.), while most modernist writers, from D. H. Lawrence and Virginia Woolf to Thomas Mann and Albert Camus, explored the multiple ways of achieving authentic self-hood. Whether they supported ideologies of the Left or Right, the great *avant-garde* movements generally agreed that social renewal would be brought about by cultural change. This affirmation of an alliance between social and artistic innovation was a lynch-pin of the whole *avant-garde* philosophy. It held that the artist was a pre-cursor, a prophet of the future, a harbinger of new and better things to come. And it is interesting to recall that the first 'cultural' use of the term *avant-garde* (a phrase originally employed in French military manuals to designate an advance party which prepares the way for the main army) was in the *Opinions Littéraires* of Saint-Simon, a utopian socialist of the nineteenth century. One of the characters of this work declares – 'it is we artists who will serve you as *avant-garde* . . . The power of the arts is in fact most immediate and most rapid: when we wish to spread new ideas among men, we inscribe them on marble or on canvas.'

The conviction that radical art could function as an agency of social subversion and reconstruction informed the development of the *avant-garde* from Courbet to Modernism. Admittedly, as it evolved, the ideal of the artist as a pioneering Public Man was gradually overtaken by the more elitist notion of the poet or painter as a dissenting outsider who abhorred the philistinism of the masses. Shedding the persuasion of a Kandinsky or Malevich that the artist could be the heralder of a New Heaven and a New Earth, *avant-gardism* took on an increasingly insular turn. For Late Modernism, the really advanced work of art was private, obscure, distant, even idiosyncratic.

Modern art thus began to lose much of its political radicalism. And as it lost confidence in the Theology of the New, in its ability to engage and transform social reality, the very ideas of innovation and change which characterized the modernist vanguard began to collapse. It is perhaps for this reason that postmodernism – as a witness to the end of modernity – is allergic to all doctrines about the inevitability of progress. Robert Hughes provides a useful account of this growing disillusionment with the modernist aesthetic:

When one speaks of the end of modernism – and it is no longer possible to avoid doing so, for the idea that we are in a 'postmodernist' culture has been a commonplace since the mid-seventies – one does not invoke a sudden historical terminus. Histories do not break off clean, like a glass rod; they fray, stretch, and come undone, like a rope. . . So it is with modernism. Its reflexes still jerk, the severed limbs twitch, the parts are still there; but they no longer connect or function as a live whole. The modernist achievement will continue to affect culture for another century at least. . . . But its dynamic is gone, and our relationship to it is becoming archaeological. Picasso is no longer a contemporary, or a father figure; he is a remote ancestor, who can inspire admiration but not opposition. The age of the New, like that of Pericles, has entered history. [18]

Thus we find the modernist view of culture as a linear sequence of phases being replaced by the postmodern idea of a synchronic polyphony of styles. Even the idea of a 'mainstream' evolving in some kind of temporal progression, which galvanized the aesthetic of the *avant-garde* up to its Late Modernist expressions, is coming undone. By the 1970s,

the sense of cultural pluralism had become so great that it dissolved the idea of the linear dialectic of new art, the sense of history unfolding along a line drawn between the first prophecy and the imagined millennium, on which so much *avant-garde* hope was predicated. . . . Instead of A leading to B, C and the rest, there was an open field where every kind of art coexisted within the same social frame. And this frame was inordinately wide. [19]

So wide, indeed, that one could no longer distinguish between the mainstream and the marginal, the progressive and the regressive, high art and pop art. It was observed that by the end of the seventies there were more commercial galleries than bakers in New York. Artists were resorting more and more to the techniques and materials of the popular consumer culture (Oldenburg's Mickey Mouse, Warhol's Coca-Cola series,

Lichtenstein's inflated comic strips, Wesselmann's Hamburger/ Budweiser collage, etc.). Or else they were mocking the very premises of *avant-gardism* by producing parodies of the great Masters (e.g. Leslie's reproductions of Caravaggio and David or Ballagh's reworkings of Goya, Delacroix and Velasquez). Art was no longer a leap into the Future but a replay of quotations from the Past.

6 From evolution to involution

The erosion of the modernist belief in a progressive mainstream of art, correlative to a process of social advancement, raises a number of unsettling questions. What, if any, is the role of the creative imagination in a postmodern age apparently devoid of a project of emancipation? If the only future is one we look back to, what can we look forward to? Has the artist or intellectual any positive contribution to make to society? Has history anywhere to turn but inside out? Has art any role apart from self-parody? And where does all this leave imagination?

While modern artists from Zola and Hugo to Sartre and Camus were committed to programmes of public action, the postmodern artist tends to believe that he is no longer capable of effective intervention.[20] Filled with a sense of incertitude about the possibility of any universal meaning, the outcome of any political project or even the identity of the human subject, postmodernism appears to have traded in the model of *evolution* for one of *involution*.[21] A postmodern culture thus becomes one which attempts to portray what is without presuming to know what it is, to analyse reflexively where we are *now* without automatically deferring to a possible future or proclaiming the present to be an advance on the past. We seem to be inhabiting a no-man's-land where authoritative statements about historical development are becoming increasingly suspect. And this is perhaps why certain intellectuals are conceiving postmodernism less as a step *beyond* modernity into something else than as a critical reworking of the 'unconscious' crisis within modernity itself.

The critical task of a postmodern imagination might, then, be to revisit and revise the infancy of modernity – this infancy being understood as a complex interplay of multiple traditions and heritages which modernism has overlooked in its impatience to surpass itself towards the New. Postmodernism might thus be seen not just as a moment of apocalyptic paralysis but as an occasion to reflect upon the inner breakdown of modernity, to expose the collapse of its millenarian ideologies and explore the causes of our contemporary dislocation. Understood in this way, as a task of critical remembrance, postmodernism would seek to re-read and re-write modernity from the point of view of its inherent end: an end *involved* in the modern project from the outset, albeit forgotten in its perpetual rush forward, its blinding obsession with the Onward March of History. Where modernity evolves postmodernity involves.

This interpretation of postmodernism admittedly upsets our accepted notions of 'periodisation'. One could see such a re-buttal of linear teleologies as a sort of 'active nihilism', a neo-Nietzschean espousal of cyclical recurrence which eliminates the idea of an historical future. But there are other ways of reading it. The postmodern task of turning back *on* history does not necessarily mean turning our back *to* it. Perhaps the determination to re-examine the unresolved crisis of Western modernity – and by extension the diversity of traditions which gave rise to it – may disclose a different way of confronting our contemporary historical dilemma. As the Jewish philosopher, Emmanuel Levinas, recently remarked, it is when we renounce the Promise that we remain most faithful to it.[22] The possibility of utopia may well require the demise of all utopianisms. For it is arguable that we will be condemned to more of the same until such time as we abandon the ideology of man as heroic master and possessor of the universe. Then something 'other' may emerge. Something to which the conventional terms of 'old' and 'new' no longer properly apply.

Such a reading of the postmodern turn is, of course, difficult to sustain. But it is one, at least, attentive to the necessity of discriminating between what is destructive in the modern legacy and what is potentially enabling. It is one, furthermore, which demands   rigorous   philosophical   reflection   and   ethical responsibility. Perhaps this is what a postmodern thinker like Lyotard is hinting at when he rejects the model of history as ineluctable Progress in favour of a more vigilant openness to the complexities and paradoxes of our contemporary condition:

Periodisation is typically modern, whereas the postmodern is a sort of permanent labour which accompanies modernity and constitutes its true value. 'Post' should not be understood therefore in the sense of a 'period which follows' but rather as a 'dynamism' which allows us to go further than modernity in order to retrieve it in a kind of 'twist' or 'loop' (*boucle*). The modern is all too easily snapped up by the future, by all its values of pro-motion, pro-gram, pro-gress . . . dominated by a very strong emphasis on wilful activism. Whereas the postmodern implies, in its very movement . . . a capacity to listen openly to what is hidden within the happenings of today. Postmodernism is deeply reflexive, in the sense of anamnesis or reminiscence, and that itself evinces what is best in modernity.[23]

Our society today, he argues, is becoming less tied to centralized ideologies in so far as it unfolds as a complex network without any single centre. And far from moving towards an homogeneous transparency in human relations, we are being increasingly oriented in the direction of a complexification which will, in Lyotard's words, 'demand of each of us a greater degree of decision and choice . . . a developed society is one where everyone must judge for himself'.

Postmodernism would thus refuse to view itself as a mere *afterword* to modernity. Instead it assumes the task of reinvestigating the crisis and trauma at the very heart of modernity; the postmodern now being understood as a testament to the fact that the end of modernity is an integral mutation within its own development, a symptom as it were of its own unconscious infancy which needs to be retrieved and reworked if we are not to be condemned to an obsessional fixation upon, and compulsive repetition of, the sense of its ending. In this respect, the task of a postmodern imagination might be to envision the end of modernity as a possibility of rebeginning.

But deprived of the invigorating humanist ideologies of universal advancement and emancipation, how can postmodernism allow for the imagining of meaningful social and cultural actions committed to the realization of a more just world? Once made aware of *both* our immense responsibility as individuals *and* our dispersion into a collective network of multiple communications, how are we to find our way? What kind of imagination can be solicited by a postmodern conscience confronting the end of modernity and grappling with its inner and ostensibly terminal crises? Where do we go from here? These are some of the key questions which motivate our inquiry into the wake of imagination.

7 The Humanist controversy

Finally, we take a preliminary look at the postmodern conviction that the very concept of a creative imagination is a passing illusion of Western *humanist* culture. The later Heidegger anticipated this view when he declared in his *Letter on Humanism*, written in 1946, that 'humanist' thinking was unable to fathom the hidden dimensions of the crisis of the human subject in the modern world. 'Should one still call "humanism" the view which speaks out against all earlier humanism, but which does not at all advocate the in-human?', he asks. 'Or should thought, resisting the word "humanism", make an effort to become more attentive to the *humanitas of the homo humanus* and what grounds this *humanitas?*'[24] Evoking a similar theme in *The Origin of the Work of Art* (1950), Heidegger explicitly questions the validity of the humanist notion of creative imagination. 'It becomes questionable', he says, 'whether the nature of poetry can be adequately thought of in terms of the power of imagination.' And he goes on to clarify his meaning by adding that 'modern subjectivism immediately misinterprets creation, taking it as the self-sovereign subject's performance of genius'.[25]

The deconstruction of imagination in post-structuralist theory is of a piece with the general announcement of the contemporary Disappearance of Man. We shall be exploring this theme in some detail in the final chapters of this work. Suffice it to note, at this point, some leading statements in the debate on humanism which has been preoccupying so many contemporary Continental thinkers. Foucault's denunciation of the 'sovereignty of the subject and the twin figures of anthropology and humanism' in the *Archaeology of Knowledge* (1969), was directed primarily against the anthropocentric philosophies which came to the fore in the nineteenth and early twentieth centuries and promoted the notion that 'human consciousness is the original subject of all historical development and all action'.[26] Foucault challenges this humanist assumption by disclosing the predetermining role played by the 'positive unconscious' of language – of which the very concept of 'man' is but an historical product! Lyotard has shown himself to be equally anti-humanist in his endorsements of a postmodern culture which enables people to look at things 'within a context where they don't begin by positing what the human sciences or liberal arts always begin by positing, which is to say the *Human Being*'.[27] And most other advocates or *avant-coureurs* of postmodern theory, from Lacan and Lévi-Strauss to Barthes and Derrida, tend to agree with the characterization of humanism as a specifically modern *Weltanschauung* which places humanity at the centre of history and makes it the privileged source of meaning.[28] The postmodern thinker disputes the claim – which held sway from the late Renaissance and Enlightenment to the modern movements of romantic idealism and existentialism – that humanity makes its own history.

Derrida, of course, extends the parameters of this critique when he argues that the philosophical tendency to construe 'man' and 'creation' in terms of *origins*, begins much earlier than the eighteenth and nineteenth centuries. In fact he traces its genesis further back to the emergence of Western metaphysics, which he equates, in Heideggerean fashion, with the onto-theological tradition. In other words, the notion of Man is said to be the inevitable counterpart of the Western metaphysical concept of the highest Being as a divine and self-sufficient presence. The death of man is thus for Derrida inseparable from the death of God, understood as absolute 'origin' or 'end'. For man and God together make up that dialectical *We* which Hegel and modern idealism established as the goal or *telos* of history. What is necessary but difficult for us today, says Derrida, is to think

an end of man which would not be organized by a dialectics of truth and negativity, an end of man which would not be a teleology in the first person plural. The *We* . . . assures the proximity to itself of the fixed and central being for which this circular reappropriation is produced. The *We* is the unity of absolute knowledge and anthropology, of God and man, of onto-theo-teleology and humanism.[29]

This deconstructionist account of the rapport between the premodern and modern epochs of Western metaphysics sheds substantial light on our own story of imagination. The creative power of imagination which biblical culture identified with Adamic man, and Greek culture with Promethean or demiurgic man, reaches its ultimate humanist conclusion with existentialist man. And the logical implication would seem to be that the human imagination will disappear as man himself disappears. The concept of imagination cannot, apparently, survive the postmodern age of deconstruction. It is slowly being erased, to adapt Foucault's vivid phrase, like a face drawn in sand at the edge of the sea.

But is there not a danger that all the talk about the demise of human imagination may in fact foment an apocalyptic pessimism which accelerates the end of humanity itself? Such a danger has, arguably, been heightened by the marked *ahistoricism* of the postmodern aesthetic: its rejection of the notion of historical progression or teleology, its tendency to construe culture as a sort of timeless and depthless space, a jumble of diverse historical styles which eclectically congregate and disintegrate. By collapsing the historical dimensions of time – recollection of time past and projection of time future – into an empty play of euphoric instants, postmodernism runs the risk of eclipsing the potential of human experience for *liberation*. It risks cultivating the ecstasy of self-annihilation by precluding the possibility of self-expression. And it risks abandoning the emancipatory practice of imagining *alternative* horizons of existence (remembered or anticipated) by renouncing the legitimacy of narrative coherence and identity – even as practised here in our own telling of the story of imagination. Finally, and perhaps most specifically, the postmodern cult of a timeless, depthless space appears to jeopardize the vocation of philosophy itself, i.e. as an investigation into the hidden or undiscovered dimension of things.

The apocalyptic inflection of much postmodern art and theory is not adventitious. The dangers are real enough. Hence the recurring image of our contemporary condition as a labyrinth of interreflecting mirrors from which there is no escape. There is not even a Minotaur lurking within to be slayed or subdued: the mythic monster is itself but a mirror reflection which refers to no 'original' reality. The danger stalking the postmodern labyrinth is *nothingness*. The empty tomb. The paralyzing fear that there is nothing *after* postmodernism. And perhaps this is why a painter like Rothko – whose work sought to protest against the 'anaesthetization of contemporary culture' but ended up as a symptom of its own 'negative space' – chose extinction.[30]

Contemporary thinkers have not remained unaware of this predicament. Lyotard proposes accordingly to interpret postmodernism in a *positive* relation to modernity. To the vexed questions 'what is the postmodern?' and 'what place does it occupy in the vertiginous questions hurled at the rules of image and narration?', Lyotard offers this reply:

It is undoubtedly a part of the modern. All that has been received, if only yesterday (*modo, modo*, Petronius used to say), must be suspected. What space does Cézanne challenge? The Impressionists'. What object do Picasso and Braque attack? Cézanne's. What presupposition does Duchamp break with in 1912? That which says one must make a painting, be it cubist. And Buren questions that other presupposition which he believes had survived untouched by the work of Duchamp: the place of presentation of the work. In an amazing acceleration, the generations precipitate themselves. A work can become modern only if it is first postmodern. Postmodernism thus understood is not modernism at its end but in the nascent state, and this state is constant (*The Postmodern Condition* 1978).

Despite Lyotard's supposedly reassuring claim that postmodernism does not represent some epistemological *coupure*, some schismatic rupture with modernist culture, he cannot so easily dispose of the problem of postmodern nihilism. Indeed his invocation of the 'inhumanity' of sublime allusions, which dismantle the productive pretensions of imagination and defy its narrative function, would seem to inflate rather than deflate the apocalyptic climate of postmodernism. One must have serious doubts as to whether the sublime excesses of rule-breaking paralogisms – recommended by Lyotard – are appropriate weapons against the postmodern paralysis.

In his Preface to *Postmodern Culture* (1985), Hal Foster also seeks to remedy the dilemma of paralysis by advocating a postmodernism of 'resistance'. This, he suggests, might serve as a counter-practice to both the official culture of modernism and to what he calls 'the false normativity of reactionary postmodernism'.[31] Such a resistant postmodernism, responding to the crisis of modernity since the fifties and sixties, would be concerned with (1) a 'critical deconstruction of tradition' as opposed to an 'instrumental pastiche of pop- or pseudo-historical forms'; (2) a 'critique of origins rather than a return to them'; and (3) a questioning rather than an exploiting of cultural codes and political ideologies. But however commendable such a discriminating postmodernism may be, we are still left with the question of whether it is feasible. In a technologized culture where the human subject is reduced to 'a pure screen for all the networks of influence' (Baudrillard), to a simulating play of commercialized images, one is compelled to wonder if the very idea of resistance is not absurd. Do not the very postmodern efforts to contest the dominance of a fetishized system of representation themselves fall victim to the system? Do they not confirm, despite themselves, the culture of pastiche they intend to mock?

In our concluding chapter we will examine a number of recent critical attempts to address this paradox, as well as advancing the model of a poetical-ethical imagination responsive to the predicaments of the postmodern age. Rejecting the nostalgic option for a return to the paradigms of onto-theology or humanism, we will be proposing the possibility of a postmodern imagination capable of preserving, through reinterpretation, the functions of narrative identity and creativity – or what we call a *poetics of the possible*.[32] Such a postmodern imagination would move beyond humanism, understood as a narrow perspective while remaining faithful to its humanitarian intentions. Indeed such a critical postmodern reinterpretation would seek to incorporate the lessons learned from the excesses of its preceding paradigms:

1. The premodern tendency to repress human creativity in the name of some immutable cause which jealously guards the copy-right of 'original' meaning;
2. The modern tendency to overemphasize the sovereign role of the autonomous individual as sole source of meaning.

The postmodern imagination we will be endorsing aims to avoid the extremes of both traditional quietism and modern volun-tarism. Entering into the labyrinth of parody and play, it dispos-sesses itself of inherited certainties. So that at the very heart of the labyrinth, it explores possibilities of an *other* kind of *poiesis* – alternative modes of inventing alternative modes of existence. To disclose how things *might be*, we must follow in the wake of imagination.

PART I

Premodern Narratives

CHAPTER ONE

The Hebraic Imagination

He spoke of the beginning, chaos and old night, and their division by God's word; He recited the vigorous, blithely plural summons of God to Himself, the enterprising proposal: 'Let us make man' . . . and indeed did God not go on to say: 'in our image, after our likeness'? He spoke of the garden eastwards in Eden and of the trees in it, the tree of life and the tree of knowledge; of the temptation and of God's first attack of jealousy: how he was alarmed lest man, who now indeed knew good and evil, might eat also of the tree of life and be entirely like 'us'. So He drove out the man and set the cherub with the flaming sword before the gate. And to the man he gave toil and death that he might be an image like to 'us', indeed, but not too like, only somewhat liker than the fishes, the birds and the beasts, and still with the privately assigned task of becoming against His jealous opposition ever as much more like as possible. . . . The very creature which was nearer to the image of the Creator than any other brought evil with him into the world. Thus God created for Himself a mirror which was anything but flattering. Often and often in anger and chagrin He was moved to smash it to bits – though he never quite did, perhaps because He could not bring Himself to replunge into nothingness that which He had summoned forth and actually cared more about the failure of than He did about any success. Perhaps too He would not admit that anything could be a complete failure after He had created it so thoroughgoingly in His own image. Perhaps, finally, a mirror is a means of learning about oneself; Man, then was a result of God's curiosity about Himself.

(Thomas Mann, *Joseph and His Brothers*)

The story of imagination is deeply informed by the ancient biblical heritage of Western culture. Together with the Hellenic sources – which make up the other most influential pole of our traditional understanding of this concept – the Hebraic account of the origin and development of imagination merits special attention. To properly grasp the founding narratives of imagination we must begin at the beginning – the Book of *Genesis*.

In seeking to comprehend what the Hebrew scriptures – both the Torah and Talmud – had to say about imagination, we are, of course, inevitably engaged in a circle of interpretation. This hermeneutic circle stems from the attempt of contemporary consciousness to reappropriate the meanings of ancient texts. How can we be sure we understand what was meant by the original authors and commentators of these writings? But it is not a question of *retrieving* some 'original' intention in its pristine state. Nor is it a matter of simply *reducing* the ancient meaning to our own contemporary context of interpretation. We are aiming at a mutual convergence of horizons, a meeting of old and new minds where each may grow from contact with the other. What is historically far removed from us may thus be brought near and *reinterpreted* in the light of contemporary commentaries and perspectives. But this act of reinterpretation remains a two-way process. If what is foreign to our present consciousness becomes familiar, by the same token, what is familiar becomes foreign. Or to put it in another way, in *appropriating* other meanings (i.e. the old Hebrew narratives) into our perspective (i.e. the current paradigm of understanding), we also *disappropriate* ourselves of our own perspective in order to open ourselves to such otherness of meaning. Each is, hopefully, enlarged by the other. In this manner, the hermeneutic circle which our contemporary reading of ancient texts entails, aims at a mutual *dialogue* in the etymological sense of *dia-legein*: welcoming the difference in order to learn from it.

1 The Adamic myth: the good and evil *Yetser*

The story of imagination is as old as the story of creation itself. In *Genesis* it is suggested that the birth of the human power of imagining coincides with Adam's transgression of God's law. The Original Sin of our first parents marks imagination from its inception. The Knowledge of Good and Evil, which the serpent promises will make Adam and Eve 'like gods', is henceforth identified with man's ability to imagine a world of his own making – a world of striving, desire, remorse and death which began with the fall from paradise into history. The Adamic myth of the first book of the Bible tells the tale of a fallen imagination. And, as we shall see, it is above all else an *ethical* tale.

The main Hebraic term for imagination is *yetser*. It is of no little consequence that this word derives from the same root *yzr* as the terms for 'creation' (*yetsirah*), 'creator' (*yotser*) and 'create' (*yatsar*). As the *Encyclopaedia Judaica* informs us: '*Yetser* as in *Ps.* 103:14 from *yatsar*, to form or create as in *Gen.* 2:8.'[1] This allusive interplay between the terms used to describe God's creation of the world and the First Man's transgressive capacity (i.e. the *Yetser*) to imitate this divine act is highly significant. When God 'created (*Yatsar*) Adam in his own image (*tselem*) and likeness (*demuth*)' (*Gen.* 2:8), He risked allowing man to emulate Him, to set himself up as His rival, to supplant Him in the order of creation (see Appendix). The *yetser*, understood accordingly as man's creative impulse to imitate God's own creation, was arguably first realized when Adam and Eve ate of the forbidden fruit of the Tree of Knowledge.[2] The wording of the serpent's temptation is apposite: 'God knows well that as soon as you eat this fruit your eyes shall be open and you shall be like Gods knowing good and evil' (*Gen.* 3:5).

The initial realization of man's imaginative potential would thus appear to correspond, in the *Genesis* account, with both an *ethical* consciousness of good and evil and an *historical* consciousness of past and future. It is coincident with the ability to project a future order of human creation (i.e. the sin of presumption and pride) and to recall the events of the past (i.e. guilt and remorse). The sin of imagination leads to the fall of Adam and

Eve into historical time where the spirit is no longer at one with itself as in the Garden of Eden. Imagination enables man to think in terms of *opposites* – good and evil, past and future, God and man. Thus bringing about the consciousness of sin and of time, the fallen imagination exposes man to the experience of division, discord and contradiction. Whereas Adam lived in harmony with God in Eden, once exiled east of Eden into history he is subject to unending conflict. Adam's transgressive act of imagination represents the alienation of God's original creation from itself – the splitting up of the pre-lapsarian unity of Paradise into the antithetical orders of divine eternity and human mortality.

But why, we may ask, should man, created in the image of God Himself and already enjoying the paradisal privileges of such a God-like creature, have succumbed to the serpent's temptation to become, as it were, *more* like God by acquiring the Knowledge of Good and Evil? And why did Yahweh create in the man and woman of his own image the potential to imagine themselves like Him even to the point of assuming themselves to be the creators of their own world? These enigmas have preoccupied commentators of the Hebraic Torah for centuries. In what follows we shall look at some of the more illuminating exegetical readings derived from rabbinical and kabbalistic sources.

In his radical commentary on the narratives of the Old Testament, *You Shall be as Gods*, the Jewish thinker Eric Fromm defines the term *yetser* as follows:

The noun *yetser* means 'form, 'frame', 'purpose' and with reference to the mind, 'imagination' or 'device'. The term *yetser* thus means 'imaginings' (good or evil) . . . The problem of good and evil arises only when there is imagination. Furthermore, man can become more evil and more good because he feeds his imagination with thoughts of evil or good. They grow precisely because of that specifically human quality – imagination.[3]

The biblical understanding of imagination is thus indelibly marked by the ethical context of its genesis – the rebellion of Adam and Eve. As a power first dramatized in man's defiance of divine prohibition, the *yetser* bears the stigma of a stolen possession. (This feature is also evident in the Promethean myth of Greek mythology examined in our next chapter.) Was this stigmatisation the price to be paid for the full exercise of human freedom? Was this the inevitable casualty of man's ability to *knowingly* choose between good and evil and thereby inaugurate an historical epoch fashioned in *his* own image and likeness?

The freedom acquired by imagination was, by all accounts, a mixed blessing. It was both a liberation and a curse. This essential ambiguity of imagination is analysed by the Jewish scholar, Martin Buber, in a work entitled *Good and Evil*. Stressing the importance of the ethical context in which the biblical concept of imagination emerges, Buber identifies the 'dream-longing' which characterizes our First Parents' act of rebellion as a longing for godliness:

The serpent promises that by partaking of it (the fruit), they would become like God, knowers of good and evil; and God seems to confirm this when he subsequently says that they have thereby become 'like one of us', to know good and evil.[4]

The God-like knowledge appropriated by Adam and Eve in this manner, is the awareness of the 'opposites implicit in all being within the world'. God Himself could legitimately *know* this oppositeness of creation; for He was its rightful and original Creator. Such knowledge did not alter or divide His nature as an omnipotent divinity. But for man there is no exemption; such knowledge is unlawful and divisive. Adam is engulfed, accordingly, in the alienating dialectic which ensues:

Good and evil, the yes-position and the no-position enter into the living cognizance; but in man they can never be temporally co-existent. . . . Through the recognition of oppositeness, the opposites which are always latently present in creation break out into actual reality. . . . One is ashamed of being what one is because one now recognizes this *so-being* in its oppositional nature as an intended *shall-be*.[5]

Split between his present being and his future possibilities of becoming, the First Man feels torn inside, out of joint with himself.

Shattering the protective dyke of paradise, Adam's transgression unleashes the flood of contradiction which fills him with 'shame'. He is ashamed of his nakedness before Eve and before God (*Gen.* 3.10). He seeks fig leaves with which to gird himself and hide his nakedness; and he thus replaces his natural condition as a created being with his first cultural artefact. This loss of innocence, of contentedness with being what he *is*, is the cost of the freedom to *become* more than he is, to make himself *other* than his given self, to imagine alternative possibilities of existence. But the curse of shame, anguish, labour and death which Adam's sin entails also contains an ironic blessing. In his presumptuous bid to equal God his father, the human son loses Eden and gains history:

The curse conceals a blessing. From the *seat*, which had been made ready for him, man is sent out upon a *path*, his own, the human path. This is the path to the world's history, only through it does the world have a history – and an historical goal . . .[6]

The freedom to choose between good and evil, and to construct one's story accordingly, is thus intimately related to the *yetser* as a passion for the possible: the human impulse to transcend what exists in the direction of what might exist. The Talmud – the Jewish tradition of exegetical interpretation of the sacred texts of the Torah or Old Testament – commonly referred to the *yetser* as the 'evil impulse' (*yetser hara*). Any deviation from the given Creation of God was looked upon as a denial of the good. It was, of course, precisely this 'impulse as a play with possibility' which became manifest in Adam's eating of the forbidden fruit – an act which, as Buber notes, thereby necessitated his expulsion from the 'divine reality which was allotted to him, from the good actuality of creation . . . out into the boundless possible which he fills with his imagining, that is evil because it is fictitious'[7].

Man's ability to project imaginatively into the future opens up an infinite horizon of possibilities. He no longer lives in the immediacy of the actual moment. And so no longer present to himself, he is cast out into the chaos of a free-floating existence. (Indeed existence as the existentialist thinkers of our own century understand it – *ex-sistere*, standing out beyond oneself in a process of endless self-surpassing – may be said to have begun with the birth of imagination. Considered in a biblical context, one could say that if Adam had not transgressed it would not have been possible for existentialist philosophy to define man as a 'being who is not what he is and is what he is not' – a being haunted by *angst* and self-division.[8]) The *yetser* is evil to the extent that man loses all sense of belonging or direction, living according to his own way rather than according to God's way – the Hebrew term *Torah* means quite literally the direction of God. In short, the human imagination becomes subject to evil in that it falls victim to its own idolatrous creations. Freed from the necessity of a divinely ordered reality, the First Man faces the arbitrariness of his own imaginings:

In the swirling space of images through which he strays, each and every thing entices him to be made incarnate by him; he grasps at them like a wanton burglar, not with decision but only in order to overcome the tension of omnipossibility; it all becomes reality, though no longer divine but his own, his capriciously constructed, indestinate reality, his violence, which overcomes him, his handiwork and fate. . . . Phantasy, the imagery of possibilities imposes its indefiniteness upon the definiteness of the moment.[9]

After the fall of Adam, the imagination would appear, logically, to be condemned to evil, transmitting the stain of its original sin to all subsequent generations. Is this not what Yahweh Himself implied when he declared that the 'imagination (*yetser*) of man's heart is evil from its youth' (*Gen.* 6:5)? It was just such a negative reading which marked a dominant tradition of Talmudic interpretation – one which deemed the *yetser* to be incorrigibly wicked and counselled suppression as the only remedy.

2 The way of suppression

The negative Talmudic interpretation of the *yetser* construes divine Law as warranting a renunciation of the imaginative impulse. Imagination is here equated exclusively with sin. This

attitude gives rise to such frequent admonitions as the following:
'To him who kills his *yetser* and confesses upon it, it is reckoned
as if he would have honoured the Holy One, blessed be He, in
two worlds, this world and the world to come.' (*Sanhedrin*,
43b).[10] In a detailed study entitled *The Evil Yezer: The Source
of Rebellion*, Solomon Schechter identifies this Talmudic
condemnation of imagination as follows: 'Sin being generally
conceived as rebellion against the majesty of God, we inquire
after the source or instigator of this rebellion. In rabbinical
literature this influence is termed the *yetser hara*. This is usually
translated as "evil imagination" . . .'.[11] One sometimes finds the
evil imagination being identified with man's corporeal nature
and particularly sexual desire. Bodily lust was seen as a symptom
of the *yetser* on account of its origin in Eve's temptation and the
subsequent fall into the historical order of sexual procreation and
shame. In other words, sin was intimately associated with the
carnal impulses of the *yetser hara* (Gen. Rab. 27, *Jalkut Shim.
Gen.* 44).[12]

In this view of things, the *yetser* could come to no good. And,
predictably, we witness numerous repressive remedies entering
the repertory of rabbinical teaching. Contemplation of death,
self-denial and other ascetic practices are recommended as curbs
to the erotic impulses of imagination. Indeed, even circumcision
is invested, on occasion, with the role of purging the evil *yetser*:
'Remove the evil *yetser* from your hearts so that ye may be all
in one fear of God . . . circumcise therefore the foreskin . . .'.[13]
A host of cautionary tales reflect such teachings. We read of the
Nazarite who had his hair cut off with the purpose of destroying
his *yetser* which had prompted him to make an idol out of his
own reflected image (*Num.* 6:18); or, more dramatic still, the
Rabbi who prayed for the decease of his nearest of kin when he
feared she would become an agent for the power of the *yetser*
(*Tannith.* 24 a). It is with similar sentiments in mind that Joch-
anan b. Nuri offered the following rabbinical account:

This is the craft of the *yetser hara*; today it says to him to do this,
tomorrow to do that, till it says to him, Go practise idolatry; and he
goes and does it. . . . What says Psalm 81:10, There shall be in thee

no strange God? What is the strange god which is within man? It is the evil *yetser*.[14]

And Rabbi Jannai provides further support for this reading when he declares that 'one who obeys his *yetser* practises idolatry' (*Jer. Nedarim*, 41b).

The Hebraic suspicion of imagination as a drive towards idolatry – the attempt to reduce God to our own 'graven images' – is thus evidenced in a particular Talmudic hostility towards bodily desire. And this tendency to condemn the idolatrous drives of imagination is probably what Freud had in mind when he wrote in *Moses and Monotheism*:

> Among the precepts of Mosaic religion is one that has more significance than is at first obvious. It is the prohibition against making an *image* of God, which means the compulsion to worship an invisible God . . . it signified subordinating sense perception to an abstract idea; it was a triumph of spirituality over the senses; more precisely a renunciation of the satisfaction of an impulse derived from an instinct (*Triebverzicht*).[15]

Freud concludes accordingly that 'the religion that began with the prohibition against making images, has developed in the course of the centuries into a religion of instinctual renunciation.[16]

But the Talmudic tradition of suppression merely served to heighten the paradox that man was originally created by God with a *yetser*. This tradition attributed to the Divine Creator such sentiments of regret as – 'Repentance came upon me that I had created man of earthly substance for if I had created him of heavenly substance he would not have rebelled against me'; or 'Repentance arose in my heart, said God, that I created in him the *yetser hara*, for if I had not done this he would not have become a rebel against me' (*Gen. R.*, 27).[17] So here once again we are confronted with the essential ambiguity of imagination as it relates to *both* a divine *and* a human source. Frank Porter offers an illuminating insight into the ambivalent origins of the rabbinical attitude to imagination in his detailed and comprehensive study of the Jewish doctrine of sin, *The Yetser Hara*:

> It is never doubted that God made the evil *yezer*, yet man is responsible

for controlling and subduing it. The word itself suggested these two
apparently contrary conceptions. The verb *yzr* means to form, or
fashion, and also, to form inwardly, to plan. It was used as the technical
word for the potter's work. It was frequently used of God's forming of
nature and of man, and also of his planning or purposing. The *yzr* of
man could therefore suggest either his form, as God made him, his
nature (so *Ps.* 103:14), or his own formation of thought and purpose,
'imagination' as the word is rendered in several Old Testament passages
(*Gen.* 6:5; 8:21; *Deut.* 31:21; *Isa.* 26:3; I *Chr.* 28:9; 29:18). In *Deuteronomy* 31:21, and probably *Isaiah* 26:3, the word is used without the
further definition, 'of the thoughts', 'of the heart', which *First Chronicles*
retains. The word had gained therefore, already in the Old Testament,
a certain independence as meaning the nature or disposition of man,
and this could be regarded as something which God made (*Ps.* 103:14)
or as something which man works (*Deut.* 31:21).[18]

This account of the fundamentally twofold character of the
biblical concept of the *yetser* points towards the possibility of a
more *benign* assessment of imagination. Such an assessment
found its place in an alternative rabbinical tradition of interpretation – the tradition of integration.

3 The way of integration

The Talmud contains a considerable number of passages which
seek to resolve the paradox of imagination by calling for the
integration of the evil imagination into a good imagination. In
its admission of a fundamentally good possibility for the *yetser*,
this Talmudic body of opinion suggests a more lenient logic
behind God's creation of man as a creature of imagination.

According to this positive reading, imagination is deemed to
be that most primordial 'drive' of man which, if sublimated
and oriented towards the divine way (*Talmud*), can serve as an
indispensable power for attaining the goal of creation: the
universal embodiment of God's plan in the Messianic Kingdom
of justice and peace. The history of idolatry is viewed accordingly
as the story of man's impetuosity. Idols are to be looked upon

as premature Messiahs, the distorted fantasies of an impatient imagination. Once re-directed towards the fulfilment of the Divine purpose (*yetser*), the human *yetser* might indeed become an accomplice in the task of historical re-creation: a task which man now undertakes in dialogue with God. In short, if the evil imagination epitomizes the error of history as a monologue of man with himself, the good imagination (*yetser hatov*) opens up history to an I-Thou dialogue between man and his Creator. This is no doubt why the Talmud declares that 'God created man with two *yetsers*, the good and the evil' (*Berach*, 61a) and prognosticates that the Messianic treaty between the Lion and the Lamb will result from an 'atoned', i.e. integrated, imagination (*Gen. R.* 48). This rabbinical teaching springs from certain suggestions about a 'good' use of imagination in the Torah (*Deut.* 31.21; *I Chr.* 28.9; 29:18) and in particular the passage in *Deuteronomy* 65, where man is urged to worship Yahweh with his 'whole' soul. Commenting on this last passage, Buber writes: 'Evil cannot be done with the whole soul; good can only be done with the whole soul.' And he explains: 'Evil is lack of direction and that which is done in it and out of it as the grasping, seizing, exploiting, humiliating, torturing and destroying of what offers itself. Good is direction and what is done in it . . . with the whole soul, so that in fact all the vigour and passion with which evil might have been done is included in it.' In this connection, concludes Buber, 'is to be recalled that Talmudic interpretation of the Biblical pronouncement of God concerning imagination or the "evil urge", whose whole vigour must be drawn into the love of God in order truly to serve Him. . . . For creation has a goal and the humanly right is service directed in the One direction.'[19]

This reading accounts for the fact that having created man with the *yetser*, Yahweh himself saw fit to declare, on the eve of his labours, that his creation was 'very good' (*Gen.* 1:31). The imagination was not therefore necessarily an evil impulse *in itself*, but only became so in the light of man's subsequent transgression. The dual nature of the *yetser* as both good and evil is attested in a variety of Talmudic and Hasidic formulations. We are told for example that the *yetser* resembles a wheat grain and is situated between the two valves of the heart – one sending life energy out from its source and the other returning it to its source (*Berachoth*. 61a). The wheat grain by all accounts refers to the legend that the Tree of Knowledge grew wheat and confirms the view that the *yetser* was closely associated with the ethical awareness of good and evil. Moreover, the locating of the grain of imagination between the two cardiac vessels alludes to the Talmudic belief that there was a good and an evil direction of the heart (*Zohar. Exod.* 107a). Other rabbinical texts confirm this bi-lateral character of the *yetser*. It was reputed to be capable of both spirituality and corporeity, masculinity and femininity, friendship and hostility (e.g. *Gen. R.* 226). And while feared, as we saw above, for its erotic inclination towards false idols (*Berach.* 17a; *I Cor.* 5:7), it was also duly recognized as the centre of all human energy and activity – the 'yeast in the dough', the divinely created ferment without which no house would be built, no trade or labour executed, no children begotten (*Eccles.* 4:4). Though David called it 'unclean' (*Ps.* 56:12) and Isaiah a 'stumbling block' (*Is.* 57:14), God Himself is said to have preferred man's song of praise to that of the angels because the former possessed a *yetser* and the latter did not.[20] And Joel – anticipating Kant and the Romantics by many centuries – called it 'the hidden one in the heart of man' (*Joel.* 2:20). Indeed at least one Talmudic commentary credits the *yetser* with the privileged role of 'accuser and witness' customarily reserved for Yahweh (*Aboth.* 4:2).

What all of these texts seem to suggest is that the *yetser* is neither good nor bad until man makes it so. It is only in the light of such ethical choice surely that we can make sense of such Talmudic passages as the following: 'In thy hand I have given the *yetser* and thou shalt rule over him both for good and evil' (*Pseudo-Jonathan. Gen.* 4:7). Thus we may understand why Joseph and Abraham are congratulated for integrating and successfully directing their *yetser* toward a good end, while David is rebuked for his inability to come to terms with this power and his subsequent renunciation of it; the implication being that in so doing he doubted the wisdom of God's creation.

This more benign reading conforms, of course, to the ultimate recommendation of the *Torah* as supreme guide for man in his efforts to integrate the inclinations of the *yetser* and reconcile them with the plan of God's creation. But, in contrast to the doctrine of suppression, this alternative Talmudic tradition refuses to identify the evil *yetser* with the body and goodness with the soul. Such body/soul dualisms are rejected. The distinction between good and evil is seen as a moral choice rather than a physical property of being. And this emphasis on the *ethical* rather than *ontological* character of the imagination is regarded by several commentators as one of the main features which differentiate the Hebraic from the Hellenic understanding of this concept.[21] According to this Talmudic tradition, evil does not pre-exist man, either as a form of cosmic being or as a pre-established given of his own corporeal being. Evil, like good, is seen in the context of man's ethical horizon of decision.

If the *yetser* in a measure displaces Satan in the rabbinical account of sin it must be regarded as a movement in the direction of a more ethical and rational conception. For the *yetser*, however vividly it is personified, always remains the tendency or disposition of a man's heart. Satan cannot be appealed to for the purpose of explaining the origin of the *yetser* . . . God made the good *yetser* also and man is responsible for the evil, or at least for its persistence . . . or the evil *yetser* itself is good, or at least inevitable in this world, and men are to turn it to good purposes.[22]

4 Imagination and history

These considerations of the *ethical* cast of the Hebraic understanding of the imagination return us finally to the question of its equally fundamental *historical* character. What is the precise logic behind the biblical equation of the birth of imagination with the origin of history?

The benign Talmudic interpretation runs thus: the Divine Potter, never unmindful of the final goal for his clay, recognized only too well that while imagination had become explicitly evil by virtue of the fall, one of its future historical possibilities remained a return to the good. Of course, this return could never signify a return to the pre-lapsarian harmony of Eden. But it could manifest itself as a covenant between man and God with regard to the future direction of history. Though contaminated by the original sin of Adam, imagination might yet serve as the midwife to an ultimately good end – the opening of a new dialogue between man and God which would issue in the Messianic Kingdom. Put in the form of an hypothesis: is it not conceivable that imagination was created by God as an invitation to join Him in the completion of His creation? Was this not part of the Potter's plan from the outset? Was this not the reason Yahweh decided to rest on the Seventh Day of Creation – so as to leave a free time and space for man to realize his creative potential by actively contributing to the venture of historical creation? Moreover, did this not signify, as one Hasidic reading has it, that 'man was created as an open system, meant to grow and to develop, and was not finished, as the rest of creation'?[23]

Such a view would certainly explain why the Jewish concept of repentance as return (*teshuvah*) was understood as an ethical act whereby 'man returns to the right way, to God' – i.e. 'return' as an independent act of man, not a passive submission.[24] Fromm offers a perceptive gloss on this whole question in line with the Talmudic tradition of integration:

The main emphasis of biblical and later Jewish religious thought is not on knowledge *about* God but on the *imitation* of God. This imitation is to be attempted by following the right way of living, which is called *halakhah*. The word has its root in the word 'to walk'. *Halakhah* means, then, the way in which one walks; this way leads to an ever-increasing approximation of God's actions.[25]

The consequence of such reasoning is that just as man's appropriation of the knowledge of good and evil was a choice of his own making, so too he may choose to return to his Creator, thereby transforming his initial evil into an ultimate good. But whether he decides to redirect his creative imagination to the way of divine creation – pursuing the way of *imitation* – or to continue his wandering through the desert of idolatrous fantasies, man's ethical choice remains a *free* one. And this very freedom belies man's oft repeated accusation, epitomized in Cain's famous complaint, that God is responsible for man's evil deeds since he created him with the evil *yetser*.[26] By choice man made his imagination evil; and by choice he can make it good. Decision for the good results in the historical realization of man's *yetser* in accordance with the plan (*yetser*) of the Original Creator (*Yotsor*) (*Baba Bathra*. 16a; *Berach*. 60b). God deliberates:

Imagination is not entirely evil, it is evil and good, for in the midst of it and from out of it decisions (man) can arouse the heart's willing direction toward Him, master the vortex of the possible and realize the human figure proposed in creation, as it could not yet do prior to the knowledge of good and evil. . . . Greatest danger and greatest opportunity at once . . . To unite the two urges (of the *yetser*) implies to equip the absolute potency of passion with the one direction that renders it capable of great love and great service. Thus and not otherwise can man become whole.[27]

In Jewish teaching the ethical notion of goodness is thus intimately related to the historical notion of becoming. This Hebraic preference for the historical category of becoming over the ontological category of being (which predominated in Hellenic culture), has radical implications. It declares that man *is* not good *per se* but may become so. But the act of becoming good means that goodness itself, as a condition of existence, is never acquired in any definitive fashion; it is never reducible to a single act in the present. On the contrary, one might say that it is an 'eschatological horizon which opens up the path of history as a dynamic movement towards the end (*eschaton*) or goal of perfect goodness – a goal which would only finally be realized in the arrival of the Messianic era, what Christianity later referred to as the Coming of the Kingdom.

The biblical concept of goodness thus calls for the action of man with man, and ultimately with *all* men, so that the Messianic era may be achieved in its proper time: at the end of history. Hence the Judeo-Christian teaching that goodness must not *show* itself in the sense of reducing itself to the realm of *being* here and now – for such is the way of pride and idolatry. Goodness, in the full sense, must always remain a promise, as it were *beyond being*, until the ultimate coming of the Messiah, that is, until man and God are fully reconciled at the end of time.[28] In contrast to the Greek understanding of time as a circular movement of recurrence – based on the cycles of the heavenly bodies, of day and night, summer and winter and the constant renewal of nature and man through birth and death – the Hebraic understanding of time is of a more linear historical path leading from the past towards the future: a path subject to alteration by human intervention. In accordance with this view of history, as Hannah Arendt observes, it was the biblical tradition which first introduced the Western concept of free will:

The Greeks had no notion of the faculty of the will, our mental organ for a future that in principle is indeterminable and therefore a possible harbinger of novelty. . . . The Hebrew-Christian credo of a divine beginning – 'In the beginning God created the heavens and the earth' – stated that man was the only creature made in God's image, hence endowed with the like faculty of beginning. . . . Augustine, it seems, drew the consequence: *Initium ut esset, creatus est homo* ('That a beginning be made man was created').[29]

The Hebraic notion of history may be summed up, accordingly, in terms of its threefold character as *creation* (both human and divine), *return* and *becoming*. Each of these features is largely specific to the biblical viewpoint, though it was later introduced into the Graeco-Roman culture, principally under the aegis of Christian thought which effected a synthesis of Greek and biblical modes of understanding. But whereas the Hellenic culture treats imagination primarily from the point of view of cognition (epistemology), the singular originality of the Hebraic concept of the *yetser* resides in its emphasis on man's free choice between good and evil (ethics). Rather than construing evil as a *cosmological* property of being, over and above man's moral responsibility, the Hebraic tradition sees it as an essentially *anthropological* act – that is, as an option which the human imagination may choose or refuse as it constructs its historical destiny. Paul Ricoeur emphasizes this basic trait of the Hebraic imagination in *The Symbolism of Evil*:

What underlies this ethical vision of the world is the idea of a liberty entirely responsible and always at its own disposal. This notion . . . is implicit in various themes of a practical rather than speculative character, which are found in all the rabbinical literature. The first of these is the theme of the two 'inclinations' or *yetser*; man is subject to the duality of two tendencies, two impulses – a good inclination and an evil inclination. The *yetser ha-ra* is implanted by the Creator in man; it is one of the things that God has made and of which he has said that it is 'very good'. The evil inclination, then, is not a radical evil . . . from which man is radically powerless to free himself; it is rather a permanent temptation that gives opportunity for the exercise of freedom of choice, an obstacle to be transformed into a springboard. 'Evil inclination' does not make sin something irreparable. This interpretation is confirmed by the Jewish literature concerning 'repentance' . . . For 'repentance' signifies that 'return' to God, freely chosen, is always open to man . . . it is always *possible* for a man to 'change his way'.[30]

Our preceding analysis has revealed the Hebraic concept of imagination in terms of four fundamental properties:

1. As *mimetic* (a human imitation of the divine act of creation);
2. As *ethical* (a choice between good and evil);
3. As *historical* (a projection of future possibilities of existence);
4. As *anthropological* (an activity proper to man which differentiates him from both a higher divine order and a lower animal order and which opens up a freedom of becoming beyond the necessity of cosmic being).

5 The Golem legend

We conclude our study of the Hebraic concept of imagination with a brief look at some Kabbalistic and Hasidic tales of the Golem – a quasi-human creature constructed by man in imitation of his divine Creator. Again here, at the level of popular Jewish folklore, we find evidence of the Hebraic fascination with the notion of creation (*yetsirah*) as a paradoxical interplay of human and divine activities. The following tale may serve as a typical example:

Ben Sira wished to study the Book Yetsirah (the Book of Creation). Then a heavenly voice went forth: You cannot make such a creature alone. He went to his father, Jeremiah. They busied themselves with it, and at the end of three years a man was created to them, on whose forehead stood Emeth (truth), as on Adam's forehead. Then the man they had made said to them: God alone created Adam and when he wished to let Adam die, he erased the Aleph from Emeth (truth) and he remained Meth (dead). That is what you should do with me and not create another man, lest the world succumb to idolatry as in the days of Enosh. The created man said to them: reverse the combination of letters by which I was created, and erase the Aleph of the word Emeth from my forehead – and immediately he fell into dust.[31]

The created man referred to in this tale was known as the 'Golem'. The parallel with the Genesis account of God's creation of Adam is no coincidence. The book entitled Yetsirah, draws its meaning – i.e. creation – from the same root yzr as the term yetser.[32] The Book of Creation (Sefer Yetsirah) was thought to have contained the secret letter-combination which God used when he created man. It was said to have been presented to Abraham by God in order that he might, together with his descendants, assist the deity in continuing his work of creation in history.[33] Despite the cautionary tone of the above account of Ben Sira's adventure – viz. its warning against man's inclination to usurp God by becoming an idolater of his own created image – one frequently finds more optimistic readings of the yetsirah legend. Thus we read in Sanhedrin. 65b: 'Rava said – if the righteous wished, they could create a world, for it is written (Isa. 59:2): Your man is saintly without sin his creative power is no longer separated from that of God.' In another rabbinical text we find a more explicit allusion to the positive connotations of the yetsirah story as a replay of Genesis: 'Rabbi Tahhuma said in the name of Rabbi Eleazer: In the hour when God created the first Adam, He created him as a Golem and he was stretched out from one end of the world to the other . . . and He showed him all the generations and their wise men, all the generations and all their leaders' (Genesis Rabbah. 24). This passage suggests that the first man, Adam, was the original Golem in which the potential of all historical creation resides, standing at both the beginning and the end of time, holding out the promise of a new and radically transfigured mankind. The Sanhedrin text, for its part, suggests how this promise might be lawfully realized by those holy men who commit themselves to the work of God. And this point is developed further by Judah Ben Barzilaii, perhaps the most celebrated exegete of the *Book of Creation*, who affirms that this holy task may only be accomplished if man resists the danger of idolatry and fully recognizes that the creation of a new history is never the result of a single human imagination but requires that men work together in community and under the strict guidance of God's law. To support his contention he cites this 'old recension' of the *Sefer Yetsirah*:

Abraham sat alone and meditated on it, but could understand nothing until a heavenly voice went forth and said to him: 'Are you trying to set yourself up as my equal? I am one and created the Book *Yetsirah* and studied it: but you by yourself cannot understand it. Therefore take a companion, and meditate on it together, and you will understand it.' Thereupon Abraham went to his teacher Shem, son of Noah, and sat with him for three years, and they meditated on it until they knew how to create a world.[34]

This conviction that the historical task of creation is essentially a collective enterprise, requiring an ongoing dialogue, not only between man and man but also between man and God, finds additional confirmation in other examples of holy partnership invoked in Hasidic texts – e.g. the rabbinical teams of Rava and Zera, Hanina and Oshaya, Jeremiah and Bena Shira and, according to some versions, Jesus and his disciples.[35] But while it is true that several Kabbalist and Hasidic accounts of the creation of the Golem entertain the possibility of a positive outcome, the mainstream rabbinical tradition remained extremely prudent. Time and again we witness the deeply rooted biblical suspicion of the mimetic powers of the creative imagination. If man, created in God's image, avails of his imagination to create a new man (Golem) in his own image, will not this act of imitation bring about the death of God by man and the idolatrous birth of man as God? Is this not the reasoning behind the admonition of Ben Shira's Golem to renounce the privilege of *yetsirah* lest the world succumb to idolatry as in the days of Enosh?

This fear of the Enosh event is, in the final analysis, paramount. The Bible tells us that Enosh was the first idolater. Questioning his father Seth about his origins and being informed that Adam had neither father nor mother but was created by God's breathing into the earth, he proceeded to make a figure from mud and to breathe upon it. As it is told, Satan came and slipped into the figure, giving it the appearance of life and the countenance of God. Enosh's idolatry, together with the identification of the evil imagination with Adam's original act of transgression (seeking to 'be like God'), are no doubt at one with the orthodox Hebraic mistrust of 'images' (see Appendix). For both accounts apprise us of the dangers attached to man's attempts to *imitate* God's power of creation. Well might the prophet Isaiah scorn the 'strange thought' of the clay scheming against the potter, the handicraft disowning its craftsman or the thing of art calling the artist fool (*Is.* 29:16); but it was just such a strange thought which occasioned the fall of the First Man from paradise and which ever after would haunt all who sought to emulate the formula of *yetsirah* in constructing a Golem.

The Jewish attitude to the Golem was, understandably, one charged with both suspicion and fascination. And this ambivalent attitude left a long and varied legacy ranging from the middle European legends of popular Jewish tradition, and beyond that to such celebrated notions as the Alchemist's 'homunculus' (a human figure made from base matter) and the various Frankenstein creatures of folk culture.[36] But it was within Jewish folklore itself that the Golem legend most conspicuously flourished. Among the most famous versions are those of the Great Rabbi of Poland and Rabbi Loew of Prague. The account of the Polish Rabbi, dating from the sixteenth century, tells how he succeeded in stopping the Golem he had made from revolting against him. But he suffered death in doing so: as the Golem collapsed back into the clay from which it had been formed, it fell upon the Rabbi and smothered him.

The account of the Prague Rabbi spells out the moral tale in more elaborate detail. Here we are told how Rabbi Loew ben Bezalel, a renowned scholar and mystic, magically produced a quasi-human figure from matter and gave it a sort of life by infusing it with the concentrated power of his mind.[37] Since this power was but a reflection of God's own creative power, the Rabbi placed a slip of paper into the completed Golem's mouth with the mystic name of God written upon it. While the seal was in his mouth the Golem remained alive, performing all kinds of useful tasks for his Rabbi master and the Jews of Prague. The Golem differed most radically from human beings in that he lacked the capacity to speak. But he was allowed to rest on the Sabbath day like God's own creatures. The Rabbi would simply remove the slip of paper from his mouth and he would become inanimate. On the eve of one particular Sabbath, however, Rabbi Loew forgot to remove the seal as he went to pray at the great synagogue in Prague. As the Sabbath dawned the Golem got restive and began to roam about in the ghetto like a madman bent on destruction. Hearing reports of this, the Rabbi rushed into the streets and confronted his own handiwork which had now outgrown him and threatened to overpower him. Stretching out his hand he grabbed the Holy Name from the Golem's mouth, whereupon the man-made creature disintegrated into his original condition of lifeless dust.

Tracing these popular legends back to the Jewish mystical writers of the Middle Ages known as the Kabbalists, Gershom Scholem makes an explicit link between these mystical commentaries and the biblical account of the creation of Adam:

The Golem – a creature created by human intelligence and concentration which is controlled by its creator and performs tasks set by him, but which at the same time may have a dangerous tendency to outgrow that control and develop destructive potentialities – is nothing but a replica of Adam, the first Man himself. God could create Man from a heap of clay and invest him with a spark of His divine life force and intelligence (this, in the last analysis, is the 'divine image' in which man was created). Without this intelligence and the spontaneous creativity of the human mind, Adam would have been nothing but a Golem – as, indeed, he is called in some of the old rabbinic stories interpreting the biblical account. When there was only the combination and culmination of natural and material forces, and before that all-important divine spark was breathed into him, Adam was nothing but a Golem. Only when a tiny bit of God's creative power was passed on did he become Man, in the image of God. Is it, then, any wonder that Man should try to do in his own small way what God did in the beginning?[38]

Each version of the Golem legend reminds us, however, that an essential difference exists between human and divine creation. While man can conjure up the forces of material nature and combine them according to the mystical numbers and letters of God's original creation – thereby producing the semblance of a human pattern – there are always at least two things lacking to the man-made Golem: *speech* and *sexual inclination*.[39] As we have already noted, in the biblical mind speech was related to the letters of Creation (*Yetsirah*) which was, in turn, reflected in the human power of the *yetser*. And sexual drives were equally related, albeit usually in a disapproved sense, to the *yetser*. This rapport was alluded to in several rabbinical texts. But it finds reinforced expression in the later Kabbalist-inspired versions of the Golem story. Thus in one saying attributed to the Rabbi of Prague we read that 'the Golem was created without the sexual urge; for if he had that instinct, no woman would have been safe from him'.[40]

There is, then, a profound paradox in the basic attitude to the Golem in so far as he is made in the image of man who is himself made in the image of God. Accordingly, the Golem both *resembles* his human creator and yet fundamentally *lacks* his creative power (that is, the *yetser* which expresses itself in imaginative projects, speech and sexual desire). The Golem is incapable of producing more Golems. And he is also incapable of morally choosing between good or evil. Yet, precisely as a quasi-human creature, the Golem remains a testament to the divine spark of creativity at work within the human *yetser*. Scholem explains some of the Kabbalist ideas behind this paradoxical attitude:

Just as the human mind remains infinitely inferior to the all-encompassing divine intelligence of God, so does the Golem's intelligence lag behind the human – that is to say, it lacks that spontaneity which alone makes Man what he is. But still, even on a subhuman plane, there is in the Golem a representation of Man's creative power. The universe, so the Kabbalists tell us, is built essentially on the prime elements of numbers and letters, because the letters of God's language reflected in human language are nothing but a concentration of His creative energy. Thus, by assembling these elements in all their possible combinations and permutations, the Kabbalist who contemplates the mysteries of Creation radiates some of this elementary power into the Golem. The creation of a Golem is then in some way an affirmation of the productive and creative power of Man. It repeats, on however small a scale, the work of creation.[41]

The more sinister side of this similar-yet-different relation between the Golem and its maker is emphasized in most accounts of the legend. This is particularly evident in a variation of the Golem story cited above where Jeremiah and his son Sira consulted the *Book of Creation*, producing a creature with the letters 'God the Lord is Truth' (*YHWH Elohim Emeth*) imprinted on his forehead. In this version, it is the Golem himself who removes the letter *alef* from *Emeth*, meaning *truth*, so that the word *meth*, meaning *dead*, remains. On seeing this, Jeremiah rents his garment because of the blasphemous implication that 'God is Dead', angrily demanding of the Golem an explanation for his action. The Golem's reply establishes a clear link between the idolatrous dangers of Golem-making and the demise of God:

'I will tell you a parable. An architect built many houses, cities and squares, but no one could copy his art and compete with him in knowledge and skill until two men persuaded him to teach them the secret of the art. When they had learned how to do everything in the right way, they began to anger him with words. Finally, they broke with him and became architects on their own, except that what he charged a guinea for, they did for ten shillings. When people noticed this, they ceased honoring the artist and instead gave their commissions to his renegade pupils. So God has made you in His image and in His shape and form. But now that you have created a man like Him, people will say: There is no God in the world beside these two!'

When Jeremiah then asked what solution there was, the Golem told him to write the alphabets backward on the earth, but this time to do so meditating not on the ways of assembling but of disassembling. Heeding his counsel, Jeremiah and his son witnessed the man-made creature return to dust before their eyes.[42]

Scholem concludes his appraisal of the Golem tale by suggesting that the contemporary technology of Western culture offers new possibilities of Golem-making which could rival or destroy God's own creative plan. Today, it appears, the Kabbalistic interpretation of the Golem story as a mystical insight into man's creative power is replaced by a pragmatic theory of technical mastery – a meaning warned against in the moral tales of Jewish folk tradition. Instead of being treated as a specifically spiritual exercise, a symbolic replay of the Genesis event, the Golem is now being taken literally as a technical servant of man's needs. In this connection, Scholem cites the modern electronic engineer or applied mathematician as latter-day disciples of the Rabbis of Poland and Prague, concocting their own kind of computerized Golem, yet without the theological and ethical context of their rabbinical ancestors. The contemporary Golems are composed on the basis of the binary computer system of numerical representation rather than on mystical combinations of the twenty-two letters of the Hebrew alphabet. And while the legendary Golems of Jewish tradition were animated by the life-energy of the creative spirit (articulated in the differential name of God), the new mechanical Golems are powered by electronic energy. But what both the Golems of Jewish legend and of advanced technology share in common is the absence of speech and of desire. And it is here perhaps that we find evidence of the Golem's continued *lack* of the creative power of the *yetser* – a fundamental safeguard against its ever becoming a perfect 'image' of man or God. Aware of this limit to the advances of technological science, Scholem issues this admonishment: 'I say to the Golem and its creator: develop peacefully and don't destroy the world.'[43]

Such an admonishment corresponds to the basic Jewish belief that the making of Golems in simulation of the divine act of creation in *Genesis*, was permissible not so much as a *real* creation but only as a 'creation of thought' (*yezirah mahshartith*) – a symbolic ritual which might serve to remind men of the inimitable greatness of God. As Judah Ben Bathyra counselled: 'Truly one should study such things only in order to know the power and omnipotence of the Creator of this world, but not in order really to practise them.'[44] Golem-making is a dangerous undertaking for it threatens to destroy the creator himself. The wisest solution to the paradox of the creative imagination is, it appears, to resist the temptation to imitate God's original act of creation. This is a simple step involving, as Ben Shira discovered, no more than the removal of a single letter from the forehead of the Golem. The life which was hailed as divine truth (*emeuth*) thus returns to its natural condition of dust, of lifelessness (*meth*).

APPENDIX

The 'Image of God' debate

The Genesis formulations about man being 'created in the image and likeness of God' have given rise to an immense body of scholarly commentary and controversy, spanning both the Jewish and Christian traditions. The Old Testament suggests that the 'image of God' is something which relates to the First Man (Adam) from the moment of creation and is not lost by the Fall. The New Testament reinterprets this reading somewhat, claiming that the 'image of God' belongs in the full sense only to Christ – the image now being seen as a perfect reflection of the Divine prototype, which the human believer may come to participate in by means of an eschatological hope.[1]

The Old Testament sources

In both biblical accounts of God's creation of man – *Gen.* 1:26–7 and 2:8 – two terms are used to express a relation of resemblance: 'image' (*tselem*) and 'likeness' (*demuth*). The former is sometimes interpreted as a concrete resemblance and the latter as a more abstract notion of relation between the human personality and God. But the matter is by no means clear cut. *The Interpreter's Dictionary to the Bible* informs us that each of the terms – *tselem* and *demuth* – are used in the Old Testament to refer to both a concrete and abstract meaning. Of the seventeen occurrences of *tselem* in the Old Testament, five are from the Genesis passages on creation mentioned above; ten carry a more concrete and material sense of 'statue', 'model', 'picture'; while the remaining two refer to a more oblique or mental sense of image as 'shadow' or 'dream'. It appears to be the more abstract/spiritual connotations of this term which determine certain later renditions of this notion as 'personality', 'consciousness', 'freedom of will' and 'immortality' (e.g. *Wisd. Sol,* , 2:23–4). The five Genesis allusions to *tselem*, which primarily concern us here, are generally located somewhere in the middle of the scale extending from the concrete to the abstract. And it is perhaps worth noting that in some of the Jewish exegetical literature, particularly of a mystical or Kabbalistic bent, *tselem* gave rise to a double interpretation based on an antithetical play of associated words: *halom* (dream image) and *golem* (material image) – the implication being that man bears a resemblance to both the spiritual and physical orders of creation.[2]

The second term used in the Genesis account of creation, *demuth*, also carries the dual sense of abstract and concrete resemblance. The paradoxical nature of this term was to preoccupy many Jewish exegetes, and Moses Maimonides, the famous twelfth-century thinker, devoted the opening chapter of his *Guide to the Perplexed* to a detailed commentary of its meanings. He concludes that *demuth* refers primarily to a spiritual or 'notional' likeness and leads to idolatry if taken in a purely 'material' sense (whence Yahweh's reproach to Israel – 'what image will you find to match me with', *Isaiah*, 40:25).[3] Not surprisingly, certain mystical Jewish commentaries explored the dual connotation of the root *DMH*, in the form of verbal associations: *dam* referring to 'blood' or man's animal/physical nature; and *damah* referring to a condition of stillness, silence or composure as in *Ps.* 131:2 (which may allude to the more spiritual activity of contemplation which man shares with the angels).

The terms *tselem* and *demuth* also appear in a curious passage in *Gen.* 5:3 where the reference is not to the relation between God and Adam but between Adam and his own son, Seth. But here the terms of resemblance are used in reverse order. Whereas God makes man according to His image (*tselem*) and likeness (*demuth*), Adam engenders Seth according to his likeness (*demuth*) and image (*tselem*). Some rabbinical commentators have taken this inversion to mean that in the properly human order of historical creation-procreation, it is man's ethical responsibility to make the 'human' likeness of *demuth* into a more divine resemblance (*tselem*).[4]

A third biblical term for 'image' (*temuna*) also contains a basic ambivalence. Whereas, for example, the Second Commandment (*Ex.* 20:4) speaks of God's prohibition of man-made 'graven images' which bear a likeness (*temuna*) to anything in the heavens above, the famous passage in *Deut.* 4:15–24, relating the fact that man saw no 'similitude' (*temuna*) of God at Horeb, does not deny that God has such a form (indeed the theophanies described in *Is.* 6 or *Ezk. I* actually imply that God does possess such a form and that it might be glimpsed in some fashion). It is no doubt to this passage that the *Wisdom of Solomon* (7:25–26) alludes when it speaks of Divine Wisdom as a 'flawless mirror of the active power of God' and the 'image of his Goodness'. Though it must be borne in mind that the *Wisdom* text was written in Greek and so was probably susceptible to Greek philosophical influences.

The authors of *The Interpreter's Dictionary of the Bible* document the various oscillations in the Old Testament texts between the view that God can be seen and that He cannot. Our attention is also drawn to the central fact that what Genesis says is,

not that man may make an image of God – this he would have strenuously denied – but that God has made man an image of himself. By stating likeness, he also implies distance. It should also be recognized that to assert external resemblance does not exclude spiritual resemblance. The OT does not treat man as a duality of soul and body.[5]

They conclude their scholarly analysis of the 'image of God' with the following interesting observations:

while much of the thought that there is an external resemblance between God and man may be present – Ezekiel, who was a priest, has it, however cautiously he states it – P seems to have reached a measure of abstraction. We may not go far wrong if we say that for him the image of God means personality, provided we remember this must not be understood in the sense of the autonomous, self-legislating self of the philosophers. Man is determined by God as his Creator. By 'image of God' may be meant what gives authority, and that God has made him to exercise such may imply responsibility.

Though the image of God must not be defined in terms of the task of ruling over the lower creation, or of ability to do so (cf. Ecclus. 17:3), the two are closely connected. This appears also in Ps. 8, which speaks of God's condescension to, and care of, man and his granting him a status little less than divine and royal honors that he may exercise his rule. The glory and honor with which man is crowned suggest both external beauty and inward dignity. The mythological account of the king of Tyre in Eden (Ezek. 28:12, 17) implies an endowment of beauty and also of wisdom. We may say that Ps. 8 implies dignity and authority and nobility of appearance as God's gift to man to fit him for his cultural task (cf. Gen. 1:26, 28).[6]

At best, the Old Testament treatment of the 'image of God' theme may be seen as allowing for the possibility of man becoming a creative vicar of God on earth. At worst, it may be read as a stern warning against man's idolatrous impulses to set himself up as a rival of God. The fact that both readings are tenable is perhaps what is most significant.

The inherent ambiguity of the three main biblical terms for 'image' (*tselem, demuth, temuna*) – in addition to that evident in the term for 'imagination' (*yetser*) – would appear to express a deep ambivalence in the very design of creation itself. In his famous treatise, *Nefesh Hahayyim (The Spirit of Life)*, published in the nineteenth century, Rabbi Hayyim of Volozhyn notes that man was made by God as a being who participates in both a superior and inferior order of creation – the heavens and the earth formed on the first day of creation. Hayyim cites a Midrash (*Genesis Rabba,* 12) which declares that when God wished to create man he was faced with a fundamental dilemma: if he formed man from the elements of the superior world only, there would be no peace in the universe (for the superior world would vanquish the inferior); whereas if he formed him from the inferior elements only, there would be no peace either (as the inferior world would constantly threaten the superior). And so God decided to create man from *both* elements at once, taking dust from the earth and then breathing a living soul through man's nostrils (*Gen.* 2:7).

It is in this creation context of man as a mediational being, stretched like a rope between the earth below and the heavens above, that Rabbi Hayyim interprets the passage from *Deut.* 32:9 – 'Because his people are one part of God, Jacob strode across (*hebel*, meaning literally a rope) his heritage'. Rabbi Hayyim makes a similar observation with regard to Jacob's dream of a 'ladder stretching towards the earth' (*Gen.* 28:12). He notes that the ladder is not reaching up from the earth, but down from the heavens. This he takes to refer to the fact that the power of creation properly derives from on high – as when God first breathed the divine spirit into man. The power of creation descends from God into the life spirit (*Nefesh*) of man and from there to the world as a whole. Thus when we read that Jacob 'dreamed and behold there was a ladder' with the 'angels of the Lord mounting and descending', we are being told, Rabbi Hayyim claims, about the spirit of the higher angelic world which depends upon human images, thoughts and actions in order to find access to the living world below. Moreover, the fact that the angels mount the ladder before descending suggests to Rabbi Hayyim that the life spirit must itself first elevate the world to the superior order of divine light before it can descend again, illuminated, to the world. The ladder, Rabbi Hayyim concludes, is in fact the 'breath of life' which God breathes into man, thereby making communication possible between the higher and lower orders of creation.[7]

The bilateral nature of creation was also commented on by the Kabbalist school of Safed in the sixteenth century as well as being discussed in detail in the introduction to the influential *Tiqqunei Zohar*.[8] In these commentaries the world of Creation (*Olam ha-Yetsira*) is seen as an indispensable process of mediation between i) the world of Emanation (*Olam ha-Atsilut*) which is still substantially one with God, and ii) the lower material world of mere fabrication (*Olam ha-Assiya*) which stands at the furthest remove from God. The midworld of Creation is inhabited by both the angels and mankind and can serve as both an agency of manifestation for the divine light and/or as a screen against it. Accordingly, the primordial man created by God (*Adam Qadmon*) was said to participate in the divine world (*Atsilut*) in so far as he reached upwards to the heavens, and in the material world (*Assiya*) in so far as he reached downwards to the earth. What is more, the intermediary world of Creation (*Yetsira* coming from the same root *YZR* as *yetser*) was said to correspond – at the metaphorical level of Adam's body – to the middle regions of the liver and the heart: the focus also of the creative life force or spirit.[9] And, by extension, the world of Creation was associated with the human power of speech and imagination – whence the biblical allusion to the 'imaginations of man's heart'.[10] Thus we find the Kabbalist commentaries relating the *theological* division of successive orders of creation to a *cosmological* division into different worlds which in turn relates to an *anthropological* division into different parts of the Adamic body (head, heart, feet).[11]

Rabbi Hayyim's most explicit interpretation of the 'image of God' motif is to be found in the opening part of his *Nefesh Hahayyim* treatise. Here we find the claim that the controversial remarks in Genesis about man's resemblance to God refer primarily to the *creative* capacity to transform the world:

Just as He, Elohim, is Master of the powers which exist in all the worlds . . . So He decided to confer on man the power of developing and restraining the myriad forces in the worlds. Every detail of man's behaviour affects all the domains at each instant, thanks to the superior roots of his actions, words and thoughts, as if he himself were master of these forces, so to speak. . . . As Rabbi Azariya put it: When Israel enacts the will of God, it reinforces the power of the Most High, because it is written that 'In the Lord, we strengthen his power' (*Psalms*, 60,14). But when Israel does not enact the will of God, man weakens, if we may so put it, the power of the Most High, because it is written: 'You weaken the rock which has engendered you' (*Deut.* 32,18).[12]

Rabbi Hayyim goes on to cite the Zohar's repeated assertions that 'man's sins make fissures On High' and the psalmist who exorts man to 'give power to the Lord' (*Ps.* 68:35). And the main implication he draws from such passages is that man has an ethical responsibility to restore and consolidate God's power by realizing the divine plan for historical creation in his everyday acts here on earth. One of the most mysterious acts of God, according to Hayyim, was to have 'given to man of the lower world, the charge of the higher worlds'.[13] And this curious blending of lower and higher is itself related to Adam, as the first created man, and his acquisition of the Knowledge of Good and Evil. Much is made of the fact that the Hebrew term for knowledge (*Da'at*) means to 'bind' together opposites. Sin is thus seen as a blurring of oppositions, as the rabbinical masters noted in their gloss on the idolatry of the Golden Calf: 'Satan came and introduced confusion into the world' (*Shabbat*, 89). And this confusion resulting from the fabrication of false images of God is seen as a consequence of Adam's original sin: 'They too, like Adam, transgressed against the Alliance' (*Hosea*, 6,7). It is in this context that Rabbi Hayyim makes the curious suggestion that Yahweh's banishment of Adam and Eve from paradise before they could eat of the Tree of Life, should be seen as a benevolent wish to save man from existing 'eternally' in sin: death is not merely a punishment but rather an opportunity for man to escape from his condition of sinful confusion and be restored, through death, to God.[14]

But if man's sinfulness results from a confusion of lower and higher, his ability to mediate in a *positive* manner between higher and lower is what constitutes his superiority to the angels. For only man 'has the capacity to elevate, bind and unify the worlds by the results of his actions, because he alone is made up of a combination of all the worlds'.[15] Indeed the angelic world can only be elevated by the good actions of men (in so far as they contain an angelic component). The angels cannot by themselves take the initiative of praising creation: they receive this power from Israel when she sanctifies the Lord by means of creative ethical actions.[16]

Man's being made in the image of God refers not just backwards to the original act of creation but also forwards to the possibility of realizing a future kingdom. Commenting on the rabbinical proposition that 'all of Israel has a portion of the future world', Rabbi Hayyim points out that such a world does not already exist but remains a task for the creative work of man 'who by his acts enlarges, augments and founds his proper portion'.[17] Similarly, hell is not something which exists independently of human action. Evil contains its own punishment as *Proverbs* (5:22) informs us: 'The evil one is caught in his sins, he is embroiled in the entrails of his crime.' Hell is created by the sinners themselves. And it is interesting to note how in rabbinical literature, as in the Greek myth of Prometheus, man's act of sinful rebellion is identified with the making of fire. As *Isaiah* (50:11) puts it: 'All of you who kindle fire, go ye into the flames of your fire'. Thus it is, according to rabbinical commentators, that whenever man breaks the commandments of God he kindles the fire of the 'evil imagination'; while the overcoming of the 'evil imagination' by the 'good imagination' quenches the fire.[18]

The implication of all this is that man is ultimately responsible for the kind of relationship which exists between the lower and the higher worlds. Although we may consider our actions and imaginings to be of little consequence, they do in fact affect the whole creation process from beginning to end. For just as Yahweh created man in his own image by breathing the spirit into his body, so too, the Zohar tells us, 'each breath of man's mouth has its importance . . . No word or sound uttered by man is vain: there is a place for each of them' (*Zohar II*, 100b).

The biblical and rabbinical texts do acknowledge, however, an essential difference between the divine and human acts of creation, no matter how much the latter may resemble, confirm or otherwise affect the former. There are two terms used for God's creation of man – *Bara* and *Yatsar*. And the first of these is attributed to God alone. In the first creation account in Genesis (1:27), the word *Bara* is employed, suggesting that here God is concerned with a creation from nothing (*ex nihilo*). In the second account in Genesis (2:7), the term *Yatsar* is used in conjunction with *Bara* – 'He created (*yatsar*) him out of dust . . . and in the Garden of Eden he put the man he had just created (*yatsar*).' Here the implication is that God creates Adam not from nothing, but from pre-existing matter. It is in the second sense of creation – and in this sense only – that man's creative power (*yetser*) may be said to resemble God's. For man's creation of images or things are always and of necessity from pre-existing created elements.

This secondary sense of creation, as an activity common to both God and man, is invoked in several telling metaphors of the craftsman or artist – as, for example, in *Isaiah*. 29:16 where *Yatsar* is employed to refer to the potter forming his clay (a connotation made clear in the Septuagint translations of *Yatsar* by the Greek term, *plassein*, meaning the artist's activity of shaping works from matter, whence the modern English use of the term 'plastic arts'). Moreover, the fact that several Jewish texts (e.g. *Abot*, 4) invoke Yahweh as both *Bore* and *Yotser*, would seem to confirm the existence of two modalities of creation. While man may be said to legitimately imitate God as *Yotser* in so far as his creative activities express his 'good imagination' (*yetser hatov*), he cannot presume to emulate God as a Creator *ex nihilo* (*Bore*).

Certain recent Jewish commentators have extended the rabbinical interpretations of the 'image of God' controversy into an affirmation of man's ethical responsibility not only for himself and the world, but for God Himself. As Emmanuel Levinas has remarked, the biblical assertion that man is created in the image and likeness of God reveals a 'God who has chosen to be dependent on human beings, who are henceforth charged with the infinite responsibility of sustaining the universe'.[19] The complex set of paradoxes arising from the various terms used to define the resemblance between the Creator and his creatures may be seen accordingly as a 'felicitous ambiguity whereby the *more* is signalled in the *less*, the *new* in the *old*, the *beyond* in the *here*'.[20] This implies that the central insight of biblical religion consists in grounding the highest aim of religious life in the *ethical*. Such insight into the dependency of God's creation on man's ethical acts of re-creation contains the following revolutionary consequences:

The all powerful God can only relate to the being of the worlds, if I as a human being, conform to the exigencies of the Torah. God associates with, or dissociates from, the being of other beings than myself by virtue of my actions; I am responsible for the universe! Man is responsible for others . . . is the soul of all the worlds, of all beings, all life, like the Creator Himself. Not in the sense of some diabolic pride or presumption, but in virtue of the will of God who did not recoil from this equality with the human and even a certain subordination to it . . . God placed his creative word into the mouth of man! Whence the conclusion of the *Isaiah* verse 50:16 – '*Imi Ata*', you are *with* me, you are with me in the act of creation; the acts, words and intentions of man have power over the created world and over the forces of creation itself![21]

2 *The New Testament sources*

While our third chapter will discuss various concepts of imagination developed by Christian philosophers from Augustine to the scholastics in the wake of the Greek influence, it is perhaps fitting to make some brief remarks here about the more biblically-inspired commentaries on the 'image of God' debate to be found in the Christian tradition of exegesis. This tradition generally involved a rereading of the Old Testament sources in the light of the New Testament.

There are at least two passages in the New Testament where the Old Testament view reappears without substantial alteration – *I Cor.* 11:7 and *Jas.* 3:9. The first of these passages uses the term *eikon* (the Septuagint rendering of *tselem*), while the latter uses the term *homoiousis* (the Septuagint rendering of *demuth*). In most other New Testament references to the 'image of God', *eikon* is employed to suggest not so much a 'likeness' in the Old Testament sense, but a 'perfect reflection of the prototype'. As the following entry from the *Interpreter's Dictionary of the Bible* explains:

Nothing could make clearer the tremendous impact of the revelation of God in Christ than the fact that it has almost completely obliterated the thought of man as being in the image of God and replaced it with the thought of Christ as being the image of God, that being understood in the sense of perfect correspondence to the divine prototype.[22]

Whereas the Jewish tradition spoke of Wisdom as a 'spotless mirror of the working of God' and the 'image of his goodness' (e.g. *Wisd. Sol* 7:25–6), the Christian texts attribute this role of privileged reflection to Christ himself, as son of God: 'He reflects the glory of God and bears the very stamp of his nature' (*Heb.* 1:3). The implication is that in Christ the image of God ceases to be a merely spiritual likeness and becomes a historically incarnate reality. To see Christ, as John affirms, is to see the Father (*John*, 1:14, 12:45, 14:9). In becoming flesh the image of God has now been made visible, for those who have eyes to see – the faithful. Paul's writings make this New Testament reading even more explicit. In *Col*, 1:15 we read accordingly that Christ is the 'image (*eikon*) of the invisible God'. Paul makes a telling distinction between the First Adam created out of dust by means of the living spirit and the Second Adam, Christ himself, 'who *is* the Spirit' (II *Cor.* 3:18). The reasoning behind the Pauline reinterpretation of the 'image of God' theme is this:

Paul's mind is filled with the thought that it is only in relation with Christ that man can attain the likeness to God which at the first (Gen. 1:26) was only man's in promise. In Phil. 2:6–8 he speaks of Christ's exchanging the form (μορφη) of God, which was his by right to assume the form of a servant and the likeness of men, μορφη – in both cases, meaning 'mode of existence'.

As Christians are in this Christ, the relationship will work itself out in the relationships existing in the Christian community. In Col. 3:15 the exchanging of the old man (nature) for the new, 'which is being renewed in knowledge after the image of its creator,' will bring about a community in which racial, religous and social distinctions will no longer have any meaning, 'but Christ is all, and in all' (cf. Eph. 4: 22–24).

Above all, Christians must 'put on love, which bonds everything together in perfect harmony' (Col. 3:14). It is in God's plan for men that they should 'be conformed [συμμσοφους] to the image of his Son' (Rom. 8:29) and therefore, since there is no distinction, to the image of God. This is an eschatological hope, but it is also in some real measure a present reality, for 'we all, with unveiled face, beholding the glory of the Lord, are being changed into his likeness from one degree of glory to another; for this comes from the Lord who is the Spirit' (II Cor. 3:18: cf. Phil. 3:20–21).[23]

The New Testament reinterpretation of the Old Testament notion of *yetser* is more difficult to determine. One of the reasons for this is that no single Greek term seems to have been thought suitable to convey the complexity of the Hebrew original.[24] The closest we get is some variation on the idea of forms/figures/ purposes/shapes (*plasma*) of the heart (*cardia*). More often than not the shorthand term *cardia* alone is used to render the ambivalent Hebrew notion of the human origin of good and evil imaginings. (Although other Greek terms were used in the Septuagint rendering of Old Testament occurrences of the term *yetser*: e.g. *plasma* for *Is*. 29:16 and *Ps*. 103:14; *dianoia* for *Gen*. 6:5 and 8:21; *poneria* for *Dt*. *31:21*; and *euthemena* for *Chr*. *I*: 28:9). The most common rendering of *yetser* in the Vulgate is *cogitatio*. But curiously enough, the English Revised Version restores the term 'imagination' for *yetser* in both the *Gen*. 6:5 and 8:21 occurrences. Here, as in the rabbinical texts, one finds the view that good and evil imaginings are elements of the human personality, even propensities to modes of action.[25]

It is arguable, however, that within the Latin tradition of Christian exegesis the Augustinian emphasis on the role of *imaginatio* (a term first employed by Augustine on a consistent basis although occasionally used by earlier Latin authors such as the Elder Pliny and Tacitus) may have borne some relation to the biblical notions of images (*tselem, demuth, temuna*) and creative imagining (*yetser*). While the influence of neo-Platonic versions of the Greek term, *phantasia*, are clearly paramount, the possibility of biblical influences on Augustine's understanding of imagination cannot be ruled out – particularly in his formulations of a theological model of the *Imago Dei* and his frequent references to a positive eschatological role for the faithful in the order of creation. One could cite here Augustine's extraordinary claim that 'we ourselves will be the Seventh Day of Creation' (*Dies Septimus nos ipsi erimus*): a claim which appears to coincide with certain radical Jewish interpretations.[26]

The eschatological connotations of the 'image of God' theme explored by Augustine and other Christian exegetes are, of course, deeply indebted to the Pauline view of the human heart (*cardia*) as the focal point of good and evil inclination (*Rom*. 1:21, 16:18; *Cor*. *II*, 4:6; *Cor*. *I*, 7:37; 1:45). The 'heart' is the place of eschatological decision where man chooses to follow God's plan for the good of creation or else close himself up in evil (*Rom.* 10:6–10; *Cor. II.* 3:14; 1:22). It is quite probable that in such passages Paul has in mind Old Testament allusions to the 'living *yetser*' (*Ezek.* 11:19) and to the command that man should love God with his 'whole heart' (*Deut.* 6:5), that is, by integrating his evil *yetser* into his good *yetser*.[27] This is surely what Paul is referring to when he counsels man to unite the impulses of his heart (*Rom.* 1:24), thereby making them one with the will of God and reconciling the desires of spirit and flesh (*Gal.* 5:7). Paul thus appears to be exploring – albeit through the detour of the Greek language – the Old Testament notion of a good and evil *yetser* in the light of Christian revelation. Instead of seeing God indirectly through images and riddles, 'through a glass darkly' (*aenigmate*), Christ promises an eschatological future where we may behold God 'face to face' (*Cor. I.* 13:12). Adam's fall, which made the 'image of God' an oblique and ambiguous rapport between man and his Creator, may be made good by the Christian promise of a New Creation where the mere reflections of images are replaced by the reality of a direct encounter. But this eschatological promise can only be realized if man undergoes a change of heart and conforms the impulses of his *yetser* to the plan of Divine Creation:

The choice between good and evil expresses itself as a choice between serving the Creator or turning one's back on Him. . . . And so, we come to understand that the ultimate sin is to believe that life is our own possession rather than a gift of the Creator, a life for ourselves rather than for God. . . . Christ reveals the possibility of life just as Adam introduced the possibility of sin and death.[28]

The choice between these rival possibilities remains the ethical responsibility of the human *yetser*. The eschatological promise depends for each man on his use of the 'imaginings of his heart'.[29]

Several Christian commentators, besides Augustine, have made significant contributions to the 'image of God' debate. Although we will be devoting a full chapter to the Christian philosophies of imagination in the medieval period, our attention there will be mainly focused on Christian reinterpretations of Greek epistemology. The explicitly biblical notion of the 'image of God' is not discussed as such. It would seem appropriate therefore to rehearse at this point – as a final consideration in this Appendix – the treatment of this biblical theme by one of the great mystical Christian thinkers, Nicholas of Cusa. We shall concentrate our remarks on one particular treatise, *Trialogus de Possest*, where Cusanus offers a Christian reading of the 'image of God' motif, not according to the ontological/substantialist categories of Augustine or Aquinas, but in terms of a mystical category of 'actualised possibility' which appears to derive more directly from the biblical tradition itself.[30]

A German thinker of the fifteenth century, Cusanus was influenced less by the mainstream of medieval onto-theology than by the mystical theories of such non-conformist thinkers as Eriugena, Bruno, Eckhart and the Rhine movement of mysticism. Departing from the orthodox scholastic definition of God as *Esse*, Cusanus redefines Him as *Possest* (i.e. absolute possibility which includes all that is actual). 'Existence (*esse*) presupposes possibility (*posse*)', says Cusanus, 'since it is not the case that anything exists unless there is possibility from which it exists.'[31] 'God alone', he claims, 'is what he is able to be';[32] and this is so by virtue of His infinitely creative power from the beginning to the end of time.

The consequences of this radical conception of the Creator for a new understanding of the 'image of God' debate are immense. Cusanus states that the idea of *Possest* leads one beyond all the senses, all reason and intellect into a 'mystical vision'.[33] Since everything created by God always exists as a possibility-to-be, man, created in God's image, may be said to participate in a special way in the ongoing process of creation. This is where the human powers of imaging and imagining come into play. In order to represent God who is 'beyond all difference and opposition', man uses particular kinds of symbols (*aptissimo trochi*) which 'lead us imagistically to the Almighty' (*ducit aenigmatice ad omnipotentem*).[34] These image-symbols point beyond what is conceivable and nameable by the intellect to the Creator as *Possest*, above the very distinction between being and non-being – 'for *there* being and not-being do not contradict each other'.[35] And it is interesting to note that Cusanus' use of the term *aenigmate*, meaning mirror-image or riddle, is borrowed directly from the Pauline reference in the First Letter to the Corinthians, mentioned above.

Cusanus thus confronts the basic theological dilemma as to how the 'invisible' God can be seen by means of images:

Since that superwonderful God of ours cannot by any ascent – even the highest ascent – naturally be viewed except through a symbolism (*in aenigmate*) when the possibility of being seen is attained and the seeker arrives at the shadowy dimness, how is it that, at last, He-who-remains-ever-invisible is seen?[36]

Cusanus responds by invoking the eschatological notion of a Kingdom where the 'foolishness' of the humble will be revealed as the highest form of 'wisdom'. And he pursues this Christian vision in terms of a mystical notion of the Creative Word of God somehow 'dwelling' in man. He even suggests the existence of an intimate and ongoing rapport between the 'Creative Art' of God and that of man.[37] This suggestion bears a close resemblance to Eriugena's view that the 'creature, by subsisting, is in God, while God, by manifesting himself . . . creates himself in the creature'.[38] And one could argue that Cusanus is implicitly alluding to the biblical rapport between the divine act of creation (*Yetsirah*) and the human creative impulse (*yetser*) when he praises man's 'ability to desire' (*desiderare*) and declares his power of speech to be capable of 'participation in the divine art of speaking' (*participatio verbi divinae artis*). Where Cusanus differs, of course, from the Jewish tradition is in his affirmation that it is Christ, the *New* Adam, who makes possible a 'Creative Art' (*ars creativa*) which perfectly reflects the 'image of God'. 'Since Christ is the Word of the omnipotent God and is the Creative Art', he writes, 'when he enters into our spirit, which receives Him by faith, He elevates it above nature into fellowship with Him.'[39] As Son of the Father, 'Christ *is* that which the Father *can*'; and by implication, all humans who imitate Christ can become sons of the Father. Because the Creative Art of Christ may come to 'dwell' in man, we may come to realize the highest goal of all our desires and inclinations – 'the knowledge of our creation' (*nostrae creationis scientia*).[40] And the equation of such knowledge with the 'knowledge by which God created the World' (*scientiam dei qua mundum creavit*), bears a striking parallel to the Jewish Kabbalist theories of man seeking to acquire the knowledge contained in the Book of Creation (*Sefer Yetsirah*) reputedly given to Abraham.

But just as the Jewish tales of the Golem warned against premature identifications of man's creative power with that of God, so too Cusanus invokes the Pauline distinction between seeing God through mirror-images (*per speculum in aenigmate*) and seeing Him directly (*facie ad faciem*). Indeed Paul's distinction derives not simply from popular Cynic-Stoic teaching but from several Jewish references to this theme (*NM.* 12:6 and *Wisd. Sol.* 25–26 for example). And the 'face to face' allusion is, of course, a common biblical motif (*Ex.* 32:20, *Ezra 4*, 7:98, *Ap.* 22:3–4). The 'face to face' vision of God, as reinterpreted by Paul and certain Christian mystics, is deemed comparable to that intuition possessed through the charismatic gifts of gnosis and prophecy.[41]

Cusanus' treatment of this matter is, however, deeply ambiguous. For while he invokes the distinction between a direct vision of God and vision through images, he affirms a positive potential for the latter. Though they cannot be known in themselves, we can know 'something' about the divine works of creation by means of certain *figurae* which express themselves through symbolic reflections (*ex aenigmate et speculo*).[42] Everyone who understands, asserts Cusanus, must behold images (*opportet enim omnem intelligentem phantasmata speculari*); and this entails a certain privileged use of 'symbolism for searching into the works of God' (*aenigma ad venationem operum dei*).[43] It is, moreover, by means of such symbolism that man is enabled to 'see the Christian theological doctrine that God is one and three'.[44] But Christ himself, of course, as the begotten Son of the Father, remains the most perfect *figura* of the 'image of God' (*solus dei filius est figura substantiae Patris, quia est quicquid esse potest*).[45]

Cusanus concludes his treatise accordingly by stating that symbolic images may serve as an indispensable guide for mankind in its efforts to approach the Unknown God. Affirming the mystical power of such images, he asserts that the investigation into the ineffable nature of the Creator requires man to use *imaginatio*.[46] Defying the orthodox scholastic distrust of images and imagining, Cusanus maintains that the 'world is the *imago* of that Beauty whose truth is ineffable' and that the unknowable Creator reveals himself to the world 'in imagery and symbolism' (*in speculo et aenigmate*).[47]

But Cusanus, even at his most mystical, retains certain reservations about the use of images. God Himself, while revealing Himself through 'figures' and 'symbols', surpasses all forms of 'imaginable and intellectual knowledge which inheres in images' (*imaginabilem . . . et intellectualem phantasmatibus inhaerentem in infinitum excedentem cognitionem*).[48] The Divine Creator exceeds the limits of our finite imagination. And whatever symbolic and creative powers we may use to reach or imitate Him are always only preludes to the eschatological 'face to face' encounter (*facialis visio*), an encounter which Scripture promises to those faithful followers of the Son of God.[49]

CHAPTER TWO

The Hellenic Imagination

Hellenic culture has provided Western philosophy with most of its formative concepts. Along with the biblical tradition of Judeo-Christian revelation, the Greek heritage of speculation has exercised an enduring influence, at almost every level, on the development of European civilization. This influence extends, of course, to the understanding of imagination. Indeed, it is arguable that the first properly philosophical categories of imagination are to be found in the writings of Plato and Aristotle. Most of this chapter will be devoted accordingly to an analysis of what these foundational thinkers had to say about the nature and role of images, imaging and imagination. But before focusing our attention on the decisive contributions made by the Platonic and Aristotelian philosophies, we shall cast a glance at the ancient Greek myth of Prometheus: a pre-philosophical narrative of how man first acquired the power to shape his world, to create arts and images capable of transforming nature into culture.

1 The Promethean myth: the art of making

The Hellenic understanding of imagination may be traced back to the mythology of ancient Greece. The biblical story of Adam's fallen imagination finds its closest Greek equivalent in the myth of Prometheus. As we move from the one culture to the other we observe a certain shift of emphasis from the *ethical* to the *epistemological* dimension of imagination. The name Prometheus, meaning fore-sight (*pro-mētheus*), designates the power to anticipate the future by projecting an horizon of imaginary possibilities.[1] Hesiod tells us in his *Theogony* how Prometheus stole fire from the gods and bestowed it upon man. Angered by his transgression, Zeus punished Prometheus by chaining him to a rock and sending an eagle to devour his liver. With the use of this stolen fire, man was able to invent his own world, creating the various arts which transmuted the order of *nature* (the cosmos of blind necessity governed by Zeus) into the order of *culture* (a realm of relative freedom where man could plan and control his own existence). The stigma of theft was thus attached to imagination, understood broadly as that Promethean foresight which enabled man to imitate the gods. It became the source, as Aeschylus noted in *Prometheus Bound*, of 'every art possessed by man'.

The Promethean imagination shares many of the traits of its Adamic counterpart. In both instances, imagination is characterized by an act of rebellion against the divine order of things; it dismantles the harmony of nature as pre-established by the gods. It is thus marked from the outset by an essential ambiguity. For while it empowers man to imitate God, it does so by means of an unlawful act. In *Thieves of Fire*, a study of the formative influence of the Prometheus myth on the Western literary heritage, Denis Donoghue has this to say about the ambivalent origins of imagination:

Above all Prometheus made possible the imaginative enhancement of experience, the metaphysical distinction between what happens to us and what we make of this happening. That is to say, Prometheus provided men with consciousness as the transformation grammar of experience. No wonder the gift also gave men a sense of the endlessness of possibility arising from the endlessness of knowledge and desire. The power of (imagination) helped men to maintain a relation between themselves and nature, but it did not bring peace between men and gods. . . . The imagination has always been a contentious power, as a result, so far as men are concerned in their relations with the gods . . .

the divine power in men, falsely acquired, stolen from the gods in the first of many similar outrages.[2]

Prometheus then, no less than Adam, was portrayed as both benefactor of man and instigator of his illegitimate desire to substitute his own arbitrary creations for the original act of divine creation.[3] Henceforth men would seek to emulate and even usurp the role of the divine demiurge who, according to Greek myth, first shaped this world from formless matter. Indeed, as we shall see below, Plato exposes the limits of this creative 'art of making' (*dēmiourgikē technē*) given to man by Prometheus in a telling passage of his *Protagoras* dialogue (320c–322d). Since man could only presume to replace the divine by means of imagination, he is always reminded that the very need for the gift of fire – to supplement his earthly existence with the promise of a celestial perfection – itself betrays an essential *lack* in mankind. In short, the Promethean origin of imagination signifies

the deficiency of one who needs fire in order to achieve a more perfect form of being. In obtaining this higher form of being for man, Prometheus shows himself to be man's double, an eternal image of man's basically imperfect form of being.[4]

Just as the serpent tempted Adam and Eve with the double-edged promise that the knowledge of good and evil would make them 'like gods', so too Prometheus' gift of imagination is at once a liberation and a curse – it makes possible a world where 'men having taken the place of the gods and demi-gods think their own imaginations divine'.[5] Prometheus was construed accordingly, in later Western literature, as a 'Greek Lucifer' to the extent that his imparting of the spark of divinity to man was also the source of divisiveness between man and God.[6]

Thus we find that, significant distinctions notwithstanding, both the biblical account of Adam's fall and the Greek myth of Prometheus' theft portray the acquisition of imagination as an offence against the gods. But both narratives are also deeply ambiguous; for they see such an offence as the precondition, as it were, of human culture. On the one hand, imagination promises to repair man's sense of lack. On the other, it transmits the taint of the original transgression (i.e. of Adam or Prometheus) to all subsequent generations of mankind. In short, imagination is a power which supplements the human experience of insufficiency and sets man up as an original creator in his own right. But because imagination deals in the realm of art rather than nature, it can never fully escape the feeling that it is merely an *imitation* of the *original* act of a divine maker (e.g. the biblical Yahweh or the Greek Demiurge) – an act which alone is deemed lawful.[7] Imagination can never forget that its art is artifice, that its freedom is arbitrary, that its originality is a simulation, repetition, *mimesis*.[8]

The Promethean imagination conforms to the ambivalent Greek model of the *pharmakos*: the sacrificial scapegoat who is neither entirely innocent nor entirely guilty. Both Prometheus and Adam fulfil the role of the sacrificial victim who, as Northrop Frye points out, 'is innocent in the sense that what happens to him is far greater than anything he has done provokes . . . but guilty in the sense that he is . . . living in a world where such injustices are an inescapable part of existence. . . . The two parts do not come together; they remain ironically apart'.[9] Although different in several respects, as we shall see below, the Adamic and Promethean myths subscribe to the sacrificial model of dying gods and aspiring men: both represent a mixture of the benign and the demonic, of nobility and crime.[10] These sacrificial heroes occupy an intermediary position somewhere between the divine and the human. They 'hang between heaven and earth, between a world of paradisal freedom and a world of bondage'.[11] Consequently, in Greek no less than in biblical culture, the imagination which devolves from the transgressions of quasi-divine heroes – Prometheus and Adam – is indelibly marked by this double nature. These mythic heroes are 'very great as compared with us, but there is something else . . . compared to which they are small. This something else may be called God, gods, fate, necessity, circumstance, or any combination of these, but whatever it is the tragic hero is our mediator with it.'[12]

This question of 'mediation' is of crucial significance. The intermediary character of imagination in the Hellenic and Hebraic myths determines its ultimately *mimetic* role. Hence in

Western classical and medieval culture – founded largely upon these two major traditions – we find that the imagination is never understood in terms of some internal, subjective power of man alone. It is always evaluated in terms of man's relation to a divine or cosmic power greater than imagination itself. Or to put it in a more technical way, the premodern imagination is *alio-relative* (defined *vis-à-vis* something *other* than itself) rather than *ipso-relative* (defined exclusively in reference to itself). It is almost invariably construed as an *imitation* of a unique divine act or state of being. And this obtains whether imagination is condemned for seeking to imitate God in the sense of replacing Him, or praised for subordinating its own creative activity to the divine order of things (as when Adam confesses his fault and resolves to obey the law of Yahweh; or when Prometheus finally becomes reconciled with Zeus in the final part of the Aeschylus tragedy). The imagination of the rebellious hero receives its identity from a higher order of *original* meaning which it flouts but is ultimately compelled to acknowledge. It has no significance independently of this relation to something beyond itself. Thus Prometheus needs Zeus, 'if for no other reason than that he needs a force at least equal and opposite and preferably greater than himself. He needs in Zeus a force sharing many of the same qualities of imagination, but more powerful . . .'.[13] And for similar reasons, Adam needed his Divine Creator, Yahweh.

But if the Promethean imagination parallels the Adamic model of conflict between the claims of human freedom and divine order, it differs from its biblical counterpart in important respects. In the Adamic myth, as we saw in the previous chapter, man's historical fate is a result of an ethical choice between a good and evil imagination. In the Greek myth of Prometheus, by contrast, man's evil fate is inscribed as a tragic destiny. It is part of a cosmological order of being which supersedes the anthropological order of freedom and responsibility. The Greek tragedy of Prometheus, as Paul Ricoeur argues in *The Symbolism of Evil*, illustrates the extreme opposition between a 'wicked god' (*kakos daimōn*) and a proud hero. The characters of Zeus and Prometheus in Aeschylus' *Prometheus Bound* are the two extremes of this polarization. Zeus represents the intrinsic 'guiltiness of being'; he exemplifies the tragic conviction that evil is somehow part of a cosmic fate to which the hero is inexorably condemned. Prometheus, observes Ricoeur,

heightens by his innocence . . . the guiltiness of being. Prometheus is the benefactor of mankind; he is the humanity of man; he suffers because he has loved the human race too much. Even if his autonomy is also his fault, it expresses first his generosity; for the fire that he has given to men is the fire of the arts and crafts . . . of culture. In that fire is summed up what it is to be a man, breaking with the immobility of nature and the dreary repetition of animal life and extending his empire over things, beasts and human relations.[14]

There is more to the Prometheus story, however, than the innocent passion of man victimized by a malign deity. In the eyes of the pious Aeschylus, the rebellion of the proud hero is an impure act. Prometheus, like the gods themselves, is ultimately contaminated by the guiltiness of being. As a Titan he is at least partially subject to cosmological evil. His creative liberty is therefore merely one of *defiance*, not of *participation*. From the beginning, Prometheus was a 'guilty innocent'.[15] The maleficent dimension of Prometheus' act is also indicated by his secret foreknowledge that a union of the King of the gods with a mortal would result in the birth of a man who would overthrow the gods. Prometheus possesses, therefore,

the secret of the fall of Zeus, the secret of the twilight of the gods; he has the means of annihilating being. A destructive freedom like this is not, for Aeschylus, the last word of freedom . . . and so the final defiance of Prometheus, as we know, provokes a thunderous reply; Prometheus trembles with his rock into the abyss. For Aeschylus, this disaster is part of a hard schooling.[16]

The Promethean myth of imagination differs substantially from its Adamic analogue, then, in so far as it attributes evil to a *pre-existing cosmic destiny* of which man and the gods themselves are victims. The Adamic myth, by contrast, offers a radically *anthropological* account of evil. Not only does the Hebrew name Adam mean 'man' (*Adameh*), but the biblical version of this First Man's acquisition of imagination places the guilt of this transgression of divine law on man. There is no question of the Divine Creator in *Genesis* being a 'wicked god' implicated in a guilty order of being. Adam does not inherit evil from the cosmic order. He is the one who makes the imagination evil by his own free choice. And by the same token, he is also free, after his fall from paradise, to put the stolen power of imagination (as a knowledge of good and evil) to good use by submitting it to the way of God (*Torah*), thereby contributing actively to God's Messianic plan for history. Adam's freedom of imagination is not merely one of defiance but of participation. The 'holiness' of God and his creation is thus preserved in the biblical account. By contrast, the tragic vision of the world which typifies Greek myth precludes the intrinsic goodness of the cosmos and 'excludes the forgiveness of sins'.[17] Prometheus and Oedipus do not seek pardon from the gods. At best, they seek to know and acknowledge their preordained fate, to stoically accept their cosmic destiny. Evil pre-dates the actions of man in Greek tragedy. The hero learns to suffer his fate. There is no question of the tragic hero actively redeeming his transgression by 'returning' to the way of God and engaging in a dialogue with his Creator for the sake of an ultimately 'good' outcome.

This 'tragic' vision of imagination is not confined to the Prometheus legend. Several other heroes of Greek mythology reenact the Promethean paradigm of crime and punishment. Indeed the recurrence of this theme in Greek myth might even be said to constitute a foundational archetype of imagination. Dionysus is torn to pieces by the Titans for revering his god-like image in a mirror. Narcissus is condemned to death because he lovingly contemplates his own reflection in nature. Orpheus is dismembered by frenzied Maenads when he dares to reconcile man and nature in a quasi-divine harmony composed by song and the music of his lyre. And Dedalus who, like Enosh in the Bible, is the first to invent the art of sculpting human figures from rock and giving them the power of speech, is banished into exile. All of these mythological rebels share the Promethean quest to usurp the gods by transmuting reality into a divine image.[18] And all suffer the Promethean fate of chastisement by wicked or angry gods who feel threatened by the allotment of imagination to the world of mortals. The mythic heroes of imagination disrupt the cosmic hierarchy by exalting the human order in imitation of the divine. They thereby commit the fault of pride which is henceforth associated with the power of imagination (*phantasia*) – that is, the power to exceed the established limits of nature. The 'tragic' fate suffered by these mythological rebels is manifest in the fact that their defiant use of imagination, in emulation of the gods, is already implicated in the evil of the cosmos itself. The ancient Hellenic heroes of imagination do not *cause* evil, they are *subject* to it – as indeed are the gods themselves who mete out cruel punishments. Their terrible fault (*hamartia*) is tragic precisely because it is inevitable. The very world which embraces both gods and men is vitiated by wickedness, jealousy, rivalry and vengeance. According to this tragic vision of Greek mythology, the whole cosmos is infected by the guiltiness of being. Thus Aeschylus could declare that 'when the gods shake a home, misfortune pursues the multitude of its descendants without respite . . . for many, hope is only a description practised by their credulous desires . . . evil seems to be a good to him whose mind the divinity is leading to destruction'.[19] In short, the hopes and desires engendered by human imagination are condemned from the outset. One may defy this verdict of being but one cannot change it. And, at best, as the tragic heroes discovered to their cost, one learns to accept it.

This goes some way to explaining why Plato, who wished to rehabilitate the 'goodness' of divine being, expressed deep indignation at the tragic vision of existence and deplored Aeschylus' portrait of the wicked god. And so he writes in the *Republic*:

God, since he is good, is not the cause of everything, as is commonly said; he is the cause of only a part of the things that happen to men and has no responsibility for the greater part of them, for the bad far outweighs the good in our lives. . . . We will not therefore allow the young to hear the words of Aeschylus: 'God implants crime in men when he wishes to ruin their house completely.' (*Rep.* 379c–380a)

The 'innocence of god', which Plato's metaphysics sought to

ensure by dividing the cosmos into two radically opposed worlds of spiritual good and material evil, was incompatible with the tragic mythology of evil. For such a mythology ultimately precluded the religious belief in divine goodness.[20] With this in mind, we may more readily appreciate the philosophical motivation behind Plato's condemnation of imagination as a 'mimetic' function confined to the lower order of human existence and divorced from divine being.

2 Plato's metaphysical verdict

With Plato, one of the founding fathers of Western metaphysics, the notion of imagination receives its first properly *philosophical* formulation. Removed from the cosmic drama of gods and heroes, the theme of imagination is assessed as a distinctly *human* mode of existence. This transition from a mythological to a metaphysical perspective was already anticipated by several pre-Socratic thinkers – e.g. Democritus, Pythagoras, Xenophanes, and Anaxagoras – who occasionally adverted to the problematic rapport between images (*phantasmata/eidōla*) and reality.[21] But Plato was the first to provide a systematic critical account of imagination. 'Up to the time of Plato', as M. W. Bundy notes in *The Theory of Imagination in Classical and Medieval Thought*, 'there was no comprehensive view of the relation of matter to spirit, of the outer to the inner, necessary for an adequate concept of the nature and function of "phantasy".'[22] It was only after Plato had developed these conceptual distinctions in his great metaphysical system that there emerged an explicit theory of imagination.

We might say, therefore, that Platonic metaphysics is to Greek myth what the Talmud is to the Torah in Jewish tradition. It offers a series of interpretations, discriminations and conceptualizations unavailable at the level of mythic narrative. Indeed, Plato's view of philosophy as a movement beyond myth towards reason itself informs, as we shall see, his negative evaluation of the activity of imagining. Plato's *epistemological* opposition between the knowing faculty of reason(*nous*) and the mimetic

knowing v imagery

functions of imagination (*eikasia* and *phantasia*) must be understood in the larger context of his *metaphysical* distinction
between being and becoming.[23] Reacting strongly against the
mythological habit of contaminating divine being with evil, Plato
elevates the original forms of being into a transcendental realm
of Ideas. These Ideas of pure being are immutable and timeless.
They comprise a hierarchy crowned by the highest form of all –
the Good. Thus sealed off from the lower order of material
becoming, the Ideas remain untainted by the human order of
transience which is now identified as the source of evil. Reason
alone has access to the divine Ideas. And imagination, for its
part, is condemned to a pseudo-world of imitations.   LIES ?

This question of imitation (*mimēsis*) is central. Plato is very
suspicious of the imitative function. He is, above all, against the
human presumption to imitate the divine. As he explains in the
Timaeus (29–31), it was in imitation of the transcendental order
of Ideas that the divine demiurge or craftsman first fashioned
the material world of becoming. And this is why man, by his
use of reason, can ultimately return from this material world to
the original world of Ideas of which it is a copy. The imagination,
by contrast, simply leads man further astray; it does no more
than imitate the material world of becoming, which is itself but
an imitation of the divine world of being. Thus Plato denounces
man-made images as 'the poor children of poor parents' – that
is, as inferior copies. In presuming to create a world in its own
image, the human imagination resides at a third remove from
truth. And in so far as it identifies itself with the shaping activity
of the divine demiurge, imagination easily leads to idolatry.
What is permitted to God is not permitted to man.

But before embarking on a detailed examination of Plato's
condemnation of imagination in the *Republic*, it is worth taking
a look at his reading of the Prometheus myth. There is a key
passage in the *Protagoras* (321–322) where Plato explicitly associates the 'art of making' (*demiourgikē technē*) with the Promethean
gift of stolen fire.[24] Plato tells us that Prometheus' act was motivated by his desire to help man emerge from the earth into the
daylight:

Being at a loss to provide any means of salvation for man, Prometheus stole from the gods, Hephaestus and Athena, the gift of skill in the arts (*entechnos sophia*), together with fire – for without fire it was impossible for anyone to possess or use this skill – and bestowed it upon man (321c–d).

Plato goes on to link man's creative power of making with his capacity to erect images of the gods and to communicate in words with his fellow men. And this capacity, made possible by Prometheus, is what raises man above the animal order and makes him resemble, in part at least, the gods themselves.

Since then man had a share (*methexis*) in the portion of the gods, in the first place because of his divine kinship, he alone among living creatures believed in gods, and set to work to erect altars and images of them. Second, by the art which they possessed, men soon discovered articulate speech and names, and invented houses and clothes and shoes and bedding and got food from the earth. (322a)[25]

Plato is quick to point out, however, that all of these creative arts bequeathed by Prometheus to man were not sufficient to save him from self-destruction. By means of the gift of fire, man acquired sufficient resources to survive and to cultivate a world of his own making, transforming thereby the animal order of nature into a human order of culture; but he *lacked* the 'art of politics' (*technē politikē*). This art was in the keeping of Zeus alone, and Prometheus had no right of entry to the citadel where Zeus dwelt. Thus men found themselves unable to live together in community and ended up committing crimes and injustices against one another. In other words, the creative arts bestowed by Prometheus proved ultimately destructive in themselves – for they were devoid of the guiding laws of 'political wisdom' which belonged to Zeus.

Plato leaves us in a little doubt as to the moral of the story. Prometheus is compelled to stand trial for his theft; and Zeus, fearing the total destruction of the human race, finally decides to send Hermes to impart to men 'the quality of respect for others and a sense of justice, so as to bring order into our cities and create a bond of friendship and union' (322c). In short, left to its own devices, the Promethean art of creation (*demiourgikē techné*) leads to the ruin of mankind. It is only by submitting himself to the guidance of a divinely ordained justice that man learns 'moderation' and develops a sense of communal respect. Plato warns that the creative arts of man stolen from the gods must be made subservient to the higher laws of the *polis* legitimately established by Zeus himself. In this way, the divine order of being, as reflected in the *polis*, preserves the privilege of goodness in opposition to the human arts of making which, left to themselves, result in the evil of destruction. By thus polarizing the rational order of Zeus and the imaginative disorder of Promethean man, Plato saves the 'holiness' of being. Such is the primary lesson of Plato's cautionary tale.

In the light of this reading of the Prometheus myth, we are in a better position to appreciate the rationale of Plato's general condemnation of imagination. For Platonism, the creator of an image (*eidōlōn dēmiourgos*) is by definition an imitator (*mimētēs*). Accordingly, every human activity which relates to the making of images – be it painting, sculpture, poetry, music, the use of rhetorical or metaphorical speech or the other creative arts of human culture – is understood as an imitation of the original act of the divine demiurge. And since the original act is the only true one, all subsequent copies of it must be false to some degree. While the demiurge produced real things, the imagination can produce no more than unreal artefacts. Mankind, in so far as it deploys the power of imaging, is characterized accordingly as a 'race of imitators' (*ethnos mimētikon*).[26]

Plato's critique of the mimetic imagination finds fullest expression in the *Republic*. In book VI of this dialogue, Plato provides an essentially epistemological account of imagination. He begins by drawing a 'Divided Line' which sections off the correct vision of knowledge (*epistēmē*) from the false vision of mere opinion (*doxa*). He then proceeds to place reason in the highest section of the Divided Line and imagination in the lowest. Whereas reason (*nous*) is accredited with the capacity to contemplate truth, imagination is relegated to the most inferior form of human opinion – what Plato calls *eikasia* or illusion. Reason alone has access to the transcendental Ideas. Imagination does no more than reflect the things of our sensory world – a world which is itself, of course, no more than a copy of the transcendental Ideas themselves. And since *eikasia* would have us take its own second-hand imitations as true, it is denounced by Plato as an agency of falsehood.

This analogy of the Divided Line, which opposes reason and imagination, corresponds to the more fundamental metaphysical division between being and becoming. Plato makes this clear in his famous Simile of the Cave in book VII of the *Republic*. The world of darkness inside the cave is presented as an illusory stage where men live in ignorance, prisoners of man-made images (*eidōla/phantasmata*). The world of light outside – to which all lovers of truth aspire by following the way of reason – is equated with the transcendental realm of spiritual being. 'Opinion is concerned with becoming and the exercise of reason with being', Plato explains, 'and what being is to becoming, the exercise of reason is to opinion' (534a). The Sun which is the original source of light beyond the cave is identified by Plato with the highest and most divine form of being – the Good. But only reason, we are told, can 'elevate the noblest part of the mind to a contemplation of the highest being' (532c). The Good remains inaccessible to those who cling to their images thereby condemning themselves to the phantasmagoria within the cave. But those who abandon the imitations of *eikasia* for the realities of *nous* behold 'no longer an image (*eikōn*) but truth itself' (533a).

In book X of the *Republic*, Plato develops his critique of the mimetic imagination into an argument for the expulsion of the artist from the ideal *polis*. First, the maker of images is accused of ignorance. Taking the example of three sorts of bed, Plato asserts that the first exists in 'the ultimate nature of things' and 'must have been made by God'; the second is made by the carpenter; and the third by the painter (597a). The artist's representation is at a third remove from reality because he simply *imitates* what the other two *make*. He trades in ignorance and deceit. Plato writes:

The artist's representation is a long way removed from truth, and he is able to reproduce everything because he never penetrates beneath the superficial appearance of anything. For example, a painter can paint a portrait of a shoemaker or a carpenter or any other craftsman without *knowing* anything about their crafts at all; yet, if he is skillful enough, his portrait of a carpenter may, at a distance, deceive children or simple people into thinking it is a real carpenter. (598b)

Plato is putting us on guard here against those imitators who pretend to be masters of every craft and to possess better knowledge than all the experts. The artist is just such a charlatan 'whose apparent omniscience is due entirely to his own inability to distinguish knowledge and opinion, reality and representation' (598c). The artist, in short, is a sophist who pretends to know more than he does. His work is, in the final analysis, no more than a lie (*pseudos*).

On the basis of this epistemological condemnation of image-making, Plato goes on to enumerate a series of related objections. His next accusation is that works of imagination are *non-didactic*, that is, they teach us nothing about the reality of things. This pedagogical objection takes the form of a trial against Homer and the poets. The evidence adduced to support the charge that Homer merely 'manufactured shadows at a third remove from reality' (699d), is that his works have not reformed the constitution of any state, as Lycurgus did at Sparta. They were, in other words, *useless*. If the poet was really a 'stage nearer the truth about human excellence, and really capable of judging what kind of conduct will make the individual or the community better or worse', then we would be able to name some city or state which owed its legal system to the poet. But no such example exists. Nor did Homer ever wage a successful war or command an army, invent any practical device, engage in public service or found a school where 'enthusiastic pupils came to hear him while he lived, and to hand on a Homeric way of life to their successors' (600b). Since Homer imparted no 'practical skills' to Greek society and no theoretical skills to Greek learning, Plato pleads for the verdict that 'all the poets from Homer downwards had no grasp of reality but merely gave us a superficial

imitation of any subject they treat, including human goodness'
(600e).

Once again we detect an epistemological basis to Plato's charge
that works of imagination possess no didactic purpose. For just
as the painter may paint a shoemaker without knowing the first
thing about shoemaking, so too the poet 'uses words as a medium
to paint a picture of any craftsman, though he knows nothing
except how to represent him, and the metre and rhythm and
music will persuade people who are as ignorant as he is . . . that
he really has something to say about shoemaking or generalship
or whatever' (601b). Once stripped of its 'natural magic', the
emptiness of poetry is exposed for all to see; the 'artist who
makes an image of a thing, knows nothing about the truth but
only about the *appearance*'. Plato concludes accordingly that 'art
has no serious value' (602b). And this condemnation of the non-
didactic character of imagination also illustrates the Greek
priority of the public over the private, of politics over art. Works
of imagination are dismissed as unproductive because they
contribute nothing practical to the realm of the *polis*. They have
no public utility. They remain within the confines of private
fantasy.[27]

The third aspect of Plato's critique of the artistic imagination
concerns its *irrational* character. The power of images is
explained by virtue of their appeal to our erotic and animal
desires. In so far as imaginary works are far removed from reality,
they pander to that part of the human psyche which is 'equally
far removed from reason' (603a). Whereas reason is conducive
to a sense of unity in man – correlative to the immutable unity
of being itself – imagination introduces 'conflict and contradiction
into the realm of vision' (603c). Instead of portraying the
'unvarying calm' of the rational soul, the images of the artist
appeal to the recalcitrant element of human experience which is
essentially 'unstable and irritable'. And so Plato insists that art
'strengthens the lower elements in the mind (i.e. *eikasia*) at the
expense of reason' (605a). It encourages the 'unreasoning' part
of the psyche by 'creating images far removed from reality' –
images which distort our sense of truthful judgement and plunge
us into confusion (605b).

But an even more serious charge against the image-creating faculty remains: its 'terrible power to corrupt even the best characters'. Art is therefore to be condemned as *immoral*. Its propagation of false imitations misleads its audience into 'imitating the faults it represents' (605d). By imaginatively empathizing with the misfortunes and misdeeds of the immoral characters portrayed in art, we ourselves become infected by an irrational *pathos*. We become slaves to our feelings and give free reign to our 'comic instinct' for laughter and foolishness which offends the laws of reason. 'Poetry has the same effect on us', bemoans Plato, 'when it represents sex and anger, and the other desires and feelings of pleasure and pain. . . . It feeds them when they ought to be starved, and makes them control us when we ought . . . to control them' (606d). If we submit to the allurements of artistic imitations then immoral desires become the rulers 'instead of law and the principles commonly accepted as best' (607a). The principles of 'political wisdom' which Zeus gave to man, in the *Protagoras* account, to counteract the 'creative arts' of Prometheus, are reinvoked in the *Republic* to vindicate the prosecution of the artistic imagination.

The fifth and final reason for Plato's hostility to imagination is its tendency towards *idolatry*. Here Plato's epistemological critique rejoins its fundamentally metaphysical basis. If image-making is a crime against *truth*, it is equally a crime against *being*. The imagination of the artist brazenly imitates the activity of the divine demiurge by holding a mirror up to the surrounding world. The artist 'takes a mirror, and turns it round in every direction . . . thus rapidly making the sun and the heavenly bodies, the earth and even himself' (596d). This use of the mirror metaphor to characterize the mimetic activity of imagination was to become a stock motif of classical theories of aesthetics. What underlies Plato's invocation of this motif is a metaphysical scruple about the blasphemous tendency of images to replace the original order of divine being (*theion*) with a man-made order of non-being (*mē on*). Imagination is idolatrous to the extent that it worships its own imitations instead of the divine original.

Plato's famous description of the mimetic image as a 'poor child of foster parents' points in the same direction. The connotation here is one of illegitimacy: images are the bastard progeny of surrogate parents (i.e. the things of nature which are themselves no more than copies of the Ideas). Images are imitations of imitations which seek to usurp the legitimate Father of all being – the divine form of the Good. The imaginative activity of imitation is, consequently, a form of parricide, and by implication, deicide. For the original Father, the transcendental source of all light as represented by the Sun in the Allegory of the Cave, is of course divine being itself. The crime of the artist is to dare to make the invisible source of truth visible in the form of representational images. Such a feat transgresses the Platonic oppositions between being and non-being, spirit and matter, soul and body, good and evil, truth and falsity – dualisms upon which the entire edifice of Western metaphysics rests. As Jacques Derrida observes in *Dissemination*, 'the absolute invisibility of the origin of the visible, of the Good-Sun-Father', which is the very essence of *Platonism*, 'is the general rehearsal of this family scene and the most powerful effort to conceal it by drawing the curtains over the dawning of the West'.[28] The mimetic image is an illegitimate son, who like the Stranger in Plato's *Theaetetus*, 'dares to lay unfilial hands on the paternal pronouncement' (*patrikoi logoi*) (241–2). And, again like the Stranger, the imagination is accused of parricide – of displacing the rightful Father, the true origin, the paternal *logos* upon which Western metaphysics is founded. The imagination is thus seen by Plato as a disobedient son who threatens to subvert the patriarchal law of the metaphysical system – a law which safeguards the rights of inheritance by outlawing the counterfeit claims of imitators, pretenders and impostors. The imagination is the alien body in the system, the fault-line in the edifice of being, the trojan horse in the City of the *logos*.

But what exactly is the *logos*? And how did it come to be associated with the concept of divine paternity? Derrida suggests that the Platonic model of the *logos* as 'silent dialogue of the soul with itself' logically entailed the correlative model of the Father as absolute origin, as self-sufficient identity and unity – in short the model of divine being as an original presence to itself. The mimetic image is a threat to this original presence, this dialogue of being with itself, for it constitutes a detour of representation – Derrida would say *écriture* – which claims 'to do without the Father of *logos*'.[29] In so far as it creates a world of imitative artifice, imagination challenges the copyright of the paternal *logos*. It breaks from the original self-identity of the Father and assumes a life of its own, an existence other than, and independent of, the Father. The Promethean gift of the 'creative arts', which as we noted above included the capacity to invent a properly human language, thus transgresses the Law of the Father – called Zeus in the *Protagoras* and the divine form of the Good in the *Republic*.

Only the divine demiurge, according to Plato, possessed the original right to form or shape a world. He was the lawful heir. He was the unique legitimate son of the Father. He alone remained an integral part of the Father's spiritual dialogue with himself. The artist who styles himself as a *human* demiurge, by contrast, becomes the 'Father's *other*'. The distinguishing mark of all artistic or imaginative discourse is, to quote Derrida, that 'it cannot be assigned a fixed spot . . . sly, slippery and masked . . . a joker, a floating signifier, a wild card which puts play into play'.[30] It is precisely because the imagination introduces indeterminacy and ambivalence into discourse that it serves to deconstruct the paternal *logos* of self-identity. The mimetic activity of imagination unleashes an endless *play of substitution*, – one where artificial *re-presentations* imitate and eventually seek to replace the original *presence* of divine being to itself.

In the pseudo-world of imagination opposites are no longer dualistically opposed, as dictated by the paternal *logos* of metaphysics; they are subversively conjoined. And this, of course, entails a further flouting of the founding laws of philosophical logic (first outlined by Parmenides though not formally articulated until Aristotle) – the law of identity (A is A) and the law of non-contradiction (if A is A it cannot be non-A). It is quite possible that Plato's hostility to art in book X of the *Republic* is motivated, in part at least, by a desire to protect the metaphysical principle of identity. For not only does the work of art, as an imaginary imitation, testify to a worrying *lack* of identity with being (*to on*), but within art itself, particularly as evinced in

Greek drama, the logic of identity is threatened by the fact that both the audience and the actors (each actor played several parts) identify with many *different* roles at the same time. Against this latter danger, Plato vehemently protests that 'the same part of us cannot hold different opinions about the same thing at the same time' (602e). In short, where reason unites the soul by conforming to the law of identity and by contemplating the transcendental unity of the Good, imagination disperses the soul into a play of contradiction.

This rejection of imagination as a play of contradiction is central to Platonism. In the *Republic* (596), *mimēsis* – or the art of mirroring – is compared to painting (*zōgraphein*). While Plato also includes poetry and written verse as forms of *mimēsis* in the *Republic*, it is in the *Phraedrus* (275d) that he most explicitly likens the act of writing (*graphein*) to the mimetic activity of painting. And writing is in turn described as a drug (*pharmakon*) (274–277). Plato uses the term *pharmakon* in an ambiguous way: it carries the connotations of both remedy and poison.[31] The mimetic image – as a form of painting/writing – may be understood as a *remedy* in that it records human experience for posterity and thus saves it from the oblivion of passing time; and it may be seen as a *poison* in that it deceives us into mistaking its imitation for the original, thereby assuming the status of an idol. This paradoxical function of the image is, of course, also evident in Plato's own writings. For does not Plato himself use imagination to denounce imagination? Does he not employ the figures of myth, simile, metaphor and analogy to convince us of the very unreliability of these modes of imaginative representation?

It is no doubt this very ambiguity of imaginative expression which prompts Plato to define painting and writing as mere playthings (*Phaedrus*, 276). A mischievous agency of confusion and changeability, play is to be regarded with the utmost of suspicion. The reality of the forms – understood as stable, permanent and self-identical – cannot accommodate the basic ambivalence inherent in play. Play is either to be outlawed altogether, or else subjected to paternal supervision. And if fathers must allow their children to play, they must do so within strict limits.

'If you control the way children play,' counsels Plato in the *Laws*, 'and the same children always play the same games under the same rules and in the same conditions, and get pleasure from the same toys, you'll find that the conventions of adult life too are left in peace without alteration. . . . Change, except in something evil, is extremely dangerous' (*Laws*, 797).

In the light of this extended commentary on the equation of divine being with the paternal *logos* of identity, we are perhaps in a better position to appreciate Plato's warning against the 'blasphemous' inclinations of imagination. Although Plato refers to this in book X of the *Republic*, it was in book II that he first made his position clear. Since divine being, he argued here, is changeless, it can never assume the variable sensible forms of imaginary representations. The attempts by artists such as Homer, Hesiod and Aeschylus to 'mimetically' portray God in mythic images are, Plato insists, conducive to blasphemy. His argument, which summarizes much of our above analysis, runs as follows:

God is the source of the Good only . . . the state of God and the Divine is perfect; and therefore God is least liable of all things to be changed into other forms . . . God is as good as possible and remains in his own form without variation forever . . . So we cannot have any poet saying that the gods disguise themselves in every kind of shape . . . We must stop all stories of this kind and stop mothers being misled by them and scaring children by perversion of the myths . . . They are merely blaspheming the gods . . . God is not the author of poetic fictions . . . God is without deceit or falsehood in action or word, he does not change himself, nor deceive others, awake or dreaming, with imaginary fantasies (*phantasia*) . . . (380–382).

Plato's critique of the artistic imagination, rehearsed above, can be summarized in the form of five main accusations: (1) *ignorance*, (2) *non-didacticism*, (3) *immorality*, (4) *irrationalism* and (5) *idolatry*. These objections derive in turn from five fundamental dualisms which characterize Platonic philosophy and subsequently inform the classical and medieval traditions of Western thought: (1) the *epistemological* opposition between truth and falsehood; (2) the *anthropological* opposition between political praxis and artistic uselessness; (3) the *moral* opposition between good and evil; (4) the *psychological* opposition between the rational soul and the material body; (5) the *metaphysical* opposition between divine being and human becoming. What essentially distinguishes the Platonic account of imagination from its Jewish counterpart is the addition of the first and fourth categories of critique – that is, the formulation of a systematic epistemology and metaphysics which allowed imagination to be defined as a threat to the basic *philosophical* principles of rational knowledge and absolute being.

3 The great paradox

Plato's metaphysical assessment of imagination is not, however, entirely negative. Beneath the official censure of the mimetic image, there runs a counter-current which surfaces in certain passages of the Platonic dialogues. Even in the *Republic*, the *locus classicus* of Plato's excommunication of image-makers, the author does allow of the occasional use of images in pursuit of truth. Thus in book VI, Plato concedes that knowledge (*epistémē*) may at times have recourse to what he terms 'thought-images' in order to enable our human understanding (*dianoia*) to give figurative expression to its abstract ideas. Such images may serve a positive heuristic purpose by providing the mind with quasi-intuitive representations of otherwise invisible truths; they help us to visualise and thereby communicate the concepts of knowledge. Plato gives the example of the mathematician who employs material drawings of a square to help his pupils comprehend the essentially invisible idea of the square. And the same principle applies to philosophers such as Socrates (and by implication Plato himself) who use similes, analogies, myths and other metaphorical tropes to convey their arguments to others in a vivid manner. But such positive uses of images are exceptions to the general rule.

What distinguishes this legitimate function of images from the normal practices of artists and sophists is that they are never treated as *ends in themselves*. They serve rather as instrumental means for mediating between our sensible experience and our rational intelligence. This *mediational* function of thought-images leads the mind from the lower to the higher – that is, from the material to the transcendental world. It thus acts as a corrective to the artistic use of images which seek to reduce the original ideas to a pseudo-realm of copies. Teachers of truth redeploy images to point *beyond themselves* to essences that ultimately transcend figurative embodiment. The image here cancels itself out. Or like Wittgenstein's ladder, it is thrown away as soon as it has permitted us to climb from the cave of error into the world of truth. As Plato himself explains, philosophers

make use of and reason about visible figures, though they are not really thinking about them at all, but about the originals which they resemble; they are arguing not about the square or diagonal which they have drawn but about the absolute square or diagonal, or whatever the figure may be. The figures they draw . . . they treat as illustrations only, the real subjects of their investigation being invisible except to the eye of the mind (510d-e).

The real aim of the philosopher remains the pure pursuit of truth by means of reason (*nous*) – the activity of spiritual contemplation which 'makes no use of images' but prosecutes 'its inquiry solely by means of Forms' (510b).

In this way, Plato appears to accept the possibility of good and bad uses of imagination. In the service of understanding, images may assist us in moving beyond the world of becoming to the world of being – but only on condition that we remain scrupulously aware that they are no more than signposts, never independent truths in their own right. Left to the devices of illusory representation, images merely confuse the copies of reality with reality itself; and they thereby deflect our attention from the Ideas. The most dangerous kind of imaging is that which does not openly proclaim that it *is* imagining – thus allowing itself to be mistaken for reality. Moreover, Plato realizes that if such a distinction between true and false image-imitations were not possible, much of language, and indeed of philosophical discourse itself, would be irredeemably condemned to error. The human mind has need of metaphorical and mythic figures to mediate between the worlds of becoming and being and thereby elevate us from our lower sensory experience to the contemplation of truth.

Plato develops this argument most comprehensively in the *Sophist*. Here he acknowledges the necessity of being able to discriminate between true and false propositions in language. This concession is granted in the form of a response to the Sophist's clever argumentation. Having accused the Sophist of using words in an 'imaginative' rather than 'truthful' way, Socrates is compelled to take stock:

> If we say to him that he professes an art of making illusory-images (*phantastikē technē*), he will return our argument against us; and when we accuse him of being an image-maker in general (*eidōlopoiētikos*), he will reply, 'what do you mean by an image?' . . . We shall doubtless tell him of the images which are reflected in water or in mirrors, also of sculptures, pictures and other duplicates . . . but he will say we are contradicting ourselves, for in maintaining this we are compelled over and again to assert being of non-being, which we claimed already to be an impossibility (239d–241a–b).

Once again, we see how for Plato the *epistemological* question of the image is inseparable from the *metaphysical* question of being. Plato is forced to admit here that imagistic modes of expression must have *some* portion of being, however small or modified, for otherwise it would be impossible to determine which propositions are false and which true. The imagistic figures of speech – be it metaphor, allegory or myth – are consequently admitted to partake of both being and non-being. Were this not so, we would be unable to distinguish between good and bad uses of imaginative discourse – understood as a linguistic means of linking the worlds of the sensible (*doxa*) and the intelligible (*epistēmē*). Bundy offers this perceptive commentary on Plato's reasoning:

> He is insisting that if the Sophist is to be answered – if we are to be able to talk about true and false propositions – there must be a sufficient modification of the old theory of ideas to establish the 'being', the reality, of error in thought, opinion, speech, in all the manifestations

of phantasy as the power of receiving and giving expression to one's impressions. . . . Henceforth he is also interested in mental processes; and not alone in the thought concerned with ideas, but also in the thought which, bound up with sense and opinion, issues in phantasies, opinions which have taken sensible shape.[32]

Faced with the Sophist's objections, Plato makes two important concessions. First, he revises his official dismissal of the image as mere 'non-being'. And second, he implicitly recognizes that images are not simply external imitations – paintings, sculptures or other works of art – but may also function as *internal modes* of thought and expression, that is, as mental images.[33] Admittedly, this latter discovery of the psychological role of images in thought and speech is merely touched upon and never receives extensive analysis by Plato. Only with Aristotle, as we shall see, was this psychological function of imagination given a comprehensive treatment. What is most significant in Plato's response to the Sophist is his observation that the image constitutes a sort of *ontological paradox*. The images of speech both *are* and *are not*. They possess a sort of quasi-existence; and this necessitates a modification of the established dualism between being and non-being. As soon as one accepts that 'opinion presented in some sensible mode of expression is what we call imagination' (*Soph.* 264a), one is forced to accept the attendant paradox that images are a mixture of *both* being *and* non-being. For if being were totally denied to spoken images, our discourse would be false; and if non-being played no role in such images 'every proposition would be necessarily true' (*Soph.* 241d). Jean-Pierre Vernant elaborates on this central paradox of Plato's treatment of the image:

Without being identical with either pole, the image places itself between being and non-being in an intermediary position which it shares with *doxa* and which allows for the possibility of error, false judgement, the attribution of being to what has no being, the confusion of the image with that of which it is an image (i.e. its original). In other words, there is no point in defining the image as an appearance or imitation if this definition does not already imply some reference to being, on the one hand, as distinct from mere appearance and as prior

metaphysical → (margin annotation)

to appearance, and to non-being on the other as the basis of a possible confounding of the image with reality.[34]

But while Plato is prepared to accept the paradoxical role of the spoken image in the *Sophist* – and also, it might be noted in his celebrated discussion of 'iconic discourse' in the *Cratylus* (423–4, 430–1) – he does so *reluctantly*. The very ambivalence of the image as a confection of being and non-being, truth and falsehood, remains for Plato a source of worry. Erroneous judgements, he tells us in the *Cratylus*, are all too often a result of the unreliability of our 'fluctuating imaginings' (*phantasmata*) (386e). And he goes on to insist that the use of mimetic images to name things in reality can never provide us with a sure knowledge of the essences of these things (423d–424a). Such knowledge is the prerogative of reason itself: pure thought which unfolds as a dialogue of the soul with itself, in silence (*aneu phōnēs*, i.e. without speech), unadulterated by words or images.[35]

But the paradoxical status of imagination in Platonic metaphysics has yet a further dimension. Apart from its mediational role in human expression, the image may also play a revelatory role. Already in his conclusion to the *Republic*, Plato conceded that imagination might be permitted a certain valid function in his ideal state if it agreed to renounce its claim to artistic autonomy and submit to transcendental guidelines, producing 'hymns to the gods and paeans in praise of the good' (607a). But this concession is altogether abrupt and the reader of the *Republic* is at pains to understand how Plato can allow such a status to imagination, having so thoroughly denounced its activities in the rest of the dialogue.

In several of the later and at times 'mystical' dialogues – particularly the *Phaedrus* and the *Timaeus* – Plato offers occasional glimpses of the divinatory function of imagination. In a description of mystical experience in the *Phaedrus*, he speaks of the Idea of Beauty itself being given to certain 'chosen witnesses' in the form of 'visionary images', *phantasmata*, which the 'soul could never perceive in ordinary daylight' (250a–d). This isolated reference to mystical vision in the *Phaedrus* receives a more extended treatment in the *Timaeus* (70–72). Here Plato speaks of divinely inspired images (*eidōla* and *phantasmata*) which arise in the sleep of certain holy seers (*Tim* 71a). Curiously, it is in the lowest part of the human body – the liver – far removed from the centres of the rational (the head) and the spiritual (the heart), that Plato locates the source of divination (*manteia*). Perhaps Plato was mindful here of the irony that in Greek myth the liver carried the stigma of Prometheus' crime and punishment (for Zeus had sent an eagle to devour Prometheus' liver in retribution for his theft of the fire of imagination)? But either way, Plato was certainly aware of the profound paradox implied in attributing the highest form of truth to the lowest part of the physical organism. Indeed the paradox is further heightened in this same passage of the *Timaeus* by Plato's equation of the liver with the mimetic functioning of a 'mirror', *Katoptron* (recalling the relegation of the mirror-images of *eikasia* to the most inferior position of human cognition in the analogy of the Divided Line in the *Republic*). Plato even seems to suggest, moreover, that the power of the liver to mirror divine images may enable visionaries to come upon truth immediately, thereby dispensing with the arduous dialectical ascent to the Ideas through philosophical argumentation (*noēsis*). In such moments of ecstatic vision, the imagination becomes the privileged recipient of divine inspiration. To the lowest faculty of falsehood – i.e. the mimetic activity of imagination – Plato appears to be according the highest form of truth![36] The reversal of the standard Platonic condemnation of imaging could hardly be more explicit.

This apparent scandal is soon dispelled however. For Plato is quick to add that these 'original' images of divine revelation are products of God, not man. What is more, these properly divine images are only accorded to holy men who enter a state of inspired ecstasy (*ek-stasis*) where they are 'beside themselves', that is, no longer in command of their own imaginations. Plato also calls this state of holy inspiration *enthousiasmos* – meaning to be infused with the divine. The fact that this occurs in sleeping visions or other forms of ecstatic non-consciousness signifies that the divine images reside *beyond the control of man*. They are at all times involuntary and unpredictable – and this in sharp contrast with the playful manipulations of the artist or sophist. Indeed Plato observes that the holy seers who receive such visions are rarely able to understand their meaning themselves. Their visions require to be subsequently interpreted by rational commentators.[37]

Plato suggests accordingly that we are no longer dealing here with 'images engendered by man'. These visions are not imitations produced by the human imagination. They are revealed to man by God Himself. And one of their main purposes, furthermore, is to 'correct and banish' the imitations produced by human imagination. Mirroring the transcendental forms themselves, these visions serve to counteract the false practices of man's image-making, to pacify its attendant bodily desires, and thereby open the soul to divine inspiration. In this way, the mind is enabled to recall the transcendental Ideas which it knew in its pre-existence (prior to its descent into this material world) and to anticipate its return to the world of divine Ideas after its death. Hence Plato's cautionary addendum that all such mystical visions must remain subject to the overall super-vision of rational interpretation and religious obedience. For man to mistake the divine images for his own creations would be the worst kind of idolatry. The human imagination is of its very nature mimetic and derivative. It can never, *by its own artifices*, lay claim to divine truth. In brief, the images of revelation are authored by God, not man. Prometheus remains safely bound; Zeus still reigns supreme.

We may summarize Plato's treatment of images – whether it concerns the mimetic phantasies of the artist or the divine visions of inspired seers – by saying that the *human* imagination is only deemed legitimate to the extent that it acknowledges the three following conditions: (i) that it is an imitation rather than an original; (ii) that it is ultimately subordinate to reason; and (iii) that it serves the interests of the divine Good as absolute origin of truth. Whenever human imagination departs from any of these three strictures it is to be condemned without hesitation and without reprieve.

4 Aristotle's psychological verdict

No account, however schematic, of the Hellenic understanding of imagination could be considered adequate without some reference to Aristotle's philosophy. We conclude this chapter, therefore, with a few remarks about how Aristotle developed and revised the Platonic theory of imaging. Though still primarily concerned with an epistemological assessment of imagination – that is, the role it plays in the promotion of truth or falsehood – Aristotle shifts the terrain of investigation from a *metaphysical* to a *psychological* level. We also witness in Aristotle's treatment of *phantasia* a transition from an idealist to a realist epistemology. And this difference from Plato means that the emphasis is now more consistently placed on the role of the image as a mental intermediary between sensation and reason rather than as an idolatrous imitation of a divine demiurge.

In the *Poetics* (1447–8), Aristotle redefines the notion of *mimēsis*. He identifies it with the positive capacity of art to portray the universal meaning of human existence. In so far as art is the imitation of action, it constitutes a *muthos* which isolates universal truths from the contingent particulars of man's everyday experience; it gives our existence a heightened sense of unity and coherence; it redescribes reality so as to disclose the 'essential' dimension of things. In this manner, Aristotle is able to redeem the artist from Platonic censure by affirming that the practice of poetic imitation is one which fosters truth rather than falsehood, which deals in essences rather than appearances.[38]

While the notion of imagination plays a marginal role in the *Poetics*, it is accorded a central place in some of Aristotle's other treatises.[39] Against the Platonic tendency to treat the image as an *external* imitation (*eidōlon* or *eikōn*), Aristotle tends to concentrate on the properly psychological status of the image as a *mental* representation (*phantasma*). Plato had, of course, touched on this function of the image in his discussion of true and false propositions in the *Sophist* and the *Cratylus*. But it is only with Aristotle that the psychological workings of imagination receive a systematic and comprehensive treatment. Thus the

Platonic paradigm of the image as a form of painting – an external copy of nature which is itself an external copy of the transcendental Ideas – is replaced by the Aristotelian paradigm of the image as an internal activity of mind which mediates between sensation and reason. *Phantasia* stands midway between *aisthēsis* and *noēsis*.[40] The image serves as a bridge between the inner and the outer. It is both a window on the world and a mirror in the mind.

Aristotle's approach to imagination is more scientific than Plato's. In *De Insomniis*, he rejects the Platonic notion of mystical images implanted in the human psyche by God. All the images of our dreams or reveries are, he asserts, ultimately derived from our sensible experience. 'With regard to their being (*einai*)', Aristotle writes, 'imagination and sensation are the same.' And he goes on to explain 'that imagination is a species of sensation, even if each expresses itself in a different way'. And so it follows that since 'a dream is a species of imagination, it is therefore a particular mode of perception, that is, an imagined mode of perception' (*De Insom.*, 459a). Every dream is thus reducible to our sensory experience of the empirical world. This 'realist' character of Aristotle's epistemology is also evident in his definition of the image in the *Rhetoric* as a secondary or modified sensation (*phantasia estin aisthesis tis asthenēs*) (1370a). The so-called divine visions of which Plato speaks in the *Timaeus* are, Aristotle dryly retorts, merely effusions of our physical impressions which rise up when reason is asleep or in a fever (*De Insomniis*, 462a). Those who claim to be inspired visionaries are simply 'confusing the representation of a perception with perception itself' (*De Memoria*, 451a). To avoid such confusion, it is necessary to recognize that the main source of our images is *memory* understood as a reservoir of images which record our sensory impressions of reality (*De Mem.* 451). 'Memory', says Aristotle, 'refers to that part of the soul to which imagination refers' (450a).

It is, however, in the *De Anima* that Aristotle offers the most elaborate account of the psychological origin of images. His common-sense realism is manifest in his consistent definition of the imagination as an intermediary faculty between our sensible and rational experience. Although imagination is seen as a species of sensation, it also differs from the latter in its capacity to relay our impressions of reality to the inner activities of reason. The image serves as the internal representation of sensation to reason. Aristotle describes this mediational role accordingly: '*Phantasia* differs from both perception and thought even though it cannot exist without perception and serves as a precondition of belief' (*De An.* 3,3, 427b). And for this reason, it is necessary that 'every time one thinks one must at the same time contemplate some image' (*De An.* 432a). In order to be able, for instance, to think of mathematical concepts such as straightness or largeness one must have an image of something that is straight or large – a line or a triangle (*De. An.* 431b).

In *De Memoria* (449b–450a), Aristotle compares this mode of image-representation to a kind of drawing or draughtsmanship:

We have already spoken of imagination in our writings on the soul; and we stated there that it was not possible to think without an image (*aneu phantasmatos*); because it is the same thing to think and to draw (*diagrāphein*). Thus in the case of a triangle, even though we have no need to determine its size we draw it in terms of size; so too he who thinks, even though he may not be thinking of size, places something of size before our eyes, and can only think of things in terms of size.

What this analogy suggests is that imagination is an inner draughtsman of the mind. Aristotle also invokes here the Platonic model of the image as a kind of painting. But he gives it a radical twist in so far as the imaging process, like the writing process, has been internalized. The 'painted image' (*zographeme*) is situated *within* the soul as an indispensable instrument of memory (*De Mem.* 450a).

It would appear then that the concept of imagination as a *picturing* activity is to be found in Aristotle as well as in Plato. But Aristotle's understanding of this picturing activity differs from Plato's in three fundamental respects. First, it is *psychologized* – that is, it becomes an interior mode of mental picturing rather than an exterior act of figuration (the favoured Platonic model of the plastic arts). Second, it serves as a precondition of all rational thought – unlike the Platonic category of *nous* which had no need of images. And third, its mediational rapport with our sensible experience is one which may result in the apprehension of truth rather than leading us into an illusory world of imitations.[41]

These differences ultimately depend, of course, on Aristotle's departure from Plato's 'idealist' epistemology. Aristotelian 'realism' has no difficulty in according imagination a positive role in the human process of knowledge; for it maintains that the forms which give meaning to reality are not confined to some transcendental other-world, but inhabit the sensible world of our human experience. Ideas are no longer deemed to be disembodied spiritual essences. They are categories of human thought which correspond, through the indispensable mediation of images, to the forms of the real world perceived by our senses. Aristotle has, so to speak, taken the transcendental Forms from their celestial heights and implanted them in reality.

For Aristotle to affirm that images are modified modes of sensory perception, is not therefore to condemn them to a pseudo-world of untruth. The sensible world of becoming so denigrated by Plato in the *Republic* and elsewhere, is now acknowledged as the very source of our knowledge of being. Aristotle's endorsement of a realist epistemology sets out to 'save the phenomena', in the famous catchword of classical antiquity. And this entails, logically, the need to recognize images as reliable agents of our phenomenal experience. Without the transitional services of imagination, reason would be unable to make contact with the sensible world of reality. Thought devoid of images is unthinkable. It would not be able to represent anything. Deprived of content, it would be directionless, pure emptiness. Reason simply cannot function without the mediation of the mental image (*phantasma noētikon*).

While Aristotle confirms the Platonic equation of imagination with the finite realm of movement, desire and time, he gives it a benign inflection. We shall take each of the terms of this triple equation in turn. Man's relationship to the world depends, firstly, on an intimate link between the image and *movement*. The image, Aristotle tells us, 'is movement based on a sensation which permits us to act or to receive experience in multiple *develop on it though* (handwritten marginalia)

ways' (*De An.* 428b). At the psychological level, the imagination is that which gives rise to movement understood as a transition from potency to act, from the inferior sensations to cognition, from lack to fulfilment.

Aristotle then proceeds to link imagination to *desire*. 'When the imagination moves it does not move without desire' (*De An.* 433a). Moreover, the fact that all men desire in this imaginative way means that 'all men desire knowledge', since knowledge is to be understood as that supreme act (*energeia*) which realizes our human potentiality (*dunamis*). Knowledge is that which all men lack; it is the goal towards which we all move. Movement is incomprehensible without the motivation of desire. And it is imagination which communicates desire from the material realm of appetite to the mental realm of our intelligence (*De An.* 433–4). Aristotle elaborates on this point in the *Rhetoric* when he defines fear as an experience of pain which 'comes from an image (*phantasma*) of evil or of pain to come'; and when he defines love as motivated by the 'imaginative anticipation of the good which all the world desires' (*Rhet.* 1, 11, 17). Imagination is thus accredited a central role in the moral orientation of behaviour: 'In the regulation of conduct the phantasy is a kind of weakened sensation aiding one in deliberating about the right course by means of concrete pictures affecting the appetite.'[42]

This acknowledgement of the regulative role played by imagination establishes, finally, its relation to *time*. Imagination is temporal by virtue of its ability to recall our experience of the *past* and to anticipate our experience of the *future*. We have already alluded to the relationship between the image and memory (i.e. as a reservoir of faded impressions). The imagination's rapport with the future is somewhat more complex. It is, of course, obvious that human behaviour is deeply affected by the capacity to imagine the outcome of our acts. We avoid certain types of action (e.g. murder) because we anticipate the pain that may result (e.g. punishment). And, contrariwise, we are propelled towards other types of action because we anticipate the good or happy outcome that may ensue. But such projections into the future would seem to suggest a certain ability of the image to move beyond the *given* sensible experience of our past in order to prefigure *possible* modes of experience. Thus we find Aristotle allowing for kinds of cognitive images which rise above sensations:

The thinking soul apprehends the forms in images, and since it is by means of these images that it determines what is to be sought and what avoided, it moves beyond sensation when it is concerned with such images . . . Moreover, it is by means of the images or thoughts in the soul, which enable us to see (the future), that we calculate and deliberate about the relationship of things future to things present (*De An.* 3, 7, 431b).[43]

One might also mention here the intimate rapport, recognized by Aristotle, between such an intellectual use of images and the illuminating and transformative powers of the 'active intellect' (nous poiētikos).[44]

In the light of such considerations, Aristotle makes an important distinction between the purely sensible imagination (*phantasia aisthētikē*) and the rational imagination (*phantasia logistikē/bouleutikē*). While the former exists in both animals and humans, Aristotle implies that the latter is the privileged possession of humans (*De An.* 429a; 433a–b). 'It is only because an animal desires that it can move and it can only desire by means of images', writes Aristotle, 'but imagination can express itself deliberatively (*bouleutikē*) as well as sensibly (*aesthētikē*), although animals share with man only the latter function' (*De An.* 433). Where the sensible imagination refers exclusively to our empirical appetites, the rational imagination is capable of uniting and combining our empirical sensations in terms of a 'common sense', which is in turn representable to reason (*De Mem.* 450a). This 'synthetic' practice – which Aristotle terms *eidōlopoiountes* (*De Mem.* 441b) – is a unique property of the rational imagination.[44] But one would probably be mistaken to see this as a properly *productive* power. The discovery of an autonomous imagination which creates meaning out of itself is a modern event. Only with Kant and the German idealists would Western philosophy officially and explicitly proclaim the existence of an imagination prior to, and independent of, both sensation and reason. For Aristotle, *phantasia* remains an intermediary faculty residing, as it were, *between* the primary and pre-existing faculties of sensation and reason. In short, it remains alio-relative: for it owes both its mode of *existence* (at a metaphysical level) and of *truth* (at an epistemological level) to either sensation or reason or both. Benedetto Croce is correct, I think, when he summarizes the classical heritage of imagination as follows in the *Aesthetic*:

Ancient psychology knew fancy or imagination as a faculty midway between sense and intellect, but always as conservative and reproductive of sensuous impressions or conveying conceptions to the senses, never properly as a productive autonomous activity.[45]

It is undeniable that Aristotle's 'realist' epistemology encouraged a more generous reading of imagination than that officially countenanced by Plato. In so far as he located the forms of truth in the real world of experience rather than in some transcendental otherworld, Aristotle situates the image at just one remove from truth. It is, to be sure, still considered as a picture or residue of our sensory experience (Aristotle uses the term *emmenein* to describe this 'remainder' character of the image in *De Anima*, 429a). But precisely as such, it is now recognized as a necessary instrument for the acquisition of knowledge. In other words, *qua* mental representation, the image still serves as a *copy* rather than an *original*; but it is now validated as a generally reliable copy rather than an illusory copy of a copy. Since Aristotle admits that the true forms of being – to which our rational categories correspond through the mediation of imagination – are to be found in *this* world rather than in some other one, he may also admit that the image can help us intuit the essential truth of things (*De An.* 402b).

Nevertheless, this admission does not mean that imagination is itself the origin of meaning. At best, it may be enlisted in the service of higher truths: truths which exist *beyond* our images of them. The legitimate function of the mental image – and it is by no means insignificant – is to represent reality to reason in as faithful a manner as possible. If the draughtsman of imagination dares to break his contract with the rational master, he is at once condemned to error. And on this decisive point Aristotle

Both d

is no less insistent than Plato that imagination must ultimately remain subservient to reason. For both these founding fathers of Greek philosophy, imagination remains largely a *reproductive* rather than a *productive* activity, a servant rather than a master of meaning, imitation rather than origin.

CHAPTER THREE

The Medieval Imagination

Traditional Western thought was largely though not exclusively composed of a blending of biblical and Greek concepts.[1] This admixture of the intellectual frameworks of Jerusalem and Athens reached most explicit expression in the famous 'Christian synthesis' of medieval philosophy. We understand the term 'medieval' here in its broad designation as a middle epoch between antiquity and modernity, one extending from the collapse of the Roman Empire in the fifth century to the taking of Constantinople in the fifteenth century. What we are seeking, however, is not a history of causal events but an epistemological paradigm (or *episteme*, to borrow Foucault's term) which might be said to inform the various concepts of imagination in the medieval epoch.

1 The Christian synthesis

Before proceeding to isolate some paridigmatic examples of the medieval imagination, it is important to say something about the overall significance of the Christian synthesis of Greek ontology and biblical theology. We call this synthesis 'onto-theological' (though we understand this shorthand term less in the Heidegerean sense of metaphysics in general, from Plato to Nietzsche, than in the more specific sense of medieval Christian thought – a sense underlined by Etienne Gilson when he spoke of the *identification of God and Being* as the 'common good of Christian philosophy').[2] In short, the 'onto-theological' character of medieval thinking refers to its bringing together of the Judeo-Christian notion of a Divine Creator and the Platonic-Aristotelian metaphysics of Being.

In both traditions of this conceptual alliance, as we have seen, the imagination was essentially interpreted as a *mimetic* activity – that is, as a second-hand reflection of some 'original' source of meaning which resides beyond man. In biblical tradition, this Origin was identified with Yahweh, the Father of all creation. While in the Hellenic tradition, it was usually equated with the highest of the Forms: something which mortals desire to emulate, contemplate or know in some way.

The conjugation of these two foundational heritages – Greek and Judeo-Christian – was by no means a foregone conclusion. When St Paul arrived in Athens from Jerusalem he debated with the Greek philosophers and subsequently declared that the truths of biblical faith, as revealed in the Old and New Testaments, could not be adequately comprehended in terms of a rational metaphysics. The mysterious relationship of God and man was, Paul held in his first letter to the Corinthians, a 'folly' for the philosophical mind. It could only be experienced in the gift of faith. Many of the early Christian thinkers subscribed to this basic suspicion of Greek reason. Tertullian, writing in the second century, for example, exclaimed that Athens and Jerusalem had nothing in common whatsoever. The Bible was the one true guide to salvation and philosophical theory merited, at most, contempt.

However, it soon became obvious to Christian apologists that the best way to defend the biblical message against the pagan thinkers of Greece and Rome was to admit that classical metaphysics may on occasion have anticipated, unbeknownst to itself, the revealed truths of biblical religion. Thus, for example, the 'unknown god' (*agnōstos theos*) of the Greeks might at last be recognized as the Creator God of monotheistic religion. Likewise it was allowed that Plato's hypothesis in the *Timaeus* of a divine demiurge may have parallels with the biblical account of Yahweh's creation of the universe in *Genesis*. And the suggestion was even advanced by certain Christian authors that the concept of the *Logos* in Greek metaphysics was equivalent to the Second Person of the Trinity – Christ himself. Frederick Copleston outlines the significance of these equations in his *History of Medieval Philosophy*:

From the point of view of the Christian writers, the search for the maker and father of the universe, as Plato put it, together with the search for the knowledge of man's final end and of the way to attain it, had reached their goal in the Christian religion . . . The Christian world-view is impregnated with the ideas derived from or suggested by Greek philosophy, so that it appears as a fusion or synthesis of Platonic elements with Christian belief. The One is the Trinity; the *Logos* or Word became incarnate in Christ; man's likeness to God, referred to by Plato, is the work of divine grace; and the human soul's return to God is not simply a solitary flight of the individual but is achieved in and through Christ as the head of the Church.[3]

While several of the early Church Fathers gestured towards such possibilities of synthesis, it was Augustine in the fourth century who first succeeded in forging a sustained and systematic concordance between Judeo-Christian theology and Greek ontology. Augustine argued that man's faith in the biblical Creator God could be positively articulated and clarified with the aid of philosophical concepts. He distinguished accordingly between propositions held as true simply on authority, as when a child believes something to be true on the word of its parents, and propositions whose truth is established by philosophical reasoning. Augustine thus advanced the view that faith could be raised to an onto-theological perspective which enabled man to reconcile his belief in the God of Revelation with a metaphysical understanding of the categories of Being. Yahweh as the God (*theos*) of Creation is seen as the ultimate origin of Being (*on*). In short, Augustine opened up the possibility of conscripting theology and ontology as joint allies in the pursuit of truth. He paved the way for the famous medieval model of 'faith seeking understanding' (*fides quarens intellectus*).

This onto-theological alliance was, needless to say, to have a profound and enduring impact on the subsequent evolution of medieval thinking about imagination. In its simplest form, the alliance served to deepen the traditional suspicion of imagination: it combined and consolidated (a) the biblical condemnation of imagination as a transgression of the divine order of Creation (i.e. as *ethical* disorder) and (b) the metaphysical critique of imagination as a counterfeit of the original truth of Being (i.e. as *epistemological* disorder). The medieval current of opinion was subsequently to carry a double negative charge. And, not surprisingly, we find the notion of a profane imagination (*imaginatio profana*) being given widespread currency by most Christian thinkers of the Middle Ages.

Augustine was, of course, an influential forerunner of the medieval theories of imagination. He was the first Latin author to use the term *imaginatio* in a consistent philosophical manner, combining the biblical distrust of images with the Greek and neo-Platonic view of *phantasia* as a hindrance to spiritual contemplation.

Augustine's philosophy, as is well known, was deeply influenced by neo-Platonism. He was surely not unmindful of Plotinus' warning that 'we cannot apprehend intelligible entities with the imagination (*phantasia*) but only with the faculty of contemplation (*noesis*)' (*Enneads*, 5,5).[4] Plotinus' verdict is equally reflected in the writings of his disciples. Porphyry relegated imagination to the lower flux of sensation – as is evident, for example, in his claim that 'the knowledge of incorporeal natures is attainable by us with great difficulty, for we remain in doubt about their existence as long as we are under the dominion of phantasy'.[5] Similarly, Proclus counselled men to 'flee images whose very divisibility and diversity . . . leads us away from the divine towards the movements of the earth.'[6] It is against this neo-Platonic background that we may best understand Augustine's statement in *De Genesi* (34) that intellectual vision alone is capable of intuiting the world in its 'essence' rather than merely in its 'corporeal image'; for as soon as one endeavours to grasp the spiritual light 'with the help of an image one is no longer grasping it as it is in itself'.[7]

Augustine's theory of imagination largely conforms to the classical schema of 'mimetic' representation. The image, no matter how interiorized or mentalized, continues to refer to some original reality beyond itself. It cannot create truth *out of itself*, but must always observe the strict limits of *reproduction*.[8] The image remains a derivation. It can never lay claim to the status of originality. That is the prerogative of the divine. And so we find that even when Augustine is prepared to acknowledge a role for imagination in prophecy, he leaves us in no doubt that such a role is permissible only on condition that our images are meticulously supervised by reason. This qualification is evident, for instance, in a passage in the *De Genesi* where Augustine observes that while the dream images of the seven ears of corn and the seven kine were given to the Pharaoh in his sleep, it was only Joseph who could *decipher* the prophetic content of such images in the daylight of reason. 'To the one', as he puts it, 'was given the *imagination* of things, to the other the *interpretation* of that imagination' (*De Gen.* 34). Moreover, Augustine's choice of an example from the Bible is surely telling. Is he not implicitly enlisting the authority of the Judeo-Christian suspicion of images to counteract the potential dangers of Plato's notion of divine images in the *Timaeus*? Although Augustine himself was later to be accused of 'ontologism' – that is, of bringing the divine and human visions of being too closely together in his notion of 'illumination' – such heresy could never be put to the account of his treatment of imagination. For Augustine, *imaginatio* is, at best, the humble servant of a higher intellect. The only true 'image of God' was Christ. Any attempt by the human imagination to substitute for this unique convergence of God and man in Christ was blasphemy.[9]

2 Medieval interpretations

We may now turn our attention to an analysis of some medieval theories of imagination. Rather than proceeding in the manner of the historian who establishes causal or consecutive connections between one philosophy and the next, we will isolate certain thinkers who, we believe, succeed in encapsulating the medieval paradigm of imagination. What particularly interests us is the specific character of the metaphors or symbols employed by medieval thinkers in order to describe imagination. Or to put it in more technical terms, we wish to discover the hermeneutic model – the typical system of interpretation – which characterizes the underlying *imaginaire* of medieval philosophies of imagination, that is, how they represent the very activity of imaginative representation.

Richard of St Victor

We begin our search for such paradigmatic metaphors with some passages from a twelfth-century text by Richard of St Victor entitled *De Unione Corporis et Spiritus*. In the first passage, Richard warns of the corruptive influence which imagination may exert on the practices of spiritual *contemplatio*. In a witty allegory he likens contemplation to a *mistress* who inhabits the inner sanctuary of reason, and imagination to a *handmaid* who frequents the outer rooms of bodily desire. This image of inner and outer, borrowed from Aristotelian psychology, is amplified by the addition of two further analogies: i) a biblical analogy which compares the mistress to Rachel and the maid to her servant Bilhah; and ii) a social analogy which identifies the mistress as a privileged member of the upper feudal class and the maid as an accomplice of the lower feudal class. The noble mistress, Rachel, cannot afford to lose touch altogether with the inferior senses. Yet being of aristocratic blood she cannot condone either that 'a servant such as one of the senses be in the habit of bursting into her private recesses'. And so she hires imagination, Bilhah, as an intermediary handmaid who may allow for communication between the higher and lower classes while preventing the necessity of direct contact. But Richard cautions us against placing too much trust in the mediational services of imagination. Bilhah's frequentation of the menial servants of the senses has rendered her basically unreliable, suspect to distraction and disloyalty:

Bilhah becomes garrulous and loquacious. Nor can Rachel rule even in her own house; with such persistence does Bilhah din in the ears of the heart that Rachel cannot live with her. So it is when we sing and pray, we ought to remove from the eyes of the heart the phantasies of thought, or what should be called the images of things. The heart, though unwilling, is perpetually calling up images of the memory.[10]

In this intriguing text, Richard endeavours to explain how imagination is both indispensable to the life of reason – since reason must have some contact with the outer world of the body – and yet a constant obstacle to the highest aim of reason: meditative contemplation. By introducing both speech (Bilhah's noisy loquacity) and spectacle (Bilhah's phantasies) into the calm silence of the contemplative heart, imagination contaminates the pure spirit with corporeal sensations of sound and sight. And she thereby threatens to subvert the triple hierarchy of i) inner mind and outer body (the epistemological model of Greek metaphysics); ii) blessed and unblessed generation (the biblical model of Hebrew prophecy – Rachel, born under the sign of the virgin, was the first and favoured wife of Jacob, mother of Joseph, and thus rightful transmitter of the seed of Israel; whereas Bilhah was the inferior maidservant who replaced Rachel as Jacob's spouse); and iii) the upper class of nobles and the lower class of serfs and peasants (the medieval model of feudal society).

By assigning imagination a 'transitional' role in each of these hierarchical systems, Richard is at once reinforcing and undermining the very dualisms which make up the system. For if it is true that the spirit needs the 'images of things' – i.e. memory – to communicate with the world of the senses, it is these very 'mimetic' mediations which impede it in its upward ascent to rational contemplation. In other words, the spiritual heart of reason cannot live *with* imagination, and it cannot live *without* it. Likewise, while Rachel requires Bilhah to represent her in her everyday dealings with the impious servants, this very strategy of substitution threatens to permit the infiltration of the impure into the pure, the gentile into the Holy of Holies. And so also *à propos* of the third hierarchical dualism, the feudal aristocracy needs to enlist the services of a 'middle class' of merchants, guildsmen and other travelling entrepreneurs so that it can dispense with all direct dealings with the lower peasant classes

– but it is this very mobile, shifting intermediary class (later to become the bourgeoisie?) which ultimately threatens to dismantle the feudal hierarchy and upset the genteel pastime of aristocratic contemplation. On all three counts then, Richard is suggesting that the higher spirit, 'though unwilling', is, despite itself and against its better interests, perpetually soliciting those very images which subvert it.

The second passage – also from Richard of St Victor's treatise *De Unione Corporis et Spiritus* – develops this paradoxical nature of imagination. Here the image is metaphorically portrayed as a 'borrowed robe'. While Richard is prepared, like Augustine, to admit a limited role to images as a means of 'clothing' rational ideas so as to make them 'presentable' and accessible to the uninitiated populace, he warns against the danger of allowing these images too much leeway. He writes:

Reason uses imagination as a vestment outside and around it; if reason becomes too pleased with its dress (i.e. imagination) however, this imagination adheres to it like a skin; and separation is effected only with great pain. . . . The mind delighted with body in this wise is deformed by the phantasies of corporeal imagination, and impressed deeply with these, it is not able to sever its union with the body.[11]

This metaphor of the vestment is telling in several respects. Firstly, it suggests that the image must be kept at a safe distance from reason lest we mistake its *artificial* apparel for a *natural* possession (i.e. skin). In other words, reason must not become so seduced by the charms of its imaginary clothing that it forgets its original condition of pure and innocent nakedness (i.e. self-presence). Thus while it may function as a useful instrument of *re-presentation*, imagination must not be confused with the original *presence* of reason to itself. But the double metaphor of clothing/skin also carries another message. It cautions against the risk of reason confounding its own ideational life with the sensory life of the physical body. In this reading, the metaphor of skin takes on a more *literal* meaning: it refers to the corporeal skin of our bodily experience which threatens to absorb reason into the lower world of movement, desire and time. Thus in either case – whether reason mistakes imagination for itself or descends through imagination to the body – the properly 'mediational' status of the image is blurred.

In short, imagination is only legitimate to the extent that it occupies an intermediary position *between* the inner mind and the outer body. Once we forget its role as a 'vestment' of the soul which communicates the inner to the outer and protects the inner from the outer, we also forget the duality which *separates* reason from sensation. And, as Richard admonishes, if we let down our guard in this way and allow reason to be 'impressed deeply' by the decorative phantasies of its clothing, these phantasies will become grafted onto the spirit; and we must then go to great pains to amputate this unnatural growth which assumes the guise/disguise of nature.

A 'deconstructive' unravelling of the contradictory connotations of this equation between *image, vestment and skin*, might demonstrate how such a play between inner and outer, mind and body, reason and sensation, ultimately serves to destabilize the very metaphysical order upon which such oppositions are based. The outcome of such a deconstructive reading would be to show how imagination opens up a gap in the strict metaphysical opposition between spirit and matter. The imagination would be revealed not as a mere re-presentation of some pre-existing original (i.e. the body or reason) but as the very play which produces the notion of such an original presence in the first place. We shall return to this suggestion in our discussion of Kant's theory of imagination in the next chapter. Suffice it for now to have at least indicated such a deconstructive textual play within the corpus of medieval philosophy.

The ultimate reason for Richard's distrust of imagination is, of course, to be found in his onto-theological vision of truth. Richard powerfully illustrates the medieval determination to reconcile classical ontology with Christian theology. The purpose of philosophy, he argues, is to justify the mind's transcending this world of sensation and imitation in search of a Supreme Being which exists of necessity in itself. In true onto-theological fashion, Richard identifies this highest of beings with God Himself as Original Cause and Creator of the universe. God, he maintains, subscribing to St Anselm's argument on degrees of perfection, is the infinite ground of all finite perfection. Richard's use of rational argumentation to lead us beyond our temporal experience of sensation and imagination to the divine origin of all existence, puts the instruments of classical philosophy (e.g. reasoning about first causes, grounds and beings) into the service of Christian Revelation. And as such, it represents, in Copleston's words, a 'considerable development in philosophical theology'.[12] Thus when discussing the Trinity, Richard declares his intention, as far as God permits, to provide not only probable but necessary reasons for what Christians believe. He proceeds to construct a dialectic of love between the three persons of the Trinity; and he argues that the Trinitarian model is necessarily required by a rational appreciation of Divine Being as the self-sufficient and self-identical origin of love. God is not simply loving but love itself. Superimposing the Christian notion of The Trinity onto the Aristotelian definition of the Highest Being as a 'self-thinking-thought', Richard concludes accordingly that it is 'only in the light of the idea of the internal love-life of Father, Son and Holy Spirit that we can do justice to the statement that God *is* love'.[13] In so far as human reason seeks to elevate the mind to a contemplation of this self-identical love, it must strive to divest itself of the mediational trappings of imagination. But is it possible for the human mind to transcend imagination altogether – and therefore also, by implication, our sensory experience – without ceasing to be human? For if imagination is a signal mark of our finitude how can we presume to surpass it without presuming to become one with God himself? Richard of St Victor has no answer to this embarrassing anomaly. Like many of his medieval confrères, he prefers to pass it over in prudent and devout silence.

St Bonaventure

One of the most celebrated philosophers of the Middle Ages to have been influenced by Richard's treatment of the soul's contemplative ascent to God was St Bonaventure.[14] The most telling metaphor for imagination in Bonaventure is that of mirroring. Bonaventure explicitly adverts to the derivation of the term *imago* from *imitando*, meaning to imitate or reflect (I, 540).[15] Images are always used analogously in the human order to express a secondary form of imitation – what Bonaventure calls *similitudo*. The true source of the Model/Image relation remains that of God the Father and Christ the Son. Here, and only here, is the Image at one with its Original (I, 542). All finite images are, accordingly, merely copies of the Divine Image of Christ which is the perfect reflection of the *Exemplar Aeternum*. By extension, human imagining is but a mirroring of the Divine act of creation (as primary imaging) (5, 385–6). The human creature is a *simulacrum* of the Divine Creator (5, 386); and his highest vocation is to faithfully 'mirror' the Supreme Artist of the universe. (See also Appendix to Chapter One on the Image of God Debate).

Bonaventure invokes the neoplatonic model of *exemplarism* to account for creation as a mirroring of the original in and through its images. In the *Commentary on Sentences*, he states that the human creature comes to know himself truly when he declares: 'I am a copy' (I, 540). The created world is to be construed by the inquiring mind as a set of mirrors all of which point towards God. This metaphor of mirror-reflection is developed by Bonaventure in the opening chapter of the *Itinerarium* when he speaks of the light and shadow of God relating to his creatures *in* and *through* a mirror. God's image is mirrored at three ascending levels: 1) the external world; 2) the natural self; 3) the supernatural. In the external world God is only seen 'through a mirror darkly'. Sensible things serve as similitudes which, at best, point beyond themselves to the source of their imaging (i.e. God). In the internal order of the self, man becomes aware of his own power as a maker of images – a power which is 'like' that of God's. At this level of internal mirroring, the self converts the natural *macrocosm* into a *microcosm* of memory and imagination. The formation of such internal similitudes 'images' God in so far as: 1) the mental species is an image of God; 2) the natural object represented is an image of God and; 3) the activity of creating the mental similitude itself mirrors the activity of God creating the universe.

Bonaventure thus locates imagination at the second step of

the *itinerarium* halfway between the sensible world and the understanding. As such, images can either lead downwards into error or upwards toward supernatural truth. Taking the option of ascent, imagination can create images which imitate God. This is particularly obvious in the case of artistic creation where 'expressed harmonies' may be produced by imagination from 'memorial harmonies' (derived from the similitudes of the senses) in accordance with the rational judgement of Eternal Truths (5, 302). Artistic images are thus seen to express the inner ideas of intellectual judgement using materials drawn from the outer senses. Bonaventure even proposes at one point a daring comparison between man's creation of an artistic image and God's creation of man:

The maker plans before making an object, and then he makes the object as planned. The maker produces an external work as close to the internal similitude as he possibly can; and were he able to produce an object that would both love and know him, he would do so by all means; and if this produced object were to know its maker, it would do so in terms of the similitude from which the artist had worked; and if the eyes of knowledge of the produced object were so clouded that it could not look up above itself in order to know its maker, the similitude from which it had been produced would have to come down to the level of a nature which the object could apprehend and know (5, 322–323).

But Bonaventure is quick to add that it is not imagination itself that makes a work beautiful but 'knowledge' which judges images in the light of truth (5, 323, 13). The judgement of beauty is a property of the 'rational soul' bestowed upon man by God; its purpose is to 'praise and serve Him' by acknowledging Him as sole Exemplar of all created images. By means of reason, which prevents imagination from cultivating images as ends in themselves, the 'arts return to the light of the Holy Scriptures, which often and rightly use images taken from them' (5, 323, 14). Similarly, while Bonaventure admits that prophecy may also avail of imagination (e.g. *secundum imaginationem est visio prophetalis imaginaria*. I, 281), he insists that contemplation must always move beyond imagination toward the light of rational intellect which alone can discriminate – both ethically and epistemologically – between images, legitimizing some, reforming others, and contradicting others again.

If imagination is not subjected to such rational scrutiny it risks leading us into evil *malae imaginationes . . . sunt tomentum concupiscentiae*, 2,232). Moreover, Bonaventure's identification of the source of evil with concupiscence rather than pride, stems from a revealing reading of Adam's original sin as a desire for forbidden knowledge. 'Concupiscence may still be alive within us in the form of curiosity', he writes. 'This vice afflicts the man who seeks to possess occult knowledge . . .' (8, 4–5). In other words, evil results from a wrong use of imagination: one which takes images as ends in themselves rather than mirror-reflections of the divine Exemplar. 'Creatures are deceived and fall into error', explains Bonaventure, 'when they take the image and the copy for the thing itself' (5, 305).

Bonaventure distinguishes accordingly between two uses of the mirroring function of imagination: a good use of *imaginatio* as participant in the ascent of the human mind toward God (4, 325); a bad use of *imaginatio phantastica* (or *phantasia*) as a pervertor of rational judgement and participant in the descent of the mind down the image chain towards evil (e.g. *imaginatio phantastica multum impedit nos a elevatione ad puritatem intelligentiae*. 4, 225). Bonaventure is acutely aware of the latter propensity of imagination; and he explicitly reads the first and second Commandments prohibiting false gods and idols as a warning against the 'demonic pacts' of imagination wherever it 'attributes to creatures what it should attribute to the creator', seeking to magically transform nature in the manner of Pharaoh's magicians.[16] Imagination inclines to idolatry when it disregards reason and produces images which confuse being and non-being (*errorem autem facet phantasia obnubilans rationem et fasciens videri esse quod non est*. 5, 514). In short, idols arise when imagination ceases to recognize images as similitudes which mirror a higher being and becomes engulfed in images which mirror themselves in an empty play of non-being.

Another telling metaphor in Bonaventure's understanding of the ascent of images toward God is that of the 'ladder'. Reformulating Plato's famous simile of the Divided Line in the light of the neo-Platonic figure of Vertical Emanation (whereby the One descends into the world and reascends again to its proper heights), Bonaventure advances the following hierarchy of epistemological faculties – *sensus*: *imaginatio*: *ratio*: *intellectus*: *intelligentia*: *apex mentis*. Without enumerating the specific function ascribed by Bonaventure to each of these faculties, we note that *imaginatio* is located beside sensation on the lowest rung of the scale (5,297). Conforming thus to the official downgrading of images in Platonic metaphysics – and particularly in Book VI of the *Republic* – Bonaventure also introduces the Aristotelian notion of imagination as a 'mediational' faculty: one which passes on our lower sensations in the form of mental representations which are then purified by the intellect into abstract ideas.

But Bonaventure's metaphor of the 'ladder' is not confined to the idioms of Greek philosophy. True to the onto-theological model, Bonaventure's trope also draws from the biblical tradition. As a transitional faculty of imaging, *imaginatio* is, of course, analogous to 'Jacob's ladder' (although Christ remains the true example of the ladder model). For just as Jacob dreamt of a ladder stretched between heaven and earth with angels descending and ascending, so too images may point towards sacred truths by mediating between the lower senses and the higher faculties of reason. But Bonaventure leaves us in no doubt about the limitations of this transitional activity. Imagination, he insists, can never reach truth *on its own*. It is merely one step in the journey towards truth – and a very low one at that. And if Jacob was indeed granted a vision of God's relation to man, receiving the 'name' of God after his struggle with the Angel at Bethel, this was a unique event in the history of Revelation: a prophetic act which ordinary mortals dare not imitate without committing blasphemy. Even Jacob, who carried the privileged blessing of Isaac and Abraham, did not survive unscathed from the encounter – he limped ever after as a reminder of the danger of coming too close to his Creator.

If such deformity was the price exacted for Jacob's prophetic dream, how much more perilous is the threat to ordinary mortals who claim to possess such divine images? Mindful of the cautionary implications of this biblical story, Bonaventure declares that Christ is the only legitimate model for the ladder analogy (5,297); and he warns that more often than not *phantasia* serves as a hindrance to truth, 'obscuring the intellect', 'impeding the freedom of will', and thereby leaving us vulnerable to 'demonic possession' (2,189; 2,631; 5,514). In this way, what appeared to be a concession to imagination quickly turns into its opposite – a further occasion for its prosecution. The possibility of a divinational role for imagination becomes instead a stern admonition against its diabolic potential. Indeed, this prosecution of the 'demonic imagination' in Bonaventure's writings in the thirteenth century was frequently invoked by later scholastic philosophers of medieval Christendom.[17]

Aquinas

Finally, we take a brief look at the contribution made to the theory of imagination by the dominant figure in medieval and scholastic philosophy – St Thomas Aquinas. Aquinas represents what many consider to be the crowning achievement of the medieval synthesis of Greek and biblical learning, rehearsing and rearranging the principle stages of Western ontology and theology in a magisterial system or *summa*.

Aquinas' discussion of imagination in the *Summa Theologiae*, written in the second half of the thirteenth century, consolidates the medieval conception of this power as a mediational faculty between mind and body. Defending the Aristotelian thesis of a plurality of psychological functions, Thomas counts imagination as one of these. He enumerates a number of different faculties ranging from perception, common sense and imagination to reason and intellect, concluding that 'since none of these actions can be reduced to the same one principle, they must be assigned to diverse powers'.[18] Aquinas' intention here is to refute all 'monist' accounts of the mind – whether spiritualist or materialist. The different cognitive acts are there to testify to the *diversity* of our mental faculties and to their complex interrelations.

Thomas in no way accords autonomy to imagination – which he designates by the synonymous terms *imaginatio* and *phantasia*.

Indeed, in certain passages, we even witness a certain diminution of the role played by imagination to the extent that it is confined to the preservation of our sensible experience in the form of derived copies. Aquinas writes,

For the reception of sensible forms the proper and common sense is appointed; but for the retention and preservation of these forms, the phantasy or imagination (*phantasia sive imaginatio*) is appointed, which are the same, for phantasy or imagination is, as it were, a *storehouse* of forms received through the senses.[19]

This metaphor of the 'storehouse' is perhaps *the* paradigmatic figure of imagination in Thomistic philosophy and, one could even argue, in the mainstream of medieval scholasticism as a whole. This storage function of the image is also underlined in Thomas' account of dreams – in sharp contrast to the Platonic theory of divinely inspired dreams in the *Timaeus*.[20]

At best, Thomistic epistemology recognizes the intermediary role of images, given the finite limits of human understanding. While the true forms of reality – whether it be spiritual ideas or the things themselves – lie beyond the grasp of imagination, man has need of images to serve as *analogies* between our rational and sensible experience. Aquinas thus cleverly combines the Platonic notion of a pure noetic realm devoid of images with the Aristotelian doctrine that forms cannot be mentally represented *without images*. He explains,

Incorporeal things of which there are no phantasms are known to us by comparison with sensible bodies of which there are phantasms. Therefore when we understand something about these things, we need to turn to phantasms of bodies, although there are no phantasms of the things themselves.[21]

Thomas' position here typifies the orthodox view of scholastic *realism*. This realism goes hand in hand with a certain kind of *rationalism*. All uses of imagination are subordinate to the superior claims of both reality and reason. Thomas is, of course, prepared to admit that certain mysteries of divine Revelation – such as the Trinity or prophecy – may well surpass the limits of human understanding. But he insists that these mysteries are on no account to be confused with the irrational workings of imagination. The latter can only lead to error unless controlled by the rational intellect. Thomas is unequivocal on this point:

There are intellectual habits by which a man is prompted rightly to judge of the presentation of imagination (*imaginatio*). When he ceases from the use of the intellectual habit, extraneous imaginations arise, and occasionally some even of a contradictory tendency, so that unless by the use of the intellectual habit these are cut down or repressed the man is rendered less fit to form a right judgement.[22]

If then, as Scripture tells us, divine visions have been vouchsafed to holy prophets in the Old Testament, such visions must on no account be confused with the mad effusions of the human imagination in sleep, lunacy or lust. The imagination simply confounds the metaphysical distinctions between being and non-being, truth and non-truth, substituting its unreal imitations for the things themselves. And so Thomas does not baulk at Bonaventure's suggestion that imagination may prove an accomplice to demonic possession. 'Demons are known to work on men's imagination', he confirms, 'until everything is other than it is.'[23] The medieval suspicion of imagination could hardly be more clearly stated. As a mimetic faculty of representation and storage, imagination has its place. But it must be kept in its place. Any departure from its mandatory subordination to reason and reality, can only lead to error – and, at worst, satanic pride.

What do the paradigmatic metaphors of medieval imagination have in common? What is the underlying epistemic *a priori* which informs these various descriptions of imagination – Richard of St Victor's insolent handmaid or borrowed vestment; Bonaventure's mirror; Aquinas' storehouse? True to its dual 'onto-theological' nature, the medieval understanding of imagination conforms to the fundamentally 'mimetic' model of both its Greek and biblical origins. In each of the philosophies examined, we note that the image is treated as an *imitation* – i.e. copy, representation, surrogate, substitute, mirage, memory-impression, secondary mental phantasm and so on. It is never considered as an *original* in its own right. The recognized mimetic function almost invariably assumes the related function of 'mediation'. Deeply influenced by Aristotelian epistemology, the medieval thinkers were, with few exceptions, prepared to accept that this mediational role of imagination could be positive or negative. Positive in the measure that it related the inner world of the mind to the outer world of the body and vice versa. Negative in the measure that it frequently deviated from the supervision of the higher intellect and confused the rational with the irrational, the spiritual with the sensible, being with non-being.

This acknowledgement of the ambiguous status of imagination on the *epistemological* plane was expressed in a general attitude of suspicion – a suspicion exacerbated by the adherence of medieval philosophy to the *ethical* condemnation of imagination found in Holy Scripture. The combination of these two foundational authorities (Greek ontology and Judeo-Christian theology) resulted in a largely hostile view of imagination. For the official thinking of the Middle Ages, truth remained the privileged possession of a transcendent Other: God or Being. And, this self-identical Other was the unique and exclusive Origin of all reality. No exceptions were to be admitted. In so far as imagination was prepared to enter the humble service of this higher Origin and honour it as the one and only Father of all things, it could be granted probation under the jurisdiction of reason. But as soon as imagination sought to surpass this limited role as a ward of court, it was to be harshly penalized. Leniency in such a case could only lead to idolatry, blasphemy or demonic possession.

This basic antipathy to imagination was, then, the *official* verdict of medieval philosophy. As such, it took little or no account of the vibrant life of imagination at the level of popular folk and vernacular culture. On the margins of mainstream medieval *theory*, but at the very heart of the medieval *life-world*, we find many cults of what Jacques le Goff and others have called the 'profane imagination'.[24] These include various celebrations of the magical powers of imagination in medieval folklore, witchcraft, and occultism. But such attitudes were, not surprisingly, frowned upon by the official authorities. They were considered deviations from the prevailing orthodoxy and exerted little influence on the approved conception of imagination in the Middle Ages. Such a divorce between attitudes to imagination in philosophy and popular culture largely perdured until the efflorescence of modern theories of the 'productive imagination' in German idealism and European romanticism generally. Only then would the philosophy of 'mimetic' imagination be definitively overturned and a more positive and humanist portrait come to occupy the centre stage of Western thinking.

3 Iconography and iconoclasm

As one might expect, the Christian understanding of Being, and more precisely of the role of imagination in the order of Being, was not without its effect on the medieval attitudes to religious art. From the outset, the Church Fathers made it clear that although there is a certain parallel between the beauty of God, expressed in the biblical notion of 'glory' (*Kabod/Doxa/gloria*), and that of the created order of being, this parallelism was never more than analogical. It was in this spirit that the Fourth Lateran Council decreed that the differences between the two were infinitely greater than the similarities. All visible forms of representation were deemed to be radically disproportionate to the glory of God they sought to express.

The biblical prohibition on man-made images of the Divine Creator was, of course, constantly referred to in the iconoclastic doctrines of early and medieval Christendom. Its influence was evident in Pope Leo III's edict on iconography in 730; the protracted controversies in the Byzantine Church; and also in the negative theologies of Philoxenes, Pseudo-Dionysius and even St Thomas. But the doctrinal reservation towards artistic representations of Christ could never be total. There was a basic ambiguity at the very heart of the matter. For on the one hand, Christianity held that the Divine had assumed visible form in the person of Christ (a notion unacceptable to the Jews) and so appeared to remove the Hebraic embargo on human images of the Godhead. Yet, on the other hand, Christianity had to be doubly cautious about the possibility of false imitations. The God-man, Jesus Christ, was deemed to be the unique and perfect representation of the Divine. And it was for this reason that Philoxenes and other proponents of negative theology held that Christianity had put an end to the 'era of images' (and not only the false idols of pagan cultures but even the prophetic visions of the Old Testament!). In short, the mystery of the Christian Incarnation appeared to *waive* the biblical prohibition on images of God and to *reinforce* it at one and the same time.[25]

While mindful of this paradox, the Orthodox Church came to cultivate the religious art form of the icon as a fitting extension of the Incarnational mystery. And in time the icon was considered to be almost as sacred as the inspired words of the Scriptures themselves. The proliferation of iconographic art in Greece and Russia after the eleventh century marked a decisive stage in the theological rift between Rome and Constantinople. This rift had been growing for centuries. It centred largely on different theological interpretations of the Trinity. Rome laid most emphasis on the relationship between the Father and the Son, seeing the Holy Spirit as a derivative or accessory expression of this privileged rapport. Hence the controversial formulation of the Nicene Creed in terms of the *Filioque*: the belief that the Spirit proceeded from the Father *and the Son*. The Orthodox Church rejected what it saw as a patriarchal privileging of the Father-Son relationship and sought to restore the Holy Spirit to a central and equal position in the Trinity. This view was expressed in the theological figure of the *perichoresis* which portrayed the Three Persons of the Trinity as a circular dance movement where each Person cedes the place to the other in a perfect symmetry of co-existence.

This re-emphasizing of the inspirational power of the Holy Spirit by the Oriental Church accounts in large part for the development of iconography as an influential sacred art in the East. The implication was that divine inspiration was not confined to the original Scriptures which bore witness to the historical event of the Incarnation but could also be reinvoked, as it were, at any stage in history through the sacramental representation of icons. The Church Father, John of Damascus, implied as much when he declared that 'however perfect a Bishop may be, he needs the Gospel on the one hand and the painted expression of the same on the other, because the two have equal value and should receive equal veneration' (*Epistles*, II, 171).[26]

Iconography thus flourished in the East at the same time as scholastic theology flourished in the West. This ecclesiastical divergence was neatly witnessed in the fact that whereas medieval scholasticism claimed the *Summa Theologiae* of Thomas Aquinas to be the standard document of the Roman Church, the Council of the Hundred Chapters in the sixteenth century deemed Andrei Rublev's icon of the Trinity, painted in 1425, to be an exemplary expression of the Orthodox Church. This did not mean, however, that the Byzantine Church issued a free dispensation to representational images of the Divine. The theological legitimacy of icons was not established until the ninth century after bitter iconoclastic debates. And, thereafter, a series of strictly defined conventions had to be observed by the holy icon makers.

Firstly, the art form of iconography was only permitted as a *sacred* practice in praise of God. It was not to be confused with a secular art which might express the human personality or creativity of its maker. For many centuries icons did not bear the name of their authors – unlike works of theology for example – and were held to be the work of the Holy Spirit rather than of an individual man. Iconography was essentially an 'impersonal' art with little or nothing in common with the classical art of Graeco-Roman civilization which preceded it, or the humanistic art of the Renaissance which followed it.[27]

Secondly, the precise *content* of religious icons was doctrinely delimited. The divine mystery of Christianity could not be expressed directly. In most cases it was to be represented through the mediation of the face of Christ. And so the Father could remain 'invisible' as biblical authority demanded. If the Christian Trinity was to be depicted, it was to be done obliquely or symbolically (as, for example, in Rublev's icon where the Three Persons are represented by the three angels who visited Abraham under a tree in the Old Testament).

Thirdly, a certain abstractness of *form* was prescribed to insure that the iconic copy would not be confused with the Divine Original. The presence of God must be only hinted at by the icon itself; otherwise it would easily degenerate into an idolatrous illusion. To avoid such a danger, the following list of conditions must be scrupulously observed:

The artist had to be a committed Christian and to perform his work almost as a liturgy, fasting and praying and obeying the various canons and regulations laid down for this specific art form. Both the subject matter of the icons and the various figures, items and placings were rigorously preordained. The fact that the icon was executed on a two-dimensional surface was an essential reminder that it was representing another reality which could not be substituted for by the art-work itself.[28]

Thus the Orthodox Church did not allow statues, for it was felt that their realistic and material qualities might occasion idolatry. Nor indeed did it permit perspective to be introduced into iconic representations. Not because their icon-makers were unaware of the early advances by the West in this direction, but because 'this geometrical trick which, by an optical illusion, allowed the beholder to imagine that a three-dimensional reality was appearing on a two-dimensional surface, might allow us to take the icon for the actual reality it was trying to lead us towards'.[29] Other formal devices used to avoid the dangers of 'realism' were the alteration of facial features (the ears and mouth of the Christ face were usually smaller than normal and the eyes larger); the absence of a frame (suggesting that the icon is not self-contained but is open to the infinite); and the use of a gold base (which was considered the most appropriate symbol for the light of the Godhead since it presented a completely flat surface eliminating the illusion of an intermediary space between it and the figures embedded in it). Gold represented the glory of the Divine which intrudes from another world absorbing into itself all natural light emanating from other colours. By virtue of these various formal conventions, the icon was considered as a means of communicating with the transcendent Godhead rather than as a dialogue between man and man – i.e. artist and audience.

Icons are not meant to create a subjective mood or even a pious response in the mind of the beholder. . . . The icon is meant to be a window onto another world, not really a thing in itself. As a material object it is no more than a prism or a focus which concentrates energy in a way that allows our vision to transcend it and go beyond . . . it should become *transparent* rather than act as a barrier to the kind of vision it is designed to encourage.[30]

The icons of early and medieval Christian art differ fundamentally from the subsequent art forms of the Renaissance. The great humanist artists – Alberti, Leonardo, Brunelleschi, Verrochio, Donatello – translated the revolutionary advances of the new sciences into the idioms of plastic representation. This produced the mathematical mastery of space, anatomical realism and the use of light and colour to express depth, both psychological and physical.[31] Thus in Renaissance painting the spectator becomes the centre of the composition through the use of three-dimensional perspective and other illusionist strategies of pictorial realism. In sharp contrast to medieval iconography, everything is now viewed from the human spectator's point of view, and every effort is made to cultivate the impression that what is depicted on the canvas is actually taking place in front of our eyes. The painting of the *Quattrocento* is, in Leonardo da Vinci's words, 'the art of offering the eye perfect simulacra of natural objects'. It matters little, in the final analysis, whether the content of such art is religious or secular – or both at once. What matters, firstly, is the personal style of the human artist who puts his signature on the art work, thereby ensuring its authentic originality; and, secondly, the aesthetic effect this work has upon the human perceiver. Renaissance humanism departs radically from medieval iconography in affirming that the primary purpose of art is to *communicate between man and man.*

One of the legacies of such Renaissance art was the cultivation of the illusion of reality. Caravaggio, for instance, had no compunction about choosing his models for St Joseph from the most destitute beggars of his town. Likewise he painted St Matthew with a bald wrinkled head and bare ugly feet, causing a scandal at the time.[32] Indeed, it was even rumoured that he took his model for Our Lady from a drowned prostitute who had been lifted from the Tiber. By the end of the Renaissance, art was less concerned with transcendent ideals than with human reality. The sacred jostled shoulders with the profane. And this was proof enough of its basic humanism. 'Nobody looks upwards in Caravaggio's pictures', notes Roger Hinks, 'they gaze at each other, they gaze out of the picture, but they never gaze at the sky – for there is no sky in Caravaggio's world. It is the difficulties of *mankind* that he underlines.'[33] Indeed one might say of Caravaggio's religious art what has been said of Milton's famous religious poem, *Paradise Lost*: though it ostensibly claimed to be vindicating the ways of God to man, it actually succeeded in vindicating the ways of man to God.[34] Between the fifteenth and the seventeenth century the humanist perspective had come to dominate most of Western art, both visual and literary. Latin had been replaced by the vernacular languages, sacred vision by secular perception, theology by science.

The Roman Church, of course, gave its blessing and patronage to the religious art of the Renaissance. Pope Julius II, for example, explicitly adopted the Raphaelesque formula, which seemed to embody a perfect synthesis of order and science. But in becoming the official aesthetic of the Roman Church, this formula had the effect of promoting a predictably 'Church' art of decorative intent rather than a specifically religious art which, as in medieval iconography, aimed beyond the art work itself toward a mystery which surpassed it. The ultimate result of this aesthetic standardization of religious art was, ironically, to diminish or even destroy its sacramental potential. It was detrimental in two ways:

On the one hand it meant that the autonomous sources of creative endeavour could no longer submit to such authoritarian attempts to direct their energies and so became divorced from the Church and, in many instances, from Christianity itself; on the other hand, religious art within the Church became an imitative and derived reflection of the model set, and, with the passing of the centuries, became weaker and paler until it became the mass reproduction of itself in prints and 'holy pictures' which technological advance has made possible in our day.[35]

Despite certain concessions granted to art by the Church in the Middle Ages, we must not lose sight of the fact that the 'onto-theological' attitude to man-made images, which prevailed during this period, was essentially one of prudence or distrust. It was Thomas Aquinas, after all, the canonized doctor of the medieval church, who claimed that the 'ultimate in human knowledge of God is to know that we do not know him' (*De Potentia*, 7, 5), thereby ultimately endorsing a 'negative theology' which exposed the inadequacy of human representations of the Godhead. As Etienne Gilson observes in *The Elements of Christian Philosophy*: 'In deep agreement with the most radically imageless mysticism that ever existed, that of St Bernard of Clairvaux, Thomas Aquinas invites us to transcend all representation and figurative description of God.'[36]

It is, however, important to recall in conclusion that the Christian attitude to imagination is not all there is to the medieval imagination. This point is made convincingly by Jacques Le Goff in *L'Imaginaire Médiéval* where he documents the existence of a significant 'a-Christian' culture beneath the established culture of medieval Christendom.[37] This unofficial culture was sustained by the popular folk arts which accorded a central place to three main areas outlawed by the onto-theological orthodoxy – *magic*, the *body*, and *dreams*. Thus, for example, while the Church in the Middle Ages invoked the warnings of Augustine and Gregory the Great against the heretical powers of dreams, the profane movements of *l'imaginaire médiéval* celebrated these very powers. And in so doing they fostered the notion of a personal human consciousness – a factor which was to assume pivotal importance in the later development of Renaissance humanism. Similarly, while medieval Christendom considered the 'miraculous' to be the exclusive prerogative of God, the profane *imaginaire* presented it as an integral part of human and natural reality. We cannot pursue such considerations here. The exploration of this unofficial *imaginaire* falls outside the chosen parameters of this chapter, namely: the analysis of the dominant paradigms of imagination in the Christian philosophy of the Middle Ages.

APPENDIX 1

The onto-theological notion of being as production

The onto-theological outlook which conditioned the official medieval theories of imagination is distinguished by several features. Perhaps the most important of these, according to Heidegger's controversial but suggestive reading, is the determination of existence as 'production'. Heidegger argues that the medieval notion of reality as *actualitas* is intimately related to the concept of production – *agere, actum.*[1] Accordingly, the 'essence' or 'nature' of something is understood in terms of an active making or bringing forth which permits the thing to be seen in its proper form. Unlike the pre-Socratic apprehension of Being as 'unconcealment' (*aletheia*), medieval metaphysics interprets the appearing of Being less as a *dis-closure* than as an act of *production*. The classical paradigm of 'mimesis' still predominates:

The model upon which this understanding of Being is based is that of the artisan, the potter, say, who aims to engender a certain form in the clay; the clay then takes on a look which conforms to the exemplar – the anticipated look – which he attempts to copy. The prototype, the exemplar, shows us how the thing is supposed to look before it is actually produced. That is why the expression *quid quod erat esse*, that which a thing was to be, is used interchangeably with *eidos* (*causa exemplaris*). The *eidos* is that from which the actual thing is descended, its kin, its *genus* (kind). The members of a genus form a group only because they have a common 'descent', belong to the same family. Hence the word *phusis* belongs to the same sphere of significance. *Phusis* (*natura*) means growth, to produce its own kind. The 'nature' of a thing is a self-producing essence.[2]

Medieval onto-theology thus reinterprets the Greek concepts of making (*technē, poiēsis, praxis*) so as to redefine the very reality of Being as a causal product. It never occurred to Aristotle, for example, that matter, understood as that 'out of which' things are made, could itself be made (i.e. by God, as in the Judeo-Christian version of creation). Moreover, the dominant metaphors of family, patriarchy, kinship, generation and genealogical descent, invoked to account for the 'productive' character of nature, serve to reinforce the onto-theological understanding of worldly reality as a copy or imitation of some pre-existing Divine Original. This transcendental Origin becomes identified in medieval philosophy with the Mind of God Himself as First Cause and Creator of all things. The 'production' of Being is consequently understood as an activity which belongs to God rather than man. The recognition of man's own original creative powers would have to await the discovery of the 'transcendental imagination' by Kant and the German Idealists in the late eighteenth century.

According to Heidegger, Medieval scholasticism effectively endorses an 'objectivist' account of Being as something which is already in existence prior to all human intervention or invention. And as such, observes Heidegger, it betrays a blindness to man's essentially productive power. In keeping with its dual allegiance to Platonic metaphysics and biblical Revelation, Christian onto-theology continues to affirm the Divine as the only legitimate Origin of the universe. Indeed, it may even be said to amplify the ancient suspicion of human creativity to the extent that it superimposes the Father-Son-Spirit hierarchy of Trinitarian theology on the Patriarchal hierarchy of the Platonic Ideas (and in particular the Neoplatonic model of emanation from the One). It is perhaps in the light of this onto-theological conception of Being as a creative/procreative lineage of descent that we should read the allusions to Jacob, Joseph, Rachel, etc. (as chosen transmitters of the prophetic tradition) in several of the medieval accounts of holy vision and contemplation cited above.

Heidegger also points to the crucial role played by Roman culture in the transition from Greek to medieval metaphysics. 'In order to realize sufficiently the scope of this transition,' writes

Heidegger, 'the Roman character must be understood in the full wealth of its historical developments.'[3] The onto-theological determination of Being as making and production was greatly assisted by the language and culture of Imperial Rome. Christian creationism, which defined God as the *actualitas omnium rerum* (*Summa Theologiae*, I,4.i), borrowed several of its philosophical terms from the Roman civilization of power and action (*actus, agere, actus, actualitas*). Heidegger detects here a connection between the 'political imperial element of Rome and the Christian element of the Roman church'. The Judeo-Christian theology of creation assimilated the Roman ontology of causal production, engineering and mastery.

Thus the medieval Christian conception of Being in terms of making and what is made is articulated in a language (Latin) which belongs to the people of making and doing. The 'Roman Church' is not just an historical appellation. It points to an inner harmony between Christian metaphysics and the metaphysics of making, which come together in the conception of Being as *Wirklichkeit* (*actualitas*).[4]

While Aristotle and Plato may be said to have preserved an echo of the pre-Socratic experience of Being as an 'original presencing', the Christian philosophers of the Middle Ages understand Being increasingly in terms of *causality* – that is, as a relationship between what effects and what is effected. So that when the scholastics declare that *scientia Dei causa rerum* (God's knowledge is the cause of things) they mean that divine knowledge is both speculative and productive. And the key concepts of reality in scholastic philosophy – *existentia* and *actualitas* – bear the trademark of this causal model. The reality of things as they appear to us is not treated as an original presencing in itself. It is seen as a second-order 'effect' produced by the transcendent Cause of all Causes, the Supreme Being who subsists in Himself (*per se subsistens*), the Divine Lord and Master of all Creation. Nothing exists in any permanent fashion unless it is made so by God himself. God as Creator is the only being who does not need to be created. All other beings have their existence bestowed upon them by the Creator (*esse receptum et participatum*).

In short, Being is conceived primarily in terms of power, efficiency, action, force, making, work:

Being comes to mean that which is responsible for, effects, or brings about the constant. This is brought out very clearly in the scholastic conception of God. The more what is present endures in its permanence, the more actual it is. But God cannot be lacking in Being. And since Being means permanence, God is the most enduring, most fully actual being, the *actus purus*. His Being is self-persisting. He owes His presence to nothing other than Himself. But this self-persisting being is the *summum ens* and as such the *summum bonum*, which makes Him the cause of causes. . . . As the highest cause, God effects (*er-wirkt*) what is real (*Wirkliche*) in its persistence. The original Greek experience of Being then is covered over by the categories of actuality (*Wirklichkeit*), causality (*Wirken*), and persistent presence. Even presence itself – the divine *omnipraesentia* – is defined in terms of causality. Thus St Thomas says that God is present to everything in virtue of being its cause (*ST*, I,8,3).[5]

Finally, Heidegger maintains that the medieval paradigm of *Being as production* prepares the way for the modern epoch of humanism and technology. The modern conception of 'nature' as a spatio-causal system of 'reality' which produces empirically verifiable effects ultimately derives from the creationist model of medieval onto-theology. The difference being, of course, that in the modern epoch this model of production has been radically secularized by the natural sciences. Likewise, the growth of the human sciences in modern Western culture has replaced God with man as first cause and creator of meaning. This is the essence of humanism. The underlying framework of modern technology – what Heidegger identifies as the *Ge-Stell* – still owes much to the scholastic model of the *causa prima*. And if it is true that the Church condemned Bruno and Galileo at the time of the first emergence of modern physics, this is seen by Heidegger as an 'inhouse controversy' which occurred within the parameters of an understanding of Being as causality and actuality.

The essential origin of Being as making possible and as causing dominates throughout the future history of Being. Making possible, causing, accounting for, are determined in advance as gathering in virtue of the One as what is uniquely unifying.[6]

The triumph of humanism in the Renaissance, Enlightenment and Romantic periods may therefore be viewed as an extension of this productionist model in so far as it installs man as the 'uniquely unifying' creator of meaning and value. And this move, as we shall see in our next chapter, was to have revolutionary implications for the Western understanding of imagination. Instead of being considered as a 'mimetic' replay of Divine Creation, the human imagination becomes a 'productive' play in its own right.

APPENDIX 2

Philoxenes of Mabboug on imagination

We have seen how Augustine and the Christian thinkers of the Latin Church displayed an attitude of caution towards imagination, bordering at times on condemnation. The thinkers of the Eastern Christian Churches were no less hostile in their views. One of the most interesting examples of the latter is Philoxenes of Mabboug, a Syriac Church father of the fifth century.

Philoxenes marks an absolute rupture between the intellectual vision of truth, which he sees as participating in the spiritual world of self-sufficiency, and the sensible world of untruth, to which human imagination and sensation are incorrigibly bound. Philoxenes writes in his *Letter to Patricius*,

> Once the intellect has contemplated truth in its own region it may no longer express this contemplation in any *lower* region, and even if it wished it could not do so since it transcends all bodily sensations. . . . What it sees and hears within itself is experienced spiritually in the region of the Spirit alone.[1]

Philoxenes' critique of the imagination, motivated by the above conviction, unfolds in several stages. First, he asserts that the complicity of imagination with our bodily passions prevents us from ever knowing the objects of the real world as they are in themselves. The world is thus fashioned according to our imaginary desires. It yields not knowledge of things but a mirage. Imagination condemns us to 'wander about in a closed confinement of mirrors'.[2] But imagination is guilty of an even greater sin to the extent that it *presumes* to escape from its own mirror-images in pursuit of divine truth itself. While it claims to be leading us into the promised land of contemplation – and away from the fleshpots of physical desire – imagination is in fact posing as a substitute for *both* the objects of our sensible experience *and* spiritual truth itself! The imagination's pretension to dispense with all sensible mediations in order to present invisible truth to us directly is, therefore, a *double* lie. As long as man's quest for contemplation remains prompted by the desires of imagination, he is condemned to vanity. For if our renunciation of the things of this world is one governed by a passion of imagination, however ostensibly spiritual, we are in fact guilty of the worst of all trespasses, pride of spirit – vainglory understood as the passion of conquering passions where man indulges in his own power as the imaginary cause of his own perfection.[3]

It is at this point in his critique that Philoxenes delivers his most serious and subtle accusation. The imagination, he charges, is *intrinsically* perverse. It is not just the *content* of images that is evil; it is their very *nature*. It is not *what* man imagines that is bad but *that* he imagines at all. The perversity of imagination, in other words, resides in its very activity as *representation* – that is, the false claim to present spiritual truth *immediately*, understood in the double sense of without mediation (spatial immediacy) and without delay (temporal immediacy). This distinction between the moral content of images and their very nature is most significant. And it may be said to mark a new phase in the traditional condemnation of imagination. The Greek theories of both Plato and Aristotle had allowed for good and bad uses of images. Indeed it had been suggested that an image is more or less neutral in itself and only becomes good or bad by virtue of our judgement concerning its mode of representation (i.e. whether it corresponds to reality or not). Aristotle even allowed of a positive *moral* role in so far as the image pictured a 'good' outcome for our actions. Likewise, the rabbinical tradition had admitted of good and evil inclinations in the *yetser*. By contrast, Philoxenes' guilty verdict allows of no defence. There were to be no alibis, excuses or attenuating circumstances. The imagination is judged evil through and through. Its very 'haste to represent' truth is the very thing which cuts off all access to truth. And it is of little consequence whether the image represents obscene degradations or celestial beatitudes. The crime is in the very act of representation itself: the occlusion of reality behind an illusory imitation. This act of substitution is, moreover, *inherently* idolatrous for it incarcerates the one who images in his own self-glorifying hallucinations.

Hence we may say that Philoxenes advances a *structural* rather than a merely *circumstantial* condemnation of imagination. Brushing aside even the limited concessions made to human imagination in Greek philosophy (e.g. Aristotle's claim that we can have no thought without images) and in biblical exegesis (e.g. the rabbinical admission that without the *yetser* man would be deprived of all inclination to construct a social or cultural dwelling), Philoxenes denounces the very structure of *phantasia* as an act of premature representation. Guy Lardreau provides this perceptive summary of the main implications of Philoxenes' analysis:

The hallucination of the Trinity or of a woman's sex do not of course derive from the same desire . . . but it is the same *haste to represent* which in both cases places an illusory satisfaction in front of truth, thereby precluding access to the knowledge of nature (*theoria physikē*) or of God (*theoria theologikē*). In both instances, fantasy is substituted for reality. Thus the whole of spiritual life can be defined as a *struggle against images*, and its progress as a gradual access to the *things themselves*.[4]

Philoxenes' position leads logically to 'iconoclasm'. His castigation of all modes of imaginative representation appear to have exerted a considerable influence on the great theological debates about iconography which prevailed in the Christian Churches of Rome and Constantinople in the early Middle Ages. The overriding premiss of Philoxenes' critique of imagining is, of course, a theological one. And the greatest weapon *against* the errors of imagination is, he insists, the Christian doctrine of the Incarnation. By assuming the form of a real man in Christ, God put an end to the era of idolatry. Once the eternal appeared in person in the unique event of the Incarnation, the quest for absolute truth no longer needed to resort to the illusory devices of imagination. Even prophecy – which Philoxenes acknowledges to have made use of *phantasia* in the Jewish tradition – is now redundant. For God has revealed, through the reality of the Christian Incarnation, that He alone is truth and that no image, no matter how inspired, may be allowed to come between the human mind and the pure contemplation of the divine. Consequently, even attempts to picture the person of Christ in images or plastic representations is forbidden. Christianity is thus seen as augmenting rather than diminishing the Hebraic prohibition against images of God. The Christian era, inaugurated by the *reality* of the Incarnation, is hailed by Philoxenes as the decisive turning point in the spiritual battle against imaginary *appearances*.

The greatest temptation facing the philosopher is to ignore the truths of Revelation and so to think he can reach truth out of his own finite resources. To submit to this temptation is to eclipse reality by enclosing onself in a narcissistic world of one's own desires. The Greek thinkers of pagan antiquity were victims of such falsehood, according to Philoxenes and other like-minded Christian commentators, for they were not yet enlightened by the truth of Revelation. Barred from access to the One – i.e. the transcendent God of creation – the 'thoughts' of the pagan philosophers were, unbeknownst to themselves, no more than idle 'imaginings' lost in an artificial world of multiplicity. Hence, even though they never actually constructed *external* images of things – statues, paintings, effigies, etc. – their very thoughts were little more than *internal* images. And this is why, Philoxenes explains, the pagan culture of classical antiquity was one which ultimately facilitated (Plato's critique of the artist apart) the proliferation of the plastic arts. For it followed that since reality was already divided and multiplied in human thought – not yet having received the Revelation of the One – the subsequent step of representing this multiplicity of images in works of the plastic arts was natural, indeed inevitable. Deprived of Christian Revelation, the desire of imagination simply reproduces itself *ad infinitum*. It is only when reality itself is fully disclosed to man by Christ that it becomes possible to escape from the artifices of human imagination and discover that truth has its unique source in God.

By equating imagination with 'original sin', Philoxenes in effect

tars all modes of pre-Christian or non-Christian philosophy with
the same brush. He cannot accept the attempts made by Greek
thought – for example Aristotle's psychology – to classify imagination as *one* of the natural faculties of the human mind amongst
others (e.g. reason, memory, perception), and on the basis of
such a division to then distinguish between false and truthful
modes of representation. The human mind remains bound to
imagination until it is redeemed by grace of Christian truth,
made possible by baptism and conversion. In short, the very
nature of the human mind is fallen and corrupt as a result of
original sin. Unless man is renewed by the grace of Christ and
thereby divested of his original nature, he can never rise above
his own subjective imitations. Falsehood cannot, therefore, be
accounted for by appeal to the discriminations of a faculty
psychology which prescribes a 'truthful' use for our mental activities. Only a theology of sin provides the explanation of all human
error and points towards the sole source of truth – God himself.
Hence Philoxenes' insistence that man cannot by his own
initiative accede to the contemplation of truth. Man does not
contemplate reality; at best, he witnesses the contemplation of
reality through the grace of God. In other words, true contemplation is not a property of human thought at all: it is the thought
of the Absolute Other who exceeds all human thought. In the
silent and imageless contemplation of truth, man ceases to be
the author of his thoughts. And by so relinquishing all sinful
desires to create, control, will or possess, he opens himself, as
an empty vehicle, to the treasures of divine meaning – 'those
marvels which receive you in the interior of the Holy of Holies
which God himself has made – and where resides the very
arche of all spiritual signs and all divine knowledge' (*Homilies*,
289–290).

Philoxenes' critique of imagination may thus be said to anticipate the 'negative theologies' of early and medieval
Christendom. Since Revelation surpasses the limits of human
representation – as circumscribed by imagination which informs
all modes of human thought – there is nothing that can be
known about divine truth as it exists in itself. God can only
be approached philosophically, therefore, by means of a *via*

negationis. Nothing may be affirmed of God. For the very act of contemplation belongs not to man but to God himself. Only that thinking which has no relation to the Divine Other can vainly presume to think about, or represent, this relation. 'We may say how God *is not*,' concludes Philoxenes, 'but we cannot say how he *is*.'[5]

APPENDIX 3

Maimonides on imagination

Although we have dealt in our first chapter with the Hebraic theories of imagination, it is important to note that certain Jewish thinkers of the medieval period succeeded in combining the biblical and rabbinic teachings on imagination with the Greek philosophies. Moses Maimonides of the twelfth century is a good case in point.

Maimonides' great work, *The Guide of the Perplexed*, may with some reservations be qualified as 'onto-theological' to the extent that it drew from both the philosophy of Aristotle and the biblical tradition. The biblical content of his writings is, of course, derived largely from Talmudic sources rather than the Christian doctrines of the Church Fathers. But this fact in no way modifies Maimonides' ability and willingness to synthesize the intellectual traditions of Athens and Jerusalem. Indeed, one of the main aims of the *Guide* is to reassure those 'perplexed' by the apparently conflicting claims of Greek philosophy and scriptural law, that the ethical and prophetic teachings of the latter may be reconciled – through careful attention to multiple and diverse levels of meanings – with the scientific reasoning of the former. Moreover, the 'non-Christian' character of Maimonides' thought did not prevent him from serving as a highly respected authority for Aquinas and the scholastics. It is fitting, therefore, that we should note some of Maimonides' key pronouncements on imagination by way of extending our treatment of the medieval paradigm and supplementing the Hebraic paradigm analysed in our first chapter.

Maimonides opens his *Guide* with a lengthy exegesis of the *Genesis* text: 'When God created man, He created him in His own image' (*Gen.* 5.1.). The term 'image' is used here, he submits, to designate a 'notional' rather than a 'material' likeness.[1] It is not a likeness of form or shape that is at issue but one of spiritual kinship. Man is made in the 'image' of God, therefore, in so far as he bears this 'notional' resemblance to his Creator; but it is precisely because of this resemblance that idols are also called 'images' and denounced accordingly. 'What we sought in idols', explains Maimonides, was 'the *notion* which was thought to subsist in them and not shape or configuration.'[2] The biblical concept of the 'image' refers, in short, to a spiritual rather than a physical property – and as such can come only from God. Once man seeks to produce such a spiritual notion in his own *man-made* images, he succumbs to idolatry. Hence when Yahweh reprimands the people of Israel with the words, 'What image will you find to match me with' (*Isaiah*, 40:25), He is affirming the impossibility of imagining a divine 'notion' in the form of a visible representation.

In accordance with rabbinical tradition, Maimonides goes on in a later passage in the *Guide* to identify man's inclination towards idolatrous images with our 'bodily appetites and desires'. Commenting on the serpent's promise that Adam and Eve would be 'like gods knowing good and evil' (*Gen*, 3:5), he observes that our first parents yielded to the temptation not only because they sought forbidden knowledge but because the fruit itself was sensually seductive – 'good for food and beautiful to the eye' (*Gen.* 3:6). In other words, man's idolatrous instinct is intimately linked to the lower drives of his sexual nature. Drawing on the Aristotelian doctrine that imagination and sensation share the same mode of existence, he imputes to the former the primary responsibility for man's anthropomorphic misrepresentations of the divine essence. Imagination, he asserts, is inherently corrupted by its association with our animal appetites and 'perceives nothing except bodies or properties belonging to bodies'.[3] The influence of Aristotelian epistemology is also evident in Maimonides' description of imagination as a mental 'faculty' which 'retains the impressions of the senses, combining them chiefly to form images'.[4] The only valid role which he accords imagination is that of a strictly *psychological* mediation

between sensibility and rational intellect (*Bun₁*): a mediation which transforms sensory impressions into mental images which reason then abstracts from their material base and judges in respect of their causal relations.[5]

But Maimonides adamantly denies any autonomy to imagination. It possesses no power to distinguish what is real from what is unreal. Any attempt, therefore, to withdraw imagination from its service to a supervisory reason leads to chaos and caprice. Allowed to operate in its own right, imagination 'yields no test for the reality of a thing'[6] – since it forfeits both its relation to external reality (via sensation) and to internal reality (via reason). Left to its impulses to reduce the spiritual to the material and to transform reality into phantasies of its own making, the imagination plunges us into a play of idolatry, the gravest of 'those errors of men guided by imagination'.[7]

PART II

Modern Narratives

CHAPTER FOUR

The Transcendental Imagination

Imagination is like Adam's dream, he awoke and found it true.
(John Keats)

What most distinguishes the modern philosophies of imagination from their various antecedents is a marked *affirmation* of the creative power of man. The *mimetic* paradigm of imagining is replaced by the *productive* paradigm. No longer viewed as an intermediary agency – at best imitating some truth beyond man – the imagination becomes, in modern times, the immediate source of its own truth. Now imagination is deemed capable of inventing a world out of its human resources, a world answerable to no power higher than itself. Or to cite the canonical metaphor, the imagination ceases to function as a mirror reflecting some external reality and becomes a lamp which projects its own internally generated light onto things. As a consequence of this momentous reversal of roles, meaning is no longer primarily considered as a transcendent property of divine being; it is now hailed as a transcendental product of the human mind.[1]

Modern philosophy reclaimed imagination as the divine spark in man. This reversal was already implicit in the general culture of Renaissance humanism – with its insistence on the primacy of anthropological over onto-theological truth. And there were, of course, numerous occult writings in praise of the magical and alchemical powers of imagination to be found in the theosophical and esoteric movements of Renaissance and post-Renaissance mysticism (ranging from Bruno and Paracelsus to Swedenborg, Boehme, Novalis and Von Baader). But such writings were largely confined to marginalized hermetic cults.[2] It was really only with Kant and the German Idealists in the late eighteenth and nineteenth century, that the productive imagination became, as it were, *officially* recognized by mainstream Western thought. Kant, Fichte and Schelling released imagination from its long philosophical imprisonment. They provided the theoretical impetus for its rise to undisputed supremacy in the romantic and existentialist movements.

This was achieved, first, by demonstrating that imagining was not merely a 'reproduction' of some given reality (the fallacy of imitation) but an original 'production' of human consciousness; second, by showing that the image was not a static 'thing' (res) deposited in memory (the fallacy of reification) but a dynamic creative act; and third, by establishing that the image was not just a mediating courier between the divided spheres of the lower 'body' and the higher 'soul' (the fallacy of dualism), but an inner transcendental unity which resists this very duality. In thus denouncing the traditional interpretations of the image as *reproduction*, *reification* and *dualism*, the modern philosophers hailed imagination as the power of the human subject to create a world of original value and truth. Man could now declare his autonomy from all given being. Meaning no longer required the orthodox mediations of reality to prove itself. It became its own guarantee – the immediate invention of imagination.

1 The Copernican Revolution

The modern reclamation of imagination first became effective, at least on an official level, with Kant. In the first edition of his *Critique of Pure Reason*, published in 1781, this thinker from Königsberg startled his contemporaries by announcing that imagination was the common 'unknown root' of the two stems of human cognition – understanding and sensation. This extraordinary admission turned the entire hierarchy of traditional epistemology on its head. Departing from the received wisdom of classical and medieval philosophers, Kant rescued imagination from its servile role as an intermediary faculty between our sensible and intelligible experience, declaring it to be the primary and indispensable preconditon of all knowledge. Nothing could be known about the world unless it was first pre-formed and transformed by the synthetic power of imagination (*Einbildungskraft*).[3]

This rehabilitation of imagination exerted a profound influence on the subsequent development of German idealism and, by extension, of European romanticism in general. Kant himself was by no means unmindful of the revolutionary implications of his discovery. He quickly became aware that such a declaration of independence on behalf of imagination meant nothing less than dismantling the traditional edifice of metaphysics and, by implication, the ultimate basis of philosophical rationalism. Indeed, so alarmed was Kant by his own arguments that he went to considerable lengths in the second edition of the *Critique of Pure Reason*, published in 1787, to take most of the harm out of his initial claims (see Appendix). But Kant's recoil from the subversive consequences of his discovery of the 'productive' imagination in no way detracts from the pivotal importance of this discovery in the history of Western thought. After Kant, imagination could not be denied a central place in the modern theories of knowledge (epistemology), art (aesthetics) or exist-ence (ontology).

Kant's radical revision of the accredited status of imagination is intimately related to his overall philosophy of being. According to the traditional perspectives of classical and medieval thought, being was the source of all human knowledge. To know reality was to secure an adequate representation of being. And this was generally to be achieved by means of a rational judgement which ensured that the human understanding was in conformity with external reality. Hence the famous scholastic definition of truth as *adaequatio intellectus ad rem* (the correspondence of the mind to things). Being was the centre of the universe and the human mind was like a planet which revolved around it. Kant reversed this model. He proclaimed a 'Copernican Revolution' in philos-ophy whose aim was to remove the human mind from its periph-eral role and place it at the very centre of the universe. Being would henceforth be conceived not as the transcendent origin of meaning, but as a representation of the human subject – or,

more precisely, as a *production* of the human imagination. This
is what Kant had in mind when he affirmed that 'being is not a
real predicate . . . but only the *positing* of a thing' (A 598).

This Copernican Revolution marked a decisive turning point
in Western thinking for it effectively replaced the old onto-
theological definitions of being as Divine Cause or First Principle
with the quintessentially modern definition of being as a projection (*position oder setzung*) of human subjectivity.[4] In short,
Kant's Copernican Revolution gave rise to the modern conviction
that being is not first and foremost some transcendent deity
which produces human meaning but is rather a product of man's
own transcendental imagination. Imagination thus ceases to be
a copy, or a copy of a copy, and assumes the role of ultimate
origin. As the poet Yeats exclaimed in his rousing Introduction
to the *Oxford Book of Modern Verse* (1936), the imagination
surpasses the constraints of 'ancient history' and opens up the
path of modern aesthetics at that crucial moment when 'the soul
becomes its own betrayer, its own deliverer, the one activity,
the mirror turns lamps'.

2 Transitional movements

Kant's revolutionary discovery was not of course entirely without
precedent. Several currents of Western thought served as
preliminary stages between the reign of the scholastic paradigm
in the thirteenth and fourteenth centuries and the emergence
of the Kantian paradigm in the late eighteenth century. Before
embarking on a detailed analysis of Kant's own treatment of
imagination in the two *Critiques*, we shall take a cursory look at
some of the most significant theories which anticipated the
Kantian turn in one way or another.

Renaissance mysticism

There were various Renaissance movements of mystical and
hermetic thinking which may be seen as precedents to the
German idealist cult of the productive imagination. Although

these movements were largely confined to marginal sects, at least until Schelling and the romantics gave them wider currency, they do make up a significant body of writing on the transformative powers of imagination – or the *virtus imaginativa* as it was frequently termed. Paracelsus and Bruno were two of the most interesting proponents of such mystical tendencies in the Renaissance period.

Paracelsus set the tone for most alchemical theories of imagination when he described it as a 'sun whose light is not tangible but which can set flame to a house'. And pursuing this solar metaphor, so central to the Copernican revolutions of the Renaissance, Paracelsus declares imagination to be the privileged expression of 'man's desire to be the sun, that is to be absolutely everything he desires to be'. 'What else is imagination,' concludes Paracelsus, 'if not the inner sun which moves in its own sphere.'5 While Paracelus and his followers generally dealt with the hermetic powers of imagination (e.g. to symbolize by means of magical substitutions, optical illusions and secret letter combinations) they did anticipate the modern tendency to emphasize the radically 'anthropological' nature of creativity. Just as Copernicus inverted the Ptolemaic system of cosmology, the alchemists reversed the traditional system of epistemology which had located reality as a transcendental sun beyond man's grasp. Imagination was now hailed as a divine flame within man. The stigma of the Promethean theft was removed. And this discovery of the human imagination as the source of universal light and power, marks one of the earliest attempts to affirm the primacy of subjectivity, to move beyond a metaphysics of transcendence towards a cult of human creativity. For Paracelsus and his alchemist disciples, the imagination is to be hailed as a child-god in its own right, born of a virgin nature and clouded in glory.

Another Renaissance figure who made pioneering efforts to establish imagination as a power of mystical insight was Giordano Bruno, an Italian thinker of the sixteenth century. Drawing from the heretical doctrines of gnosticism, Bruno hailed the human imagination as the creative source of the 'forms' of thought. Bruno championed the idea of a *spiritus phantasticus* which enables mortals to transcend their finite condition and become one with the secret rhythms of the cosmos. The material world, he contended, is there to be transformed by man's own imaginative power (*vis imaginativa*) in accordance with a hidden cosmic design. And this contention was coupled with Bruno's belief – also shared by other Renaissance gnostics such as Marsilio Ficino – that the imagination is the privileged vehicle of the Holy Spirit. Even the material shape of the human body is deemed to be an external product of man's spiritual imagination (*ergo phantasia instar virtutis vivificae format et ipsa proprium corpus*). Revising Richard of St Victor's metaphor of imagination as a borrowed vestment which obscures the rational soul and contaminates it with the body, Bruno insisted that the imagination is the 'first vestment' of the Spirit which precedes and indeed creates both reason and the body. For Bruno, as one commentator observes, 'imagination is living, fecund, personal and conceived for the first time as the positive essence of art'.[6] And it has even been suggested that the theories of Bruno and Ficino represent a sort of humanist rewriting of the Platonic notion of mystical vision outlined in the *Timaeus* – the crucial difference being, of course, that the inspired imagination is now held to be properly human rather than divine.

Bruno's thinking was condemned as heresy by the Church: he was burnt at the stake. His theory of imagination failed to make any direct impact on the mainstream of Western philosophy in his own time.[7] But despite the hostility of the philosophical and theological orthodoxies one does find continuing echoes of the mystical theory of human imagination as privileged possessor of the 'secret signatures' of creation. The precise links are difficult to ascertain due to the fundamentally occult nature of such doctrines. But a number of commentators, including Jean Starobinski, have attempted to trace a subterranean line of influence extending from the gnostic theories of Renaissance thinkers like Bruno and Ficino through the mystical writings of Paracelsus, Boehme, Stahl and Mesmer to the modern theories of German idealism and romanticism.[8] If such an undercurrent of thought did persist through the centuries, it certainly remained outside the mainstream tradition of philosophical rationalism. Kant may well have been acquainted with such a counter-tradition of mystical thought; but since he made little reference to it (apart from a negative assessment of Swedenborg), one can only assume that such a putative influence was, at best, indirect. Subsequent German Idealists, and particularly Schelling, did acknowledge this mystical-hermetic heritage in a positive and explicit manner.

Cartesianism

A second transitional stage between scholasticism and Germa idealism which merits some mention is *Cartesianism*. Descartes, it must be recalled, was the first modern thinker to mark a decisive rupture with scholasticism. His theory of the *cogito* signalled a major change in Western understanding in that it located the source of meaning in human subjectivity (the act of the 'I think') rather than in the objective world of reality or transcendent being. Whereas medieval onto-theology had spoken of truth as a referential correspondence of subject to object, Descartes argued that truth results from the reflexive conformity of the subject to his own thought.[9] The human mind is given priority over objective being: 'I think *therefore* I am.' On the basis of this formula, Descartes sought to vindicate man as the 'master and possessor of nature'. Despite his provision of proofs for the existence of God, the Cartesian theory of the *cogito* contains stirrings of the modern project to provide an anthropological foundation for metaphysics.

Although Descartes and his followers blazed the trail of modern humanism, they remained captive to the traditional bias against imagination. In spite of his assertion of the central role of human subjectivity, Descartes continued to subscribe to the received view of imagination as a mere intermediary between mind and body. Moreover, Descartes' commitment to rationalism prompted him to consider the image as no more than a quasi-material residue of sensory experience which, in fact, obscures the self-reflection of the *cogito*. The act of imagining remained bound to the errors of corporeal contingency.[10] In short, while Descartes was incontestably 'modern' in his positive evaluation of the *cogito*, he was essentially 'pre-modern' in his negative assessment of imagination. The image was still construed according to the mimetic paradigm. It was considered an unreliable copy rather than an original creation in its own right. Whence Jean-Jacques Rousseau's famous quip – 'the philosophy of Descartes has cut the throat of poetry'.[11]

This Cartesian hostility to imagination was shared by such rationalist philosophers of the seventeenth century as Leibniz, Spinoza and Malebranche. In his essay *On The Improvement of the Understanding*, for example, Spinoza declared that 'imaginary ideas' are always inferior to the 'ideas of reason' in so far as they are concerned with merely 'possible' (logically contingent) rather than 'necessary' (logically certain) entities. And since imagination is unable to distinguish between existing and non-existing things, it leads the mind towards 'contradiction' and away from 'eternal truth'.[12] Spinoza concludes accordingly that imagination is incompatible with freedom: for freedom can only be achieved when the mind has dispelled all 'imaginative illusions' (*auxilia imaginationis*) of a temporal past, present or future and discovered that being exists necessarily according to the logic of Reason.[13] (Curiously, it was this very connection between imagination and temporality which was to provide Kant with one of his main reasons for celebrating imagination as the origin of knowledge.)

Leibniz's attitude to imagination also bears the hallmark of Cartesian intellectualism. In a letter to Arnauld in 1686, Leibniz puts his friend on guard against the deceptive 'ideas of imagination' which frequently resemble those of reason. No matter how 'intellectualized' the image may become, he insists, it can never lay claim to the rational status of 'logical necessity' – *a priori* or *a posteriori*.[14] In *New Essays in Human Understanding*, Leibniz asserts that since imagination always falls short of reason, it is also lacking in true being.[15] Here again we witness the basic Cartesian conviction that because the *cogito* is the autonomous source of judgement there is little or no need to represent our truth through the mediation of images.

This rationalist view was shared by many other thinkers of the late Renaissance and early Enlightenment. The Cambridge idealist, John Smith, denounced imagination as a 'deforming lens'; Gravina called it a 'witch' and Muratori a 'drunkard';[16] and even the intellectualist aesthetic theories of Wolff and Baumgarten in the eighteenth century disregarded its creative potential. The attitude towards imagination bequeathed by Descartes was far from flattering. Croce, in his *Aesthetic*, observed

The French philosopher abhorred imagination, the outcome, according to him, of the agitation of the animal spirits; and though not utterly condemning poetry, he allowed it to exist only in so far as it was guided by intellect, that being the sole faculty able to save men from the caprices of the *folle du logis*. He tolerated it, but that was all; and went so far as not to deny it anything '*qu'un philosophe lui puisse permettre sans offenser sa conscience*'. . . . The mathematical spirit fostered by Descartes forbade all possibility of a serious consideration of poetry and art.[17]

This was the main tenor of Cartesian rationalism which Kant inherited and radically transformed. Confirming Descartes' primacy of human subjectivity, Kant would substantially revise its intellectualist premiss by reuniting understanding and sensation on the common basis of a transcendental imagination which grounds both.

Empiricism

A third transitional stage in the development of the philosophy of imagination from scholasticism to Kantian idealism was David Hume's empiricist account. Kant avows that it was Hume who awoke him from his 'dogmatic slumbers' and compelled him to rethink the whole basis of Western metaphysics. Hume had proposed, in typical Enlightenment fashion, to show how knowledge could dispense with all appeals to transcendent beings or deities, how it could establish its own foundation in the immanence of human reason. But while he set out as an advocate of positivist rationalism, Hume ended up a radical sceptic. He was to discover that once one divests reason of its metaphysical scaffolding and seeks to found it on a purely empirical basis, the very edifice of rationalism collapses into an arbitrary fictionalism.

Hume's sceptical conclusions were all the more alarming given the staunchly scientific character of British empiricism established by John Locke. Basil Willey informs us,

Locke's philosophy was the philosophy of an age whose whole effort had been to arrive at 'truth' by exorcising the phantoms of imagination, and the truth standards which the eighteenth century inherited through him involved the relegation of the mind's shaping power to an inferior status.[18]

So wary was Locke of the irrationalist effects of imagination on the scientific ideal that in his *Thoughts concerning Education*, he actually counselled all parents who discovered a 'fanciful vein' in their children to 'stifle and suppress it as much as may be'. The romantic poets who came after Locke were, not surprisingly, quite enraged by his attitude. Blake accused him of 'petrifying all the Human Imagination into Rock and Sand'; Coleridge of reducing the mind to a cold mechanism; and pursuing this romantic legacy of denunciation, Yeats would later claim that 'Locke took away the world and gave us its excrement instead.'[19]

Hume basically accepted Locke's empiricist description of the image as a 'faded impression of the senses'. But he developed it in the direction of an extreme fictionalism which threatened to subvert the very basis of Enlightenment reason.[20] One might even say that Hume pushed the 'mimetic' model of imagination to its final and unjustifiable limits. Discarding both the 'innate ideas' of Descartes and the unknowable 'substance' of Locke (a leftover from scholasticism), Hume declared that all human knowledge was derived from the association of image-ideas. The cognitive process was no longer to be considered in terms of necessary metaphysical laws. It was reduced to a series of purely psychological regularities (i.e. *resemblance*, *contiguity* and *causality*) governing the connection between image-ideas.[21]

Hume never actually renounces, however, the accredited paradigm of the image as a mimetic representation of our sensory experience. On the contrary, he accords this representational function of the image such an inflated role in all modes of cognition that traditional epistemology begins to burst at the seams. Hume thus accelerates the shift from the received notion of 'substance' (the priority of reality over consciousness) to the modern notion of 'subjectivity' (the priority of consciousness over reality). While retaining the mimetic model of the image as a mental copy of sensation, he goes on to insist that this subjective world of representation is the only reality we can know. Reason is thereby deprived of any autonomous role, its ideas simply differing from sensory images by their degree of 'force or vivacity'. The rational self or *cogito* is voided of substantial identity. And by the same token, the external world loses its independent existence. Hume makes this point forcefully in *A Treatise of Human Nature* when he asserts that it is the principle of imagination which 'makes us reason from causes to effects, and it is the same principle which convinces us of the continued existence of external objects'.[22] His argument proceeds:

> the illusion of the identity and endurance of the self is based on the relations of contiguity and resemblance that we experience among our perceptions. Identity is nothing really belonging to these different perceptions and uniting them together, but is merely a quality we attribute to them, because of the union of their ideas in the imagination . . .'.[23]

The worlds of reason and of reality, it seems, are both fictions of imagination.[24] The mimetic image no longer refers to some transcendent origin of truth; it becomes an end in itself, an exercise of pure immanence.[25] The only truth we can know is that of our image-representations. And this means no truth at all.

Hume insists, however, that if reality is no more than a bundle of fictions, we must nonetheless cling to these fictions *as if* they were real. For without them, our everyday lives would lack all sense of 'unity and continuity'. Imaginary order is preferable to disorder. This is a crucial point in Hume's argumentation. And it places him before a veritable crisis of conscience. The moment ordinary mortals are awakened to the truth that there is no truth, is the moment anarchy is loosed upon the world. In other words, if people no longer believe in the illusions of permanence, substance, identity and so forth, the very basis of all enlightened society, dedicated to the pursuit of 'peace and happiness', is threatened. Even such a simple matter as keeping a promise, for example, would lose its 'objective' foundation – for the person who made a promise on one day might logically reply that he is no longer the same person the next (the very idea of a permanent or enduring identity being no more than a subjective fiction). For Hume then, 'the illusion of fantasy is the reality of culture'.[26]

Under such circumstances, the only legitimate role left to reason is one of vigilant but discreet scepticism. Without reason, the philosopher would be unable to discover that the so-called 'realities' of culure are fictions. But this discovery, Hume reluctantly concedes, must be kept to the philosophers themselves. If the populace at large were to be apprised of the fact that the king wears no clothes, that the principles guiding all our social systems of authority from law and education to morality, religion and government, have no *objective* validity, life would beome unlivable. The rational sceptic thus feels himself to be, in Hume's poignant words, a 'strange and uncouth monster' who 'not being able to mingle and unite in society has been expelled from all human commerce, and left utterly abandoned and disconsolate'. Alienated from the fellowship of ordinary men and women, and carrying within his breast the intolerable realization that the world is but a mess of mimetic shadows manipulated by imagination, the philosopher observes a self-imposed silence. To speak out is to endanger the possibility of peaceful coexistence between mortals. Thus for Hume, as for Plato in his allegory of the cave, the imaginary world is one of comfortable illusion. But the all important difference between Hume and Plato is that the former no longer believes in a 'transcendent' reality existing *beyond* the dark cave of imitations. All men who participate in human culture are, Hume sardonically admits, liars; and poets and artists are unique only in that they are 'liars by profession'.[27]

Hume's account of imagination issues, finally, in this fateful dilemma: accepting that the world is a collage of fictions, how are we to distinguish between good and bad fictions, between those which lead to benighted ignorance and those which preserve the indispensable order of society? And since reason itself can only play the negative role of shattering fictions, how is one to choose between the exigencies of reason which make life impossible but 'real', and those of imagination which make it possible but 'unreal'. Having brought the mimetic theory of imagination to the limit of an unfounded subjectivism, Hume is compelled to conclude that he is totally at a loss. He has driven himself to the following impasse:

The question is how far we ought to yield to these illusions. This question is very difficult and reduces us to a very dangerous dilemma, whichever way we answer it. For if we assent to every trivial suggestion of the fancy; beside that these suggestions are often contradictory to each other, they lead us into such errors, absurdities and obscurities that we must at last become ashamed of our credulity. Nothing is more dangerous to reason than the flights of the imagination, and nothing has been the occasion of more mistakes among philosophers. . . . If we embrace this principle and condemn all refined reasoning, we run into the most manifest absurdities. If we reject it in favour of these reasonings, we subvert entirely the human understanding. We have therefore, no choice but betwixt a false reason and none at all. For my part I know not what ought to be done in the present case.[28]

The great pioneer of Enlightenment thinking finds himself, in the final analysis, in the 'most deplorable condition possible, invironed with the deepest darkness'. The only remaining strategy of survival is that of evasion. Hume decides to close his books and join his local friends for a game of backgammon. Kant's solution to this dilemma was, as we shall now see, of a very different order.

3 Kant and the transcendental imagination

What does Kant mean when he speaks of a 'transcendental imagination'? He means that imagination is the hidden condition of all knowledge. In the *Critique of Pure Reason* (B, 138), he speaks of it as an 'art concealed in the depths of the human soul'. The transcendental imagination is that which grounds the objectivity of the object in the subjectivity of the subject – rather than in some 'transcendent' order beyond man. It preconditions our very experience of the world.

For Kant, then, the term 'transcendental' is concerned with the presuppositions of experience – that which makes experience possible in the first place.[29] In contrast to Platonic metaphysics, Kant situates this transcendental realm in the human mind and not in some other-world of Eternal Forms. 'I entitle *transcendental*', explains Kant, 'all knowledge which is occupied not so much with objects as with the mode of our knowledge of objects in so far as this mode of knowledge is to be possible *a priori*' (*CPR*, A 11). The revolutionary modern paradigm of the imagination arises, therefore, in Kant as a response to the transcendental question: how is knowledge possible?

The philosophies of Descartes and Hume had, of course, already established the primacy of subjectivity *vis-à-vis* substance. So doing, they had paved the way for modern idealism. Where Kant differs from his Cartesian and empiricist predecessors is in his provision of a radically transcendental basis for the claims of human subjectivity. Descartes might be said to have gestured in this direction when he formulated his principle of the *cogito* as the origin of meaning; but his rationalist metaphysic came to grief on the insurmountable obstacle of mind/body dualism. Hume, one could argue, also beckoned towards a transcendental position in his recognition that imagination is the inner source of our ideas; but he was finally hampered by his refusal to acknowledge the *a priori* productive power of imagination, a refusal which became manifest in the totally foundationless character of his 'fictionalism'. Only Kant was prepared to take the final step towards the disclosure of the transcendental imagination, thereby obviating both the Charybdis of Cartesian dualism and the Scylla of Humean scepticism.

The imagination, Kant argued, must no longer be conceived exclusively according to the *mimetic model of representation*. It is to be reconceived in terms of the *transcendental model of formation* – hence the need to distinguish between the 'reproductive' and 'productive' functions of imagination. The latter function alone can explain how the act of imagining is not merely a secondary mediation between sensation and intellect but the common 'root' of both these forms of knowledge. Roused from his slumbers by the challenge of Hume's scepticism, Kant resolved to rehabilitate the validity of objective knowledge by establishing the validity of the subjective imagination – as a 'transcendental synthesis' of our sensible and intelligible experience. Imagination thus ceases to be an arbitrary or relativizing function. It becomes instead the *sine qua non* of all genuine knowledge.

How did Kant legitimize imagination in this way? To answer this question we must rehearse some of the more technical arguments of the *Critique of Pure Reason*. Kant begins by examining the empiricist thesis that all human knowledge is derived from experience. Granting that there is no knowledge without sensible experience, he affirms that it does not therefore follow that it arises out of our experience alone. 'It may well be', he writes, 'that even our empirical knowledge is made up of what we receive through the impressions (of the senses) and of what our own faculty of knowledge supplies from itself.'[30] In other words, if our sensory experience is what supplies the 'content' of cognition, it is the faculty of our understanding which supplies the 'form' in which we grasp it. Sensation without understanding is blind; and understanding without sensation is empty.

The next step is to show how these two branches of knowledge – *sensibility* which provides the manifold of experience, and *understanding* which provides the formal categories for uniting this manifold – may be conjoined in a 'synthesis'. How is one to ground their mutual correlation? Since sensory appearance can never be for us an object of knowledge except through its relation to consciousness, which combines the various appearances occurring in the mind separately and singly into a coherent totality, there must exist in us 'an active faculty for the synthesis of the manifold'. This active faculty is what Kant calls *imagination* (*Einbildungskraft*). We cannot come upon impressions of the world which are not already *pre-cast* in a certain mould and connected with others. And it is precisely the *a priori* function of imagination to present our actual experience in the particular form laid down by the pure concepts of the understanding.

To avoid the traditional error of construing imagination as a secondary mediation between mind and body, Kant introduces his famous distinction between its 'productive' and 'reproductive' aspects. The reproductive function enables the mind to connect the diverse impressions of the senses by reinstating a preceding perception alongside a subsequent one, thereby forming a sequence of perceptions.[31] But this reproductive role is in turn guided by a more fundamental role which provides the 'rule' according to which certain 'combinations' of perceptions are preferred to others independently of their empirical order of appearance. And it is this *autonomous* act of synthesis which Kant ascribes to the productive imagination.

Kant then proceeds to extend the productive role of imagination into what he terms the 'unity of transcendental apperception'. The synthesis of perceptions might well remain arbitrary unless its rules of 'association' and 'affinity' (provided by the imagination) were themselves related to a connected whole of understanding. But this is only possible if the productive synthesis of my *perceptions* is coupled with the productive synthesis of my *consciousness of myself* as the ultimate source of unity. For it is only because I ascribe all perceptions to *one* consciousness (i.e. original apperception) that I can say of my perceptions that I am conscious of them. This consciousness is an *a priori* rule of transcendental imagination; and, as such, it precedes and governs the empirical rules of the reproductive imagination. It is that 'unity of apperception' which ensures that every perception apprehended by my understanding has a proper and necessary place with respect to all knowledge that is mine.

We shall be returning to this crucial point in the Appendix to this chapter. Suffice it here to observe that for Kant the unity of *perception* presupposes a unity of *apperception* in the form of a 'transcendental ego' intimately related to the transcendental imagination. As Kant explains,

The affinity of appearances and with it their association, and through this, in turn, their reproduction according to laws, and so experience itself, should only be possible by this transcendental function of imagination. . . . For without this transcendental function no concepts of objects would themselves make up a unitary experience.[32]

Without the imaginative synthesis of our sensible intuition (of temporal and spatial objects) on the one hand, and of our intellect (or an abiding transcendental ego) on the other, the so-called 'objective' world would be bereft of coherence. 'The order and regularity in appearance', concludes Kant, 'which we entitle nature, *we ourselves introduce*. We could not find them in appearances, had not we ourselves . . . originally set them there.'[33] Imagination is thus hailed as the common 'root' of both sensation and understanding.

4 Kant's aesthetic

If Kant retracted many of his claims for the productive imagination in his revised second edition of the *Critique of Pure Reason*, he appears to have allowed himself further leeway in his aesthetic theory of the *Critique of Judgement*. No doubt, the lower metaphysical profile of this third *Critique* afforded Kant something of a 'poetic licence'. He could come out of hiding again, as it were, and resume his crusade for imagination. But even here, we shall see, Kant was to eventually temper his own enthusiasm and set definitite limits to the powers of imagination.

Most of the third *Critique* is devoted to the analysis of aesthetic judgement. Kant begins by dividing the mind into three faculties: i) *understanding* (whereby we apply scientific concepts to the necessary experience of nature); ii) *reason* (whereby we apply principles both to the understanding and to our moral experience of freedom) and iii) *judgement* (which participates in both reason and understanding in that it allows us to bring together the particular situations of experience and the universal rules of reason). Although Kant admits of different kinds of judgement, he seems to privilege aesthetic judgement where the ideas of freedom are intimately connected with the works of creative imagination. As Herbert Marcuse observes,

In the *Critique of Judgement* the aesthetic dimension and the corresponding feeling of pleasure emerge not merely as a third faculty of the mind, but as its *centre*, the medium through which nature becomes susceptible to freedom, necessity to autonomy. . . . Beauty symbolizes this realm in so far as it demonstrates intuitively the reality of freedom. Since freedom is an idea to which no sense-perception can correspond, such demonstration can be only indirect, symbolical, by analogy.[34]

What exactly does Kant mean by an aesthetic judgement? An aesthetic judgement is expressed whenever we say that an object is 'beautiful'. And beauty – the primary term of Kant's aesthetic – results from our experience of a 'pattern' or 'finality' in an object. Whether we are concerned with a painting, poem or piece of music, the aesthetic judgement of both artist and audience depends upon the recognition of an *inner finality of form*. The beauty of an object, in other words, derives from the sense of autonomous freedom which the imagination enjoys in beholding it. The goal of art is not to be found in an external or transcendent world, but within the artistic experience itself – what Kant calls the 'free play of imagination'.[35] Thus liberated from all outer constraints, the mind becomes auto-telic; it becomes its own means and its own end, the mirror turned lamp. This is the aesthetic condition which Kant describes in his famous phrase – 'purposiveness without purpose' (*Zweckmässigkeit ohne Zweck*). Art differs from a tool or other practical instrument in so far as its 'inner finality' precludes any purpose outside of itself. For something to be beautiful, insists Kant, means that we can no longer ask the question – *what is it for?* But to say that art is without external constraint is not to say that it is without order. On the contrary, our pleasure in the freedom of beauty depends on the capacity of imagination to create its own order and thereby defy the chaos of the outer world. Imagination does indeed observe rules. But these rules are self-imposed. Here we find the seeds of the great modern aesthetics of romanticism, symbolism and the art-for-art's-sake movement of the *fin de siècle*.

Every aesthetic experience is a response to a particular object. But this in no way denies its universality. Beauty, for Kant, is not simply in the eye of the beholder. The aesthetic judgement of 'taste' is inherently universalizable to the extent that creative imagination is possessed by every human being. The 'harmonious activity' of imagination, Kant insists accordingly, is an experience of 'universal communicability postulated by the judgement of taste'.[36] It is not the prerogative of a few extraordinary 'geniuses'. Aesthetic pleasure possesses a 'quasi-objective' quality; it is shared by everyone who perceives the inner finality of an art work.

Aesthetic objects differ radically from the objects of everyday experience. Only with the former does imagination find its 'finality' *within itself*. In ordinary experience, as we saw, we recognize an object – say a pair of shoes – by first forming an image of an object *like* the one we are now applying to the relevant concept (i.e. of shoeness). We can only apprehend this object in front of us as a pair of shoes because we can form other images of other pairs of shoes. It is when the pair of shoes ceases to be perceived in the real world and becomes instead an imaginary object of art – as in Van Gogh's painting of the peasant shoes – that we experience *aesthetic pleasure*. Now the imagination is free to work with itself alone. It is no longer bound to any external reference. Its end is exclusively internal, autonomous. Here imagination can exult in the plenitude of its freedom *prior* to any application to general concepts of understanding or to perceptions of actual objects. In this aesthetic role, imagination is revealed as a 'productive activity of its own'.[37]

When Kant speaks, therefore, of imagination's power to create a *second* nature out of the material supplied to it by nature,[38] he does not see this second nature as a mere imitation of the first. It is a totally new creation which transforms the given appearances of things. In aesthetic judgement, writes Kant, 'imagination freely produces its own law. It invents a concept . . .'.[39] So that when we look at Van Gogh's painting of shoes and judge this painting to be beautiful, we are not worried about general concepts of 'shoeness', nor about whether such shoes *really* exist. On the contrary, 'we are judging that it displays perfectly a satisfying pattern, that it manifests a certain completeness in itself . . . produced by the imagination in its free play with the object before it'.[40] The work of art is a 'finality

without end', in Kant's phrase, precisely because it is account-
able to no authority beyond itself – neither to understanding nor
to empirical reality.

The opposition between the classical and modern philosophies
of art could hardly be more evident. Where Plato condemned
the self-referential and impractical character of art, Kant
celebrates it. Where the ancients scoffed at the presumed
autonomy of aesthetic imagination, Kant commends it as a pre-
eminent virtue. The free 'play' of imagination ceases to be
denounced. It is championed as the privileged expression of
human freedom. Indeed from Kant onwards, this notion of 'free
play' was to become one of the pivotal concepts of modern
theories of art.

5   From beauty to the sublime

But however affirmative Kant is in the third *Critique* about the
creative powers of imagination, it would be a mistake to read this
as an unqualified vindication of his claims for the transcendental
imagination in the first edition of the first *Critique*. For Kant has
now effectively circumscribed the creative role of imagination;
he has confined its full freedom within the boundaries of art.
This was to have a deep impact on the romantic movement, and
especially its tendency to separate the world of artistic creativity
from the increasingly uncongenial world of social reality and
industrialized nature. A further hint of this division is manifest
in Kant's admission in the third *Critique* that the 'harmonious
interplay between imagination and understanding', which art
embodies, is something we cannot 'conceptualize' but only 'feel'.
By dissociating reason from the life of feeling, Kant is ultimately
reducing imagination to the latter and thereby anticipating the
romantic opposition between science and art.

The romantic dimension of Kant's aesthetic is perhaps most
obvious in his movement from the 'beautiful' to the 'sublime'.
Kant did not actually invent this distinction. Addison, Burke and
Hutcheson had already spoken in such terms. But he was the
first to define both notions sytematically in relation to the

creative activity of imagination.[41] In *The Critique of Judgement* the faculty which takes pleasure in the contemplation of both beautiful and sublime objects is that which forms images. But whereas the experience of the beautiful results from the imagination's freedom to create images without constraint, that of the sublime results from our confronting the *limits* of our representations. 'The feeling of the sublime', writes Kant, 'may appear in point of form to contravene the ends of our power of judgement, to be ill-adapted to our faculty of presentation, and to be, as it were, an outrage on imagination.'[42] Why an outrage? Precisely because the sublime surpasses not only the concepts of understanding but even the images of imagination itself. The pleasure the imagination takes in the sublime is one of challenge, defiance, risk, excess, even shock. The sublime threatens the formal adequacy of the harmony of beauty. It opens imagination to new heights yet to be scaled and new depths yet to be plumbed. It provokes imagination to venture into strange unchartered continents, to seek new forms of order in new forms of disorder. Mary Warnock offers this useful account of the Kantian sublime:

The creative imagination has, as one of its functions, the exciting in us a sense of the sublime precisely in that it excites in us ideas which we realize *cannot* be represented by any visible or other sensible forms – ideas which cannot be restricted or brought down to size by any image-making power of the imagination.[43]

Kant is not, as might first appear, reverting here to a traditional proof of the existence of a transcendent being beyond human subjectivity. The sublime serves rather to deepen and extend our sense of subjective interiority – as Kant reminds us 'sublimity is discoverable *in the mind*'.[44] One could say therefore that the sublime is, paradoxically, the discovery of the infinite depth of imagination which cannot be presented in terms of adequate images. And this is why the sublime experience of overwhelming super-abundance produces a sense of 'awe' rather than 'pleasure':

We are in awe precisely of the human power to frame ideas which cannot be intuited. Imaginatively we stretch out towards what imagination cannot apprehend. We realize that there is *more* in what we see than meets or can ever meet even the inner eye.[45]

The theory of imagination outlined in the *Critique of Judgement* is deeply ambiguous. In relation to beauty, the imagination reveals its power as freedom and autonomy. In relation to the sublime, however, imagination displays its power by betraying its own powerlessness; it surpasses the self-sufficient limits of beauty and points to a vastness which it is unable to embody. And yet this very testimony to the inadequacy of its own images enables artistic imagination to serve as a 'symbol' which directs us towards what Kant terms, rather vaguely, the 'mind's suprasensible province'. Art becomes sublime to the extent that it produces 'symbols' (analogues to the ideas of reason) which *signify* something which our mind cannot actually grasp; and this, in turn, induces in the beholder an awareness of 'something mysteriously great in the human mind itself'. But the precise identity of this mysterious greatness is left in suspension. At best, Kant hints at some undefinable rapport between the 'ideas of reason' and what he terms the 'aesthetic ideas' of imaginative 'genius'. But although these latter ideas of imagination are capable of 'inducing much thought', they *lack* 'the possibility of any definite thought whatever, i.e. *concept*, being adequate to (them)'.[46]

The most that one can say is that aesthetic ideas function according to the *symbolic mode of analogy*. They point beyond themselves to the noumenal depths of transcendental subjectivity. The artistic genius is, therefore, one 'who can find new ways of *nearly* embodying ideas; and in his attempts imagination has a creative role'.[47] In paragraph 59 of the *Critique of Judgement*, Kant even goes so far as to compare these aesthetic symbols with the moral experience which in the second *Critique* had been confined to practical reason. And here once again, Kant's opposition to Platonism is striking. Instead of seeing art as incompatible with the moral good, as in Plato's *Republic*, Kant suggests they are mutually inclusive if not identical. By allowing for a certain ambivalence of emphasis in his treatment of the sublime in *The Critique of Judgement* – relating it both to ideas of reason and to the aesthetic ideas of imagination – Kant appears to be having it both ways. It is as if he wishes to remain faithful to both the primacy of imagination established in the first edition of the *Critique of Pure Reason* and the primacy of a limiting reason re-established in the second edition. This conflict of fidelities remains unresolved in Kant. The German idealists and many of the romantics who followed Kant sought to overcome the dilemma by means of an absolute conflation of reason and imagination. They dispensed with all compunctions and unreservedly embraced the revolutionary consequences of the humanist celebration of imagination.

6 German idealism: Fichte and Schelling

The influence of Kant on the movement of German idealism is generally recognized. What is less frequently explored is the continuity between Kant's initial theory of the transcendental imagination and the subsequent idealist theories of Fichte and Schelling. This oversight is no doubt due to the official 'rationalist' interpretation of Kant which prevailed in neo-Kantian philosophy in the nineteenth and early twentieth century. Heidegger was one of the first modern commentators to advert to this neglected connection; even if it is only in the form of a note in his *Kant Book*:

The specific characterization of the imagination as a fundamental faculty must have enlightened Kant's contemporaries as to the significance of the faculty. So Fichte, Schelling, and in his own way, Jacobi, have attributed an essential role to imagination.[48]

This cursory allusion deserves to be developed.

Schelling and Fichte may be said to have inflated the power of transcendental imagination to such a point that the canonical distinctions of traditional epistemology dissolve. Kant himself, as we saw, was moving in this direction. But he ultimately drew back on glimpsing the subversive implications. Kant's conservative scruples are, moreover, plainly evident in his deference to traditional classification in the tri-partite division of his own critical philosophy: *The Critique of Pure Reason* (scientific theory); *The Critique of Practical Reason* (moral theory); and the *Critique of Judgement* (aesthetic theory). The German idealists who succeeded Kant tended to erase these demarcation lines and subsume all these faculties of mind under the common rubric of 'the productive imagination' (*Die Produktive Einbildungskraft*). This radical departure from the more rationalist character of Kantian philosophy was also, of course, motivated by the growing influence of the revived occult movements of esotericism and mysticism on the post-Kantian idealists.

In *The Vocation of Man*, Fichte brushes aside Kant's famous division between the 'phenomenal' world which can be known, and the 'noumenal' world which cannot. He declares that even being-in-itself – 'the one and infinite' – is a direct possession of 'genuine transcendental idealism'.[49] And in his first *Wissenschaftslehre*, Fichte makes his position clear when he hails imagination as 'the very possibility of our consciousness, our life and our being'. Extrapolating the implications of Kant's discovery of the intimate rapport between imagination and the 'transcendental ego', he claims that all the syntheses of subjectivity, including those of reason, are rendered possible by the productive imagination. Reason itself thus becomes identified with the power of imagination to provide access to 'the spiritual order of essential being', an order where it operates as 'pure activity, absolutely by itself alone, having no need of any instrument outside of itself – absolute freedom'.[50] The humanist equation between imagination and freedom could hardly be more unequivocal.

Schelling, the other great exponent of German idealism, appears to go even further. In his monumental work, *The System of Transcendental Idealism*, published in 1800 some nineteen years after Kant's first *Critique*, Schelling makes the exalted claim that the 'productive and synthetic imagination is the organon and pinnacle of all philosophy'.[51] This text, which was to serve as a sort of philosophical manifesto for many romantic artists and poets, goes on to define imagination as that creative power which reconciles the age-old oppositions of Western metaphysics –

freedom and necessity, being and becoming, the universal and the particular, the eternal and the temporal, and even the human and the divine! There would seem to be nothing that is not, in the final analysis, founded upon or redeemable by imagination. It is presented as the panacea of all our problems, the order behind disorder, the coherence within confusion – the very alpha and omega of the universe itself. Indeed one would not be mistaken in supposing that Schelling has here replaced the onto-theological definition of God as creative being with the humanist definition of man as creative imagination.

Schelling himself recognized that transcendental idealism was the end of the old metaphysical dispensation and the beginning of a new romantic era. This decisive turn would, furthermore, enable one to reinterpret the history of philosophy in an original way. It would enable one to retrieve neglected and marginalized trends of Western thinking and rehabilitate them in the main-stream of a new 'scientific philosophy'. Thus, for example, what former mystical, gnostic or heretical thinkers had said about imagination 'on the basis of subjective sentiments and supposed revelations', could now be reclaimed by transcendental idealism in all its scientific and essential truth.[52]

Schelling's deep determination to reconcile mystical and scientific thought was also manifest in the very style and form of his presentation. Where most traditional philosophers, and even Kant himself, had proceeded by means of rigorous and painstaking argument, Schelling and his followers tend to offer us incantatory formulations, enigmatic aphorisms and sententious repetitions. Logical syllogism, it seems, has given way to visionary rumination. This formal approximation of philosophy to the language of poetry is not accidental. It bespeaks a significant alteration in the very *content* of philosophy. Thus, writes Schelling, 'the objective world is only the original still unconscious poetry of the spirit'. The common task of both art and philosophy is to produce a form of *conscious* poetry which articulates the *unconscious* poetry of being itself. And this unconscious poetry or *poiesis* (creation of everyday existence) is one in which all men participate as possessors of the 'productive imagination'. Schelling's notion of unconscious poetry is, almost certainly, an echo of Kant's description of imagination as the 'root *unknown to us*'. But Schelling takes an additional step. By spelling out the relation between the unconscious creativity of imagination in everyday life and its conscious creativity in art and philosophy, Schelling is dismantling the opposition between nature and art which prevailed from Plato to Kant himself. Schelling leaves us in no doubt that imagination creates *both nature and art*, both the real objects of the world and the ideal objects of culture – including the ideas of reason itself. It is, in short, imagination which creates poems *and* universes.

The artistic genius, concludes Schelling, only differs from ordinary men in so far as he has realized the unity of his unconscious and conscious imagination. And the 'pleasure' which results from the composition and appreciation of art is due to the experience of this 'harmony' between hidden and overt creation. Imagination may be said to be 'freer' in art than in nature for the simple reason that it is more at one with itself, in possession of itself. 'In all natural beings', as Schelling explains,' the living idea is manifested in blind operation only; and if it were the same in the artist, he would differ in no way from nature.' But this does not mean that the artist simply 'subordinates himself to nature and reproduces the existent with servile fidelity' – for he would, in that case, merely 'produce masks but no works of art'.[53] On the contrary, the business of the poetic mind is to rise above the unconscious creation of nature in order to produce a conscious 'vision' of this creation in the work of art. The philosopher thus takes his cue from the poet who not only interprets the creative design of the world but actively joins in this creation and *freely* extends its horizon of application.

However, the highest claim of all is surely the identification of human imagination and the Divine Mind. Schelling frequently equates 'divine ideas' with the 'symbols of imagination'. By so collapsing the onto-theological dichotomy between divine and human creation, Schelling put an end to the traditional understanding of imagination as a second-hand imitation of God's original being. And this elevation of imagination to the rank of divine omnipotence was also, by implication, a defiant challenge to the

Enlightenment insistence that imagination remain subservient to reason.

While the romantics welcomed this reversal of both traditional and Enlightenment rationalism, many philosophical commentators have viewed it with circumspection, alarm and even hostility. In her book *Imagination*, Mary Warnock sees here a 'tremendous deterioration in the rational climate'. This was due, she believes, to the fact that the sharp distinction which Kant continued to draw between what could and could not be known, between legitimate thought and impossible empty metaphysical speculation, had been done away with.[54] Once the German idealists who came after Kant amplified the power of imagination to include not only reason and sensation but the world and even God Himself, the question arose – is not philosophy now at an end? For if we are to credit imagination's revelation that all is one and everything is everything else, then surely there is nothing left *beyond* us to be interpreted or known? There is nothing except imagination creating and recreating itself in an endless play of freedom.

7 Romanticism

This was indeed the message which many romantics took from the idealist philosophy of transcendental imagination. The English romantic, Samuel Taylor Coleridge, exemplifies this attitude in his *Biographia Literaria*, an influential text published in 1817, and widely considered a *locus classicus* of romantic theory. Coleridge's immense debt to Schelling is acknowledged by the author himself and has been extensively analysed by a host of commentators – most notably Abrams, *The Mirror and the Lamp*, Orsini, *Coleridge and German Idealism* and Marcel in *Coleridge et Schelling*.[55] It would be quite superfluous to rehearse the evidence here. Instead we shall merely isolate some key passages from Coleridge's writing which illustrate romantic thinking in a paradigmatic way.

In chapter ten of the *Biographia*, Coleridge coins the term 'esemplastic' to refer to the imagination's power to 'shape into one'. He admits a direct correlation between this term and the German Idealist notion of the productive imagination: 'How excellently the German word *Ein-bildungskraft* expresses this prime and loftiest faculty, the power of coadunation, the faculty that forms the many into the one, *In-Eins-Bildung*. Esenoplay . . . is contradistinguished from fantasy or mirrorment, repeating simply or by transposition.'[56] Coleridge shows himself quite as resolved as the German Idealists to separate the creative imagination from its traditional role of mimetic representation. The mimetic function is now called 'fantasy' while the productive function is reserved uniquely for the term 'imagination'. In a well known passage from the *Biographia*, he goes on to distinguish in turn between two modes of productive imagination – primary and secondary.

The primary imagination I hold to be the living power and prime agent of all human perception and as a repetition in the finite mind of the eternal act of creation in the infinite I AM. The secondary I consider as an echo of the former, coexisting with the conscious will, yet still as identical with the primary in the *kind* of its agency, and differing only in *degree* and in the *mode* of its operation. It dissolves, diffuses, dissipates, in order to recreate; or where this process is rendered impossible, yet still at all events it struggles to idealize and unify. It is essentially vital, even as all objects (*as* objects) are essentially fixed and dead.[57]

There are a number of observations to be made about this dense and rather convoluted text. First, the author appears to be equating the *primary* function with the idealist notion of 'transcendental imagination': a notion originally defined by Kant as the 'root unknown to us' which forms our apprehension of the objects of our world, and redefined by Schelling as an 'unconscious poetry' operative in our everyday natural existence. The *secondary* function, by contrast, is reserved for the properly artistic work of imagination, one which Kant identified with aesthetic judgement and Schelling with the 'conscious' productions of the poet. Moreover, Coleridge's attribution of the quality of 'conscious will' to the secondary function seems to support this correlation.

Second, the author confirms the idealist emphasis in according priority to the secondary over the primary activities of imagination. Even though he describes the primary function as a 'repetition' in the finite mind of the eternal act of creation, he limits this function to our 'perception' of nature. Furthermore, his reference to the infinite I AM, which ostensibly implies the superiority of Divine Creation (the I AM WHO AM of the Bible) over human creation, may well be a veiled allusion to the 'transcendental I' (which both Kant and Schelling related to the role of *human* imagination in the transcendental unity of apperception).

The noted practice of uniting the finite and infinite powers of imagination in transcendental idealism would suggest as much. Coleridge was certainly aware of this practice; and it is surely not insignificant that he makes no explicit mention in this passage to a transcendent 'God' as such. While such a hypothetical equation between the 'eternal act of creation' and the transcendental I of human subjectivity is at variance with the standard interpretations of this text, it finds strong supporting evidence in other passages of the *Biographia*. The following account by Coleridge of Schelling's view on this matter is just one example:

The position which not only claims but necessitates the admission of its immediate certainty, equally for the scientific reason of the philosopher as for the common sense of mankind at large, namely, I AM, cannot so properly be entitled a prejudice. It is groundless, but only because it is itself the ground of all other certainty. Now the apparent contradiction, that the . . . existence of things without us, which from its nature cannot be immediately certain, should be received as blindly and as independently of all grounds as the existence of our own being, the transcendental philosopher can solve only by the supposition that the former is unconsciously involved in the latter; that it is not only coherent but identical, and one and the same thing with our immediate self-consciousness. To demonstrate this identity is the office and object of his philosophy.[58]

If Coleridge's allusion to the 'infinite I AM' which primary imagination 'repeats' in finite acts of perception, is indeed a reference to the transcendental I AM of human subjectivity, as the passage just quoted implies, then primary imagination is *prior* to secondary imagination in chronological order – but not necessarily in the order of importance. To say that man's transcendental creation of natural objects occurs *before* the transcendental creation of aesthetic objects is merely stating that our 'unconscious' acts of imagination in everday existence precede, at a temporal level, our 'conscious' acts of imaginatively producing a work of art. It does not imply that the former is *superior* to the latter. Indeed if Coleridge's adherence to the position of transcendental idealism is anything to go by, the opposite is true. While Coleridge appears at first to conform to tradition by describing poetic imagination as a secondary echo of our natural experience, this deference to the 'mimetic' model is no more than apparent.[59]

It is in this light that we should take Coleridge's admission that the secondary imagination is identical with the primary in *kind* (i.e. as a creative act) and differs only in *degree* (i.e. as a conscious rather than unconscious mode of application). The difference in degree does not signal a *diminution* of power; it actually establishes the superiority of the secondary function over the primary. For while the primary apprehends the given objects of nature according to the *a priori* laws of perception and apperception, the secondary transforms these 'fixed' objects in the full freedom of artistic invention. It is this secondary imagination which Coleridge describes as a 'synthetic and magical power' capable of surpassing 1) the formal logic of non-contradiction, by 'balancing and reconciling opposite or discordant qualities'; and 2) natural perception, by injecting a 'sense of novelty and freshness' into 'old and familiar objects'. What at first glance seemed a rather confused distinction between primary and secondary functions turns out, on further consideration, to be a coherent reformulation of the transcendental capacities of imagination.[60]

The modern paradigm of creative imagination was also endorsed by many other romantic writers. Wordsworth celebrates imagination in book XIV of the *Prelude* as 'another name for absolute power . . . and Reason in its most exalted mood'. Blake hails it as the 'spiritual fountainhead divine' which 'liveth forever'. And in *A Defence of Poetry*, written in 1821, Shelley defies tradition in affirming that 'reason is to imagination

. . . as the shadow to the substance', adding that 'the great instrument of moral good is the imagination'.[61] This paradigm of productive imagination was by no means confined to the Germanic and English-speaking worlds. It extended to the romantic movements in France (e.g. Nerval, Hugo, Verlaine, Baudelaire) and in most other European cultures.[62]

8 Conclusion: the imagination in retreat

With German idealism and romanticism the modern elevation of imagination would seem to have reached its apogee. Having conquered the universe, there appeared to be nothing that imagination could not do. But this rise to unlimited heights was soon to be followed by a fall. The seeds of this fall were patent within romanticism itself. Given the extravagant claims for man's creative power, it was inevitable that disillusionment would set in sooner or later. The romantic imagination could not possibly deliver on its promises. Confronted with the increasingly disabling realities of modern existence – the crushed political revolutions, the industrial devastation of nature, the bureaucratization and mechanization of society promoted by market and monopoly capitalism – the humanist hopes of both the enlightenment and of romanticism were steadily eroded. Imagination soon found itself, like Napoleon after Moscow, beating a reluctant retreat.

This recession of imagination was already intimated by many of the romantics themselves. Indeed, Wordsworth provides one of the exemplary metaphors for the romantic imagination in straits, when he writes of the poet withdrawing from the hostile world to the 'watchtower' of his solitary spirit. Henceforth, it seemed, the creative imagination could only survive as a recluse. It could continue to form *images*; but it could no longer hope to transform *reality*. Romantic fiction could not be translated into fact. The modern world of political turmoil and social conflict remained incorrigible. It was only by erecting a partition between the worlds of reality and unreality, that imagination could resort to some limited preserve in order to express its impossible aspirations.

This partitionist aesthetic was by no means confined to the English romantics. It was witnessed, in differing degrees, in all the European movements of romanticism, and not least the German. The writings of Frederick Schiller powerfully anticipate this growing divorce between the imaginary and the real. In his *Letters on the Aesthetic Education of Man*, for example, this German romantic speaks of imagination creating an un-real realm 'in the full liberty of aesthetic play'.[63] Only by making a 'leap' out of the world of everyday reality is the imagination free to invent a world of pure 'illusion' (*Schein*) – what Schiller calls the 'joyous kingdom of play'. This strain of messianic humanism, characteristic of much romantic idealism, is further evidenced in the author's claim that 'in the unreal kingdom of imagination, beyond all real experience and practice, man possesses his own sovereignty'. The reasoning here seems to be that the traditional dualisms between mind and body, freedom and necessity, may be overcome in art if not in history. The messianic kingdom is no longer something to be revealed by God. It is an aesthetic project of man's imagination. The 'fiat' of divine creation is thus appropriated by the human mind; it takes the form of a *creatio ex nihilo* where man becomes lord and master of his own supreme fictions. Perhaps Hegel was making a similar point when he reduced all reality to the humanising power of absolute spirit (*Geist*)?[64] Or as the belated romantic, Wallace Stevens, would defiantly remark: 'Imagination is the value by which we project the idea of god into the idea of man. . . . Imagination is the only genius.'[65]

The romantic apotheosis of imagination as a world unto itself, a self-engendered *paradis artificiel*, may thus be understood largely as a reaction to historical circumstances. With nature becoming increasingly dominated by the mechanistic principles of the positive sciences, and society riven apart by the industrial strife and exploitation of expanding capitalism, imagination felt more and more compelled to recoil into a magical world of its own making. In this way, human subjectivity could ostensibly continue to be creative *in spite of history* – by negating history.

An alternative realm of ludic appearances is proposed by romantic art: a proposal predicated upon the radical dissociation of 'reality' and 'culture'. Hence the restoration of Prometheus as an exemplary hero. Condemned in Greek mythology and metaphysics for bestowing the creative fire of God upon man, Prometheus is reclaimed from ancient obloquy and enshrined as a leading figurehead of romantic literature. Denis Donoghue outlines the logic behind the return of this repressed hero:

The Promethean poet feels that the fate of the world depends upon him alone, he must not seek help or sign treaties. In Romantic literature generally Prometheus becomes 'the poet', guardian of intellectual beauty, the mind speaking its own case against an increasingly materialist world. . . . It will hardly be denied that the Promethean motive is active in the Romantic imagination generally: . . . it is found in close relation to certain motives which are hard to distinguish, except in extreme cases: idealism, Satanism, symbolism, the poet's hostility to bourgeois society. The myth of Prometheus, like the Satan of *Paradise Lost*, is almost too readily available to poets who place supreme value upon the Romantic figure of the hero: too readily available, because Prometheus does not criticize himself, does not detect himself. The first quality of this rebel is that he thinks his rebellion self-evidently justified; he sins, but condemns the justice which punishes him. He does not confess himself even partly at fault. This means that he reduces all his motives to one, which then becomes his identity; there is no remainder because he has no misgivings. He is the force concentrated in his name.[66]

Romantic humanism rehabilitated the accursed rebels of ancient mythology. Apart from the paramount case of Prometheus (see for example Shelley's rewriting of the myth in *Prometheus Unbound*), one might also cite the romantic reinterpretations of Dionysius, Orpheus, Dedalus and Narcissus, not to mention such heroes of folk legend as Faust or Don Juan. Defying the strictures of transcendence, romantic humanism championed the resources of creative *immanence*. The 'divine spark' was now to be sought in the inner depths of human will and desire. Is this not what Blake suggests in *Jerusalem* when he announces that the task of the prophetic poet is 'to open the immortal eyes of man inwards onto the worlds of thought . . . the Human Imagination'? Is this not what Schiller commends in a letter to Körner in 1788, where he dares creative genius to rely solely upon itself? Or what Joachim Gasquet implies in his claim that '*le monde est un immense Narcisse en train de se penser*'? The mythic rebels return triumphant, liberated from all ethical and epistemological stigmata. One is no longer troubled whether their transgressions deny transcendent truth or goodness. What matters is the energy of defiance itself. Suspending the relation to an omnipotent deity which kept man in bondage, romanticism allows the transcendental imagination to exult in its own self-referential play.

Many of the romantics chose to remain unaware of the deleterious consequences of such self-reference. But these consequences could not be deferred indefinitely. The mythological rebels, 'unbound' by romanticism, were soon to find another, and particularly modern, kind of nemesis. The mythic rise would once again be followed by a mythic fall. This return of the mythic pattern in the Romantic version of the Narcissus story is perceptively glossed by Jean Starobinski:

Ultimately unable to open up a space in the world for imagination and unable to sustain the ambition of a magical rapport with reality, (the Romantic) falls back on himself in an interior space, he translates cosmic dreams into private dreams, and thereby embroils himself in the idealist secession. To imagine no longer means to participate in the world, it means to haunt one's own image in terms of the indefinitely variable illusions this image can fashion for itself. Imagination conforms to the myth of Narcissus.[67]

The collapse of imagination's dream before the encroaching realities of historical existence, is the point where romantic idealism ends and existentialism begins.

APPENDIX

Heidegger's interpretation of the Kantian imagination

In his controversial work, *Kant and the Problem of Metaphysics* (1929), Martin Heidegger claimed that the Kantian theory of imagination represents a watershed in Western philosophy. Heidegger analyses here how in attempting to lay the foundations for a new scientific metaphysics, Kant hit upon the discovery that all our knowledge of being derives from the 'finitude of human subjectivity'.[1] This 'finitude' was necessarily demonstrated by the fact that pure reason could not reach the objects of experience except through the sensible intuition of time and space: that is, through the finite limits laid down by imagination. Whereas many orthodox interpreters chose to read this as confirmation of the traditional 'mediational' role of imagination, Heidegger insisted that Kant had radically redefined imagination as the 'formative centre' of both intuition and thought. To vindicate his conviction, Heidegger conducts a lengthy exploration of the Kantian treatment of the transcendental imagination in the first edition of the *Critique of Pure Reason*.

In order to prove that Kant was not merely reiterating the traditional view of imagination as a faculty which servilely mediates between mind and body, it was first necessary to show how Kant had established the 'productive' role of imagination in both sensation and understanding. In other words, the imagination must be exhibited as a productive power *presupposed* by sensation and understanding rather than a derived intermediary function which comes *after* them. Heidegger points out that Kant did indeed recognize imagination's positive, as well as merely reproductive, role in sensory intuition.[2] Imagination can intuit 'images' which it produces itself, rather than relying upon representations of empirical perceptions.

Sensible intuition owes to the productive imagination its capacity to pre-form its perceptions of actual objects in the light of possible objects which may never yet have been experienced. This freedom to intuit possible objects was explicitly attributed by Kant to the 'pure productive imagination, independent of experience, which first renders experience possible'.[3] It is essentially a transcendental freedom in that it serves as the *a priori* precondition of objectivity in general. And it is also, Heidegger reminds us, the origin of our intuition of time:

The imagination forms in advance and before all experience of the object, the aspect in the pure form (*bild*) of time and precedes this or that particular experience of an object . . . . In offering a pure aspect in this way, the imagination is in no wise dependent on the presence of an object. It is so far from being thus dependent that its pre-formation of a pure schema, for example, substance (permanence), consists in bringing into view something of the order of constant presence. It is only in the horizon of this presence that this or that 'presence of an object' can reveal itself.[4]

In other words, time is a *pure intuition* which *preforms* the horizon of all that is experienced in *empirical intuition*. But since this act of pure intuition belongs to transcendental imagination, what is pre-formed therein must also be imaginative. It is in fact an *ens imaginarium* which is 'something', though not of course an 'object' in the sense of a thing empirically present here and now. This strange 'something' – which is 'nothing' in comparison with empirical things – is time itself understood as the *horizon of possibility*, presupposed by the empirical intuition of all *actual* objects.[5] Consequently, since empirical intuition is made possible by the pure intuition of time, which is now identified with pure imagination, Kant has effectively demonstrated that sensibility is indeed rooted in transcendental imagination. This Kantian correlation between imagination and time is, as we shall see, central to Heidegger's 'existentialist' interpretation.

Even at the most primary level of sensible intuition, therefore, imagination enjoys a certain creative autonomy. Heidegger notes,

As a faculty of intuition, imagination is formative in the sense that it produces an image. As a faculty not dependent on objects of intuition, it produces, i.e. forms and provides, images. This 'formative power' is at one and the same time receptive and productive (spontaneous). In this 'at one and the same time' is to be found the true essence of the structure of imagination. However, if receptivity is identified with sensibility, and spontaneity with understanding, then imagination falls in a peculiar way between the two.[6]

This 'peculiar way' in question refers, of course, to that transcendental quality of imagination which *pre-exists* both sensibility and understanding. It suggests that imagination is an *original* power of production, in whose absence neither sensation nor understanding could have meaning. Kant calls it '*originarius*' (from the latin, to 'let spring forth').

But Heidegger has still to show how it is that for Kant imagination is not just presupposed by sensation but also by *understanding*. As we have already observed, understanding owes to imagination its capacity to 'compare, shape, differentiate and connect in general (synthesis)'.[7] This very power of synthesis points to a primordial unity of sensation and understanding brought about by the imagination prior to the functioning of either faculty. The synthetic role of imagination, presupposed by both faculties, is indeed so primordial that it operates behind our backs, as it were, unconsciously. A startling consideration this, which may explain why it took Western philosophy almost two thousand years to officially recognize its existence, and which prompted Kant to this curious admission:

Synthesis in general is the mere result of the power of the imagination, a blind but indispensable function of the soul, without which we should have no knowledge whatsoever, *but of the existence of which we are scarce ever conscious*.[8]

How exactly does this act of synthesis precondition the exercise of understanding? The first thing to recall here is that understanding is defined by Kant as a 'faculty of rules'. As such, the understanding must 'pro-pose in advance those unities which guide all possible modes of unification in the act of representation'. But the representation of these regulative unities – or 'categories' as Kant usually calls them – must in turn be 'included in advance in an abiding unity by means of an act even more primordial'.[9] This abiding unity is nothing other than the 'unity of apperception': the 'I think' which makes possible the conceptualization of the many in terms of the one. And for Kant, as Heidegger argues, this 'I think' or transcendental ego does not exist in its own right but is itself rooted in the productive imagination which projects the unification of all actual and possible representations. Kant makes this plain in the third section of the famous 'Transcendental Deduction' when he writes that 'the principle of the necessary unity of pure (productive) synthesis of imagination, *prior to apperception*, is the ground of the possibility of all knowledge'.[10] What this clearly states is that the deduction of the categories of the understanding originates in the synthesizing act of imagination.

Heidegger himself acknowledges a profound debt to Kant's theory of transcendental imagination. He hails it as a decisive anticipation of the analysis of existence (*Dasein*) outlined in his own *Being and Time* (1927) as a temporal projection of possibilities. Kant made a significant contribution to the overcoming of metaphysics. He was perhaps the first Western thinker to indicate that the traditional notion of being as permanent 'presence' was no more nor less than a 'product' of the temporalizing projection of man's finite existence. For we can only form a metaphysical notion of being as enduring 'presence' on the basis of our experience of a temporal horizon of possibilities, past, present and future. Presence, Kant thus appears to have conceded, is not some objective transcendence which pre-exists time; it is a construct of our transcendental ability to move freely through time and thereby abstract, synthesize and totalize the notion of an abiding presence. The horizon of objectivity formed by transcendental imagination – as the 'preformative form of the pure intuition of time' – is revealed accordingly as the *sine qua non* of our comprehension of being. All the onto-theological definitions of being as an eternal and permanent entity derive from man's finite power of temporal projection. Kant's discovery of the transcendental imagination is credited by Heidegger as the first modern attempt to interpret *being* in terms of *time*. In the following passage from *Kant and the Problem of Metaphysics*, Heidegger suggests how all metaphysical determinations of being are ultimately related to time:

What is the significance of the fact that ancient metaphysics defined the *ontos on* – the Being which is Being to the highest degree – as *aei on* (timeless Being)? The Being of beings is obviously understood here as permanence and subsistence. What projection lies at the basis of this comprehension of Being? A projection relative to time, for even eternity, taken as the *nunc stans*, for example, is as a 'permanent' *now* conceivable only through time. What is the significance of the fact that Being in the proper sense of the term is understood as *ousia, parousia*, i.e., basically as 'presence', the immediate and always present possession, as 'having'? This projection reveals that 'Being' is synonymous with *permanence in presence*. In this way, therefore, that is, in the spontaneous comprehension of Being, temporal determinations are accumulated. Is not the immediate comprehension of Being developed entirely from a primordial but self-evident *projection of Being relative to time*? Is it not then true that from the first this struggle for Being takes place within the horizon of time'[11]

While Heidegger admits that Kant never explicitly formulated the exact relation between primordial time and imagination, his intentions to this effect were, he claims, evidenced in his threefold description of imagination as: 1) a *facultas formandi* which forms images of the present; 2) a *facultas imaginandi* which recalls images of the past; and 3) a *facultas praevidendi* which anticipates images of the future.[12] Moreover, by according priority to the third of these imaginative faculties – the anticipative pre-formation of the future horizon of possibilities – over the other two, Kant disclosed the 'existential' character of human being as that which temporalizes itself out of the future.[13] By thus linking imagination with the primordial origin of time, Kant was the first modern thinker to prefigure the existentialist account of being as established in *Being and Time*.

Kant's suggestion that the transcendental imagination is the ultimate origin of our comprehension of being had immense implications for the system of Western philosophy as a whole. It challenged the entire hierarchy of oppositions which had supported man's metaphysical view of things. First, Kant dismantled the dualistic antithesis of reason and sensation by showing that reason is, from its origin, sensible and sensation rational, since both derive from imagination which is at once receptive (sensible) and spontaneous (rational). Second, Kant undermined the traditional opposition between a permanent self (*cogito*/intellect) and a transient temporal self (the body or animal soul) by revealing that the transcendental 'ego' only secures its 'abiding' character in so far as imagination first proposes an horizon of identity and permanence (for it is only by virtue of the synthesizing horizon of imagination that something can be experienced as necessarily the same through change). Third, and as a consequence of the second, Kant challenged the absolute dichotomy between being and non-being by indicating how all our understanding of being as eternal presence is, at root, produced by the temporal projections of imagination (projections which are 'nothing' in relation to empirical or transcendent being). Fourth and finally, Kant overturns the polar opposition of theoretical and moral reason; for even though he separated his *Critique of Pure Reason* from his *Critique of Practical Reason*, the moral notion of selfhood outlined in the latter presupposes the formative powers of imagination quite as much as the theoretical notion of the transcendental self advanced in the former. As Heidegger perceptively notes, by defining the moral self as the 'feeling of respect', Kant was effectively equating the self-imposition of the law with its 'receptive'/intuitive function:

It is only by rooting practical reason in the transcendental imagination that we are able to understand why neither the moral law nor the moral self are objectively apprehended but rather become manifest in a non-objective way as duty and action.[14]

Kant, it appears, was not entirely unaware of the 'de-structive' implications of this reversal of metaphysical priorities. While the basic thrust of the first edition of the *Critique of Pure Reason* pointed to the central role of imagination, the author was reluctant to recognize the consequences of his position. Furthermore, this reluctance is surely not unrelated to the fact that in the second edition of this work, Kant rewrote several key passages and removed others so as to re-emphasize the more traditional role of imagination as a subservient mediation of understanding. In this manner, Kant seems to have finally recoiled from the revolutionary discovery that imagination is the temporalizing origin of not only all our knowledge, but indeed of the very concepts of selfhood and of being. Heidegger portrays Kant's dilemma in all its dramatic intensity:

Does not everything fall into confusion if the lower is put in place of the higher? What is to happen to the honorable tradition according to which, in the long history of metaphysics, *ratio* and *logos* have laid claim to the central role? Can the primacy of logic disappear? Can the architectonic of the laying of the foundation of metaphysics, i.e., its division into transcendental aesthetic and logic, be preserved if the theme of the latter is basically the transcendental imagination? Does not the *Critique of Pure Reason* deprive itself of its own theme if pure reason is transformed into transcendental imagination? Does not this laying of the foundation lead to an abyss? By his radical interrogation, Kant brought the 'possibility' of metaphysics before this abyss. He saw the unknown; he had to draw back.[15]

CHAPTER FIVE

The Existentialist Imagination I – Kierkegaard and Nietzsche

Existentialism is, above all else, a philosophy of human finitude. It describes man in his concrete situation in the world. Thus while it inherits the romantic cult of subjectivity, it exposes the existential limits of man's creative powers. As such, existentialism tempers the initial optimism of romantic idealism. It clips the wings of the transcendental imagination and lays bare the everyday obstacles which obstruct its flights and fiats. Against romanticism's claim for the unlimited and quasi-divine potential of imagination, the existentialist sounds a note of irony – even pessimism. He brings imagination back to earth. The operative terms of existentialist philosophy speak for themselves: *anguish, dread, bad faith, absurdity, nothingness, nausea*. In short, existentialism speaks of the creative imagination less in terms of a plenitude than of a predicament.

1 The critique of affirmative culture

If romantic idealism may be generally said to have dominated Western theories of imagination in the late eighteenth and early nineteenth centuries (say from Kant's first edition of the *Critique of Pure Reason* published in 1781 to Shelley's *Defence of Poetry* published in 1821), existentialism was to succeed it as the most

influential philosophy of imagination between the mid nineteenth and mid twentieth centuries (from Kierkegaard and Nietzsche to Jean-Paul Sartre). A substantial degree of continuity
notwithstanding, the succession marks a shift from an 'affirmative' to a 'negative' culture. And, like all mutations in the history
of ideas, this modern shift does not occur in a sealed vacuum
of mind. It is intimately bound up with specific socio-historic
circumstances.

A close link has been identified by Herbert Marcuse and
others between the reign of romantic idealism and the rise of
the Western bourgeoisie. Here, it is argued, was a social group
who played off the spiritual world of imagination against the
material world of toil and necessity, elevating culture as an
'affirmative' realm of autonomous ends in opposition to the
everyday treadmill of utilitarian means. Marcuse explains,

By affirmative culture is meant that culture of the bourgeois epoch
which led in the course of its own development to the segregation from
civilization of the mental and spiritual world as an independent realm
of value that is also considered superior to civilization (i.e. the world
of material production). Its decisive characteristic is the assertion of a
universally obligatory, eternally better and more valuable world that
must be unconditionally affirmed: a world essentially different from the
factual world of the daily struggle for existence, yet realizable by every
individual for himself 'from within', without any transformation of the
state of fact. It is only in this culture that cultural activities and objects
gain that value which elevates them above the everyday sphere. Their
reception becomes an act of celebration and exaltation.[1]

Romantic culture concealed the condition of *social* existence
at the same time as it affirmed the condition of *aesthetic* existence. It internalized the demands for universal beauty, freedom
and unity. The antagonistic relations prevailing in the real world
were thus 'pacified' within a purely imaginary realm. Affirmative
culture was not, however, without its virtues. It did foster a new
demand for individual happiness – even if fulfilment was confined
to the order of the unreal. Such a demand was unthinkable
in older (e.g. feudal) societies where the human subject was
permanently subjugated to a pre-ordained hierarchy which it

accepted without question. If romantic idealism felt it necessary therefore to posit an autonomous world of subjective freedom and beauty, it was because of a deep anxiety about the *insufficiency* of the given political order. Rejecting the constraints of a dehumanizing social mediation, the romantic individual sought his happiness in and through the immediacy of the creative imagination. 'Anxiety stands at the source of all idealistic doctrines that look for the highest felicity in ideational practice', notes Marcuse. He continues:

Nonetheless, anxiety about happiness, which drove philosophy to separate beauty and necessity, preserves the demand for happiness even within the separated sphere. Happiness becomes a preserve, in order for it to be able to be present at all. What man is to find in the philosophical knowledge of the true, the good, and the beautiful is ultimate pleasure which has all the opposite characteristics of material facticity: permanence in change, purity amidst impurity, freedom amidst unfreedom. The abstract individual who emerges as the subject of practice at the beginning of the bourgeois epoch also becomes the bearer of a new claim to happiness, merely on the basis of the new constellation of social forces. No longer acting as the representative or delegate of higher social bodies, each separate individual is supposed to take the provision of his needs and the fulfillment of his wants into his own hands and be in *immediate relation* to his 'vocation', to his purpose and goals, without the social, ecclesiastical, and political mediations of feudalism. . . . To this extent, the bourgeois liberation of the individual made possible a new happiness.[2]

But as the emerging bourgeois society established itself as the new status quo, the 'affirmative' character of its culture lost much of its protest potential. While freedom, happiness and beauty remained the triadic goal of the modern bourgeoisie, the realization of this goal continued to be denied in the social world. It became hypostasized as a mere fiction. It served, more and more, as a strategy of evasion. The pure humanity of art became the counter-image of what obtained in reality. The bourgeois belief in progress, in a better future for all in defiance of the old restrictive and unchanging order, gradually betrayed its universalist pretensions. Freedom did not extend beyond the privileged interests of the bourgeoisie, a class which, instead, came into growing conflict with the interests of the majority of society. The 'idealist' nature of the established bourgeois culture thus began to function as a largely compensatory illusion:

To the need of the isolated individual, the bourgeoisie responds with general humanity, to bodily misery with the beauty of the soul, to external bondage with internal freedom, to brutal egoism with the duty of the realm of virtue. Whereas during the period of the militant rise of the new society all of these ideas had a progressive character by pointing beyond the attained organization of existence, they entered increasingly into the service of the suppression of the discontented masses and of mere self-justifying exaltation, once bourgeois rule began to be stabilized.[3]

The philosophical signs of affirmative culture were manifest in the transcendental doctrines of Kant and the German idealists. It was here that humanity was first defined as an inner state, history as an affair of the individual soul, and mortality as the result of the 'law in man's own breast'. Kant provided us with a blueprint of this transcendental philosophy when he wrote that man 'partakes of no other happiness or perfection than that which he provides for himself'.[4] With the discovery of the transcendental imagination each individual dispenses with all worldly and heavenly mediations and becomes the immediate source of value. But by the same token, the human subject is transformed into an abstraction: its spiritual interiority and freedom become those of 'Man' rather than of concretely existing men and women. However elevated the transcendental self, each individual remains of course as historically bound to his everyday existence as before. The subject can only present himself as a self-sufficient being to the extent that he is divorced from his living humanity. If he pursues the abstract idea of *Man*, he

must think in opposition to facticity. Wishing to conceive this idea in its philosophical passivity and universality, he must abstract from the present state of affairs. . . . In every act of cognition, the individual must once again re-enact the 'production of the world' and the categorical organization of experience. However, the process never gets any further because the restriction of 'productive' cognition to the transcendental sphere makes any new form of the world impossible.[5]

Even though it continues to assert the creativity of the human subject, existentialism distances itself from the abstract affirmations of transcendental idealism. Existentialism reintroduces the baggage of cumbersome distress which idealism sought to leave 'outside'. And in so doing, it explodes the monadic isolation of the transcendental 'I', dragging the individual by the heels back into the harsh weathers of quotidien existence. We thus find Kierkegaard rebuking the optimism of speculative idealism and announcing that human life, left to its own devices, is a 'sickness unto death'. And there is Nietzsche who declares that all 'truth is illusion', and that the greatest act of individual courage is to embrace the arbitrary cycle of existence as an 'eternal recurrence of the same'. But it is probably with Sartre and the twentieth-century existentialists that the affirmative cult of imagination is most strikingly inverted. While Sartre endorses the *humanist* premiss of romantic idealism he pushes this premiss to its absurd extreme. Man is indeed what he makes of himself, Sartre concedes, but this very act of self-creation is without any foundation or purpose. Sartre denounces the benevolent abstraction of a universal human nature, promoted by Kant and the German idealists, insisting that we are born without reason and exist without justification. Those who continue to subscribe to the illusion that existence is necessary when it is merely 'an accident of the appearance of the human race on earth', are derided by Sartre as 'scum'.[6]

But in spite of this opposition between romantic idealism and existentialism, there also exist similarities. Both philosophies agree that imagination is a productive power which precedes both sensation and intelligence. And both interpret this priority in the modern perspective of a *humanist subjectivism* – however at variance their respective interpretations may be in point of emphasis. The way in which the existentialist philosophy of imagination – from Kierkegaard and Nietzsche in the nineteenth century to Camus and Sartre in the twentieth – evolved in such a dual rapport of continuity and discontinuity with its idealist predecessors, is what we must now examine.

2 Kierkegaard

The Danish thinker, Soren Kierkegaard, was one of the pioneers of the existentialist movement. Kierkegaard grants that the aesthetic attitude constitutes the first stage of existence. It is here that the human self discovers his power of imagination as infinite desire. This initial wakening to imagination is likened by Kierkegaard to a youthful 'passion for the possible'. It is the feeling that nothing is prohibited, that the vistas of existence are inexhaustibly exciting. In so far as he accepts that our quest for truth begins with the endless desires of the subjective imagination, Kierkegaard is effectively equating the 'aesthetic stage' with the attitude of romantic idealism. And this equation is supported by the fact that his chosen representatives of this stage are all canonized heroes of the romantic period – Don Juan/ Johannes the Seducer, Faustus and Prometheus.

But Kierkegaard also marks a definite rupture with the romantic paradigm. The 'aesthetic' is, he insists, only one of three 'stages on life's way'. The other two – the 'ethical' and the 'religious' – cannot be subsumed under the aesthetic, as romantic idealism supposed. The three stages represent dialectical options which the human individual is compelled to choose between if he is to attain an authentic existence. To remain forever within the aesthetic phase of creative imagination is, for Kierkegaard, to remain inauthentic; for it is to refuse the either/or choices which constantly confront us in our everyday experience.[7]

The ethical and religious stages set limits to the creative imagination. The ethical presents the aesthetic subject with a number of urgent responsibilities: 1) responsibility to the *individual* other (demanding a transition from the unrelenting play of seduction and desire, embodied by Don Juan, to the commitment of enduring friendship or marriage); 2) responsibility to the *social* other (demanding a transition from the empty freedom of aesthetic immediacy to an acceptance of such universal mediations as law and reasonable judgement, embodied by Judge Wilhelm).

The religious stage transcends and dialectically recapitulates the first two movements. It retrieves the character of subjective immediacy and inwardness initially revealed in aesthetic experience – but by way of a radical transformation (*Aufhebung*) which cancels the irresponsible quality of the aesthetic attitude in favour of a 'leap of faith' towards the absolute.[8] The religious option also surpasses the universalist mediations of law and reason while retaining the character of commitment. But it does not, as one might be tempted to suspect, entail a return to the onto-theological paradigm of medieval thought. Kierkegaard is a religious dissenter in his assertion that the leap of faith is made 'by virtue of the absurd'. Religion is now interpreted as a matter of existential choice which defies the speculative arguments of traditional metaphysics. He who still seeks to prove God's existence by means of logical syllogisms is denounced by Kierkegaard as being *ipso facto* a heathen. Existential faith is a project shot through with doubt, anxiety and desire. It can only be assumed by each solitary individual responding to what he believes to be a divine summons *even though he lacks any objective evidence to support this belief*. An absurd faith, therefore, but a faith nonetheless.

Kierkegaard takes Abraham as an exemplary figure of this faith. He responded to God's call to sacrifice his son; but he did so in 'fear and trembling' since only his inward belief could assure him that this absurd command – which transcended the universal norms of law and reason – was not some private hallucination but a mysterious sign of God's love. Abraham's faith was of course vindicated. His son, Isaac, was returned unharmed and the rite of human sacrifice banished forever. Abraham trusted that even while his faith was a 'crucifixion of the understanding', it would ultimately succeed in making the impossible possible – that is, remain faithful to both God and man.[9]

The religious act of faith bears certain similarities to the aesthetic act of imagination – as one might expect from a dialectical model. Both resist the objective norms of universal law;

both are expressions of individual will; and both are existential projects without rational guarantee. But faith differs from imagination in that its 'subjective inwardness' posits, however absurdly, a relation to a transcendent Other beyond human subjectivity. And this God of existentialism, as we noted, is radically opposed to the God of onto-theology: the former is a free project whereas the latter is a necessary possession. For the existential 'knight of faith' there is no way of knowing whether the religious choice is *objectively* true or false. Hence Kierkegaard's portrait of faith as a leap into the dark fraught with risk and uncertainty.

Indeed, it is perhaps here that we touch on a key reason for Kierkegaard's refusal to erect his dialectic of the three stages into a systematic hierarchy governed by necessary laws of speculation. The three stages co-exist as it were at all points in the existence of every individual. There is no linear chronology at work here. Imagination, reason and faith are not mechanically succeeding phases. Each must presuppose the possibility of the other if the existential choice is to be *free* rather than pre-ordained. This accounts for Kierkegaard's use of pseudonyms throughout his works – some representing the aesthetic attitude, some the ethical, some the religious, and others a combination of all three. There could be no single unambiguous viewpoint, no absolute authorial overview commanding the development of the dialectic. (And here, of course, Kierkegaard differed radically from the other great masters of dialectical thought in the nineteenth century, Hegel and Marx). The author, himself, Kierkegaard insisted, should remain *incognito*.[10] He should not impose his solutions on others. Each reader must be left, in the final analysis, alone with the conflict of pseudonymous viewpoints. For only in this way can his choice between imagination, reason and faith be a totally free one.

In the light of this summary of Kierkegaard's dialectic, we will now analyse his specific pronouncements on imagination. Kierkegaard's treatment of this term – in Danish *Phantasi* or *Indbildning* – is sporadic rather than systematic. The rejection of an overall system is consistent with his accusation that Hegel and the German idealists had taken the sting out of experience, abstracting it into a crystalline palace of ideas. Kierkegaard dismissed the transcendental idealists as 'loose thinkers' who 'with an air of superiority claim to reconcile the finite and the infinite in a dialectical synthesis of absolute spirit'. Such an ideal synthesis leaves out 'temporal existence and reality'.[11]

The Kierkegaardian philosophy of imagination unfolds accordingly less in terms of a single sequential argument than of anecdotal descriptions scattered throughout his writings. In the interests of economy, we confine our remarks to two main motifs which illustrate Kierkegaard's attitude. The first is his portrait of an aesthetic youth in pursuit of an ideal (sketched in *Training in Christianity*, written in 1848 and published in 1850); the second deals with his account of the Promethean character of imagination as a story of hope and despair (outlined mainly in *Either/Or*, published in 1843, and *Sickness unto Death*, published in 1848). What links these two motifs of the imagination is Kierkegaard's basic concern to unravel the relationship between man's aesthetic and religious experience.

The portrait of perfection

The tale of imagination narrated by the author of *Training in Christianity* is subtle and complex. Imagination, we are first informed, is that special possession of youths, poets and lovers who seek to surmount the obstacles of existence. It is the inward face of will and desire before whose gaze all the contradictions and sufferings of reality seem to disappear. Just like an impatient child who propels himself towards a glittering object to the exclusion of all else in the vicinity, so too imagination obsessively pursues its goal. The imperious nature of the aesthetic impulse thus appears incompatible with religious faith. Imagination has no problem disregarding the inherent 'offence' of the Christian mystery of the Incarnation – what Kierkegaard calls the impossible paradox of the God-Man – for the simple reason that it identifies with the *splendour of the divine* at the expense of the *suffering of the human*. 'The imagination ignores the offence', warns Kierkegaard.[12] And without the 'offence' there can be no genuine Christian faith. Moreover, since imagination overlooks the humanity in Christ, it follows that it can even more easily ignore its own existential humanity, and thus presume to be God! Kierkegaard writes,

It is not unthinkable that a man in whom imagination predominates, a man who typifies childlike or childish Christianity (since for a child the offence does not exist and for this reason Christianity does not properly exist for the child) – it is not unthinkable that such a man might ingenuously entertain the notion that he believed this individual to be God and discover no offence in it. [13]

Kierkegaard goes on to explain that such an aesthete has no 'explicit conception' of God, but merely a lofty ideal which involves no leap of faith over the 'offensive' paradox of the Christian God-Man.

In the concluding section of *Training in Christianity*, Kierkegaard's pseudonym, Anti-Climacus, refers to the relation between imagination and the God-Man in somewhat more congenial terms. The author now seems to acknowledge that imagination may serve, on occasion, as an initiating force in the dialectical opening towards faith. Because the human subject is 'not like the God-Man but a frail creature' he may often find it necessary to make his way to a religious commitment by *indirect* means, by a series of gradual intermediary steps. [14] 'Man's upbringing in the school of life', Anti-Climacus admits, frequently begins with the youthful imagination seizing upon a 'perfect idea' which he then proceeds to follow. Every human subject possesses to some degree this power of projective imagination which the author calls 'the first condition for determining what a man will turn out to be'. [15] It is his 'passion for the possible'.

To illustrate this point, Anti-Climacus presents us with a youth who imagines an 'ideal picture of perfection'. The youth desires this image; he wants to become one with it. It accompanies him everywhere, in his waking and sleeping hours. And sometimes it draws him so forcefully that he cannot sleep at all. And yet however much it haunts and eludes and tortures him, he cannot let it go. The youth falls in love with the image, an image which is nothing less than the possibility of realizing a synthesis of his opposing selves – the finite and the infinite: the possibility of the '*most perfect self*', the God-Man.[16] The image, having thus become the exclusive object of his enthusiasm, commands the youth's total attention: 'As imagination one beholds only the perfection, even the striving for perfection is seen only as completed.'[17] Here we are dealing with a proleptic imagination which leaps ahead of itself, which strives to jump out of its existential skin and perceive the end of the story even as it begins.

The inevitable tragedy of this aesthetic youth is that he blinds himself to the finite and painful reality of the world in which he must live. He desperately contrives to negate those divisions which constitute his 'out-of-joint' existence. The youthful imagination feels no real need for faith for the world offends him not; and the world offends him not because he simply does not *experience* it. Everything appears as a mere shadow when held against the brilliant iridescence of the 'ideal picture'. 'Imagination which is the faculty of representing perfection', as the author explains, 'has to do essentially with exaltation, perfection and only imperfectly deals with imperfection.' And since the youth is engaged solely with the desire to resemble the picture, this 'exercises its power over him, the power of love, which indeed is all powerful, especially to bring about likeness'.[18] Consequently, the youth's whole inward being is reconstructed little by little and 'it is as if he were beginning, however imperfectly, to resemble the picture for the sake of which he has forgotten everything else'.[19]

This aesthetic obsession to identify with the image of the 'perfect self' is, of course, doomed to failure. What seemed like the quest for a higher reality is in fact no more than a self-projection – a fiction of the idealist's own productive imagination. Reality eventually wrestles itself back into focus. The picture is shattered. And things could not have turned out otherwise; for the idealist picture only tells, at best, *half* the story. 'The expressing of the picture of perfection with the inclusion of suffering as well', Kierkegaard insists, '*cannot* be done.'[20] The bloom of youthful idealism thus fades before the invasion of our concrete existence – 'the suffering of reality and the reality of suffering'.[21] Imagination, to borrow Yeats' memorable expression, 'withers into the truth'. Anti-Climacus sums up this tragic tale of the imaginative youth as follows:

Life's seriousness consists in the will to be and to express perfection in everyday reality . . . this inevitably involves suffering since the picture he would still resemble is one of perfection and the reality in which he finds himself is anything but perfect . . . no hope came in the direction he had hoped.[22]

The Promethean project

This allusion to mistaken 'hope' brings us to Kierkegaard's second major motif of imagination – the Promethean project. In one of his journal entries, Kierkegaard links this hope to the Promethean desire to 'reform the whole world forcing oneself to be demonically stronger than one is'.[23] We shall now look at a selection of passages from *Either/Or* and *Sickness unto Death* which develop this equation between Promethean hope and the dialectic of imaginative desire and despair. Here once again we witness Kierkegaard's concern to explore the complex relationship between the aesthetic and religious attitudes.

Our first passage is from *Either/Or*. It issues a warning to all those romantic enthusiasts who have fallen under the spell of Promethean hope:

Hope precludes self-limitation. It is a very beautiful sight to see a man put out to sea with the fair wind of hope, and one may even use the opportunity to be taken in tow; but one should never permit hope to be taken aboard one's own ship, least of all as a pilot; for hope is a faithless shipmaster. *Hope was the dubious gift of Prometheus*; instead of giving men the foreknowledge of the immortals, he gave them hope.

'Whoever plunges into his experience with the momentum of hope', concludes the author, 'will remember in such wise that he is unable to forget. *Nil admirare* is therefore the real philosophy.'[24] Kierkegaard's existentialist irony is clearly in evidence here, his determination to deflate the 'affirmative culture' of modern idealism quite explicit. And of course the choice of Prometheus – one of the reclaimed heroes of the romantic imagination – is by no means accidental.

Our second passage is from one of his later works, *Sickness unto Death*. Here the author dismisses the various attempts of romantic idealism to reconcile the opposed selves of the human subject – the temporal and the external – within the realm of transcendental imagination. Such exercises in 'Promethean hope', Kierkegaard admonishes, invariably culminate in despair.[25] Faced with the existential reality of a self which is divided against itself, man experiences 'dread'. But 'dread' is itself ambiguous – 'the first reflex of possibility, a glimmer and yet a terrible spell'.[26] It is at once a portal to hope and to despair. Indeed it is highly significant from the point of view of our own genealogy of imagination, that in this same text Kierkegaard relates dread not only to the Promethean paradigm of hope and despair but also to the Adamic paradigm of temptation and fall. He invokes these two foundational myths as premonitions that man can never overcome the limits of his existential finitude and unite his divided selves by the efforts of his imagination alone. Any human subject who, 'acknowledging no power over it', attempts such a secular salvation is, he insists, doomed to 'will in despair to be itself'. To engage in such a project is to become indeed a king – but a king without a kingdom. Here is the passage in question:

Like the fire which Prometheus stole from the gods, so does this (i.e. the self's refusal to acknowledge a power over it) mean to steal from God the thought which is seriousness, that God is regarding one, instead of which the despairing self is content with regarding itself, and by that it is supposed to bestow upon its undertakings infinite interest and importance, whereas it is precisely this which makes them mere experiments. For though this self were to go so far in despair that it becomes an experimental God, no derived self can by regarding itself give itself more than it is: it nevertheless remains from first to last the self, by self-duplication it becomes neither more nor less than the self. Hence the self in its despairing effort to will to be itself labours itself into the direct opposite, it becomes really no self. In the whole dialectic within which the self acts there is nothing firm (. . .) This ruler is a king without a country, he rules over nothing.[27]

There are two insights in this passage of a singularly modern nature. First, the observation that the Promethean project to replace God with man is a fictional experiment in self-duplication. In striving to construct God out of his own subjective imagination, man is in fact condemning himself to self-reflection. This for Kierkegaard is the final lesson to be learnt from the German idealists and Hegel. The second particularly modern insight of this passage is that man's self-image is essentially a *nothingness*. The Promethean hope of romantic idealism inevitably collapses into existentialist anguish: the terrifying discovery that the human imagination is, at bottom, a gaping void. Rebuking the optimism of the transcendental idealists, Kierkegaard asserts that the inner essence of human subjectivity is an 'empty contentless *I*' – a vaporous ghost which can never succeed, despite all its efforts, in escaping its 'accidental finitude'.[28] Here Kierkegaard anticipates the existentialist analysis of 'nothingness' which was to become a central theme of twentieth-century thinkers such as Heidegger, Camus and Sartre.

In the same work Kierkegaard draws a parallel between the tendency of speculative idealism to deify imagination and the pantheistic abolition of the *qualitative distinction* between God and man: a pantheism typified by established Christendom. What separates authentic Christianity from such a pantheistic Christendom is, Kierkegaard argues, the existential stumbling block of the 'offence'. It is the 'slack orators' of the romantic imagination who seek to by-pass the offensive discrepancy between man and God – even in the paradox of the God-Man, Christ. Never anywhere has any doctrine on earth brought God and man so near together as has Christianity, concedes Kierkegaard. But he adds:

Only God himself can do this, every human invention remains after all a dream, a dubious *imagination*. Nor has any doctrine ever so carefully defended itself against the most shocking of all blasphemies, that after God had taken this step it then should be taken in vain, as though God and man coalesced in one and the same thing – never has any doctrine defended itself against this as Christianity has, which defends itself by the help of the offence.[29]

It is by trying to forget sin – and its origin in Adam's presumption and fall – that men suppose they can become one with the divine. But imaginary abstractions never fully succeed in evading the existential reality of man's finite condition – our sinfulness and our mortality.[30]

The imagination's forgetfulness of man's finitude is witnessed in the Romantic attempts to exonerate Adam's original transgression and Prometheus' original theft. Perhaps indeed it is with Plato's account of the mythological 'kinship' between Promethean man and the gods in mind (i.e. *The Protagoras*, 322a), that Kierkegaard declaims the 'abstraction which presumes to claim kinship with God'.[31] The view that the human race is akin to God is 'ancient paganism', and all idealist efforts to revive this error 'exhibit the profundity of optical illusion'.[32] But such idealist presumptions are not confined to the aesthetic attitude. They are also manifest, as noted, in the religious attitude of inauthentic Christendom – in so far as it tries to reduce the mysterious heterogeneity of God's relationship with man to the temporal mediations of doctrinal speculation or power. 'As soon as Christ's Kingdom comes to terms with the world,' asserts Kierkegaard, 'Christianity is abolished.'[33]

Kierkegaard leaves us in no doubt that the gravest error of the modern spirit is to confound human imagination with what he calls divine 'invention'. Such a confusion betrays at once the existential finitude of mankind and the eternal infinity of God. Returning to his story of the idealist youth, Kierkegaard establishes a direct connection between the Promethean excesses of imagination and the ideological excesses of Christendom:

As it is almost universally observable that children and youth desire to experience *by anticipation the whole of life* leaving nothing for manhood and old age, so has the human race, or Christendom, with like impatience desired to anticipate eternity, and (instead of what is God's invention with regard to existence as a whole, that the temporal, this life of ours here, is the period of probation, eternity the period of triumph) – instead of this they would introduce triumph *within* the temporal, which means to abolish Christianity.[34]

Affirmative culture, in both its aesthetic and religious aspects, stands rebuked. Existentialist man is a being exposed in all his anguish, solitude, dividedness and disillusionment. There is no salvation to be found either in the world or in the self. For Kierkegaard, there remains of course the leap of faith. But even that is made in fear and trembling – in what he calls the risk of 'objective uncertainty'.

3 Nietzsche

Frederick Nietzsche, the other dominant figure of nineteenth-century existentialism, also sponsored the view that man's imagination is confronted with the absurdity of his existential situation. He interprets this absurdity, however, in a different manner to Kierkegaard. Nietzsche acknowledges the fundamental anguish of modern man while declining all compensatory leaps of faith. The creative imagination is indeed foundationless, a free-floating nothingness, pure will and desire. But therein lies its virtue. Therein reposes the incontrovertible challenge of modern man to exist without alibi or reprieve, without any recourse to higher values. Imagination, for Nietzsche, is the demand to 'live dangerously'.

'If God is dead all is permitted', wrote Dostoyevsky. Nietzsche deleted the 'if' and embraced the consequences. The 'death of God' is proudly proclaimed in *The Gay Science* (para. 125), published in 1882, and hailed as the precondition for the full liberation of man.[35] Only when the last lingering belief in a transcendent deity disappears can creative imagination come into its own. Then at last man is free to invent the project of the super-man (*Uebermensch*): the great individual who dares to make his arbitrary existence into a work of art. The productive imagination thereby assumes its existential vocation as a will to power in a meaningless world. This unmitigated voluntarism takes, in Nietzsche, the form of a 'transvaluation of values' which dismantles the traditional notions of truth and morality.

Nietzsche first outlines the implications of this transvaluation in *The Genealogy of Morals*.[36] He declares that all so-called 'objective' notions of good and evil are no more than cultural inventions of man. The transcendental values of traditional philosophy are unmasked as disguised expressions of the will to power. Far from being timeless entities, such values are relative to the historical period in which they are defined. In both Platonism and Christianity (which Nietzsche denounces as 'Platonism for the people'), Western man negated existence by affirming the superiority of a supersensible world. The idea of 'absolute value' was nothing other than a strategic fiction: an invention by 'men of resentment' whose 'herd mentality' jealously sought to deny the creative greatness of free minds. Absolute value was a mask for the denial of life. It was an excuse for what Nietzsche contemptuously dismissed as 'green-meadow gregariousness' and 'bovine mediocrity'.

Heidegger has described Nietzsche as the 'last metaphysician' – the philosopher who announces the end of onto-theology.[37] Nietzsche's role here was primarily iconoclastic. He argued that the traditional concepts of God as First Cause, Perfect Being and Transcendent Good were, at root, projects of the human will. And 'nihilist' projects at that, for in attributing the origin of value to a non-existent otherworld, traditional metaphysics concealed from man that he alone was and is the creator of values. Nietzsche proposes to expose this 'nothingess' lurking at the heart of Western civilization. And instead of recoiling from it, he resolves to celebrate the feeling of 'weightlessness' which this exposure produces, seeing it as a challenge to create everything anew – out of nothing.

Nietzsche's project of transvaluation effected not only the moral question of good but also the epistemological question of truth. The age-old quest for absolute truth is now exposed as a hidden will to power. 'The so-called *thirst for knowledge*', claims Nietzsche, 'may be traced to the lust of appropriation and conquest.'[38] The metaphysical search for truth is ultimately motivated by the desire to master and control being. This was concealed from man by himself up to the modern era of existentialism when everything was put in question, nothing accepted at face value. 'Truth was not allowed to be a problem', Nietzsche explains, 'because up to the present the ascetic ideal dominated all philosophy, because Truth was fixed as Being, as God, as the supreme court of appeal . . .'.[39] Kant, of course, had come close to acknowledging the problematic nature of metaphysical truth. But, as Heidegger noted, 'he saw the abyss and had to draw back'. And the subsequent movement of German idealism and romanticism also served to deflect attention away from the existential abyss – elevating man's imagination to a new quasi-divine 'transcendental' status which turned a blind eye, for the most part, to the contingent absurdities of reality. Kierkegaard did, for his part, disclose the void at the heart of human existence. But he took some of the harm out of it by allowing for the possibility of a leap of faith – even if it was by virtue of the absurd.

Nietzsche refuses all such consolations. He takes a leap not upwards towards an absent God but downwards into the very depths of the abyss itself. The nothingness of existence is at last to be confronted in all its terrifying and magnificent nakedness. The authentic self 'dares to gaze into the darkest abyss'. According to Nietzsche, the 'will to truth' is 'already a symptom of degeneration'; and the 'one who tells the truth ends up by revealing that he always lies!'[40] In this manner, Nietzsche reverses Kierkegaard's model of the three stages. The *aesthetic* stage is now hailed as the highest expression of existence, beyond both ethics and religion.

Such considerations characterize Nietzsche's theory of imagination. The creative imagination is inauthentic to the extent that it allows its illusions to be taken for truths. And it is authentic to the extent that it acknowledges its illusions *as illusions* and thereby exults in the freedom of its own creativity. 'Truth is more fatal than error', says Nietzsche, in that it seeks to conceal the purely arbitrary nature of imagination; but we cling desperately to truth for 'it is more gratifying to think "I possess truth" than to see darkness in all directions . . .'.[41] Only by embracing this darkness as our ineluctable destiny can we begin to exist authentically. The inventive use of imagination presupposes therefore the liquidation of all established notions of truth. And from the grave of absolute truth rise up the multiple and ever-changing 'truths' of imagination – as many truths as there are interpretations of truth. The self-contained infinity of God is thus replaced by the open infinity of human interpretation.[42]

It is in this context that we must read Nietzsche's enigmatic formulation that 'truth becomes woman'. What he means by this is that the patriarchal hierarchy of metaphysics, predicated upon the principle of the absolute Father as self-identical origin of truth, is being subverted by the existential disclosure of truth as illusion (i.e. a playful dance of veils, in which woman reveals herself paradoxically in her very concealment). Here we have a telling instance of what Derrida calls the 'deconstruction' of truth. In book fifteen of the *Will to Power*, Nietzsche himself spells out some of the critical consequences of this position for traditional metaphysics and indeed for transcendental idealism. He argues that the metaphysical quest for a unified and absolute truth – symbolised by the Platonic equation of the Sun-Father-Good – is still preserved, in however altered a form, by Kant, Fichte and Schelling. Truth is not abandoned by the modern idealists; it is simply transposed into a sublime mystery. 'It is basically the old sun,' observes Nietzsche, 'but seen through haze and scepticism; the idea rarefied, grown palid, nordic, königsbergian.'[43] Where the idealists could speak of the unity of truth and art, reason and imagination, Nietzsche speaks of their 'raging discordance'.

Nietzsche unbolts the last remaining hatches of metaphysics. He proclaims truth to be no more nor less than an 'army of metaphors'. At best, existence is revealed as a palimpsest of fictions which the human imagination invents for itself in order to experience an endless multiplicity of meanings. This existentialist pluralism of subjective viewpoints is what Nietzsche calls 'perspectivism'. Gone is the traditional spirit of 'seriousness' which fed off the illusion of One Truth. Now one exults in the free play of experimentation. Metaphysics is denounced as a mythology which has forgotten its mythological origins. The implications of this reversal of traditional metaphysics are boldly stated in paragraph 539 of the *Will to Power*: 'Parmenides said – "One can form no concept of the non-existent"; we are at the other extreme, and say – "that of which a concept can be formed is certainly fictional".' And in paragraph 552 of the same work, Nietzsche offers an even more bracing version of this position: ' "Truth" is not something which is present and which has to be found to be discovered; it is something *which has to be created*, and which gives its names to a process, or better still, to the will to overpower, which in itself has no purpose: to introduce truth is a *process in infinitum*, an active determining – it is not a process of becoming conscious of something, which in itself is fixed and determined. It is merely a word for the will to power.'

Nietzsche, like Kierkegaard, never developed a systematic philosophy of imagination *per se*. Faithful to the anti-speculative impulse of existentialism, Nietzsche's pronouncements on imagination are scattered throughout his writings. It is in his views on art, however, that he offers his most consistent thinking on the subject. Nietzsche took the romantic claim that philosophy should give pride of place to art at its word. So literally indeed that he would probably have scandalized most of the romantics themselves. His extremist approach is evident in the famous catchcry of the *Will to Power* – 'art and nothing but art'. The choice is no longer between truth or fiction, but between two kinds of fiction: fiction which masquerades as truth and fiction which knows itself to be fiction. The self-acknowledged lies of art differ from the self-concealed lies of science or philosophy in that they enhance the creative playfulness of existence. 'Art is more powerful than knowledge,' affirmed Nietzsche in 1872, 'for art desires life, and knowledge achieves as its ultimate goal only destruction.'[44] But if the artistic imagination is indeed the 'great ennobler of life', it is so only to the degree that it is prepared to let *nothingness be*! This is not nihilism. For Nietzsche, nihilism is, on the contrary, the covering up of nothingness by Christianity, morality and speculative philosophy – i.e. the perverted expression of nothingness as a will to transcendent truth which in fact denies the reality of our existential world. Nihilism, in short, is the negation of *this* life in favour of another one.

Nietzsche holds that the great virtue of Greek tragedy and of certain forms of modern art – including Wagner's music – is its 'pessimism of strength'. Scorning the quest of German idealism for a transcendental unity which tries to harmonize the contradictions of reality by ignoring them, Nietzsche praises those rare artistic imaginations which dare to express the multifaceted complexity of existence. The humanistic optimism of German idealism is incompatible with Nietzsche's existentialist pessimism. Where the transcendental imagination saw coherence and totality, the existentialist imagination sees conflict and fragmentation. Moreover, the existentialist insistence on the fundamental absurdity of life – epitomized for Nietzsche in the discrepancy between man's creative will to power and the unyielding character of nature's 'eternal recurrence of the same' – is quite intolerable for the transcendental idealist. This basic contradiction in Nietzsche's dual affirmation of 1) the limitless desires of imagination and 2) the incorrigible limits of our concrete existence, is a hallmark of his existentialism. Peter Pütz accurately identifies this conflict between existential freedom (imagination) and fate (nature) as follows:

On the one hand, man has an urge to self-overcoming and self-aggrandisement – i.e. will to power – yet on the other, nature . . . admits only of the aimless repetition of the eternally identical. But how can the will to power rise above itself if the cycle of eternal recurrence obtains? How are we to conceive of Nietzsche's hoped-for 'new man' whose advent he announces, if 'eternal recurrence' only allows of a perpetuation of man as he is and has been.[45]

Nietzsche provides no solution to this dilemma. The existentialist imagination he portrays is an imagination in straits. It lives at odds with itself and with the world, even as it celebrates both. It delights in the play of its fictions, exposing at the same time the meaninglessness of the play and the emptiness of the fictions. The existentialist imagination is, for Nietzsche, one which says 'yes' to the 'no', which dances gaily on its own grave.

In section thirteen of the *Will to Power*, entitled *How the 'True World' finally became a Fable: The History of an Error*, Nietzsche states that Western philosophy is a story of how the supersensible Idea of truth, first posited by Plato as eternal Being, is not only gradually reduced from the higher to the lower, but eventually dissolves into pure fiction. Announcing the last phase of this history, a modern (perhaps even postmodern?) phase where philosophy dismantles itself altogether, Nietzsche writes: 'The true world we abolished – which world was left? The apparent one perhaps? . . . But no! Along with the true world we have also abolished the apparent one.'[46]

Several and many questions remain. Has Nietzsche really succeeded in debunking the romantic claims for creative imagination? Or has he merely replaced the optimism of romantic idealism with his own special brand of romantic pessimism – a sort of Wagnerian existentialism?[47] Furthermore, is the Nietzschean cult of the creative artist a reaffirmation of modern humanism? Or is it a subtle erosion of such humanism which already prefigures the postmodern diagnosis of the death of man? Can one still speak of imagination in terms of an individual human subject if one has effectively equated this power of creation with an activity of uncompromising negation – a defiant nothingness which reaches its fullest expression in a paradoxical *amor fati*, an act whereby the creative will of man stoically embraces the arbitrary flux of the world? These are some of the questions to which the twentieth-century existentialists would have to address themselves.

CHAPTER SIX

The Existentialist Imagination II – Sartre

The existentialist philosophy of imagination which developed in the twentieth century is, in many respects, a critical prolongation of Nietzsche's 'pessimism of strength'. If the nineteenth-century existentialists may be said to have exposed the void at the root of the romantic imagination, Sartre takes this equation of *l'imaginaire* and *le néant* as his point of departure – adding, as we shall see, a new 'phenomenological' rigour. Sartre brings the modern philosophy of imagination to its ultimate humanist conclusions. He disregards the Kierkegaardian paradox of the *leap of faith* in favour of a radical atheism. And he dismisses the Nietzschean paradox of *amor fati* by restoring the imaginative subject as an act of perpetual renovation through negation – scorning the idea of an 'eternal recurrence of the same' as a leftover from mystical paganism. Sartre's existentialist view of imagination takes the form of an unconditional humanism. The last of its kind.

Existentialism was a philosophy of dark times. If this was true for Kierkegaard and Nietzsche, it was even more true for the second generation of existentialists. By the time Sartre and his contemporaries were grappling with the meaning of existence, the 'affirmative' dreams of the enlightenment and idealist thinkers had degenerated into the nightmare of a global warfare which shook European civilization to its very foundations. The belief in the inevitable progress of history, or indeed of human consciousness, was no longer tenable after the holocaust and the barbaric consequences of modern totalitarianism.

Twentieth-century existentialism was both a symptom of, and a reaction to, these unhappy times. And so what might appear like a morbid concentration on the themes of death and *angst* cannot simply be dismissed as the passing fashion of an intellectually decadent bourgeoisie.[1] Existentialism was more than a play of abstract ideas. It was a concrete expression of the historical circumstances in which it arose. And if it is true that Sartre admitted in an interview in *Le Nouvel Observateur* shortly before his death, that he had spoken about the existential experience of 'nausea' because everybody in the Paris cafés of the thirties was speaking of it, this was not an admission of intellectual irresponsibility but a sign of how his writings were committed to a concretely lived situation.

Sartre's philosophy of imagination was, not surprisingly, a powerful testimony to these *temps modernes*. Most of this chapter will be devoted to a study of the Sartrean interpretation of imagining as a function of pure negation (*néantisation*). But Sartre was not the only thinker of our century to develop an existentialist theory of imagination. Two of his intellectual contemporaries, Martin Heidegger and Albert Camus, also made significant contributions in this field. A brief account of these contributions may usefully serve to preface and highlight Sartre's own treatment of the subject.

1 Camus

Of the twentieth-century existentialists, Camus was probably the most indebted to the Nietzschean legacy. He proclaimed the necessity of facing up to the meaninglessness of existence. But he refused to see this confrontation as in any way diminishing the 'humanist' character of the creative imagination. In an essay entitled 'Man in Rebellion' Camus asserted that to 'say yes to the world . . . is at the same time to recreate the world and oneself, it is to become the great artist, the creator.' Camus differed from the romantic idealists, however, in that he – like Nietzsche – had no illusions about the intrinsically 'absurd' nature of human creation. His various literary works from the

Stranger and *The Plague* to *The Fall* and *Caligula*, testify to
his lucid consciousness of the 'nothingness' inhabiting modern
Western culture. But it was in his philosophical essay *The Myth
of Sisyphus*, written in 1940 amid what he calls the 'French
and European disaster', that Camus most directly addressed the
contemporary crisis of nihilism. The primary aim of this essay
was, he stated, 'to meet the problem of suicide face to face'.[2]

The only authentic way of combating nihilism for Camus is to
reassert the creative power of human imagination – while
candidly admitting the 'absurd' nature of this creation. Why
absurd? Because the gap separating the imagination's desire to
transform the world and the refusal of the world to be transformed is unbridgeable. The absurd is defined, accordingly, as
the incorrigible discrepancy between man's search for meaning
and the meaninglessness of the universe.

Two of the great masters of absurd existence invoked by
Camus are Dostoyevsky and, of course, Nietzsche. The main
lesson which Camus takes from the writings of Dostoyevsky –
particularly *The Possessed* and *The Brothers Karamazov* – is that
romantic humanism is doomed to pessimism.[3] The strange virtue
of Dostoyevsky's 'absurd men', Stavrogin and Ivan Karamazov,
is that they have learned to live in this 'absurd, godless world
. . . without future and without weakness'. Their nobility resides
in the fact that they 'think clearly and have ceased to hope'.[4]
But if Dostoyevsky's characters represent, as it were, absurd
creatures, Nietzsche embodies the 'absurd creator'. In a section
of the *Myth of Sisyphus* entitled 'Absurd Creation', Camus sums
up the Nietzschean vision of existentialist imagination:

There is a metaphysical honour in ending the world's absurdity.
Conquest or play-acting, multiple loves, absurd revolt are tributes that
man pays to his dignity in a campaign in which he is defeated in
advance. . . . War cannot be negated. One must live it or die of it. So
it is with the absurd: it is a question of breathing with it, of recognizing
its lessons and recovering their flesh. In this regard the absurd joy par
excellence is creation. 'Art and nothing but art', said Nietzsche,' we
have art in order not to die of the truth.'[5]

The existentialist imagination knows that existence is a

nothingness. Yet 'even within the limits of nihilism', as Camus writes, it resolves to 'find a means to proceed beyond nihilism'.[6] And what distinguishes this existentialist imagination from its romantic predecessor is its dogged refusal to believe that its fictions are anything but fictions – its acceptance that every struggle is in vain, that every passion is ephemeral, that nothing has any real meaning. Herein lies its freedom. A negative freedom, to be sure; but a freedom nonetheless. The existentialist creators celebrated by Camus are those who 'consummate the utter futility of any individual life. Indeed, that gives them more freedom in the realization of that work, just as becoming aware of the absurdity of life authorized them to plunge into it with every excess.'[7] The greatness of the absurd creator lies in the fact that he no longer presumes to produce universal truths. He is content to produce myths – albeit 'myths with no other depth than that of human suffering and, like it, inexhaustible'.[8]

The particular myth chosen by Camus to exemplify the absurd imagination is that of Sisyphus. In Greek legend, Sisyphus was condemned by the gods to repeatedly push a rock up a mountain, knowing that on each occasion the rock would roll back again before he reached the top. And yet in this story of a man who endlessly reembarks upon an impossible task, embracing the struggle without hope of victory, Camus finds sufficient grounds for the refusal of suicide. Here at the very heart of the absurd, Camus asserts the possibility of outliving the absurd. Sisyphus *knows* his fate and actively commits himself to it. His fidelity is one that 'negates the gods and raises rocks'. Having abandoned the false consolation of metaphysical abstractions – First Causes and Absolute Origins – Sisyphus bravely accepts his destiny. Camus concludes:

There is no fate that cannot be surmounted by scorn. Thus, convinced of the wholly human origin of all that is human, a blind man eager to see, who knows that the night has no end, he is still on the go, the rock is still rolling. . . . The struggle itself towards the heights is enough to fill a man's heart.[9]

We must '*imagine* Sisyphus happy', insists Camus, even though in *reality* such happiness is an absurdity.

This opposition between imagination and reality was also a central preoccupation for Sartre. But where Camus told the story of the absurd imagination largely from a literary perspective – drawing many of his examples from Dostoyevsky and Kafka – Sartre offered a more rigorously philosophical argument based on the phenomenologial method. This difference of emphasis and method did not of course prevent these two leading exponents of French existentialism from endorsing a common humanist project – a project which comprised their intellectual debates in *Les Temps Modernes* (one of the most combative journals of post-war France); their shared, if not always harmonious, commitment to a radical politics of protest; and, above all, their common fidelity to the struggle of imagination in a meaningless world.

2 Heidegger

Sartre's philosophy of imagination was greatly inspired by the German founder of phenomenological existentialism, Martin Heidegger. This influence is most clearly in evidence in the Postscript to Sartre's early work *The Psychology of Imagination* (1940) and in his Introduction to *Being and Nothingness* (1943). Curiously, the Heideggerean text most quoted by Sartre – the monumental *Being and Time* (1927) – never explicitly deals with imagination. This enigma may be explained, however, by recalling that the concept of *Dasein* outlined in *Being and Time* is, by Heidegger's own admission, an existential reinterpretation of the Kantian concept of transcendental imagination. This admission is made in the concluding sections of Heidegger's *Kant and the Problem of Metaphysics* (see our Appendix to chapter four). Here Heidegger points out that his reading of the Kantian analysis of imagination in *The Critique of Pure Reason* is based on what Kant 'intended to say' rather than on what he actually did say – and as such involves a certain 'violence' of interpretation. Such a procedure was necessary, claims Heidegger, in order to convert Kant's 'idealist' analysis into a properly 'existential' one – i.e. a 'fundamental ontology of Dasein' which reveals that our metaphysical concepts of Being ultimately spring from the temporalizing projections of imagination. As we have already dealt with this point in some detail, we shall content ourselves here with a few summary quotations from Heidegger's conclusion to the *Kant Book*.

Heidegger writes:

Kant's laying of the foundation of metaphysics leads to the transcendental imagination. This is the common root of both stems, sensibility and understanding. As such, it makes possible the original unity of the ontological synthesis. This root itself, however, is implanted in primordial time. The primordial ground which is revealed in the Kantian laying of the foundation is time . . . The question as to Being, the fundamental question of the laying of the foundation of metaphysics, is the question of *Being and Time*.[10]

Heidegger links this discovery of the temporality of imagination with the discovery of the metaphysical abyss of Being. The existential nothingness which lurks at the heart of Being is something which Kant hit upon but was finally unprepared to confront. 'Kant's recoil from the ground which he himself revealed, namely the transcendental imagination, is', notes Heidegger, 'that movement of philosophical thought which makes manifest the destruction of the base (of metaphysics) and thus places us before the abyss (*Abgrund*) of metaphysics.'[11]

The fundamental ontology of *Dasein*, developed in *Being and Time*, is presented as an uncompromising effort to plumb the depths of this abyss. But Heidegger was of the conviction that the conversion from a transcendental to an existential perspective required a change of terminology. And this is why he replaced the term 'imagination' – which he deemed excessively charged with metaphysical connotations – with the more neutral term *Dasein*. This latter concept embodies the temporalizing activity of imagination while avoiding the idealist and romantic characteristics attached to this term by Kant and his successors (as well of course as the epistemological prejudices of traditional philosophy). By means of this change of terminology Heidegger is able to define the temporal activity of human existence as a finite being-towards-death which projects itself out of nothing towards nothing. And he is able, by the same token, to transcend the essentially 'humanist' character of the productive imagination. This point is crucial. One of Heidegger's most cherished aims is to move beyond the *anthropological* basis of modern idealism to a philosophy which reveals that human being, qua *Dasein*, is in fact grounded on the non-ground of nothingness (*Das Nichts*), a non-ground which gapes within Being. 'More primordial than man is the finitude of *Dasein*', insists Heidegger. And 'if man is only man on the basis of *Dasein* in him, then the question as to what is more primordial than man can, as a matter of principle, not be an *anthropological* one'.[12] By thus bringing the humanist philosophy of imagination to the point of its own self-overcoming as *Dasein*, Heidegger anticipates the end of imagination – and by implication the end of man. In this respect, Heidegger may be said to point beyond the modern perspective of imagination to its postmodern deconstruction.

Sartre's option to retain the concept of imagination, even in the wake of its Heideggerian overcoming, must be viewed accordingly as an option for humanism. His phenomenology of imagination is the last attempt of modern philosophy to restore an anthropological basis to the creative imagination. While he fully accepts Heidegger's equation of imagination with the radical finitude of *Dasein*, as a temporal projection from nothingness into nothingness, Sartre parts company with his mentor on the fundamental question of humanism. For Sartre, the beginning and the end of man is still man. This divergence of views is unequivocal. Indeed at the same time as Sartre was vehemently defending the absolute primacy of man in his *Existentialism and Humanism* (1946), Heidegger was arguing against this very primacy in his *Letter on Humanism* (1947).[13]

3   Sartre and the negating imagination

Sartre's first two major works, *Imagination* (1936) and *The Psychology of Imagination* (1940), were devoted to a painstaking and comprehensive description of the existential act of imagining. It was, moreover, on the basis of these two formative texts that Sartre went on to formulate his famous existentialist theories of *le néant* (*Being and Nothingness*, 1943), of freedom (*Existentialism and Humanism*, 1947) and of writing (*What is Literature?*, 1947).

In *Imagination* Sartre contents himself with a critical commentary on some modern theories of imaging, culminating in Husserl's phenomenological account of the image as an *act of consciousness* rather than a *thing in consciousness*.[14] Husserl it was, moreover, who declared in his *Ideas* (1913) that 'fiction is the source whence the knowledge of "eternal truths" draws its sustenance'.[15] This line of thinking was of tremendous consequence for Sartre. And he puts his debt to the Husserlian method squarely on record in his conclusion to *Imagination*. He affirms:

Husserl blazed the trail and no study of images can afford to ignore the wealth of insights he provided. We know that we can start afresh attempting above all to attain an intuitive vision of the intentional structure of the image. . . . The way is open for a phenomenological psychology.[16]

While *Imagination* was not an original work as such, it did enable Sartre to clear the ground and lay the stakes for his own phenomenological analysis in *The Psychology of Imagination* – the original French title of which was *L'Imaginaire: Psychologie Phénoménologique de L'Imagination*.

Sartre announces the purpose of his second book to be a 'description of the great function of consciousness to create a world of unreality – imagination'.[17] He takes as his point of departure the phenomenological disclosure of the *essential* life of consciousness as an *intentional activity*. The phenomenologist, says Sartre, is not interested in imagination as an empirical state of mind but as a phenomenon of human *significance*.[18] His task is to describe images as they first appear (*phainesthai*) to us in the form of intentional projections of consciousness; for it is only by means of such primary descriptions that we can grasp the 'essential characteristics' of the imaginative activity. Sartre isolates four such characteristics.

Firstly, the image is an *act of consciousness*. The image, in other words, is not a 'thing' deposited in memory; it is a productive activity which intends an object in a specific way. Detailed phenomenological analysis shows that the image and the percept are not so much different *objects* of consciousness as different *ways of being conscious of objects'* – i.e. the percept as a 'real' presentation of its object and the image as an 'unreal' one. When we imagine a tree, for example, we are not attending to some 'image-thing' stored as a faded impression *within* the mind (a view which Sartre rejects as the empiricist 'illusion of immanence'); we are directing ourselves towards an object by means of an intentional 'image-act'.[19]

The image is not, therefore, something which first exists in the mind – either as an innate acquisition, impressional residue or unconscious upsurge – and which subsequently becomes invested with a 'symbolic meaning'. The symbolic function is never superadded from the outside, as it were, *after* the event. It is of the very essence of the image and so cannot be detached without destroying the image itself.[20] Images are symbolically meaningful in and of themselves. Their meaning is not derived from either some *antecedent* or *subsequent* act of conceptual understanding.

The image is defined by Sartre, accordingly, as a *sui generis* act of consciousness independent of both the percept and the concept. It differs from the latter in that it provides some kind of 'intuition' of the presence of an object (whereas a concept merely intends an object in an empty non-intuitive manner). And it differs from the percept in so far as it posits its object not as really existing here and now, but (paradoxically) as being *present* in its *absence*.[21] The imaginative consciousness presents its object *as if* it were real.

This brings us to the second characteristic of the image: *quasi-observation*. Because the imaginative consciousness projects what it imagines *as if* it were real, it does not yield a perceptual observation but an unreal or *quasi* observation. It does not therefore teach us anything new, for it contains nothing that we did not already put into it, nothing that we did not know already.[22] Perception, by contrast, allows us to increase our 'knowledge' of a given object through a gradual and progressive apprehension. I can, to take Sartre's example, actually count the columns of a temple which I perceive before me as an existing reality. But I cannot count the columns of a temple which I imagine – unless, that is, I *already* know how many columns there are before I project the image. 'I can do nothing with this object which I believe myself able to describe, decipher, enumerate. The visible object is there, but I cannot see it, it is tangible but I cannot touch it, audible but I cannot hear it.'[23] The quasi-reality of the image is thus fundamentally distinct from the literal reality of the percept. The imaginary is a paradoxical phenomenon which presents things in their absence. And it is by virtue of this 'as-if' paradox that the image may be said to possess a 'certain fulness with a certain emptiness'.[24]

Thirdly, the image is a *spontaneity*. Whereas perception is essentially a 'passive genesis' of meaning which 'receives' its object, imagination is an 'active genesis' which spontaneously creates its meanings out of itself. The image is spontaneous in that it posits nothing but itself – and so is always immediately present to, and identical with, itself. Spontaneity is of the essence of imagination as a 'magical act by which one seeks *all at once* to possess an object, which for perception presents itself only gradually, by degrees and never as a whole'.[25]

Because of this unmediated access of imagination to its own meanings, consciousness discovers its *freedom*. The imaginative consciousness is free to the extent that the existence of the image and its meaning are identical. It is not determined by anything outside of itself; it enjoys, as it were, an absolute independence from the objective constraints of the perceptual world.[26] Imagination is a spontaneity of free subjectivity left entirely to its own devices. Sartre does admit, however, that this freedom can also lead to a kind of enslavement – the enslavement of consciousness to itself. This occurs whenever the spontaneity of imagination is confronted with a counter-spontaneity which it has generated from within itself. The counter-spontaneity is not 'caused' by some external, or indeed unconscious, 'influence' but results from a disintegration or alienation of spontaneity (what Sartre calls a 'resistance of the self to itself'). Thus while one often thinks of hallucinations, obsessions or evil temptations as coming from some extraneous force beyond consciousness, they are in

fact no more than a spontaneity of our own imaginary consciousness which has become divided within itself, turned back upon
itself. 'It is not that the nonthetic consciousness of imagining
ceases to grasp itself as a spontaneity,' explains Sartre, 'but it
grasps itself by means of a spellbound spontaneity'; as in a dream,
'the events occur as not being able not to happen, in correlation
with a consciousness which cannot help imagining them.'[27] We
shall be returning to this central consideration below.

Fourthly and finally, Sartre reveals the image to be a *nothingness*. Imagination differs from perception and understanding in
that it posits its object as 'nothing'. This enigmatic act of non-
positing is what Sartre defines as the 'negating' or 'unrealizing'
activity of imagination – *néantisation*. Sartre gives this example:
'To say I have an image of Pierre is equivalent to saying not only
"I do not see Pierre" but "I see nothing at all". . . . Alive,
appealing and strong as an image is, it presents its object as not
being.'[28] To project an imaginary world is *ipso facto* to negate
the real world. This nothingness of the imaginary world manifests
itself in three main ways: a) as *temporal unreality* (unlike real
time, the imaginary time of reverie, dream, fiction or art, etc.
can be slowed down or accelerated at will; it can also be reversed,
repeated or synthesized into numerous configurations of past,
present and future); b) as *spatial unreality* (the rapport between
the imaginary object and its background world is not one of
contiguity or exteriority as in the real world, but one of 'magical
interdependence' whereby a change in the object immediately
implies a change in its imagined surrounding world); c) as *inner-
worldly unreality* (unlike a real thing which is logically individu-
ated, imaginary things can assume the form of illogical and
contradictory combinations of perspectives – e.g. a Picasso or
Chagall figure can be presented upside down or back to front –
and frequently dissolve into entirely opposed images without
any causal or coherent transition).[29]

Sartre thus concludes his description of the essential characteristics of imagination by affirming that the image is an 'essential
nothingness' which must not be confused with real objects
existing in the real world. To imagine something (e.g. a tree or
the person Pierre) I must be able to negate both this thing as it

really is and the world in which it really is; for it is only by
means of such a double negation that I can intuit the *unreal*
thing in an *unreal* world. I must, in short, posit the thing as a
'nothing'. This does not of course prevent us from reacting to
the image *as if* its object were before us here and now. But,
insists Sartre, 'we seek in vain to create in ourselves the belief
that the object really exists by means of our conduct towards it;
we can pretend for a second but we cannot destroy the
immediate awareness of its *nothingness*.'[30] Sartre's discovery of
the intrinsic nothingness of the image in his opening phenomenological analysis in *The Psychology of Imagination*, provides the
basic premiss of his subsequent descriptions of the solipsistic
expressions of one's imaginative consciousness – in the realms of
art, dream, sexual passion and obsessional neurosis.

4 Figures of the solipsistic mind

If imagination is essentially an act of *negation*, it is also an act
of *fascination*. These are two sides of the same coin. It is by
nihilating (*néantir*) the real world that we become enthralled by
an imaginary one. Our fascination is related to what Sartre terms
the 'magical' quality of an imaginary object. This quality is what
allows us to possess something or to become possessed by it.
What refuses to give itself in reality can be granted to us in
unreality. Imaginative consciousness is thus described as an
'incantation destined to produce the object of one's thought, the
thing one desires, in a manner that one can take possession of
it.'[31]

   Sartre seeks to explain this complex dialectic of imaginative
fascination and possession with a number of vivid metaphors.
While these occur more or less at random throughout his
phenomenological analysis, we shall try to regroup them here in
some kind of ordered sequence of classification. These metaphorical figures offer, we believe, paradigmatic illustrations of the
existentialist imagination.

The actor

How is it that an audience comes to respond to an actor on stage *as if* he or she was a person in reality? How are we to account for that strange 'suspension of disbelief' which allows us to passionately identify with the actions and sufferings of imaginary characters? It is, replies Sartre, by means of an act of imaginative 'fascination'. Neutralizing our perceptual consciousness of a real actor (e.g. Lawrence Olivier) on a real stage (e.g. The Old Victoria Theatre), we magically transform him into the imaginary personage he represents (e.g. Hamlet). 'It is not the Prince of Denmark who becomes real in the actor,' notes Sartre, 'but the actor who becomes *unreal* as the Prince.'[32] The gestures, words, costumes and make-up of the actor cease to be *literally* perceived: they are, as it were, negated by the imagination, in their *empirical* presence, so as to allow an 'absent' or 'non-existent' *persona* – Hamlet – to appear before us in the form of a *magical* presence. The actor's face ceases to be that of Olivier in order to become that of Hamlet. Imagination brings about a 'synthetic union' of the various facial or spoken signs giving them *another life* – the life of the fictional character they embody. And the actor himself, says Sartre, experiences this imaginative transition from his *actual* self to this other *impersonated* self as a 'consciousness of *being possessed*'.[33]

This dialectic of fascination and possession is not confined to the dramatic art of the actor or impersonator. Sartre also gives examples from painting. It is, he argues, only when we become fascinated by the portrait of King Charles hanging in the gallery that we cease to perceive the actual presence of lines and colours on the material canvas and become imaginatively conscious of the quasi-presence of the dead King – who momentarily possesses the canvas *as if* he were a living presence here and now.[34] And Sartre makes a similar point in one of his essays when he argues that Guardi's paintings of Venice make us imagine the original life and power of this city 'as we have never actually *seen* it'.[35]

Midas

But if the imaginative act is thus a way of magically possessing a person, place or object in their absence (and *in spite of* their absence), this act may also have dangerous consequences. While imagination gives us a basic *freedom from* the constraints of the real world, it can easily result in our *enslavement to* an unreal one. There is, Sartre insists, something 'imperious and infantile' in the refusal of imagination to take 'distance or difficulty into account'.[36] The fascination of imagination is, after all, with the imaginary entities it has invented. It can therefore degenerate into a form of self-fascination which knows no limits, no curbs to its own desire. Condemned to his imaginings, the human subject may find himself, like Midas, imprisoned in the solipsistic circle of a self alone (*solus ipse*). Sartre writes,

Just as King Midas transformed everything he touched into gold, so consciousness is itself determined to transform into the imaginary everything it gets hold of: hence the fatal nature of the dream . . . the odyssey of consciousness dedicated by itself, and in spite of itself, to build only an unreal world.[37]

Pygmalion

The ironic character of the solipistic imagination derives from the fact that the human subject is the initiator of his own enslavement. We are not only the actors of our fictions, we are also the author. Man is a creator who becomes enthralled by his own creations. To illustrate this predicament, Sartre alludes to the motif of Pygmalion – a figure who has commanded the attention of modern artists (most notably Shaw) and who finds an ancient ancestor not only in Greek myth but also in the biblical figure of the Golem-maker. The tragedy of Pygmalion epitomizes the absurd condition of the modern imagination in so far as it seeks to fulfil its desires by means of fictions projected by its own desires. In a particularly vivid passage, Sartre explains:

The faint breath of life we breathe into images comes from us, from our own spontaneity. If we turn away from them they are destroyed . . .

Kept alive artificially, about to vanish at any moment, they cannot satisfy desires. But it is not entirely useless to construct an unreal object for it is a way of deceiving the senses momentarily, something like the effect of sea water on thirst . . . It is but a mirage, and in the imaginative act desire is nourished from itself. More exactly, the object as an image is a definite want; it takes shape as a cavity.[38]

The solipsistic imagination invites us to evade the world of reality itself. It incarcerates us in an 'anti-world' of our own making.

Narcissus

The anti-world of imagination is described by Sartre as a labyrinth of desire in which the narcissistic lover becomes obsessed with his own images. In order to possess the ideal object of our desires we may resort to an imaginary form of love – a love for love's sake. The narcissistic lover is infatuated with nothing other than himself. This gives rise to an ambivalent affection that cannot actually be *felt* (since it is no longer another person that moves me but my own fictional construct). Pure spontaneity without the slightest hint of receptivity, the object of desire becomes an icon projected from the inner void of the imaginer. Devoid of contact with the other, the narcissistic imagination becomes a monologue of the soul with itself. Unlike a real person whose inexhaustible and independent existence resists possession, the imagined *persona* of erotic fascination offers me nothing, and refuses me nothing I do not already possess. It is not the beloved who produces my feelings of desire for her; it is my desire which produces the magical presence of the beloved in the first place. Indeed this kind of imaginative infatuation presupposes the absence or intangibility of the beloved. Sartre describes this narcissistic obsession in terms of a dance around an inanimate aesthetic object:

One could speak of a dance before the unreal in the manner that a corps de ballet dances around a statue. The dancers open their arms, offer their hands, smile, offer themselves completely, approach and take flight, but the statue is not affected by it: there is no real relationship between it and the corps de ballet. Likewise, our conduct before the imaginary object cannot really touch it, qualify it, any more than it can touch us in return; because it is the heaven of the unreal beyond all touch.[39]

Narcissistic love, in short, is the symptom of man's isolated imagination. And I can only engage in it by 'unrealizing' myself in it.

The neurotic

The various metaphorical descriptions of the solipsistic imagination culminate in the figure of the neurotic. And here Sartre expresses his conviction that the modern imagination is basically *pathological* – an aspiration condemned to failure, an impossible quest to project beyond oneself to some 'other' that would be more than just a projection. Sartre cites the example of the neurotic who is his own victim and his own executioner. He believes he suffers from diseases but these are no more than symptoms of his own anguish. He seeks to bring this anguish to the surface, to give it an exterior existence, an objective embodiment. But he cannot ultimately escape from the realization that his illness is caused by nothing other than himself: 'He cries out to bring on anguish, he gesticulates to bring it into his body. But in vain: nothing will fill in that annoying impression of emptiness which constitutes the reason and basic nature of his outburst.'[40] The other side of this pathological self-suffering is, of course, the neurotic's propensity for illusions of grandeur. But the neurotic's imaginary life as, for example, a romantic Don Juan enjoying multiple amorous affairs is, Sartre insists, just another symptom of his schizophrenic imagination: he lives out a fictional scenario of sexual prowess and conquest because of his inability to love in the real world. Sartre describes this life of neurotic self-obsession as one in which the

same scenes keep on recurring to the last detail, accompanied by the same ceremonial where everything is regulated in advance, foreseen; where, above all, nothing can escape, resist or surprise. In brief, if the schizophrenic imagines so many amorous scenes it is not only because his real love has been disappointed, but because he is no longer capable of loving.[41]

Such pathological obsessions are not confined to clinically diagnosed schizophrenics. They are part and parcel of human existence as an *intrinsically imaginative project*. Sartre thus scotches the romantic fallacy that imagination is an exceptional or exalted activity of poetic genius. Every human existence takes the form of some imaginary project. Each one of us, without exception, possesses the capacity of the 'dreamer to choose from the storeroom of accessories the feelings he wishes to put on and the objects that fit them, just as the actor chooses his costume'.[42] We are captivated by the imaginary projects of our everyday experience in the same way as we are enthralled by the imaginary heroes or heroines of our aesthetic experience when we read a novel or watch a play. Thus while Sartre allows that our fictional projects – both in life and art – allow us to transcend the determining constraints of reality, this freedom is often purchased at the cost of a certain fatality.

It is here, in his early phenomenological analysis of imagination, that we find the seeds of Sartre's existential conviction that human existence is a useless passion condemned to its own nothingness, a foundationless desire to project beyond what is real to what is unreal, a captive to an absurd world where the self is never enough and 'hell is other people'. This is the world inhabited by the alienated anti-heroes of Sartre's drama and fiction: Hugo of *Les Mains Sales* who affirms *'Je vis dans un décor'*; Franz of *Les Sequestrés d'Altona* who negates the present by obsessively reliving his past; Roquentin of *La Nausée* who seeks to flee the brute contingencies of existence by aspiring towards the impossible condition of pure eternal Being – in short, all those disconsolate and fatherless creatures of Sartrean art who, negating all that preconditions them, strive in vain to create some meaningful project out of their own emptiness.[43]

5 Ontological considerations

Sartre's phenomenological description of imagining led him to the conclusion that it is not simply a 'neutralizing' of reality – as Husserl, for example, had thought – but its radical 'nullification'. In the Postscript to the *Psychology of Imagination*, he explores some of the ontological implications of this discovery of the 'nothingness' of the imaginary. How, he asks, does imagination relate to what Heidegger calls our *being-in-the-world*?

Sartre insists that the negating act of imagination cannot be dismissed as a merely 'contingent specification of the essence of consciousness'. It must be seen as the 'constitutive function of that essence'. [44] It is not a *part* but the very *basis* of consciousness. To be in the world is already to have employed the negating powers of imagination. For being-in-the-world means that we are conscious *of* the world; and this, in turn, presupposes our consciousness of *not being* in this world. The intentional 'of' distances us from objects at the same time as it relates us to them. Our capacity to withdraw from the world in order to be conscious of it derives ultimately from imagination. Without the negating power of imagination, even the real world itself (not to mention the imaginary) could not exist as a meaningful 'synthetic totality'.

Man's being-in-the-world, Sartre claims, is an act of free transcendence which surpasses actual 'facts' towards possible 'meanings'. And it is thanks to this distancing act that man ceases to be a mere 'being-in-the-midst-of-things', immersed in brute actuality. To acknowledge this omnipresent activity of imagination is to acknowledge our freedom from the given reality. And, by contrast, to ignore this 'surpassing and nullifying' power of imagination, is to become 'swallowed up in the existent'. Deprived of imagination the human subject is 'crushed in the world, run through by the real'; he is reduced to the condition of a mere thing in the midst of things. [45] 'However, as soon as he apprehends in one way or another, the whole as a situation, he retreats from it towards that in relation to which he is a lack' – i.e. the imaginary. [46] Human consciousness is, therefore, to be equated with freedom to the extent that it is always moving beyond the real towards the imaginary. Sartre says:

We may conclude that imagination is not an empirical and superadded power of consciousness; it is the whole of consciousness as it realizes its freedom. Every concrete, real situation of consciousness in the world is big with imagination in so far as it always presents itself as a withdrawing from the real.[47]

It is impossible to conceive of a human consciousness which would not be 'imaginative'; for such a consciousness would no longer be *human* but a mere thing engulfed in the world.[48] Reinterpreting the Kantian notion of imagination in existentialist terms, Sartre affirms that it is only because man is transcendentally free that he can imagine, and only because he can imagine that he is transcendentally free. It is the possibility of the unreal which provides us with the freedom to found the real. It is the hint of an absent world which pulls our present one into shape and endows it with meaning. Sartre writes:

The imaginary appears on the foundation of the world but reciprocally all apprehension of the real as world implies a hidden surpassing towards the imaginary . . . So imagination, far from appearing as an actual characteristic of consciousness turns out to be an essential and transcendental condition of consciousness.[49]

The imaginary world of art differs radically, however, from the everyday world of existence in so far as it is the result of a double negation. It is, as it were, the most complete expression of imagination in that it presupposes both a primary and secondary act of 'nullification'. Art is a state of pure 'nothingness' utterly irreducible to the universe of perceptible things. 'What is beautiful', affirms Sartre accordingly, 'is something which cannot be experienced as a perception and which by its very nature is out of this world.'[50] And it is precisely this mutual exclusiveness of aesthetic imagination and everyday perception which accounts for that peculiar discomfiture one experiences on leaving a theatre or concert hall or on closing a novel. As Sartre puts it: 'Aesthetic contemplation is an induced dream and the passing into the real is an actual waking up.'[51]

Here again, Sartre displays a marked Kantian influence. He insists in the Postscript to the *Psychology of Imagination* that art possesses its own finality – a purposiveness without purpose – which solicits in the beholder an attitude of 'disinterestedness'. He thus repudiates those traditional philosophers who, like Plato, rebuked art for its uselessness or immorality. The gulf separating the imaginary and the real means that the aesthetic order is totally removed from the ethical. Artistic beauty is 'untouchable, beyond our reach'. And this, concedes Sartre, is why, 'we cannot at the same time place ourselves on the plane of the aesthetic where the unreal . . . which we admire appears, and on the realistic plane of physical appropriation'.[52]

The conclusions to *The Psychology of Imagination* serve, in many respects, as the premises of *Being and Nothingness*, published just three years later in 1943. The basic phenomenological dualism between the 'real' and the 'imaginary' lies at the root of Sartre's famous ontological dualism between being-in-itself (*en soi*) and being-for-itself (*pour soi*). While the former category comprises the brute material facticity of things (e.g. a table or a tree), the latter designates the power of consciousness to negate the *en soi* and thereby achieve a distance or freedom from it – that is, an existence *pour soi*. But this free consciousness is only free because it is a 'nothingness' – that is, a perpetual negation of the outer world of the *en soi* which it is *not*. The ultimate goal of consciousness is to remain free and yet to fill in the basic lack of being which makes up its nothingness. It seeks to combine the inner freedom of existence *pour soi* with the outer necessity of being *en soi*.

Such a synthesis of pure freedom and pure necessity – of the lack of consciousness and the fullness of reality – is defined by Sartre as the project to be God. God represents the ideal synthesis of *pour-soi-en-soi*: the freedom which is the cause of its own necessity as *ens causa sui*. But while Sartre admits that such an ideal project of divine existence is what every human subject desires, he declares such a project to be impossible. Nothingness and being are opposites which can never be reconciled: each category exists by virtue of an absolute negation which separates them. God does not exist, Sartre concludes, and man (as the project to be God) is a futile desire in an absurd world. As the now celebrated formula runs:

Every human reality is a passion in that it projects losing itself so as to found being and by the same stroke to constitute the in-itself which escapes contingency by being its own foundation, the *Ens Causa Sui*, which religions call God. . . . But the idea of God is contradictory and we lose ourselves in vain. Man is a useless passion.[53]

The ultimate human project to be God is a mere fiction that can never be realized. It possesses all the 'unreality' of an imaginary object. It is a *nothingness* projected by an imaginative consciousness.

This so-called 'nihilistic' conclusion to *Being and Nothingness* may be seen as the logical consequence of the conclusion to the *Psychology of Imagination* – i.e. that 'the imaginary is the something towards which the existent is surpassed'.[54] While he had already acknowledged in *The Psychology of Imagination* that 'there can be no developing consciousness without imaginative consciousness', it is only in *Being and Nothingness* that he explicitly identifies the *goal* of our negating consciousness (which he now rechristens the *pour-soi*) as *value*. Human existence, he now states, 'cannot appear without being haunted by value and projected towards its own possibilities'.[55] Value is thus defined by Sartre as the possibility of a meaningful and unified existence: an always *absent* possibility which we imagine in order to try to make some sense of our experience, what is not yet determining what is.[56] This *possibility* of value is precisely what consciousness *lacks* (and so can only present to itself in the form of an imaginary absence). It is the imaginary 'something' which every human existence *is not*, but desires to *be*.[57]

And here's the rub. This imaginary 'something' is in fact 'nothing'. The possibility of value does not exist. It is that which *is not*. It cannot be defined as *being*. For, as Sartre makes clear, 'being in-itself cannot have potentialities for in itself it is what it is – the absolute plenitude of its identity'.[58] And furthermore, being in-itself is precisely that which cannot have *meaning* because it is exactly the opposite of intentional consciousness (which alone projects 'possibilities' out of itself as an act of negation). Sartre is thus led to the unavoidable conclusion that meaning is nothing other than the *nothingness* projected by the imagining subject himself.

Unlike Heidegger's post-humanist definition of 'nothingness' as a 'veil of being' which is irreducible to human consciousness (*What is Metaphysics?*, 1933), Sartre insists on a radically humanist appraisal of *le néant* as a gratuitous product of man's existence. To posit value as an independently existing entity is, for Sartre, to threaten the sovereignty of human freedom. In short, that value which man projects beyond himself (as a possibility of total meaning towards which he surpasses himself and his world) ultimately originates from the empty negating consciousness of his own imagination.[59] The coveted possibility of value, which all men lack and struggle to realize, must perpetually remain an absence. Sartre is thus compelled to admit that, even on an ontological level, the human subject is caught in the vicious circle of his own nothingness. And so if man is indeed free he is, by the same token, 'an unhappy consciousness with no possibility of surpassing his unhappy state'.[60] He is condemned to be free because he is condemned to himself. In the kingdom of the absurd the solipsist reigns supreme.

6 Humanism revisited

In subsequent writings Sartre endeavoured to modify the ontological conclusions of *The Psychology of Imagination* and *Being and Nothingness*. Having demonstrated that the existentialist imagination is predicated upon a negation of reality which appears to deprive man of meaning and make moral action virtually impossible, Sartre resolved to defend his philosophy as a fundamental *humanism*. He would try to argue that the existentialist imagination still remains a 'humanist' imagination.

The question of ethics

Existentialism and Humanism (1946) was written just after the war with the express purpose of countering those critics who held that the Sartrean description of man as a 'useless passion' threatened the very basis of Western humanist culture. (The original French title of this work – inexplicably altered in the English translation – makes this polemical intent clear: *L'Existentialisme 'est' un Humanisme*). The author does not deny his original conviction that man is, by virtue of his imagination, a being who creates himself *ex nihilo*, that is, out of the sole resources of his own subjective consciousness. But he now affirms that such a conviction is compatible with a 'fundamental anthropology' which allows for an ethical humanism.

How does Sartre justify this claim? If imagination is indeed 'the transcendental condition of all consciousness' then it follows that man's 'existence precedes his essence', that each subject makes himself what he is. And this means that man is not only aesthetically, but also ethically, *responsible* for what he does. There is no such thing as a given human 'essence' which would predetermine the subsequent acts of our 'existence'. Each one of us is alone responsible for what we become: we are entirely free to choose the values we wish to have for our existence. Man is what he is, therefore, not because he was born like that (i.e. genetically conditioned); nor because he was so determined by external environmental factors such as social upbringing or class conditioning. Man is what he is for the simple reason that he has chosen to be so. And he is always free to choose otherwise.

Sartre does not, of course, deny that each human consciousness finds itself in a particular place (society) and time (history) which pre-exists his free choices. We are all born into an existential *situation* not of our choosing: this is what Sartre, following Heidegger, calls our 'facticity'. But within such factual circumstances each individual remains free to give to his situation whatever meaning or value he decides. And this comprises, as we have seen, a project of imagination which negates what is in order to open up possibilities of what is not yet. 'What is alarming in the doctrine I am proposing', comments Sartre, 'is that it confronts man with a possibility of choice.'[61]

Sartre's humanist doctrine of absolute freedom necessarily implies atheism. And not simply because God is a logical or ontological contradiction, as had been argued in *Being and*

Nothingness. God's existence cannot be affirmed, Sartre now implies, for the ethical reason that to do so is to deprive man of his existential freedom. Man is only free to create his own essence, and to take entire responsibility for this creation – to the extent that there is no Divine Mind to preconceive it 'following a definition and a formula'. Rejecting Kierkegaard's theistic existentialism, Sartre states that the truly authentic individual is one who makes not a 'leap towards God' but a 'leap towards existence', willing himself to become what he imagines himself to be. This unconditional affirmation of the creativity of man is, Sartre insists, a necessary consequence of the existentialist repudiation of theism. The ethical individual is henceforth to be defined as a humanist subject who accepts that he 'first of all exists and defines himself afterwards'.

'Authenticity' becomes the key moral category of Sartrean existentialism. In contrast to the traditional notion of 'sincerity', which determined the self by its relation to others (God, society, family, nation, etc.), the authentic self is 'auto-creative' (*auto-hentes*): it relies on no other meaning outside of its own autonomous subjectivity.[62] The first ethical effect of existentialism, Sartre asserts accordingly, is that it puts every man in possession of himself and places the total responsibility for his existence squarely on his own shoulders. The great moral lesson of humanist existentialism is: 'You are free, therefore choose.'

Sartre at no point revokes the original claim of his early works that imagination is the creative source of all meaning. What he does wish to alter, however, is the observation made in his Postscript to *The Psychology of Imagination* that the aesthetic projects of imagination are incompatible with morality. Reinterpreting the aesthetic model of experience, Sartre now affirms that the human act of self-creation is in itself an act of moral commitment: 'In life man commits himself, draws his own portrait and there is nothing but this portrait.' And he goes on to explain this telling analogy as follows:

Moral choice is comparable to the construction of a work of art . . . Does anyone reproach an artist when he paints a picture for not following rules established *a priori*? Does one ever ask what is the

picture that he ought to paint? As everyone knows, there is no pre-
defined picture for him to make; the artist applies himself to the composition of a picture, and the picture that ought to be made is precisely
that which he will have made. As everyone knows, there are no aesthetic
values *a priori*, but there are values which will appear in due course in
the coherence of the picture, in the relation between the will to create
and the finished work. No one can tell what the painting of tomorrow
will be like; one cannot judge a painting until it is done. What has that
to do with morality? We are in the same creative situation. We never
speak of a work of art as irresponsible; when we are discussing a canvas
by Picasso, we understand very well that the composition became what
it is at the time when he was painting and that his works are part and
parcel of his entire life. It is the same on the plane of morality. There
is this in common between art and morality, that in both we have to
do with creation and invention.[63]

But the argument is not yet won. Sartre has still to answer
the vexed question: what actually *justifies* such acts of individual
creation? If everything is permitted, as Sartre's existentialism of
freedom demands, then what makes one man's moral choice of
self-creation any better than another's? What, in other words,
determines whether our moral inventions are good or bad,
useless passions or ethically meaningful actions? What is there
to prevent Sartre's humanist vision of morally self-determining
individuals from degenerating into Raskolnikov's nightmare in
Crime and Punishment:

Never had men believed themselves to be so wise, so sure of possessing
truth. Never before had they such confidence in the infallibility of their
judgements, their theories, their moral principles. . . . But all were
victims of their own anguish and unable to comprehend each other.
Each individual however believed himself to be the sole possessor of
truth and became depressed at the sight of his fellows. . . . They could
no longer agree among themselves as to what sanctions to adopt towards
good and evil, and knew not who to condemn and who to absolve. They
ended up killing each other in a sort of absurd fury.[64]

Faced with this prospect of the collapse of morality into an
absolute relativism of conflicting values, Sartre takes a step back

from his existentialist theory of imagination – though he does not explicitly acknowledge this – and has recourse to the Kantian doctrine of practical reason. Only by resorting to the Kantian doctrine of the 'categorical imperative' (i.e. that every individual must always act in a way that is universalizable for others), can Sartre hope for a solution to his dilemma. To save his humanism, Sartre feels himself obliged to invoke the 'universalist' principles of Kant and the enlightenment thinkers. But in so doing, Sartre is faced with another dilemma: the choice between the primacy of imagination and reason. For while the appeal to the universality of reason does indeed provide necessary and objective grounds for moral judgement, it appears to do so at the expense of the primacy of the creative imaginative subject.

The question of literature

Sartre admits as much in his subsequent work *Existentialism and Literature* (1947). Here he begins by making a distinction between two kinds of writing: 'poetry' based on the opacity of imagination, and 'prose' based on the transparency of signification. Only the latter, he now asserts, is capable of ethical commitment. Imaginative literature is deemed *non-engagé* to the extent that it becomes engrossed in its own poetic fictions rather than directing our attention to the world itself. Returning somewhat to the position of *L'Imaginaire*, Sartre describes how the works of poetic imagination 'enchant' and 'fascinate' their audience, lulling them into a state of magical unreality and passive contemplation. The very idea of a 'poetic engagement' is, Sartre admits, a contradiction in terms – for the poet uses words not as *signs* of the real world but as *images* of his own consciousness.[65] 'The word which tears the writer of prose away from himself and throws him into the midst of the world', he says, 'sends back to the poet his own image.'[66] The poetic imagination does not seek to communicate a message but rather to induce a state of intuitive silence – one which withdraws us from the world.

Sartre affirms accordingly that it is only prose literature which is capable of a moral or political commitment; for it alone explodes the pretence of imaginative autonomy and points beyond itself, as writing, to the world of social reality. The authentic writer is therefore, Sartre suggests, one who renounces imagination out of an ethical fidelity to reality. At certain moments Sartre almost seems to be endorsing the moralist doctrine of Socialist Realism – as, for example, when he states that 'prose is in essence utilitarian' and defines the prose-writer as one who 'makes use of words';[67] or when he asserts that the 'engaged writer knows that words are actions . . . that to reveal is to change';[68] or again when he compares words to 'loaded pistols' and describes the committed author as someone who 'fires when he speaks', aware that 'since he has chosen to fire, he must do it like a man, by aiming at targets, and not like a child, at random, by shutting his eyes and firing merely for the pleasure of hearing the shots go off'.[69] The prose writer, in short, is he who has laid aside the charms of the solipsistic imagination in order to 'reveal man to other men so that the latter may assume full responsibility before the reality which has been laid bare'.[70]

But this ability of prose writing to lay bare the reality it writes about, also requires a renunciation of the emotive or 'passional' character of the imagination – a character which, as Sartre had demonstrated in both *The Psychology of Imagination* and his *Sketch for the Theory of Emotions* (1939), makes us captive to a 'magical' world of unreality. 'Freedom is alienated in the state of passion', Sartre now insists, adverting to the fact that the etymological origin of this term, *patio-patiri-passum*, carries the meaning of a passive suffering of things rather than an active transformation of them.[71] Prose differs from poetry in that it invites us to move beyond the blindness of imaginative passion – where 'freedom becomes caprice'[72] – to the lucid transparency of reflective consciousness. Only *prose* literature can commit us to moral outrage and political struggle. And there is little doubt that Sartre would have endorsed Adorno's conviction that after Auschwitz *poetry* is no longer possible.

The question of history

It is in this post-war manifesto of *la littérature engagée* that Sartre first hints at the necessity of moving from an existentialism of subjective imagination to a Marxism of dialectical reason – a move which was to determine the basic thrust of most of Sartre's philosophical writings from the fifties onwards, and in particular his two volumes of *The Critique of Dialectical Reason*. The final aim of all committed writers, says Sartre in his conclusion to *Existentialism and Literature*, is the 'self-reflective awareness of a classless society'.[73] The isolationist consciousness of imagination must give way to a 'collectivity which constantly corrects, judges and metamorphoses itself'.[74] Authentic freedom is now projected as a 'utopian' goal of historical revolution where aesthetics and ethics would no longer be opposed. And a committed literature is defined as one which aspires to the collective subjectivity 'of a society in permanent revolution': a society capable of transcending the antinomy of word and action, image and reality, to which the solipsistic imagination was condemned. Only with such a goal in mind, concludes Sartre, can we 'discern the moral imperative at the heart of the aesthetic imperative'.[75]

Some commentators have remained very critical of Sartre's shift from an 'individualist' to a 'collectivist' perspective. René Girard, for example, sees this move as intrinsic to the very logic of the existentialist imagination which, having negated all others and indeed the world itself, ends up as an empty nothingness indistinguishable from all others. The contemporary heroes of existentialism believe themselves to be perfectly autonomous, dependent on no one but themselves, and thereby prolong what Girard calls 'the Promethean dreams to which the modern world is desperately attached . . . and which one obstinately pursues in the name of liberty, in the very midst of anguish and chaos'.[76] But this modern dream of individual autonomy and universal separation easily leads to its opposite – anonymous collectivity. The existentialist subject, argues Girard, is never 'closer to *others* than when he believes himself totally separated from them. *Me, I'm alone and they are all* . . . the interchangeable nature of the pronouns (in this typically existentialist catch-cry) abruptly turns from the individual to the collective. Modern petit-bourgeois individualism has completely emptied itself of any content whatsoever.'[77] The existentialist 'myths of solitude – sublime, scornful, ironic or even mystical', concludes Girard, 'regularly alternate with the opposite and equally false myths of total abandonment to the social and collective forms of historical existence.'[78]

Whatever one may think about the accuracy of Girard's analysis, one ought not to forget that Sartre's transition from individualism to collectivism was deeply motivated by an ethical desire to defend the values of humanism. He was keenly aware that if the negating imagination is left to its own resources it ultimately collapses into the darkness of the existential void. The lamp of idealism grows dim; and the humanist adventure of modern man comes to grief on the barren rocks of pure negativity. And so Sartre came to believe that only an appeal to a philosophy of history, which makes the freedom of the solitary subject answerable to the freedom of the collective subject, could salvage the dignity of humanism. This is surely what he had in mind when he stated in the first volume of *The Critique of Dialectical Reason* (1960) that Marxism was the unsurpassable horizon of modern philosophy. Such an horizon of collective commitment could alone preserve the humanist project by setting limits to the existentialist project.

And, curiously, we find Sartre's line of argument here leading him away from the idealist paradigm of the 'lamp' and back to the mimetic paradigm of the 'mirror'. This traditional paradigm had of course been radically 'humanized' by the Marxist turn: it no longer referred to a subservient mimesis of some transcendent meaning but to a revolutionary mimesis of our historical struggle. All morally or politically committed art now becomes, in Sartre's words, 'the flaming mirror which burns everything reflected in it' by way of prefiguring the 'outline of a future order'.[79]

This self-cancellation of the existential imagination – in the guise of the lamp returned mirror – is reflected in a number of related reversals. 'Committed' art is finally considered superior to a purely 'imaginary' art in that it asserts the priority of a) reflective reason over pre-reflective passion; b) social utility over aesthetic uselessness; and c) the collective over the private subject. It is as though Sartre believed it necessary to radically rethink existentialism in order to save humanism – taking a step back into enlightenment rationalism or sideways into revolutionary Marxism.[80]

7 Conclusion

Sartre seems to have realized that it was not possible to remain faithful to both the 'individualist' claims of his early philosophy of imagination and to the 'universalist' claims of humanism. The existential imagination's will to absolute autonomy led to the imprisonment of each individual in its own self. It gave rise to that malady of modern anguish so vividly portrayed in Sartre's literary descriptions of the solitary subject pitting himself against an anonymous mankind, crippled by nausea, paralysed by inaction and weighed down by the absurdities of existence.

With Sartre, the existential imagination found itself incorrigibly bound to a life of pathological negation, a life which ruled out the possibility of ethical commitment to others. *L'enfer, c'est les autres*, proclaimed Sartre in *No Exit*, a play which explores how the individual imagination seeks to retain its freedom by negating the threat of the other. The negating consciousness cannot be free and at the same time sustain ethical relationships with other human subjects. This point was amply demonstrated by Sartre in *Being and Nothingness* when he described how all attempts to establish such relations degenerate into *sadism* (where the free subject negates the other as an unfree object) or *masochism* (where the subject surrenders his freedom and submits himself to the negating will of the other). The only remaining alternative to this intersubjective dialectic of sadism and masochism, is *indifference*. But Sartre points out that the human imagination can never succeed in remaining completely indifferent to the existence of others. For as a temporal projection which perpetually recalls the past and anticipates the future, human consciousness is condemned to imagine the possible presence of the other – even in his absence.[81]

This condemnation of the self to others is our *facticity*. It is the reverse side of our *freedom* as a condemnation of the self to itself. While the romantic imagination sought to ignore the obstacles of human facticity, the existential imagination is compelled to confront the absurd limits of its existence as a being-in-the-world-with-others. It can, of course, choose to *negate* these limits. Indeed its very illusion of absolute autonomy is constructed on the basis of such negation. But negation, as Sartre reminds us, is also and in all cases a mode of relating, however destructively, to the other. Even the nullifying consciousness which prides itself on its solitary freedom is haunted by the relentless presence of the other which it must forever negate in order to preserve its freedom. We cannot live with the other and we cannot live without him. And all efforts to resolve this absurd paradox are no more than exercises in 'bad faith'. The existential imagination can only be authentic, it seems, if it accepts its ineluctable condition as a 'useless passion'. And the unavoidable conclusion of such a condition, as Sartre conceded in *Being and Nothingness*, is that it makes no difference whether one gets drunk in a bar or joins the revolution.

Try as he might to revise this conclusion in *Existentialism and Humanism*, Sartre failed to reconcile the conflicting claims of an existentialist imagination and a humanist ethics. The choice which Sartre ultimately faced was between the sovereign nothingness of an isolated imagination and the affirmation of a collective commitment to revolutionary action. By ostensibly opting for the latter, Sartre no doubt believed that he could give a second wind to the beleagured project of humanism. And even though Sartre himself never explicitly admitted as much, his arguments all point to the same unavoidable conviction: the existentialist imagination must die for humanist man to live on . . .

To live on for a while, at least. The postmodern philosophers, as we shall see, would put a stop to such hopes of a humanist revival. The Sartrean project would be dismissed as man's last gasp, the defiant death-rattle of the anthropological era. Viewed from the postmoderm perspective, the demise of imagination would be deemed inseparable from the demise of man. And neither would be regretted.

PART III

Postmodern Narratives

CHAPTER SEVEN

The Parodic Imagination

What has become of the concept of imagination in the post-modern era? In our Civilization of the Image might we not expect to find imagination accorded a privileged place by contemporary philosophers? The very opposite is the case. Right across the spectrum of structuralist, post-structuralist and deconstructionist thinking, one notes a common concern to dismantle the very notion of imagination. Where it is spoken of at all, it is subjected to suspicion or denigrated as an outdated humanist illusion spawned by the modern movements of romantic idealism and existentialism. The philosophical category of imagination, like that of 'man' himself, appears to be dissolving into an anonymous play of language. For many postmodern thinkers, it has become little more than the surface signifier of a linguistic system.

Curiously, the collective term 'the imaginary' survives to some extent the philosophical decline of the subjective term 'the imagination'. This former term increasingly carries the conno-tation of an impersonal entity. The 'imaginary' is seen as a mere 'effect' of a technologically transmitted sign system over which the individual creative subject has no control. In a colloquium held in January 1986 in the Beaubourg Centre in Paris, on the role of the contemporary artist and intellectual, one contributor, Max Gallo, anxiously observed that we are living in a society 'traversed by an *imaginaire* which comes from elsewhere and which we no longer master'.[1] Seduced by the summary ideol-ogies of the latest media cult or craze, we seem to have entered an age where reality is inseparable from the image, where the original has been replaced by its imitation, where our understanding of the world is preconditioned by the electronically reproducible media of television, cinema, video and radio – media in which every 'live' event or performance is capable of being mechanically recorded and retransmitted *ad infinitum*.

The postmodern experience of the demise of the creative humanist imagination and its replacement by a depersonalized consumer system of pseudo-images is, of course, intimately bound up with the historical impact of the Graphic Revolution. This revolution, initiated by the technological advances in both the print and televisual media, has radically transformed our ability to construct, preserve and communicate images. As printed matter was supplemented by, and eventually subordinated to, photography, radio and television, the representational image soon began to overshadow reality itself. History became a pale replica of its own reproduction: the Western cowboy an inferior imitation of John Wayne or Robert Redford; the Vietnam battlefield or Belfast riot a mere representation of sensational television reports. Similarly with the introduction of the 'press release' device by news managers: one finds news events becoming performances in which the politician or celebrity simply act out scripts prepared beforehand for 'future release'. In short, the technological innovations in image reproduction have made the imaginary more persuasive than the real world. The citizens of our post-industrial society, as Daniel Boorstin remarks, live in a world 'where fantasy is more real than reality, where the image has more dignity than its original. We hardly dare face our bewilderment, because the solace of belief in contrived reality is so thoroughly real.'2

Postmodern philosophies, as we shall see, reflect this crisis of the imaginary in a variety of ways. But we may say, by way of anticipation, that a central feature of such philosophies is the undermining of the humanist imagination understood as an 'original' creation of meaning. The postmodern philosophers deny the very idea of 'origin'. Meaning is deconstructed into an endless play of linguistic signs, each one of which relates to the other in a parodic circle. There is no possibility of a single

founding reference. Language, as an open-ended play of signifiers, is no longer thought to refer to some 'real' meaning *external*
to language (i.e. some 'transcendental signified' called truth or
human subjectivity). Deprived of the concept of *origin*, the
concept of imagination itself collapses. For imagination always
presupposed the idea of origination: the derivation of our images
from some original presence. And this position obtained regardless of whether the model of origination was situated *outside* of
man (as in the biblical God of creation or the Platonic Ideas) or
inside of man (as in the model of a productive consciousness
promoted by modern idealism and existentialism).

The deconstruction of the category of 'origin' is heralded by
the famous *textual revolution*. The humanist concept of 'man'
gives way to the anti-humanist concept of intertextual play. The
autonomous subject disappears into the anonymous operations
of language. Truth is replaced by parody, and the diachronic
pattern of narrative history (with a beginning, middle and end)
by achronic patterns of repetition and recurrence. The modern
philosophy of the creative imagination – whether it be in the
form of Kant's transcendental imagination or Sartre's absurd
passion – cannot, it would seem, survive this deconstructive
turn.

This paradigm shift is evident once again at the level of dominant metaphors: a level where imagination offers, as it were, an
interpretation of its own epochal mutations. While the
premodern paradigm was expressed by the metaphor of the
mirror (which reflected the light of a transcendental origin
beyond itself), and the modern by the metaphor of the *lamp*
(which projected an original light from within itself), the postmodern paradigm is typified by the metaphor of the *looking glass*
– or to be more precise, of an interplay between multiple looking
glasses which reflect each other interminably. The postmodern
paradigm is, in other words, that of a labyrinth of mirrors which
extend infinitely in all directions – a labyrinth where the image
of the self (as a presence to itself) dissolves into self-parody.

The parodic paradigm recurs time and again in postmodern
works of art and literature. The idea of the text as a labyrinthine
mirror-play constructed in terms of its own *mise en abîme* is a

common obsession of writers such as Borges, Beckett, Pynchon or Calvino. And one might also mention in this connection, Jean Genet's *Adame Miroir*, where Adam's original desire to create a new world out of his imagination degenerates into a mockery of itself 'embracing perversely images in a mirror within a mirror'.[3] Visual artists have been equally aware of the parodic paradigm. Marcel Duchamp announces the end of humanist art as an expression of the creative imagination: art becomes an anti-art which ironically mimics the dehumanizing tendencies of our mechanistic age. The works of Lichtenstein, Beuys, Ben Vautier, Ballagh and Warhol confirm this conviction. Warhol, for example, represents the dissolution of the personality of the artist in the mechanical gesture of reproducing media images. He uses a seriographic technique which replaces the notion of an 'authentic' original with that of a multiple series. Here art derides itself by playing on the idea of the image as an artificial imitation of another equally artificial image. Reflecting the consumerist ideology of interchangeable cultural objects, Warhol's pop art negates the humanist notion of creative subjectivity. Hence Warhol's response to the news that Picasso had produced four thousand paintings in his life was to declare: 'I can do as many in twenty four hours – four thousand works which will all be the same work and all of them masterpieces.'[4] The phenomenon of a unique human imagination producing a unique aesthetic object in a unique time and space thus collapses into a play of infinite repetition. The work becomes absolutely transparent, a mechanically reproducible surface without depth or interiority, a copy with no reference to anything other than a pseudo-world of copies.[5]

We shall be offering a more extensive critique of the parodic paradigm of postmodern art, literature and cinema in our next chapter. But first we wish to pursue our analysis of this paradigm within the parameters of contemporary philosophy. The postmodern turn of deconstructionist thinking pushes the model of *reflexivity* beyond the modern preoccupation with subjective inwardness. Reflexivity, as the reference of something back onto itself, ceases to apply to the individual subject as in Kant or Sartre – it becomes, as it were, an end in itself: a mirroring which mirrors nothing but the act of mirroring. Consequently, imagination can only affirm itself as a parody of itself, an affirmation which is its own negation, a truth which – like the Cretan liar of the sceptics – knows itself to be a lie. Thus we find Derrida, for example, tilting the Nietzschean maxim that 'truth is a woman' towards its postmodern conclusion: 'If woman is truth, *she* at least knows that there is no truth, that truth has no place here and that no one has a place for truth. And she is a woman because she herself does not believe in truth itself, because she does not believe in what she is, in what she is believed to be, in what she thus is not.'[6]

Postmodernism presents us, in a curious way, with a return of the *mimesis* model. But a return which is an inversion, a self-parody. For now we are concerned not with the imitation of some pre-existing truth, but with an imitation of an imitation which avows that there exists no original beyond itself. And this parodic reversal is, of course, echoed in the very style of deconstructionist discourse, in its brand of self-erasing writing where the images and metaphors of traditional metaphysics are turned inside out until they cancel each other, where the very process of representation is revoked as soon as it is posited. Hilary Lawson puts this point well in *Reflexivity: The Post-Modern Predicament*:

Derrida is forced into saying that he is playing among the webs of language – parodying himself and then parodying the parody. He is no longer trying to write of the end of the metaphysics of presence, for that description was itself just a play and a parody of others. Thus there is no centre of Derrida's writing, no sentence or portion of the text that can be considered the core of his thought.[7]

This gives one some idea of the difficulty of identifying any dominant concept of the imagination or the imaginary in the philosophy of deconstruction. But Derrida is, so to speak, the final stage of such a philosophy. Before embarking on a more detailed examination of Derrida's own writings on parody, we shall first look at some of the preceding phases of the postmodern critique of the humanist imagination.

1 Lacan: the dismantling of the imaginary

One of the prime factors in the postmodern erosion of the humanist subject has been the discovery of the unconscious. Freud himself appears to have recognized this in later writings such as *Civilization and Its Discontents* when he alerts us to the destructive potential of unconstrained libidinal desire. Humanist civilization, he warns, may well collapse if the conscious *Ego* loses its grip on the unconscious *Id*. The orthodox movement of psychoanalysis has generally adhered to this admonition. And one even finds humanist philosophers such as Sartre rejectimg the very existence of the unconscious altogether on the grounds that it represents a denial of the human subject's freedom and responsibility. For Sartre, the unconscious is totally incompatible with the autonomous consciousness of man founded in the self-projecting acts of the imagination.

Certain postmodern thinkers of a structuralist or post-structuralist persuasion have, however, chosen to interpret the discovery of the unconscious in a quite different way. Lacan, Althusser, Foucault, Lévi-Strauss and Derrida seem to celebrate the disclosure of an unconscious system of language as a key to the dismantling of the humanist imagination understood as an autonomous entity. Lacan was the first to challenge the humanist reading of Freud. Citing Freud's famous dictum – *Wo Es war, so will Ich werden* (where the unconscious Id was, there the conscious Ego will be) – Lacan takes this to mean that consciousness must open itself to the unconscious: *là où fut ça, il me faut advenir.* He thus opposes the standard humanist recommendation that the conscious Ego should triumph over the unconscious Id, thereby controlling and mastering its desires. On the contrary, he insists, it is the self-contained Ego (*Ich*) which must give way to the self-dissolving Id (*Es*). Lacan's celebrated 'return to Freud' takes the form of a basic anti-humanism.

The radical character of Lacan's position is summed up in his structuralist formula – 'the unconscious is structured like a language'. Structuralist linguistics, as initially outlined by Saussure, subordinated the speech of the individual subject (*parole*) to the impersonal system of language as a whole (*langue*). Lacan called for an analogous subordination of individual consciousness to the hidden structures of the unconscious. He staunchly repudiated the 'ego psychology' propagated by Heinz Hartman and the orthodox school of American psychoanalysis whose primary aim was to 'adapt' so-called 'ab-normal' citizens to the established norm of humanist society. Lacan denounced this cult of the 'normal man'. He saw it as a reactionary form of 'human engineering', a 're-education programme' devoted to the production of well functioning citizens with fortified cognitive egos '(.e. egos based on a false sense of *identity* and *autonomy*).[8]

Instead of cultivating the humanist ideal of self-identity, Lacan sought to expose it as an 'imaginary' contrivance. The *imaginary* level of illusion must, he believed, be unravelled in order that the *symbolic* language of unconscious desire be heard. Taking his cue once again from the structuralist model of linguistics, Lacan held that in the language of the unconscious the 'signifier' (word) is freed from any fixed reference to a 'signified' (idea). Each signifier refers to other signifiers in an endless chain of associative play. The signifiers are not tied to any determinate truth existing beyond the language of unconscious desire. There is no fixed point of 'origin' either in the conscious self or in the outside world. And any attempt to establish such an origin is simply an illusion – a fall back to some *imaginary* construct which freezes desire into an obsessional neurosis. The genuine aim of psychoanalysis, retorts Lacan, is to enable the self to i) explode the *imaginary* ideal of self-identity and ii) enter the self-differentiating language of unconscious desire. In short, the *imaginary self* must die in order for the *symbolic other* to live.

Rimbaud's controversial claim in his *Lettre au Voyant* that the 'I is another' (*Je est un autre*) serves as a sort of leitmotif for Lacan's interpretation of the relation between conscious and unconscious. The self only escapes illusion when it accepts that it is not sufficient to itself, when it begins to listen to 'other' voices which it did not create and over which it has no definitive mastery. But the erosion of the *imago* of self-sufficiency is a painful and prolonged process requiring, as Rimbaud knew, a 'derangement of all the senses'. Modern man can only be released from the 'false meaning of the ego' by submitting to a kind of purgatorial death:

He reaches the unknown, and when, bewildered, he ends by losing the intelligence of his visions, he has seen them. Let him die as he leaps through unheard of and unnameable things.[9]

Lacan's own writings obey Rimbaud's poetics of the unconscious, employing puns, conundrums and veiled allusions which challenge the presumed sovereignty of the humanist ego. They illustrate how the unconscious structures of language defy translation into the idioms of linear consciousness. Lacan's purpose here is to debunk the fantasy of a unified 'total personality' – leading the speaking/reading subject back to the unconscious depths of language as a play of multiple meanings which subverts all ego-formation. The self-contained subject is thus *decentred*, exposed as a split or divided self. The model of autonomy (that the self is itself) gives way to that of heteronomy (that the self is *other* than itself). There are no 'individuals', insists Lacan, only 'dividua' or 'divided ones'. And he expands on this point as follows in his text 'Agency and the Letter in the Unconscious':

If we forget the self's radical ex-centricity to itself with which man is confronted, we shall falsify both the order and the methods of psychoanalytic mediation. . . . The radical heteronomy that Freud's discovery shows gaping within man can never again be covered over without whatever is used to hide it being profoundly dishonest.[10]

Why does Lacan equate the illusion of self-autonomy with the 'imaginary'? Might one not reasonably expect that Lacan's view of psychoanalysis as a 'liberal art', whose exploratory methods are analogous to those of poetics and at odds with those of the empirical sciences, would result in a *positive* identification of the imaginary as an expression of the unconscious? Was this not what Kant was intimating when he described imagination as an 'unknown root' and an 'art concealed in the depths of the human soul'? Or what Schelling suggested when he actually spoke of imagination as an 'unconscious' drive in man?

Like Heidegger, whom he frequently cites, Lacan appears to consider the whole concept of the creative imagination as fundamentally bound up with humanist anthropology. The notion of imagination is deemed synonymous with the idea of a point of origin from which the self produces or reproduces its ideals. Hence Lacan's negative definition of the *imaginary* as an idealized ego formation which it is the business of analysis to dissolve. Lacan traces the genesis of the *imaginary* ego back to what he calls, quite significantly, the 'mirror phase' of child development. The human infant first experiences itself as a 'fragmented' body. To overcome its feeling of dispersion it constructs an *imago* of unified selfhood. This *imago* results from the child's need to produce a double of himself as 'he will have been' (i.e. when he has realized himself as a total personality). The imaginary double takes the form of a mirror reflection. For it is in response to the desire of the other – expressed, for example, through the look of the mother – that the infant seeks to become a self-possessed identity. Lacan describes the *imaginary*, accordingly, in terms of a 'specular ego' which imitates the look of the other and constructs its *imago* 'like another'. Thus from the outset, the *imago* is not an autonomous creation of the child's own desire, as the self would subsequently like to believe, but a reified simulation of what the mother desires the child to become.

The child's passionate identification with this idealized ego is, for Lacan, the basis of narcissism. And this narcissism is not confined to childhood. It can perdure throughout one's adult life. Indeed, extended into the realm of culture, narcissism is just another word for humanism; since a primary purpose of bourgeois humanist society is the provision of supposedly self-sufficient individuals. The narcissistic model of the *imaginary* is the lynchpin of the humanist ideology which prevails in modern industrial society based as it is on the cult of the efficient productive subject. And existential and depth psychologies merely reinforce this ideology by promoting the ideals of individuation and autonomy. The *imaginary* thus serves as a repository of the falsehoods of the 'self' at both a psychological and social level. And this is why Lacan maintains that to disrupt the *imaginary* is to undermine the modern apotheosis of 'humanist man'.

But how is the imaginary to be supplanted? How is one to counter the ego's strategies of self-defence and reveal the unconscious heteronomy underlying its *imago*? In the psychoanalytic context, this means breaking the fascination of the *imaginary* so as to allow the symbolic order of the unconscious to speak. To this end, the analyst must renounce the orthodox idea of a 'cure' which would restore the human subject to himself as an 'integrated personality'. He must work against this humanist panacea by placing the analysand in situations where he/she may be surprised by the language of the unconscious, by lapses of tongue (parapraxis), puns and other tropes of speech which mean something 'other' than what we intend them to mean. This transition from *imaginary* self-possession to the *symbolic* language of the unconscious amounts to a discovery of the *otherness of the self*: the recognition that the unconscious always speaks according to the 'desire of the other'. 'The art of the analyst', says Lacan, 'must be to suspend the subject's certainties until their last mirages have been consumed.'[11] Only then can the *imago* of self-identity surrender to the unconscious desire for self-differentiation where the *I is always another*.

The human subject remains a prisoner to the *imaginary* order to the extent that it conceals from itself its unconscious relation to the other. By confronting us with the hidden language of difference, dislocation and desire – which the humanist imagination seeks to suppress – psychoanalysis reminds us that the dynamic of the unconscious lies not in the individual self but in the 'transindividual' space between self and other (i.e. the *symbolic* order). Decentred by the language of the unconscious, the human subject becomes aware of himself as a *split-I (Ich-Spaltung)*. And he thereby acknowledges that his 'desire finds its meaning in the desire of the other'. Once exposed to the fundamental void lurking behind the *imaginary*, the subject discovers that he is a pure lack, a relentless desire for the other. In short, the 'unconscious is the discourse of the other' which, if given voice, dispossesses us of the *imago* of self-completeness.

The great error of humanist thought was to have clung to the 'mirage of the individual, the human subject as truly autonomous', to have gone on believing that somewhere in that mirage resides 'the little man within man who operates the whole business'.[12] Man is not the author of the language of the unconscious; he does not speak it, but is spoken by it. And so against those existentialists who held that the human subject makes himself and his world out of his imagination, Lacan retorts that the self 'does not even know what he *says*, and for the good reason that he does not know what he *is*'.[13] 'Freud is not a humanist', concludes Lacan, and his greatness lies in the discovery that 'man is not altogether in man'.[14] Nor is Lacan unmindful of the feminist implications of this discovery – i.e. as a critique of the narcissistic male *imago*.[14a]

For Lacan, the *imaginary* is at the root of *narcissism* which is in turn at the root of *humanism*.

2 Althusser: the imaginary as false consciousness

If Lacan's rejection of the *imaginary* focused primarily on a critique of humanist psychology, Althusser's takes the form of a critique of humanist ideology. Althusser equates the *imaginary* with the 'false consciousness' of the bourgeoisie. He defines ideology, accordingly, as the 'representation of the subject's *imaginary* relationship to his or her *real* conditions of existence'.[15] The destruction of this *imaginary* relationship will coincide, he believes, with a revolutionary change in the whole dialectic between knowledge and history.

Althusser was also identified with the structuralist movement of the sixties. And however much he sought to dissociate himself from its fashionable Parisian connotations, he certainly shared structuralism's repudiation of man as an individual creative subject.[16] But where Lacan had based his crusade against 'humanist man' on the Freudian discovery of the unconscious, Althusser held that such a critique must ultimately be founded upon the Marxist discovery of the hidden laws of 'social formation'. This discovery of the laws of 'structural causality' (which govern the relations between the material infrastructure and political-cultural superstructure) made a new science of history possible: the science of historical materialism. This science is radically opposed to the ideology of autonomous man which Althusser denounces as a 'petit-bourgeois world outlook' – and whose spiritual complements are 'ethical idealism (today humanism) and existentialist-phenomenological subjectivism'.[17]

Althusser is particularly vigorous in his opposition to Hegel and Sartre. He considers them as typical exponents of the humanist myth of subjectivity. Against the ideologies of idealism and existentialism – which as we noted in our previous chapters were prime promoters of the modern philosophy of imagination – Althusser declares that the very concept of human *subjectivity*, understood as an original condition of creative freedom, is nothing less than an ideological strategy of *subjection* to the status quo. This strategy, he argues, summons human individuals into existence by subjecting them to the fiction that they are freely creating their own world – whereas, in fact, they are merely responding to 'false representations' of the established social order. 'There is no ideology', claims Althusser, 'except by and for subjects.' The very purpose of ideology is to represent each individual as an imaginary *subject of* freedom in order that he remain *subject to* the prevailing socio-political system. Exploiting this ambiguity in the notion of the 'subject' – meaning both freedom and subordination – humanist ideology contrives to isolate human beings in order to prevent them from joining together in a collective revolutionary mass.[18] Hence Althusser's declaration of an 'epistemological rupture' between humanism and Marxism, between the *ideology of imaginary representations* and the *science of structural relations*. Only by abolishing the *imaginary* order can we begin to construct a theory of the 'real object' of history.

Of particular interest for our present purposes is Althusser's development of Lacan's analysis of the *imaginary*. In an essay entitled 'Freud and Lacan', Althusser commends this analysis as a useful critique of the 'family ideology' of bourgeois culture. By extrapolating the radical implications of Freud's disclosure of the unconscious as a decentering of the humanist self, Lacan has, in Althusser's view, challenged the ideological misuse of psychoanalysis as 'the social magic of modern times' – that is, as a ploy to bolster up the illusion of the self-contained individual. The great virtue of Lacan's account of the structural language of the unconscious is its refusal to deploy psychoanalysis as a 'technique of emotional or affective re-adaptation or re-education'.[19] The attempts by existentialist thinkers like Sartre and Merleau-Ponty to reduce the unconscious to an instrument of subjective consciousness are dismissed by Althusser as 'ideological misunderstandings'. They utterly fail to move beyond the 'imaginary' order of illusion. Only Lacan's structural account grasps the significance of the transition from a) the pre-oedipal relationship between child and mother (where the ego's narcissistic identification with the other prevents it from taking up the objectifying distance of the 'third' *vis-à-vis* the other and itself) to b) the oedipal relationship where the 'third', the father, dispels the *imaginary* fascination of the child with the mother and introduces the *symbolic* order where the child can situate itself in a world of adult 'thirds'. But Althusser goes further than Lacan. He affirms that the psychoanalytic critique of the 'family ideology' (of childhood-maternity-paternity-conjugality) needs to be grounded upon a more fundamental critique of the socio-historical *preconditions* of this ideology. And this is a task for historical materialism.

Althusser praises both Freud and Marx for their insistence that human consciousness is not the centre of the universe. Indeed he suggests that this debunking of the 'ideological image of "man" as human subject' represents a new Copernican Revolution which supersedes the Copernican Revolution announced by Kant and the modern philosophy of humanism. Humanist ideology merely sought to obstruct the radical disclosure of the hidden laws which condition the familial and social formation of 'man'. Hence the necessity of a postmodern critique of the unconscious to counter the errors of the modern critique of consciousness. Marx and Freud are the true inheritors of the Copernican campaign to de-centre our *imaginary* view of things:

Since Copernicus, we have known that the earth is not the 'centre' of the universe. Since Marx, we have known that the human subject, the economic, political or philosophical ego is not the 'centre' of history – and even, in opposition to the Philosophers of the Enlightenment and to Hegel, that history has no 'centre' but possesses a structure which has no necessary 'centre' except in ideological misrecognition. In turn,

Freud has discovered for us that the real subject, the individual in his essence, has not the form of an ego, centred on . . . 'consciousness' or on 'existence', that the human subject is de-centred, constituted by a structure which has no 'centre' either, except in the imaginary misrecognition of the 'ego', i.e. in the ideological formations in which it 'recognizes' itself.[20]

Lacan's critical account of the *imaginary* as a 'structure of misrecognition' is seen to provide historical materialism with novel insights into the workings of ideology. It helps us, Althusser notes, to identify ideology as an 'imaginary assemblage' which bourgeois society utilizes in order to vindicate its own eternal self-image – its 'empty dream' of humanism which denies the structural laws of history pre-determining it. Thus where the modern ideology of humanism saw history as a narrative continuity which the human imagination creates and posits for itself, the anti-humanist science – formulated by Lacan's Freudianism and Althusser's Marxism – demands a complete break with this ideology. It calls instead for a postmodern deconstruction of the human subject as origin of meaning.

Where does this leave the role of the *imaginary* in art? Althusser argues that 'real art' is not necessarily reducible to the ideological deformations of the *imaginary* – if rescued by the right reading! While incapable of giving us *knowledge* of the world, great works of literature can provide *perceptions* of the ideology they represent. Since ideology invests all experience, art can at best enable us to 'see' a particular ideology as it is *spontaneously lived*. But it cannot of its own accord actually go beyond the *imaginary* level of 'ideological spontaneity'. What determines the truth content of art is its capacity to offer ideological representations which may then be *scientifically known* (i.e. by historical materialism). For as long as it is misinterpreted by the humanist theories of idealism or existentialism, art remains within the order of the *imaginary*. Only an anti-humanist reading can bring its hidden structures to light.[21]

Althusser's triple equation of the *imaginary, ideology* and *humanism* is no less suspicious of philosophy than of art. For philosophy, like art, is considered party to the bourgeois illusion that history is made by human subjects rather than determined by structural causes. This consideration has prompted one commentator to accuse Althusser of falling victim to the 'fetishism of social laws'.[22] Certainly the new *science* of 'structuralist Marxism' did not hesitate to announce the end of *philosophy*. And Althusser even goes so far as to affirm that the 'teacher of philosophy, like every intellectual, is a petit-bourgeois' and that 'every time he opens his mouth it is the petit-bourgeois ideology which speaks'.[23] In *For Marx*, Althusser hails the 'scientific discovery of Marx' as an 'anti-humanist theory' which signals a definitive 'rupture with all anthropology and all humanist philosophy' and reduces 'the philosophical myth of man to ashes'.[24] There can be no room for imagination in this scenario, one where history definitively dispenses with the human subject. Imagination cannot exist, it would seem, without 'man'.

3 Foucault: the end of man

Foucault provides further arguments for the postmodern debunking of the humanist imagination. Though he never directly attacks the concept of imagination in its own right, his ominous pronouncements of the 'death of man' clearly imply the dissolution of the philosophy of creative imagination as promoted by modern idealism and existentialism. Whereas Lacan offered a *psychoanalytic* critique of the humanist subject and Althusser a *Marxist* critique, Foucault concentrates on its *epistemological* dimensions.

Foucault's critique finds its most cogent formulation in *The Order of Things*, first published in 1966. Here he proposes an 'archaeology of the human sciences' whose purpose it is to reveal a 'positive unconscious' of knowledge. This epistemological unconscious eludes the consciousness of the scientists themselves, even though it structures their discourse from beginning to end. The human subjects deemed responsible for their discourse are, Foucault argues, themselves pre-conditioned in their perceptive or imaginative capacities by underlying codes over which they have no say. It is Foucault's intention, therefore, to 'explore scientific discourse not from the point of view of the individuals who are speaking . . . but from the point of view of the rules that come into play in the very existence of such discourse'.[25] Foucault's substitution of a postmodern paradigm of the structural unconscious for the modern paradigm of creative consciousness presupposes, therefore, the rejection of the 'phenomenological approach which gives absolute priority to the observing subject, which attributes a constituent role to an act, which places its own point of view at the origin of all historicity – which, in short, leads to a transcendental consciousness'.[26]

The modern reign of transcendental consciousness extended, as we have seen in preceding chapters, from Kant's epochal account of the productive powers of imagination in the first edition of the *Critique of Pure Reason* at the end of the eighteenth century, to Sartre's existentialist exposé of these powers in *The Psychology of Imagination* and subsequent works. In chapter seven of *The Order of Things*, Foucault himself adverts to Kant's inaugural role. He acknowledges that it was the Kantian critique which brought the classical era of knowledge to an end by demonstrating how the mimetic model of objective 'representation' was ultimately founded upon a productive model of transcendental subjectivity. In this way, Kant signaled the decisive rupture between the classical and modern eras. Foucault writes:

The Kantian critique marks the threshold of our modernity, it questions representations . . . on the basis of its rightful limits. Thus it sanctions for the first time that in European culture which coincides with the end of the eighteenth century: the withdrawal of knowledge and thought outside the space of representation. That space is brought into question in its foundation . . . .[27]

This critical withdrawal suspends the dogmatic metaphysics of classical thought. But, so doing, it opens up the possibility of another metaphysics – that of modern idealism 'whose purpose will be to question, apart from representation, all that is the *source* and *origin* of representation'.[28] The emergence in the nineteenth century of the human sciences of life (biology and natural history), language (philology and grammar) and will (political economy) is, Foucault insists, correlative to the modern founding of transcendental philosophy. The affirmation of man's transcendental consciousness as the original centre of all knowledge is the decisive feature of the modern epoch. And this transcendental consciousness, as we noted in our analysis of Kant, is but another name for the productive power of *imagination*.

Foucault claims that it was on this transcendental threshold of modern thought that the 'strange figure of knowledge called man' first appeared and revealed a space proper to the human sciences. Here, at this decisive point in history, humanist thought enters into its own. For as 'things became increasingly reflexive, seeking the principle of their intelligibility only in their own development, and abandoning the space of representation, man enters in his turn, and for the first time, the field of Western knowledge'.[29] But Foucault's archaeological excavation of the strata of Western knowledge does not end there. It points to the imminence of a new postmodern era where the figure of man will once again disappear. If man is indeed an invention of recent date, he is one that now appears to be nearing its end. Nor is this to be regretted. Foucault's anti-humanist stance is unequivocal. He avows:

Strangely enough, man is probably no more than a rift in the order of things, or, in any case, a configuration whose outlines are determined by the new position he has so recently taken up in the field of knowledge. Whence all the chimeras of the new humanisms, all the facile solutions of an 'anthropology' understood as a universal reflection on man.[30]

Foucault actually declares it a relief to think that man is just a 'new wrinkle in our knowledge', not yet two centuries old, and that he will 'disappear again as soon as that knowledge has discovered a new form'.[31] This new form, Foucault implies, is of course already being prepared by his own archaeology of the unconscious of knowledge, and indeed by the whole structuralist critique of the human subject. But Foucault contents himself, in his apocalyptic conclusion to The *Order of Things*, with vague intimations about what exact shape this demise of man will take. We can merely 'sense the possibility' of this event without knowing precisely 'what it promises'.[32] The archaeology of human knowledge, in other words, brings us to the point where human knowledge itself comes to an end.

Such a conclusion was already anticipated by Foucault's prefatory admission in *The Order of Things* that the idea for the book first arose when he read a passage from Borges – a postmodern author *par excellence* – which shattered all the familiar landmarks of humanist thinking. The Borges passage in question cited an encyclopaedia where it was written that

animals are divided into: (a) belonging to the Emperor, (b) embalmed, (c) tame, (d) sucking pigs (e) sirens, (f) fabulous, (g) stray dogs, (h) included in the present classification, (i) frenzied, (j) innumerable, (k) drawn with a very fine camelhair brush, l) *et cetera*, (m) having just broken the water pitcher, (n) that from a long way off look like flies.

What struck Foucault about this taxonomy was the very *otherness* of its thought system, the sheer impossibility of thinking it in terms of our accredited order of things. We are confronted here with an alien system whose linking of heteroclite elements explodes our established modes of thinking in 'one great leap', appearing to us as some kind of monstrous disorder. And Foucault explains that what provokes in us the distinctively postmodern response of a 'laughter that shatters' is not so much the exotic animals themselves, but the insane way they are brought together in an alphabetical series (a, b, c, d), a series that utterly transgresses 'the boundaries of all imagination, of all possible thought'.[33]

Foucault proceeds finally to contrast the *utopias* of the humanist imagination (which afford modern man consolation and confirmation) with the *heterotopias* of a postmodern art (which expose the limits of our anthropocentric imagination and bring both human thought and language to the threshold of their impossibility). Heterotopias, such as those to be found in Borges, 'dessicate speech, stop words in their tracks, contest the very possibility of grammar at its source, dissolve our myths and sterilize the lyricism of our sentences'.[34] Modern art becomes postmodern when it parodies its own pretensions, when it upends the traditional distinctions between the imaginary and the real, the possible and the impossible, that which can be thought or said and that which cannot. Borges' own metaphor of art as a sprawling labyrinth with no entrance or exit, where man loses himself in circular self-mirroring paths, aptly illustrates the postmodern paradigm. 'Sleeping is like dreaming death, just as waking is like dreaming life,' Borges confesses. 'I can no longer tell which is which.'[35]

But Foucault also recognizes the existence of such *heterotopias* in the visual arts. In a study entitled *This Is Not A Pipe*, Foucault playfully unravels the paradoxes of Magritte's painting of a pipe with the words *ceci n'est pas une pipe* written underneath. In such visual-verbal non sequiturs, Foucault finds evidence of the contemporary disclosure of the arbitrariness of the sign. He makes much of this tendency to subvert the Western tradition of representation, one which extends from the Greek model of the *logos* as a correspondence between reality and language to the general European project of rediscovering the pre-lapsarian language of Adam where names inhabited the things they represented. The paintings of Magritte or the billboard reproductions of Warhol are for Foucault confirmations, at the level of visual art, of the Saussurian discovery that signs do not refer to objects in any fixed way. Such images assault the established conventions of reference by refusing to allow of any unique or original model. Using familiar images – pipes or soup cans – in such a way that the viewer is compelled to question the rapport between such images and their originals, artists like Magritte and Warhol undermine the very notion of representation. Magritte's pipe is not a pipe; Warhol's Campbells soup cans are reproductions of a commodity that is itself the product of an advertising image.

In order to explain how such images can be both familiar and non-representational, Foucault makes a distinction between *resemblance* and *similitude*. Resemblance, as the traditional model of representation, presupposes a 'primary reference' of image to reality: here the image is a copy which faithfully imitates

René Magritte, 'Ceci n'est pas une pipe'

its original. Similitude, by contrast, abandons the whole idea of reference with its hierarchy of primary and secondary, origin and imitation: here the copy is deprived of any privileged model, parodying itself in a series of lateral repetitions. Similitude 'circulates the simulacrum as the indefinite and reversible relation of the similar to the similar'.[36] Relating this specifically to Magritte's painting, Foucault writes:

Magritte knits verbal signs and plastic elements together, but without referring them to a prior isotopism. He skirts the base of affirmative discourse on which resemblance calmly reposes, and he brings pure similitudes and nonaffirmative verbal statements into play within the instability of a disoriented volume and unmapped space . . . similitudes multiply of themselves, refer to nothing more than themselves . . . the 'This is a pipe' silently hidden in mimetic representation has become the 'This is not a pipe' of circulating similitudes'.[37]

And extending this reading to Warhol's reproductions of consumer images, Foucault suggests that here we are confronted with the total dissolution of the idea of a unique model: 'by means of similitude relayed indefinitely along the length of a series, the image itself, along with the name it bears, loses its identity. Campbell, Campbell, Campbell, Campbell.'[38]

To enter the postmodern era we must, as Foucault explains in *Language, Counter-Memory, Practice,* 'renounce the will-to-knowledge' and be prepared instead to 'revere a certain practice of stupidity'. And this point is made even more forcefully in the closing pages of *Madness and Civilization.* Here Foucault celebrates those visionary 'fools' and insane 'artists' who reveal that *other* order of the unconscious which the modern age of humanism has sought to confine within the order of the *same* (i.e. the familiar system of knowledge). It is the madness of art which, he suggests, may finally deliver us from the modern tyranny of *man*:

Henceforth and through the mediation of madness, it is the world that becomes culpable (for the first time in the Western world) in relation to the work of art . . . Madness is contemporary with the work of art since it inaugurates the time of its truth. The moment when, together, the work of art and madness are born and fulfilled is the beginning of the time when the world finds itself arraigned by that work of art and responsible before it for what it does. Ruse and new triumph of madness: the world that thought to measure and justify madness through psychology must justify itself before madness.[39]

Only when the age of humanism dissolves into the apocalyptic age of madness might Foucault's final wager in *The Order of Things* be fulfilled – 'that man would be erased, like a face drawn in sand at the edge of the sea'.

4 Barthes: the death of the authorial imagination

Roland Barthes adds a new dimension to the postmodern critique of the humanist imagination. Drawing from the combined resources of his structuralist contemporaries – Lacan and Althusser in particular[40] – Barthes breaks new ground by exposing the hidden codes at work in the popular mythologies of our mass-media society.

In his 1970 preface to *Mythologies,* Barthes describes his work as an 'ideological critique bearing on the language of so-called mass-culture'. Developing the structuralist suggestion that images are no more than surface signs of an unconscious language, Barthes sets out to demystify the representations of the collective imaginary which 'transform petit-bourgeois culture into a universal nature'. The imaginary is thus treated as mere myth, an epiphenomenon of concealed linguistic structures. Barthes' aim is thus to transform 'semiology' (the science of signs) into a 'semioclasm' (a critique of signs) which will shatter the ideological *imaginaire* of Western bourgeois man, i.e. of a subject who still prides himself as the source of universal meaning. To this end, he analyses a series of typical myths of French daily life propagated by such diverse media as newspaper articles, TV advertisements, commercial films or the covers of mass-circulation magazines.

The great imposture of bourgeois man is to present himself as an eternal and autonomous *cogito* – thereby concealing the fact that he is no more than a symptom of the historical process. Hence the necessity to demystify those popular mythologies which seek to reduce 'history' to the uncritical condition of 'nature'. Barthes resolves accordingly to track down in the imaginary 'display of what *goes-without-saying* the ideological abuse which is hidden there'.[41] A famous example of such demystification is his analysis of a *Paris Match* cover showing a black soldier saluting the French flag. Behind the apparently natural image of the negro saluting is the hidden ideological message: France is a great colonial empire and all her sons, regardless of colour, faithfully serve under her flag (i.e. French patriotism is compatible with colonialism). Barthes argues that popular myths are sustained by unconscious codes which structure the production of meaning – behind our backs, as it were. And here he would appear to be in agreement with Lévi-Strauss's reading of myths as collective strategies for resolving the contradictions of everyday social life at an 'imaginary level'.[42] As the formula goes: 'It is not man who thinks myths but myths which think man.' The primary goal of the semioclast is thus to destroy the fetishistic power of the imaginary so that its covert ideological strategies be laid bare. Mythological images, for Barthes, are never innocent.

Sarcasm is, Barthes asserts, the appropriate attitude for the demythologizer in our postmodern age.[43] Why? Because it is not sufficient to demystify the collective imaginary *out there*; one must also be prepared to demystify the demystifying subject himself. There is no transcendental sanctuary of truth either outside or inside man. Sarcasm is the recognition that there is no such thing as truth at all. Barthes thus concludes *Mythologies*, as Foucault concluded *The Order of Things*, by admitting that we no longer *know* what truth is or what awaits us in the postmodern era when the myths of bourgeois humanism have been destroyed. The demythologizer can only affirm what truth is *not*. The idea of a creative imaginative subject is just as 'mythic' as that of a collective *imaginaire*. And having disabused ourselves of these ideological illusions, we have no choice but to enter the 'dark night of history' – an empty space of disorientation. There is nowhere to turn. For as the imaginary disappears, so too does the reality of the objective world. 'We constantly drift between the object and its demystification, powerless to render its wholeness,' notes Barthes. 'For if we penetrate the object, we liberate it but we destroy it; and if we acknowledge its full weight, we respect it, but we restore it to a state that is still mystified.'[44]

Here again we witness that distinctively apocalyptic tone which characterizes the postmodern dismantling of the imaginary. The demythologizer cannot return to the imaginary; and yet there is no positive reality he can turn to either. 'The havoc he wreaks in the language of the community is absolute for him,' Barthes admits, 'it fills his assignment to the brim: he must live this assignment without any hope of going back.' And at the same time,

it is forbidden for him to imagine what the world will be concretely like when the immediate object of his criticism has disappeared. Utopia is an impossible luxury for him: he greatly doubts that tomorrow's truths will be the exact reverse of today's lies. . . . He is not even in a Moses-like situation: he cannot see the promised land. For him tomorrow's positive it is entirely hidden by today's negativity. All the values of his undertaking seem to him as acts of destruction.[45]

The postmodern vision of history, Barthes ominously concedes, is one in which 'the potent seed of the future is *nothing but* the most profound apocalypse of the present'.[46]

Barthes' apocalyptic attitude is not confined to his debunking of popular mythologies. It also informs his writings on the contemporary character of art and literature. In his polemical essay, 'The Death of the Author', Barthes vigorously reasserts the dereliction of the humanist imagination. A work of literature, he argues, should not be conceived as an 'expression' of a creative subject (the author) but as an impersonal play of linguistic signs (writing). The life of the text presupposes the death of the author. Our understanding of texts must therefore be *de-psychologized*. And this in effect means *de-humanized* in the sense of dispensing with the humanist claims of romantic idealism and existentialism. Viewed from a postmodern perspective,

writing is the destruction of every voice, of every point of origin. . . . It is that neutral, composite, oblique space where our subject slips away, the negative where all identity is lost, starting with the very identity of the body writing.[47]

In *Writing Degree Zero*, Barthes had already observed a contemporary tendency towards modes of 'multiple' writing – a tendency which subverts the bourgeois belief in a sovereign individual imagination. The experimental forms of writing opened up by Mallarmé, Joyce, Beckett or the *nouveau roman-ciers*, were eroding the humanist view of literature as a privileged expression of a creative author in favour of the view that there is no origin or end of meaning outside of writing itself.[48] Here at last, says Barthes, is literature openly exposed to the problem-atic of language. And this return of language to itself, in what Mallarmé described as the 'texte impersonifié', debunks the idea of an authorial imagination which uses language to express its inner intentions.

Barthes thus confirms the postmodern maxim that the 'author is a modern figure'. The notion of the *human person* is, he insists, a mere by-product of our Western society as it emerged from the Middle Ages and discovered the 'prestige of the individual' with the European Enlightenment and Reformation. As such, Barthes agrees with Althusser and Foucault that the cult of the creative subject is a symptom of bourgeois ideology. He writes:

It is logical that in literature it should be this positivism (of the human person), the epitome and culmination of capitalist ideology, which has attached the greatest importance to the 'person' of the author. The *author* still reigns in histories of literature, biographies of writers, interviews, magazines, as in the very consciousness of men of letters anxious to unite their person and their work through diaries and memoirs. The image of literature to be found in ordinary culture is tyrannically centred on the author, his person, his life, his tastes, his passions, while criticism consists for the most part in saying that Baudelaire's work is the failure of Baudelaire the man, Van Gogh's his madness, Tchaikovsky's his vice. The *explanation* of a work is always sought in the man or woman who produced it, as if it were always in the end, through the more or less transparent allegory of the fiction, the voice of a single person, the *author* 'confiding' in us.[49]

Structural linguistics, Barthes claims, furnishes us with a valuable analytic weapon in the destruction of the author. The discovery of language as a total system of enunciation which functions independently of the *persons* of the interlocutors, shows that the author is never more than the 'instance writing, just as *I* is nothing other than the instance saying "*I*" '[50]. This enables us to replace the modern notion of the *book* (as a project of the authorial imagination) with the postmodern notion of the *text* (as an impersonalized process of writing where the author is absent). We can consequently dispense with the model of a patriarchal consciousness which was thought to exist prior to the text and to procreate itself by means of the text. Language comes to substitute itself for the productive subject who previously had been considered its owner and master. Or to put it in another way, the authorial imagination is no longer the subject with the book as its predicate, the father whose writing is its child. The opposite is the case. Language is revealed as a self-referential process with nothing *before* or *after* it. And as such it is never *original* – for there is no 'origin' outside of itself, i.e. no transcendent reality or transcendental imagination to which it could refer. The postmodern paradigm of writing does away with both the mimetic and productive models of imagination.

If, therefore, one still wishes to speak of a postmodern imagination (which Barthes does not), one would have to speak of an imagination which is no more than a parody of itself. For once the idea of an original source of meaning is renounced, every act of so-called imagination is revealed as a mere 'effect' of the endless *intertextuality* of language itself. Every text, as Barthes points out, is made up of 'multiple writings . . . entering into mutual relations of parody'.[51] What we have then, is a mirror-play between texts where every text is an imitation of another, and no text an original – an interminable rewriting of writing devoid of any guiding authority.

The postmodern death of the author, Barthes claims, follows from the death of God and announces that of Man. He does not bemoan this situation. On the contrary, he sees it as heralding a new kind of an-archy, an absence of origin (*arche*) where every act of writing traces a field 'which has no other origin than language itself, language which ceaselessly calls into question all origins'[52]. He offers this striking account of postmodern textuality:

We know that a text is not a line of words releasing a single 'theological' meaning (the 'message' of the Author-God) but a multi-dimensional space in which a variety of writings, none of them original, blend and clash. The text is a tissue of quotations drawn from the innumerable centres of culture. Similar to Bouvard and Pécuchet, those eternal copyists, at once sublime and comic and whose profound ridiculousness indicates precisely the truth of writing, the writer can only imitate a gesture that is always anterior, never original. His only power is to mix writings, to counter the ones with the others, in such a way as never to rest on any one of them. Did he wish to *express himself*, he ought at least to know that the inner 'thing' he thinks to 'translate' is itself only a ready-formed dictionary, its words only explainable through other words, and so on indefinitely. . . . Life never does more than imitate the book, and the book itself is only a tissue of signs, an imitation that is lost, infinitely deferred.[53]

The end of the author also implies, of course, the end of the critic. To deny the validity of authorial *imagination* is also to deny that of critical *interpretation*. For both presuppose the possibility of a human subject existing before or after the text. Hermeneutics (the science of deciphering the hidden meanings of texts) is thus replaced by what Susan Sontag has called an 'erotics' of textuality. Here each reader defies the solemn authority of the critic and exults in a plurality of possible meanings. Since there is no author to place a true 'message' in the text – some 'original signified' for the critic to disclose – each reader is at liberty to take from it whatever pleasure he wishes, abandoning himself to a play of multiple fragmentation and dissipation.

This kind of 'erotic' reading shatters the expedients of the homogeneous ego. It results in a disruption of all textual authority and closure, yielding an experience which Barthes terms *jouissance*. One may no longer speak of some truth residing *beneath the surface* of writing. The very superficiality of a text's limitless mirror-play is its greatest virtue. The postmodern experience of playful parody is in direct defiance of both the onto-theological and humanistic models of meaning. And Barthes does not shrink from the consequences. He revels in them:

In the multiplicity of writing, everything is to be *disentangled*, nothing *deciphered*; the structure can be followed, 'run' (like the thread of a stocking) at every point and at every level, but there is nothing beneath: the space of writing is to be ranged over, not pierced; writing ceaselessly posits meaning ceaselessly to evaporate it, carrying out a systematic exemption of meaning. In precisely this way literature (it would be better from now on to say *writing*), by refusing to assign a 'secret', an ultimate meaning, to the text (and to the world as text), liberates what may be called an anti-theological activity, an activity that is truly revolutionary since to refuse to fix meaning is, in the end, to refuse God and his hypostases – reason, science, law.[54]

And, one might add, *authorial imagination*.

In several essays, Barthes extends his analysis of 'textuality' beyond literature to photography and cinema. This is what one might expect, given the capacity of such media to mechanically reproduce images in an infinite series of 'copies'. For this capacity challenges the cult of 'originality' which hallmarks the traditional arts. Photography and cinema are typically postmodern to the extent that they are able to introduce breaks and ruptures into our habitual patterns of narrative consciousness.

This potential to disrupt the human experience of continuity entails a deeply 'traumatic quality'. In a study entitled 'The Photographic Message', Barthes speaks of traumatic photographs which 'block meaning' and leave us with nothing to say. Such images, he explains, are by their very structure *insignificant*: 'no value, no knowledge, at the limit no verbal categorization can have a hold on the process instituting the signification'.[55] The trauma serves to undermine the mythological connotations which society wishes to confer on our images in its efforts to integrate man and reassure him of his given identity.

Elsewhere, in an essay called the 'The Third Meaning', Barthes elaborates on this idea of subversive images when he analyses some shots from an Eisenstein film. He speaks here of the power of certain frames to carry a third level of impact (*signifiance*) beyond the conventional levels of informational *message* or symbolic *reference*. This tertiary meaning is described as erratic, obstinate, incomplete, a sort of inexplicable fragment whose very gratuitousness breaks up the narrative flow of consciousness. Barthes calls it an 'obtuse' signifier which extends beyond the established norms of culture, knowledge and information. There is something peculiarly postmodern about it:

opening out into the infinity of language, it can come through as limited in the eyes of analytic reason; it belongs to the family of pun, buffoonery, useless expenditure. Indifferent to moral or aesthetic categories (the trivial, the futile, the false, the pastiche), it is on the side of the carnival.[56]

This obtuse image which Barthes identifies as an essentially 'filmic' quality, resists critical interpretation. It appears to dispell the very content and practice of meaning. And it also frustrates the efforts of human subjectivity to structure experience in a linear or referential narrative. Provoking in the viewer an unsettling feeling of dislocation, the obtuse image has a 'de-naturing effect with regard to reference (to *reality* as nature)'[57]. As such it exposes us to a 'counter-logical' view of things: a view whose very strangeness opens onto a vertical space of sublime silence, one where we are compelled to leave behind the false securities of the egological imagination. Barthes speaks accordingly of a mode of representation which cannot be represented, an indescribable and inarticulate surplus of meaning which cannot be reduced to the constraints of narrative order or time. At once 'parodic and disseminatory', this traumatic dimension of the filmic image calls for a radical 'mutation of reading and its object, text or film', a mutation which Barthes claims is one of the most crucial problems of our time.[58] Indeed, Barthes adds laconically that the power of such impertinent images to transgress the comfortable confines of bourgeois imagination points to a revolutionary potential, an omen which 'does not *yet* belong to today's politics but *already* to tomorrow's.[59]

Barthes ultimately resists the modernist habit of opposing popular culture (magazines, TV programmes, etc.) to High Culture (avant-garde literature and Eisenstein films). In keeping with the postmodern tendency to blur such distinctions, to deny the possibility of discriminating between *authentic* or *inauthentic* imitations, Barthes acknowledges the existence of 'third meanings' in the most popular forms of contemporary mass culture. Citing the examples of the photo-novel and comic-strip, he avows that their very 'stupidity' actually produces in us a 'trauma of *signifiance*'. He even ventures the suggestion that there may well be 'a future truth in these derisory, vulgar, foolish, dialogical forms of consumer subculture'.[60]

What is at once remarkable and disturbing about this supposition – particularly for a humanist mind committed to an ideal of evaluation – is the implication that *every* text is of equal importance. Barthes appears to confirm this implication in a late essay, 'Change the Object Itself: Mythology Today' (1971); here he speaks of the existence of a 'generalized writing' which pervades all levels of our contemporary culture. 'The world is written through and through', Barthes admits. But does this extension of the definition of *writing* to include everything, not mean that *writing* has become co-terminous with '*mythology*'

– i.e. the ideological realm of the *imaginary*? How is one to discriminate between the revolutionary power of *writing* and the mystifying power of the *imaginary* if, as Barthes asserts, 'the mythical is present everywhere sentences are turned, stories told, from inner speech to outer conversation, from newspaper article to political sermon, from novel to advertising image – all utterances which could be brought together under the Lacanian concept of the *imaginary*'?[61] In other words, does not the post-modern tendency to collapse the old oppositions between truth and falsehood, the real and the imaginary, the authentic and the mythical, not preclude the possibility of ethical judgement or critical discernment? And must Barthes himself not therefore revoke the claim made in *Mythologies* to offer a 'critical decipherment' of ideologies by 'upending the mythological message'? For if *writing* is everything, and if everything is charged with the *imaginary*, from what non-ideological standpoint can the human subject (if he still exists at all) take up a critical standpoint?

Barthes sees the problem, but not a solution. At best, as he advises in his *Inaugural Lecture at the Collège de France* (1977), we may try to subvert the mythological system of language from *within*. Since we cannot actually step outside the artificial labyrinth of mirrors, our only chance is to become pleasure-loving terrorists seeking out 'unclassified, atopic sites' within the anonymous play of language, residual spaces where we may still speak 'according to our perversions, rather than according to the Law'. Our last remaining hope is to seek to transform knowledge into desire by using the words of the omnipresent sign system, not as messages of 'truth' or 'interpretation', but as 'explosions' and 'vibrations'. Barthes thus advocates a 'deconstruction' of linguistic artifice whereby we may exult in the *impurities* of language, the crumbling bits and pieces of the imaginary, finding in these discarded left-overs the pleasure of certain traumatic shudders, exquisite moments of *jouissance* which defy the tyranny of myth. The aim of the postmodern semiologist, concludes Barthes, is to experience instances of absolute fragmentation where there is 'no power . . . and as much flavour as possible'. This is, in the final analysis, what the postmodern

subversion of the imaginary promises – 'a moment at once decadent and prophetic, a moment of gentle apocalypse. . . .'[62]

5 Derrida: mime without end

It is no doubt in the writings of Jacques Derrida – the deconstructionist *par excellence* – that the postmodern critique of the
imagination reaches its most incisive formulation. Derrida shares
the view of his structuralist and post-structuralist colleagues that
humanism must be dismantled; and he resolutely urges that we
think through the 'end of man'.[63] Applied to the humanist category of the imaginary, this requires deconstructive readings of
metaphysical modes of representation. We shall examine
Derrida's readings under two main headings: i) *mimesis without
origin*; ii) *apocalypse without end*.

Mimesis without origin

The most effective way to deconstruct the metaphysics of origin,
in both its traditional and modern guises, is, says Derrida, to
engage in a methodical investigation of the operations of 'writing'
(*écriture*). Like Barthes, Derrida does not just mean writing in
the conventional sense of literature or, more simply, inscriptions
on a page. He too refers to a 'generalized writing' which is
not confined to the accepted opposition between inscribed and
spoken language, but includes every aspect of experience which
is marked by signifying traces – that is, by a *textual* play of
meaning which lacks any reference to some original truth. This
means for Derrida that there is no primordial 'presence' (foundation, reality, truth, idea) of which writing could be said to be
a re-presentation at second hand. There is no such thing as an
original event of meaning. On the contrary, it is the practice of
repetition and reiteration, which generalized writing embodies,
that first gives rise to the illusion of an original presence. Writing
is therefore a kind of *mimesis* – but one lacking any originary
model, any transcendental anchorage outside of itself.

Western metaphysics, beginning with Plato, was deeply

suspicious of writing. It denounced it as a poison (*pharmakon*) to the extent that the written text threatened to a) remove man from the ideal of an original presence (e.g. the model of the soul in silent dialogue with itself) and b) thereby replace the original moment of self-identical truth with a mere copy – or worse a copy of a copy (since the moment of human truth is itself modelled on the eternal Idea of the Good as a pure presence to itself). Platonic metaphysics, as we noted in our second chapter, insisted on the priority of the *origin* (Sun-Father-Idea) over its *supplement* (the mimetic play of writing which repeats this origin). And yet the paradox is that the origin of truth cannot be adequately understood without the mimetic activity of repetition. Origin cannot exist without imitation. For as even Plato recognized, the transcendental Idea of presence is only intelligible to us if it is *remembered*; and such remembrance (*anamnēsis*) presupposes that it be *repeatedly* represented as that which is the *same* as itself, stable, timeless, self-identical. The very truth of origin thus requires the non-truth of repetition – understood as a generalized *mimesis* of writing. Only that which is recorded in words and images can be repeated over time and thus recollected in spite of time. In a study entitled 'Plato's Pharmacy', Derrida outlines this deconstructive paradox of *mimēsis* which lurks at the very heart of Western metaphysics:

(Truth) appears, in its essence, as the possibility of its own most proper non-truth, of its pseudo-truth reflected in the icon, the phantasm, or the simulacrum. What is is not what it is, identical and identical to itself, unique, unless it adds to itself the possibility of being *repeated* as such. And its identity is hallowed out by that addition, withdraws itself in the supplement that presents it.[64]

This account of writing as a *mimesis-without-origin* has decisive implications for the concept of imagination. Derrida teases out some of these implications in his essay 'The Double Session' where he contrasts Plato's definition of *mimēsis* in the *Philebus* with Mallarmé's in *Mimique*. Derrida informs the reader that the guiding question of his analysis is 'What is Literature?' As treated here, the question becomes eminently self-deconstructive; for Derrida has no intention of trying to relate literature to truth in the manner of previous philosophical reflections on this subject from Plato to Sartre. On the contrary, he will show that the very opposition between literature (the imaginary) and truth (the real) is without foundation. From the first elaboration of the concept of *mimēsis* with Plato to its end with Mallarmé, a whole history has run its course: a history of metaphysical truth which in turn made possible a history of literature understood as a representation of truth. The entire development of the interpretation of the arts of letters has, Derrida claims, 'moved and been transformed within the diverse logical possibilities opened up by the concept of *mimēsis*.[65]

Derrida begins by commenting on a passage in the *Philebus* (38e–39e) where Plato compares the human soul to a book (*biblos*) which copies and illustrates human experience. This activity of mimetic writing, carried out by an internal scribe (*grammateus*) and painter (*zōgraphos-dēmiourgos*), records passing events and thereby confers a certain permanence on them: it enables the past to be recalled in the present. Here again Derrida underscores the metaphysical paradox of *mimēsis*. Without its capacity for remembrance, the soul would be unable to intuit meaning as an enduring essence (*eidos/idea*). But this very capacity presupposes the mimetic activity of duplication which in fact *replaces* the original events which it imitates. Since Plato equates *mimesis* with imagination, as we have already seen, the same paradox obtains for the latter. Derrida explains:

The element of the thus characterized book is the *image* in general (the icon or phantasm), the imaginary or the *imaginal*. If Socrates is able to compare the silent relation between the soul and itself, in the 'mute soliloquy', to a book, it is because the book imitates the soul or the soul imitates the book, because each is the image or *likeness* of the other ('image' has the same root as '*imitari*'). Both of the likenesses, even before resembling each other, were in themselves already reproductive, imitative, and pictorial in essence. *Logos* must indeed be shaped according to the model of the *eidos*; the book then reproduces the *logos*, and the whole is organized by this relation of repetition, resemblance, doubling, duplication, this sort of specular process and play of reflections where things (*onta*), speech and writing come to repeat and mirror each other.[66]

It would appear, then, that *logos* (truth) needs *mimēsis* (imitation) if it is to be preserved in the soul and intuited as an essence. Thus Plato is compelled in the *Philebus* to accord a central role to mimetic imagination in our knowledge of truth, even though he has made it clear, in the *Republic* and elsewhere, that mimetic imagination – be it that of the painter, scribe or poet – is that which removes us from truth and provides us with mere copies. Derrida argues accordingly that Plato's description of *mimēsis* as both truth and non-truth points to its own deconstruction, and by extension, to the deconstruction of the metaphysical concept of imagination. For what Western metaphysics has always struggled to establish is the primacy of *logos* over *mimēsis*, of being-present over its representation, the imitated over the imitation, the real over the imaginary. The whole order of metaphysical logic has been based on the ability to establish that 'what is imitated is more real, more essential, more true, etc., than what imitates . . . anterior and superior to it'.[67]

Derrida admits that there have been several attempts made during the course of the Western history of aesthetics to contest the 'logocentric' model of *mimēsis* (i.e. that the image imitates an original which precedes it). But Derrida denies that any metaphysical system, however idealist or subjectivist, has ever succeeded in dispensing with a) the old distinction between the original and its imitation and b) the attendant habit of according primacy to the former over the latter. Even those romantic idealists who proposed a theory of 'productive imagination', and thereby sought to oppose Platonism, still clung to the idea of a transcendental origin of meaning which enjoys priority over its 'imitations'. The famous romantic dichotomy between a primary (productive) and secondary (reproductive) imagination still conforms to the metaphysical opposition between 'origin' and 'derivation'. Derrida insists that such idealist efforts to reverse traditional 'mimetology' do not in fact escape from the metaphysical system of truth. It is, of course, the case that the romantic imagination refused to 'imitate any thing or action, any reality already given in the world existing before and outside its own sphere'.[68] And Derrida readily grants as much. But he argues that the model of the 'original' is simply *interiorized*. The metaphysical idea of divine origin as the *presence of what is to itself* is now converted into the transcendental consciousness of the creative subject: 'the ideality, for the subject, of what is'.[69]

To declare, as the romantic idealists and existentialists did, that art no longer copies nature but productively transforms it, is nonetheless to remain captive to a metaphysics of presence. The extra-value or the extra-being attributed to the 'original' creations of imagination simply make 'art a richer kind of nature, freer, more pleasant, more creative; more natural'.[70] Thus, regardless of whether reality is taken as the original and imagination as the copy (Platonism) or vice versa (romantic idealism), the old origin-imitation model prevails. Both in its role as a production of truth (as original presence) and as a reproduction of it (as the re-presentation of original presence), art is still considered to take the 'presence of the present' as its norm, order and law. In both cases, it is in the name of *truth* 'that mimesis is judged, proscribed or prescribed'.[71]

The deconstruction of the metaphysical concept of mimesis is, therefore, logically contingent upon that of *origin*. It is just such a double deconstruction which occurs, Derrida believes, in Mallarmé's text *Mimique*. Here we are concerned not with a 'neo-mimetologism', but with a play of *mimesis* which completely explodes the traditional notion of imitation. We are confronted with a mime which has no original, a representation without presence, pure mimicry. Of this self-deconstructing *mimesis*, Derrida comments:

There is no imitation. The mime imitates nothing. And to begin with he doesn't imitate. There is nothing prior to the writing of his gestures. Nothing is prescribed for him. No present has preceded or supervised the tracing of his writing. His movements form a figure that no speech anticipates or accompanies. They are not linked with *logos* in any order of consequence . . . We here enter a textual labyrinth panelled with mirrors.[72]

Derrida's description of Mallarmé's *mimique* as a labyrinthine play of mirrors is, as we have seen, paradigmatic of the post-modern *imaginaire*. The mime in question makes up a gestural writing which no pre-established script or authorial voice has determined. The *mimique* is a form of writing which imitates nothing which pre-exists it – neither author, event nor world. It is a 'mute soliloquy', as Mallarmé says, which does not illustrate 'any actual action'; it is a writing which parodies itself as writing. 'The mime ought only to write himself on the white page he is,' explains Derrida, 'he must *himself* inscribe *himself* through gestures and plays of facial expressions. At once page and quill, Pierrot is both passive and active, matter and form, the author, the means and the raw material of his mimodrama.'[73]

Let us take a closer look at Derrida's detailed argument. In writing his text, *Mimique*, Mallarmé would appear to be himself writing on a white page. But what is he writing about? Mallarmé is in fact writing about another text – a pantomime booklet about the mime of *Pierrot Murderer of his Wife*. But this booklet was itself written as a sort of record *after* the event of the mime performance. And the performance was itself a sort of text: a gestural mimodrama in which Pierrot wrote himself on a white page (i.e. on himself as a white body and face).

The process of mimetic reference does not, however, end even here. We still have not hit upon an 'original' event which would bring the process of mimicry to a full stop. For what, we may now ask, is the referent of Pierrot's own gestural body-writing? Does it not refer back to the crime of Pierrot who murdered his wife – an event which the mime serves to recall? But this supposedly past crime which the mime artist *represents* for us in his present performance is, as Mallarmé notes, merely 'under the false appearance of a present'. For it is precisely the act of miming the 'past' crime in the 'present' which makes the crime appear in the first place. There is and was no crime outside of the mime itself. The mime, in other words, reproduces a past crime which never occurred before the mime production. Pierrot's mime of the crime refers, in short, to nothing other than the mime of Pierrot's crime. Derrida spells out the decon-structive implications of Mallarmé's *Mimique* as follows:

The center of presence is supposed to offer itself to what is called perception, or generally, intuition. In *Mimique*, however, there is no perception, no reality offering itself up, in the present, to be perceived. The plays of facial expression and the gestural tracings are not present in themselves since they always refer, perpetually allude or represent. But they don't represent anything that has ever been or can ever become present: nothing that comes before or after the mimodrama . . . .[74]

Mallarmé's text, *Mimique*, thus constitutes an absolute extension of the play of writing which nothing escapes, a *mise en abîme* of the whole notion of intentional reference upon which Western metaphysics, from Plato to Sartre, is based. *Mimique* pushes the labyrinthine play of textual mirroring to the point where nothing which *is* lies beyond it. For what Mallarmé is actually describing is 'a scene of writing within a scene of writing and so on without end, through a structural necessity that is marked in the text. The mime, as "corporeal writing", mimes a kind of writing and is himself written in a kind of writing.'[75]

One might be tempted here to reintroduce the notion of imagination. May we not suppose that the mime which imitates nothing resembles a sort of transcendental act which produces an original meaning out of itself, creating out of nothing the very thing it is representing? But this idea of an originary production is, Derrida insists, a contradiction in terms. One could push Mallarmé's *mimique* back into an originary metaphysics of meaning only if the cycle of mimicry could be traced back to some fixed point of origin. But such is not the case. What we are faced with is a mimicry imitating nothing –

a double that doubles no simple (origin), a double that nothing anticipates, nothing at least that is not itself already a double. There is no simple reference. It is in this that the mime operation does allude, but alludes to nothing, alludes without breaking the mirror, without reaching beyond the looking glass.[76]

Derrida's deconstructive account of *Mimique* thus leads us beyond both the premodern paradigm of the mirror (Platonism) and the modern paradigm of the lamp (idealism) to the postmodern paradigm of the looking glass. The story of mimesis has come full circle and, as it were, cancelled itself out. Deprived of an original point of reference – either in transcendental reality or the transcendental imagination – mimesis voids itself into its own limitlessness.

Mallarmé himself prefigured this postmodern turn of events when he observed: 'That is how the mime operates, whose act is confined to a perpetual allusion without breaking the ice or the mirror.' For he here recognized that the world as text is a looking glass which reflects no reality but only gives rise to 'reality effects'. Reality no longer exists except through the simulacrum. What we are left with is the 'mirror of a mirror . . . a reference without a referent, without any first or last unit, a ghost that is the phantom of no flesh, wandering about without a past, without any death, birth, or present'.[77] And Mallarmé appears to have reinforced this motif by introducing the metaphor of the *lustre*. In opposition to the figure of the 'sun' as an original source of light – which Platonism held was reflected in the mirror and modern idealism held was identical with the power of human imagination – Mallarmé proposed the figure of the 'lustre': a chandelier with multiple glass pendants endlessly reflecting each other. With this trope of the multi-faceted lustre which is nothing beyond its own intra-fragmenting light, we discover that there is no essential distinction between 'the image and thing, the empty signifier and the full signified, the imitator and the imitated'.[78]

The postmodern figures of the labyrinth of multiple mirrors, the impenetrable looking glass and the fragmentary lustre, all serve to undermine the metaphysical paradigms of the imaginary as 1) the copy of an original (onto-theology) or 2) the original of a copy (romantic idealism). In other words, the paradigm of parody – as an endless play of a copy copying a copy and so on *ad infinitum* – not only deconstructs Platonic models of *mimēsis*, it also deconstructs modern idealist attempts to posit the transcendental imagination as an original production of meaning in its own right. All such efforts, from Kant and Schelling to Sartre, to 'reverse mimetologism or escape it in one fell swoop by leaping out of it with both feet, only amount to an inevitable and immediate fall back into the system (of truth as origin). In striving to suppress the model of the double altogether, one simply reverts to the metaphysical model of direct intuition: the production of presence or truth'.[79]

The postmodern deconstruction of the metaphysical opposition between the imaginary and the real opens up an alternative logic – the logic of 'dream', of the unconscious play of language which defies the logocentric principle of non-contradiction. This dream logic of 'doubling' is frequently found in literary works, e.g. Mallarmé's notion of *mimique* or Joyce's portrayal (especially in *Finnegans Wake*) of a 'nighttime consciousness' which permits us to have 'two thinks at a time'. It is also anticipated by Nietzsche's talk of 'truth becoming woman' (a pure play of appearances without any reference to an underlying reality), and by Freud's description of the unconscious as a play between the strange (*unheimlich*) and the familiar (*heimlich*). Such models undermine the *either/or* logic of metaphysics in their insistence upon 'the paradoxes of the double and of repetition, the blurring of the boundary lines between *imagination* and *reality*'.[80] And Derrida suggests that one even finds instances of this postmodern logic of deconstruction in the mathematical discovery of the concept of 'undecidability'. (Gödel demonstrated in 1931 that a proposition is undecidable when, given a system of axioms governing a multiplicity, the proposition is neither a consequence of these axioms nor in contradiction with them, is neither true nor false with respect to these axioms).

The paradigm of parody is undecidable, as Derrida concludes, because it is 'at once image and model, and hence image without model, without verisimilitude, without truth or falsity, a miming of appearance without concealed reality, without any world behind it . . .'[81] This deconstruction of the opposition between imagination and reality – by parodying one in terms of the other in perpetual mimicry – is most fittingly expressed, says Derrida, in the postmodern figure of *play*. The practice of play casts aside the whole system of truth. For in the play of parody, imitation mimes imitation in an endless circle of allusion that has no ground. And 'one can never know what the allusion alludes to, unless it is to itself as a process of alluding. . . . Wherein allusion becomes a game conforming only to its own formal rules. As its name indicates, allusion (from the latin, *ludere*) plays.'[82]

What are the main conclusions to be drawn from Derrida's deconstruction of the metaphysical distinction between the imaginary and the real? Firstly, we can no longer legitimately ask the question: *what is imagination?* Such a question presupposes that there is some 'essence' of imagination which would distinguish it from a real world existing beyond it or before it. But Derrida's extension of the notion of writing to include *everything* means that the opposition between imagination and reality dissolves into the textual play of undecidability from which nothing escapes. The world becomes a never-beginning, never-ending text where 'everything is reflected in the medium or speculum of reading-writing *without breaking the mirror*'.[83] This implies, furthermore, that the question *what is literature?* is also meaningless. We can no longer speak of a decidable being of literature, one which might be distinguished from some notion of 'truth' which it is supposed to imitate (as copy) or create (as origin). Literature is *both* true *and* false. And following the deconstructive logic of undecidability this also means it is *neither* true *nor* false.

Secondly, we can no longer ask: *who imagines?* Once the notion of an origin of meaning has been done away with, it makes no sense to speak of a transcendental or existential subject who produces or reproduces images. There is no *author* of the text, no human centre from which the imaginary emanates, no father of writing, no one, in short, to intend or intuit meaning. Nor can one speak any more of the *reader* as some decidable identity existing outside of the text. Father and son, author and reader, mirror each other in a textual interplay of mutual dispossession. Or as Philippe Sollers puts it in *Numbers*, his parody of Mallarmé and Joyce: 'all of us are thus turning about inside the cage . . . are ceaselessly placed in echo-positions' (*Numbers*, 3.11). And this typically postmodern sentiment is further elaborated on by Derrida himself when he asks the so-called reader:

But who is it that is addressing you? Since it is not an 'author', a 'narrator', or a 'deus ex machina', it is an 'I' that is both part of the spectacle and part of the audience; an 'I' that, a bit like 'you' . . . functioning as a pure passageway for operations or substitutions, is not some singular and irreplaceable existence, some subject of 'life', but only, moving between life and death, reality and fiction, etc., a mere function or phantom.[84]

It is not really surprising, therefore, to find Derrida applying a deconstructive reading to his own practice of philosophical writing in such experimental works as *Glas*. Here he presents us with a text made up of multiple parodic texts, a text without preface or conclusion, without, it would seem, even the possibility of an identifiable author or reader – a form of writing which appears to write itself, and to undo itself as it does so.[85]

Thirdly, we can no longer ask the question: *how does one escape from parody?* There is no escape. The imagination which is deconstructed into a parody of itself abandons all recourse to the metaphysical opposition between inner and outer. There is no way out of the cave of mirrors, for there is nothing *outside* of writing. Or, in Derrida's own phrase, there is no *hors-texte*. As an endless mimicry of itself, the text cannot be transcended in the direction of some extra-textual *beyond*. Postmodernism may thus be said to return us to Plato's cave of imitations, but with this crucial difference: it is no longer the inner world of mimetic images which imitates the outer world of truth, but the contrary. And this, of course, amounts to saying that the whole Platonic hierarchy of the imaginary and the real is finally dissolved into parody. Derrida offers this graphic account of the self-deconstructing imagination:

Imagine Plato's cave not simply overthrown by some philosophical movement but transformed in its entirety into a circumscribed area contained within another – an absolutely other – structure, an incommensurably, unpredictably more complicated machine. Imagine that mirrors would not be *in* the world, simply, included in the totality of all *onta* (things) and their images, but that things 'present', on the contrary, would be in *them*. Imagine that mirrors (shadows, reflections, phantasms etc.) would no longer be *comprehended* within the structure of the ontology and myth of the cave – which also situates the screen and the mirror – but would rather envelop it in its entirety . . . The whole hierarchy described in the *Republic*, in its cave and its line, would once again find itself at stake and in question . . .[86]

The history of the Western philosophy of imagination is brought to its end. Not in the sense of being completed, but of being displaced into *another* order of representation – the postmodern order of perpetual allusion. Thus displaced, the cave of mirrors ceases to be an inferno of darkness and falsehood. Parody becomes, ironically, the only *paradis* (to borrow Sollers' pun) left to us in the age of deconstruction.

Apocalypse without end

Is the dominance of the parodic paradigm in contemporary culture merely an intellectual accident of our times? Or does it perhaps signal the approach of a postmodern apocalypse? In his lecture *La Différance*, delivered to the *Société Française de Philosophie* in 1968, Derrida admits that the increasing emphasis on the deconstructive logic of undecidability in literature, science and philosophy, epitomizes the 'juncture of what has been most decisively inscribed in the thought of what we conveniently call our epoch'.[87] Derrida shows himself reluctant to subscribe to the Heideggerean view of the end of metaphysics as a new dispensation in the destiny of Being. And he pointedly declares himself wary of negative theology and prophetic post-structuralism. Yet he does concede that the rapport between deconstruction and the crisis of our contemporary world is a 'formidable question'.

If deconstruction takes place everywhere it takes place, where there is something (and is not therefore limited to meaning or to the text in the bookish sense of the word) we still have to think through what is happening in our world, in modernity, at the time when deconstruction is becoming a motif . . . with its privileged themes, its mobile strategy etc. All my essays are attempts to have it out with this formidable question. They are modest symptoms of it, quite as much as tentative interpretations.[88]

To thus acknowledge deconstruction as a symptom of the

break-up of Western culture and its metaphysical foundations, is to tempt a postmodern vision of apocalypse. And Derrida ultimately seems to recognize as much. The most explicit expression of this recognition to date comes in the form of a spirited defence of the use of apocalyptic strategies of discourse in a lecture on the *Apocalyptic Tone in Philosophy*, delivered at the Cérisy conference on his work in 1980. The term apocalypse, Derrida here reminds us, actually means to 'un-cover' (*apo-kaluptein*). But in unmasking the logocentric language of power and authority, apocalyptic discourse is, paradoxically, often compelled to mask itself in order to evade official censure. The cyphered and cryptic character of much apocalyptic writing is, therefore, to be understood as a ruse to defy the authoritarian status quo. Such subversive discourse – whose multiple meanings Derrida compares to an argus with a thousand looks – resists assimilation to the established order of domination. It hijacks the accredited system of communication and undermines its legitimized conceptual oppositions. As such, there is for Derrida nothing less conservative than the apocalyptic genre. Confusing codes and confounding conventional expectancies, this genre poses a radical challenge to the dominant ideological consensus. The apocalyptic strategy is the final word in the demystification of ideology. But, as practised by Derrida himself, one suspects that it is also more than that – it is demystification itself brought to the point of self-deconstruction!

Derrida accepts that his own writings have at times been charged with an apocalyptic tone. This he sees as an inevitable consequence of the fact that to write *about* the 'end' of the Western system of understanding – that is, about an apocalypse of human consciousness – is itself apocalyptic. With particular reference to his text *Glas*, which deploys two 'doubled' columns – one literary, one philosophical – deconstructively played off against each other, Derrida grants the existence of an 'apocalyptic laughter about apocalypse': a laughter resulting from the textual juxtaposition of the sacred apocalypse of St John and the profane apocalypse of Jean Genet. And in *La Carte Postale*, Derrida detects traces of apocalyptic play in the disseminating world of postmodern communications, a world where 'humanist' man has become a 'post'-man. This is a text, by Derrida's own admission, in which the

> allusions to the Apocalypse and its arithmosphy are multiplied, where everything speculates (*spécule*) on numbers and particularly the number seven, the 'written 7', the angels, 'my angel', the messengers and the postmen, the prediction, the announcement and the news, the 'burning' holocaust and all the phenomena of *Verstimmung*, of changes of tone, mixing of genres, wanderings of destiny or of *clandestination* – so many signs of a more or less bastard apocalyptic filiation.[89]

Derrida concludes his apocalytic commentary on his own apocalyptic commentaries on other apocalyptic commentaries (Genet, St John, etc.), with a deconstructive analysis of the word 'Come'. This word, which recurs at several key points in the Apocalypse of the New Testament, as well as in some of Derrida's own texts (e.g. *Pas, Survivre* and *En ce Moment même dans cet Ouvrage me voici*), is said to exemplify the apocalyptic tone. It transgresses the whole order of Western thought – what Derrida calls 'onto-eschatotheology' – in so far as it opens up a deconstructive play without ever becoming an object, theme or representation subsumable under the logocentric order. 'Come' is the gesture of a word which cannot be retrieved or interpreted in the analysis of that word. It is an address *without a subject*: we do not know who speaks it or whom it is spoken to. Nor do we know whether it is uttered in the past, present or future tense. A citation which cannot be temporally situated, it undoes the linear narrative time of the human imagination.

'Come' is a paradigmatic figure of postmodern apocalypse because it deconstructs every conceptual or linguistic attempt to *decide* what it means. It hails from an altogether *other* order. And what it puts into play is an apocalypse *without* apocalypse – since we cannot say or know or imagine what the 'truth' of apocalypse means. Derrida thus confronts us with the word of an apocalyptic writing which can only be grasped, if at all, as an *ending without end*. He leaves us with this undecided and undecidable conclusion:

> We cannot say what it *is* . . . 'Come' does not address itself to an

identity determinable in advance . . . and it is derivable from nothing
which could be verified, presented, decided or appropriated as an
origin . . . . What here announces itself as promise or threat, is an
apocalypse without apocalypse, an apocalypse without vision, truth or
revelation, dispatches without message or destination, addresses
without any fixed addresser or addressee, without last judgment,
without any eschatology other than the tone of 'Come' itself . . . an
apocalypse beyond good and evil . . . the apocalypse of apocalypse,
'come' is in itself apocalyptic. Our *apocalypse now*.[90]

After the holocaust of the second world war, Adorno asked,
who can write poetry? After deconstruction, we may well ask,
who can write philosophy? In our postmodern era of apocalypse
both the poetry and philosophy of the human imagination would
seem to have reached their end. What is to come is, apparently,
beyond the powers of imagination to imagine.

APPENDIX

A note on postmodernism and computer science

The terms of 'play', 'undecidability' and 'bricolage' have come to occupy a dominant role not only in postmodern philosophy – Lévi-Strauss, Lacan, Barthes and Derrida – but also in some contemporary theories of Computer Science.

One of the most cherished ideals of the pioneers of Artificial Intelligence is a *self-programming computer system*. The basic word units of a computer memory can, like monetary units in an economic system, serve a wide variety of functions, depending on the use to which each is put to in the overall program: as numbers in binary notation, as dots on a TV screen or as letters in a text, etc. Each word possesses an 'address' where, as in a postal coding system, it can be 'located' by the Central Processing Unit or memory bank. But cybernetic research is moving more and more in the direction of decentralized data processing and since the 1950s has established sophisticated *programs that translate programs*. This gave rise to the idea of new *compiler languages* (e.g. 'algorithmic' language as opposed to the more primitive 'machine' or 'assembly' languages). The function of these 'compilers' is primarily to translate from a higher to a lower language, taking 'input' (a finished algorithmic language) and producing 'output' (an elaborate sequence of machine language). And at a more advanced level again, there has emerged the practice known to the *aficionados* of computer research as 'bootstrapping' where a compiler is used to compile extensions of itself – rather like a child who acquires speech by using language to acquire more language, that is, by pulling himself up by the bootstraps.

Alongside this recent movement in the direction of *self-*

programming, there is also the curious phenomenon of mimetic *'emulation'*. With the introduction of microprogramming, a computer of one manufacturer can now be configured so as to possess the same machine language instruction set as a computer of another manufacturer. Hence one talks of the microprogrammed computer 'emulating' the other computer. By way of conveying the immensely sophisticated electronic operations which now exist in computers, one might cite Hofstadter's useful comparison with the advanced telephone system:

> You have a choice of telephones to connect to. But not only that, many different calls can be handled simultaneously. You can add a prefix and dial into different areas. You can call direct, through the operator, collect, by credit card, person-to-person, on a conference call. You can have a call rerouted or traced. You can get a busy signal. You can get a siren-like signal that says that the number you dialled isn't 'well-formed', or that you have taken too long in dialling. You can install a local switchboard so that a group of phones are all locally connected – etc., etc. The list is amazing. . . . Now sophisticated operating systems carry out similar traffic-handling and level-switching operations with respect to computer users and their programs.[1]

Computers have now reached such a stage of development that the experts are talking about 'automatic programs' which can even second-guess their own programmers. 'The space of all possible programs is so huge that no one can have a sense of what is possible', and that is one of the main reasons for the drive towards languages of ever higher levels.[2]

For most people today the computer system is something mysterious, amorphous and remote, an entity whose power, like that of money, has grown to such proportions that one is no longer likely to give full credence to Lady Lovelace's reassuring dictum that 'computers can only do what they are told to do'. With the outstripping by computer 'software' (the program) of 'hardware' (the physical computer apparatus itself), the question is increasingly posed: who is it that tells the computer what to do? Does the programmer run the program or does the program run itself?

Returning to the comparison with the monetary system of late capitalism, we might think of the man in the street, puzzled by the enigma of inflation, deferring to his National Central Bank, which in turn defers to the International Investment Banks which in turn defer to the Dow Jones Average in New York and the other financial exchange markets of Tokyo, Paris, London, etc – which in turn defer to each other or back to themselves in a seemingly endless recursive circle. Here the 'software' of money flow has massively outstripped the 'hardware' of metal assets and institutional frameworks. It is as though the entire monetary system of late international capitalism is without any single centre, a criss-crossing network of connections, a hall of mirrors reflecting and multiplying the diverse market forces from around the globe. The money exchange model, like that of the self-programming computer, is essentially ex-centric to itself, an interplay of forces without any identifiable source, origin or centre. The core of the network appears to be empty, absent, decentred.

It is perhaps not surprising, then, that we find so many contemporary artists and commentators of the growing high-tech paranoia beginning to wonder whether in the year 2000 it will be the human imagination which plays the computer game or the computer game which plays the imagination. Is what we call imagination becoming no more than an 'epiphenomenon' – a mere 'effect' of an overall systems organization?[3] Or is it still meaningful to talk of a creative imagination at all when the human subject feels caught up in a 'multiplicity of circuits difficult to master, a society constituting a sort of web extending to infinity which no centre seems to control'?[4] These are, as we shall see, some of the central questions which increasingly preoccupy the postmodern imagination in search of itself.

CHAPTER EIGHT

Postmodern Culture: Apocalypse Now?

The deconstruction of imagination is by no means an isolated concern of philosophy. As we have had occasion to remark in our preceding review of structuralist and post-structuralist critiques, the tendency to undermine the basic metaphysical relationship between the imaginary and the real is a recurring feature of contemporary Western culture in its broadest aspects. Hitherto we have concentrated on *theoretical* accounts of this deconstructive tendency. The fact is, however, that many post-modern works of art, literature and cinema themselves manifest a critical preoccupation with the imminent death of imagination and testify to a keen worry about its apocalyptic consequences. Before proceeding to assess some of the social and ethical impli-cations of this theme, it may be useful to examine some recent examples of its *aesthetic* development at first hand. This should help us to more fully appreciate the extent to which the decon-struction of imagination is a global phenomenon and not merely the rarefied invention of a few Parisian intellectuals. To this end, we select for analysis six representative samples of postmodern culture: two from literature (Pynchon's *V* and Beckett's *Imagin-ation Dead Imagine*), two from cinema (Fellini's *Ginger and Fred* and Wenders' *Paris, Texas*), and two from the plastic arts (*Le Magasin de Ben* at the Beaubourg centre and the *Palace of Living Arts* in California). These works testify, in their different ways, to the erosion of the modernist conviction that avant-garde art is the expression of unique and innovative personalities who can somewhow redeem society by an elitist fiat of imagination. They mark the emergence of a postmodernist aesthetic of *undecidability* wherein it becomes increasingly difficult to distinguish between art and artificiality, culture and commodity, imagination and reality.

1 *V.* (Pynchon)

Thomas Pynchon's *V.* (1963) is one of the most arresting examples of postmodern writing. This novel, or rather anti-novel, bears witness to several characteristics of deconstruction: the sovereignty of the void replaces the sovereignty of the creative subject; a random chain of arbitrary signs disrupts the continuous narrative of events; the 'tradition of the new', which typified the modern age, begins to disclose an anti-tradition of parody at its very centre; the project of the transcendental imagination to transform reality falls victim to a non-human system of disorder (which Pynchon frequently identifies with the anonymous laws of entropy); a feeling of encroaching apocalypse drowns out the humanist belief in history as a progressive development towards a better world. In all of these respects, *V.* is a powerful illustration of the self-negating aesthetic of postmodernism, an aesthetic according to which, in Susan Sontag's words, 'art tends towards anti-art, the elimination of the subject . . . the substitution of chance for intention, the pursuit of silence'.[1]

The eponymous Lady V. of Pynchon's text exemplifies the annihilation of the humanist model of consciousness. She has no identity. She is a 'nobody' who exults in catastrophe and chaos, floating from one persona to the next with a deranging logic which contravenes all novelistic conventions of character and plot. V. is metamorphosis without motive, a shifting multiplicity of masks with no decidable expression: Leda and St Anne, a blood-sucking vampire and Queen Victoria, a perverse Maltese priest, an English convent girl, a plague-bearing rat in the sewers of New York, and a Parisian dressmaker who conducts a fetishistic lesbian relationship with a ballerina entirely by means of mirrors. V. cannot be determined in terms of time, place or gender. What we are confronted with is an endless play of representations without presence. A phantom of disassembly.

Pynchon's anti-hero, Herbert Stencil, pursues the fleeting figure of V. She has become for him an idealized fetish which he wants to pin down and possess. This obsessive search serves as a parody of the *quest structure* of both the premodern epic and the modern novel. And the very name, Stencil, is itself a mock-heroic allusion to the image-making power of man. But imagination is impotent in this apocalyptic world of fracture and failure. The alchemical will to transmute the dross of reality into the gold of imagination is reduced to pitiless self-irony. Romanticism is shipwrecked on the rocks of its own emptiness. We find ourselves in a pseudo-world where the false reigns supreme, where the dividing line between the imaginary and the real has been abolished.

V. represents the disconcerting consequence of such a vision. S/he is at once the goal of perfection and the epitome of depravity, the confusion of the animate with the inanimate, a postmodern golem without God or Man, a living body in the form of a streamlined automaton with ivory limbs and a navel of sapphire. The great humanist ideal of Renaissance art has here declined into anti-humanist pastiche – a point brought home to us with disturbing force in a scene where Botticelli's *Birth of Venus* is torn from its frame and mercilessly mocked.

Pynchon's text is a good instance of the postmodern practice of 'mixed writing'. V. constitutes a sort of intertextual collage which mimics the major narrative genres of bourgeois fiction: adventure novels, detective novels, political or spy novels, romantic and erotic novels. Indeed, one critic, Tony Tanner, claims to have identified mock stylistic allusions to over nine distinguished fiction writers including Cervantes, Conrad, Faulkner and Waugh.[2] Similarly, Pynchon defies the standard novelistic conventions of time and space. He reduces narrative temporality to a series of discontinuous episodes – as evident in the lack of connection between the various chapters and the fragmentary sequences of war, genocide and international violence. And the norms of spatial continuity are equally made a nonsense of by the manner in which the text shifts abruptly from one city, country or continent to another without any predictability. While *V.* ostensibly presents itself as a riddle to be solved, according to the traditional expectancies of the novelistic plot, it soon becomes evident that what we are concerned with is a labyrinthine anti-plot without identifiable beginning or end. Moreover, Pynchon's habit of mixing together diverse literary genres with the even more random discourses of advanced technology, multi-national commercialism and multi-media communications, further heightens the reader's sense of disorientation. A gulf opens up between the reader's deciphering intentions and the almost innumerable fields of signification which the text sets in play.

In this way, we, the readers of *V.* are compelled to share the same feeling of dislocation experienced by the characters described in the text itself. And in this mirror-play between the worlds of reading and writing, the line separating the 'inside' from the 'outside' of the text becomes blurred. Within the text, the most obvious case of the failure of human imagination to come to grips with the cyphers of meaning is that of Stencil. As the name suggests, Stencil is a carbon copy of the postmodern age which he, and we the readers, inhabit. He is, as Pynchon tells us, 'the century's child'. His repeated efforts to interpret reality in terms of his obsessional quest for *V.* lead him deeper and deeper into a maze of mimetic simulacra where the clues multiply to the absurd point where they cancel each other out. By coming to mean *everything*, *V.* comes to mean *nothing*. And no matter how much Stencil strives to adhere to the consoling conviction of his father, a British secret agent, that 'events would fall into ominous patterns', he cannot escape the growing uncertainty that anything actually *is* what it *seems*. The paternal metaphysics of being disintegrate into an anarchistic play of appearances. And as the enigmas incessantly multiply rather than resolve themselves, Stencil himself becomes a paradigmatic figure of the fatherless and traditionless postmodern imagination.

But Stencil is not the only anti-hero of *V.* There is also Benny Profane, an obese roadworker of no fixed abode who potters about in the debris of post-industrial society – without hope, without desire, without a project. Benny has given up the quest for a transcendental ideal of perfection. He is not only a 'man without qualities' but a 'man without imagination'.[3] Oblivious to clues and cyphers, Benny is content with the surfaces of things. He doesn't seek ulterior meanings because he knows there aren't any. He dissipates himself in meaningless chaotic parties – symptomatic of the breakdown of communal existence – or else moves around aimlessly from no-place to no-place in a pastime called 'yo-yoing'. Benny differs from Stencil in that he has abandoned the attempt to make sense of the fragments of meaning which surround him. On the contrary, he surrenders to them, propelled passively back and forth like a yo-yo on a string that is held by no one. He is, in short, a typical representative of the Whole Sick Crew of Contemporary America – 'a motiveless wanderer up and down the generic street of the twentieth century, going nowhere and seeing only separate objects in a disintegrating world.[4]

The text itself displays no preference for either Stencil or Benny. All options remain open. Is Stencil a madman or a creative visionary? Is Benny a down-to-earth realist or a dim-witted dullard? And at a broader thematic level, the issues remain equally undecided. 'Are we surrounded by plots – social, natural, cosmic; or is there no plot, no hidden configuration of intent, only gratuitous matter and chance? . . . Is everything "patterned", ominously or otherwise; or is everything sheer accident?'[5] These undecidable enigmas of Pynchon's text are similar to those which haunt many other postmodern writers from Joyce and Borges to Beckett and Calvino. Here, as there, one finds that the undecidability of theme is echoed at the level of form. V is, as we noted, a palimpsest of multiple modes of writings. The book is made up of different styles, tongues, dialects, vernaculars and languages. And since there is no omniscient narrator or dominant authorial voice to guide us, it is impossible to know which writing is true and which false, which main-text and which sub-text. By thus generating an open series of diverse and often conflicting interpretations, Pynchon makes the reader an accomplice to the textual play of indeterminacy.

As the reader proceeds he discovers that the traditional divide between form and content, style and character, collapses

altogether. This is perhaps most obvious in the indeterminable
nature of V. S/he represents a process of limitless signification –
or what the deconstructionist philosopher would call a *floating
signifier without a signified*, a written trace without identifiable
origin. Hence we find Stencil's quest to decipher the meaning
of the 'letter V.' taking the form of an endless paper chase of
signs leading nowhere – from the V-note jazz clubs to the fantasy
land of Vhessin to Vesuvius, Venus, Venezuela, the Vatican,
Valetta and so on. Stencil, we are given to suppose, is also in
search of his own origins, his own parental beginnings. His
mother disappeared in mysterious circumstances. And Stencil
has no way of knowing whether she 'died in childbirth; ran off
with someone or committed suicide'. Indeed, this uncertainty is
heightened by Stencil's father's cryptic memo about V. – 'Not
who, but what: what she is.' Assuming the form of a neutralized
shifting sign, V. becomes (and perhaps always was) no more than
an anonymous *what*. The text informs us that Stencil 'doesn't
know who she is, nor what she is. He's trying to find out. As a
legacy from his father.' But this quest to ascertain *V's* original
identity is doomed to failure. It may even be seen as an impossible attempt to 'humanize' the contemporary void by pursuing
the traditional question of origins – a question which deeply
informs the entire history of Western metaphysics (as Heidegger
reminds us in the *Letter on Humanism* when he declares that
'every humanism remains metaphysical').

In proportion to the failure of the humanist quest of Stencil's
imagination, V. grows increasingly inhuman. And this breakdown
of humanism is also portrayed as a breakdown of ethics. Stencil's
incapacity to imagine V. in any human shape or form is seen as
a symptom of her absolute 'divorce from moral intention'. In the
persona of the Bad Priest or Anti-Christ, V. celebrates the cult
of the inanimate and warns her/his admirers against the foolishness of childbirth. V. hails the anti-virtues of 'mineral symmetry'
and the 'immortality of rock'. And the only form of love allowed
is that of a narcissistic mirror-play which, like the irreversible
law of entropy, leads to a slow decline into sameness – to the
'Kingdom of Death'. Thus the relation between V. and her
fetishized double, the ballerina Melanie, is described ironically

as an 'ageless still-life of love'. The love-play is portrayed as an 'impersonation of the inanimate, a transvestism not between sexes but between quick and dead; human and fetish'. Pynchon offers us this chilling account of their necrophiliac voyeurism:

Mélanie watching herself in the mirror; the mirror-image perhaps contemplating V. from time to time. No movement but a minimum friction . . . V. needed her fetish, Mélanie a mirror, temporary peace, another to watch her have pleasure. . . . With the addition of this other – multiplied also, perhaps, by mirrors – comes consummation: for the other is also her own double. . . . As for V., she recognized – perhaps aware of her own progression towards inanimateness – the fetish of Mélanie and the fetish of herself to be one.[6]

Pynchon suggests that this play of doubling is symptomatic of the general contemporary trend towards an impersonalized society. He compares the pseudo-love which V. and Mélanie engage in through the 'mirror's soulless gleam', to a 'version of tourism'. Tourism is also a kind of mirror-play of sameness, for the tourist group is one which 'creates a parallel society of its own in every city'. By virtue of its ability to reduce a multiplicity of unique places to a multi-national, transpersonal abstraction, tourism is ironically defined as 'the most absolute form of communication we know on earth'. But Pynchon pursues a further analogy: he relates the demise of the humanist imagination to the increasing mechanization of life in our computerized age. V. thus represents the *end* of the modern imagination in the double sense of being *both* the absolute goal *and* the absolute negation of Stencil's transcendental quest. S/he is a postmodern technological madonna who annihilates the life-giving impulse of humanity. In one of his many daydreams Stencil pictures her thus:

Skin radiant with the bloom of some new plastic; both eyes glass but now containing photoelectric cells, connected by silver electrodes to optic nerves of purest copper wire leading to a brain exquisitely wrought as a diode matrix ever could be. Solenoid relays would be her ganglia, servo-actuators move her flawless nylon limbs, hydraulic fluid be sent by a platinum heart-pump through butyrate veins and arteries. Perhaps even a complex system of pressure transducers located in a marvellous vagina of polythene. . . .[7]

It is not difficult to see the link between such a passage and Marinetti's disturbing claim in the *Futurist Manifesto* that 'war is beautiful because it initiates the dreamt-of metalization of the human body'.[8]

Stencil's search for the 'ultimate plot' of origins thus appears to find its nemesis in a nightmare of mechanistic inhumanity. Apocalypse Now. But perhaps the matter is not so simple. ('Perhaps' is one of Pynchon's favourite terms.) The apocalyptic vision offered in this text is fundamentally ambivalent. Towards the end of the novel Stencil's father speaks of a 'Third Kingdom', one of postmodern apocalypse which will replace both the premodern kingdom of the authoritarian Father and the modern kingdom of the libertarian Son. This Third Kingdom, he surmises, may well announce the 'Paraclete as Mother'. 'Comforter, true', he muses, 'But what gift of communication could ever come from a woman. . .' Does such a figure of pentecostal comfort and communication exist? Is such a figure just another of V.'s many disguises for the Kingdom of Death? Or is this Third Kingdom only something which can be discovered by renouncing the romantic-messianic quest for V. altogether, espousing instead another quite different (post-metaphysical) myth – 'a myth rickety and transient as the bandstands and the sausage-pepper booths of the street . . . only a temporary interest, a spur-of-the-moment tumescence'?[9]

Between the apocalyptic kingdom of abstract death and the gentle humdrum apocalypse of the everyday street, the fate of the human imagination appears to hang. The former promises the destruction of imagination from an excess, as it were, of its own romantic desire to pursue a metaphysical truth which no longer exists, to dissolve into the emptiness of its own idealist dreams. The latter promises the possibility of a quite different form of imagination: one which disavows metaphysical quests and resolves to discover some other kind of meaning in the random debris of the postmodern landscape. Pynchon's text remains, on this crucial question, as on all others, undecided and undecidable.

2 *Imagination Dead Imagine* (Beckett)

If Pynchon's *V.* is an anti-novel, Beckett's *Imagination Dead Imagine* might be described as a sort of post-novel – or at least a post-script to the novel. Having apparently exhausted the traditional resources of the novel genre, Beckett turned in the sixties to another kind of prose writing (in addition of course to his plays), an experimentation with minimalist texts called variously, *écrits manqués, residua* or *texts for nothing. Imagination Dead Imagine*, published in 1965, is such a text. And the reason we choose to comment on it here is that it impressively confronts the postmodern dilemma of the deconstruction of imagination.

One of the avowed aims of Beckett's work has been to 'deanthropomorphize' the writing process.[10] This could best be achieved, Beckett affirmed in an early essay, by investigating the contemporary 'rupture of the lines of communication' – a rupture consequent upon the 'breakdown of the object' on the one hand, and the evacuation of the 'author's own interior existence' on the other.[11] Such an investigation might succeed, Beckett believed, in disencumbering us from the romantic idea of imagination, exposing it as an anthropocentric 'eye of prey' which reduces the world to its own solipsistic fictions.

It is with a similar scruple in mind, that Beckett contrasts 'involuntary memory' which yields a 'revelation of reality' to 'voluntary memory or imagination' which impedes such a revelation. Voluntary memory, writes Beckett in his *Proust* essay of 1931, 'is of no value as an instrument of evocation and provides an image as far removed from the real as the myth of imagination'.[12] The danger of fiction is that it denies the otherness of being by transforming experience into the aesthetic project of the authorial subject. Beckett would appear to be endorsing the postmodern call for a disassembling of the humanist imagination, therefore, when he affirms that 'art', which had for so long been hailed as the 'one ideal and inviolate element in a corruptible world', is in fact quite 'as unreal and sterile as the construction of a demented imagination'.[13] No amount of imaginative activity can recreate a genuine experience of things: imagination is a wilful process wherein a human subject casts its pre-conceived patterns onto what is other than itself. The voluntary imagination is thus denounced by Beckett as the 'inevitable gangrene of romanticism'. It is nothing more than the 'dream of a madman', a fiction which can never escape from the closed circle of its own representations. As Beckett puts it: 'Reality . . . remains a surface, hermetic. Imagination, applied *a priori* to what is absent, is exercised *in vacuo* and cannot tolerate the limits of the real.'[14]

The paradoxical task of Beckett's writing is to dismantle fiction by means of fiction. 'The same lie lyingly denied', as he expresses it in one of his *Texts for Nothing*. Hence one finds Beckett's various narrators undermining their own narratives. They do this by means of self-critical asides (e.g. 'What a misfortune, the pencil must have slipped from my fingers' or 'This is awful writing') and by other strategies which undermine the fictional conventions of plot and character. One even finds the narrator of one text making cross-textual allusions to the narrators of other texts in a mirror-play without ostensible exit:

Let us leave these morbid matters and get on with that of my demise. . . . Then it will all be over with the Murphys, Merciers, Molloys, Morans and Malones, unless it goes on beyond the grave.

Even the self-mocking imagination cannot, it seems, escape itself: an infernal predicament conjured up by one of Beckett's narrators, Malone, who significantly compares himself to a Prometheus devoured by the vulture of his fiction! What Beckett appears to be hinting at here is that the power of imagination, which the mythic figure of Prometheus first unleashed upon the world, has ceased to serve man and become instead a power which incarcerates man within himself. The crime has returned to plague its inventor.

Beckett's writings may be read accordingly as repeated attempts to bring imagination to an end. But such a project is condemned to fail from the outset. For fiction is a self-reflexive play which cannot undo itself except by inventing another fiction. And so Beckett stoically resolves to make a virtue of necessity. He advances a postmodern aesthetic of failure – i.e. the failure of the artist to transcend art by parodically exposing its artifice. Beckett explains as much in the last of his *transitions* dialogues with George Duthuit in 1949:

To be an artist is to fail, as no other dare fail, that failure is his world and to shrink from it desertion. . . . I know that all that is required now is to make of this submission, this admission, this fidelity to failure, a new term of revelation, and of the act which unable to act, obliged to act, he makes, an expressive act, even if only of itself, of its impossibility . . .[15]

This failure of imagination to escape from itself is the central preoccupation of *Imagination Dead Imagine*. The self-referentiality of the title makes this plain. This short text takes the form of a monologue in which an unnamed narrator describes a rotunda-shaped skull which reduces the outside world to a hot white light that comes and goes. We are presented with a mathematical emblem of colourless, expressionless, zero degree writing – Beckett's metaphor, it would seem, for the postmodern imagination. All that is left of Western humanist culture is an impersonalized space where the very distinction between the imaginary and the real has collapsed. Imagination has self-destructed into a void. It has ceased to function as a human agency of expression, will and creativity and become instead a mechanical drift towards sameness. Even the two white automatons slowly expiring within the rotunda are mere doubles of each other, lying back to back, head to tail, in a condition of suspended animation where the only hint of life is to be found in mist on mirrors held before their faces. These golem-like 'doubles' of the dying imagination are disconcertingly inhuman. They might well pass for inanimate, the text tells us,

but for the left eyes which at incalculable intervals suddenly open wide and gaze in unblinking exposure long beyond what is humanly possible. . . . The faces too, assuming the two sides of a piece, seem to want nothing essential.[16]

Struck by the absolute stillness and silence of these moribund figures, the narrator still remembers a time when things were otherwise. But it is no more than a memory, a memory without images. And there is, apparently, no way back.

Beckett presents us here, as in his *Texts for Nothing*, with an abstract phantasmagoria which fails to convert itself into recognizably human forms. We are exposed to a text which refuses to satisfy our readers' appetite for representation – a featureless writing which bespeaks the vanishing of all forms of language, an anti-narrative where action is reduced to the technical repetition of an alegbraic formula (a,b,c,d).[17] But this entropic decline of imagination into emptiness cannot even bank on the finality of death as a solution. What we have is an ending without end, an apocalypse without apocalypse to use Derrida's phrase. For even in imagining imagination dead, we still find ourselves caught in the reflexive spiral of imagining. Life and death have become indistinguishable:

No trace anywhere of life, you say, pah, no difficulty there, imagination not dead yet, yes, dead, good, imagination dead imagine . . . world still proof against ending tumult. Rediscovered after what absence in perfect voids it is no longer the same, from this point of view, but there is no other.[18]

The last phrase says it all. There is no *other*: no other perspective, no other reality, no other world, no other being *tout court* – human or divine. Only a dying imagination which cannot die, affirming one moment that 'there is better elsewhere', only to deny it the next: 'there is nothing elsewhere'. The old metaphysical quest for some original experience, some lost holy grail, some transcendental truth, seems irreversibly suspended: 'no question now of ever finding again that white speck lost in whiteness . . .'.[19]

Beckett's deconstruction of imagination is significantly accompanied by a parallel deconstruction of the metaphysical metaphor of the *sun*. The use of the solar trope to signify the transcendental origin of light and life was, as we noted in former chapters, a key feature of both Platonic and modern theories of imagination. For Platonism the sun represented that other-worldly source of truth which the mimetic activity of imagination contrived to 'copy'. For modern idealism, romanticism and existentialism, by contrast, this figure became identified – in the wake of Kant's Copernican Revolution – with the power of the creative imagination itself. In Beckett's postmodern scenario we can no longer trace the 'rise and fall' of the sun back to any source. We do not know whether it comes from *within* the white skull of imagination or from *without*: 'The light that makes all so white no visible source, all shines with the same white shine, ground, wall, vault, bodies, no shadow.'[20] Indeed, the very movement of the sun itself – 'from white and heat to black and cold' – defies all human expectations, for it is regularly reversed, 'the rise now fall, the fall rise'. Imagination is thus reduced to a skeleton of itself – imagining, as it were, its own posthumous existence, its life after death. No longer able to represent the transcendental sun in imitational copies (as in Platonism) or to project the sun's light from within itself (as in romantic idealism), the postmodern imagination of Beckett's text is the seemingly inconsolable manipulandum of an electronically computerized world – a world where an artificial light comes and goes according to a logic of mathematical precision and technical reversibility which it is beyond the powers of human subjectivity to comprehend.

But Beckett's verdict on the future of this postmodern imagination is ultimately as 'undecidable' as that of Pynchon's. He refuses in the final analysis to opt either for hope (imagination lives even in death) or for despair (imagination is dead even as it lives). Like the doubled partners in the rotunda-skull, Beckett's images are suspended halfway between a grave and a womb, at one moment resembling half-dead corpses, the next half-living embryos. Beckett's paradoxical attitude is perfectly summed up in the negative/affirmative phrase of one of his unnamable narrators – 'I can't go on, I'll go on.'[21] The fate of the postmodern imagination remains for him fundamentally uncertain: 'Where we have at once darkness and light, there we also have the inexplicable. The key word of my work is *perhaps.*'[22]

The undecidable status of imagination in Beckett's work may be extended to the more general question of narrative – understood as the capacity of man to transform history into stories. Already in the 1930s, the German critic, Walter Benjamin, was predicting that the advent of the mechanical age of mass reproduction and technological communications would threaten the traditional practices of imaginative creation (the idea of an 'original work' giving way to that of a reproducible copy) and, more broadly, of storytelling as a whole. Benjamin defines storytelling as the 'ability to exchange experiences'. And the crisis of narrative in our time is construed accordingly as a symptom of the decline of communicable experience.

The transition from epic storytelling to the novelistic modes of narration had already signalled a shift from communal to solitary experience – that is, from a feudal to a bourgeois culture. But it is with the arrival of the new mass-media society that the fundamental function of narrative, in both its epic and novelistic guises, is most decisively undermined. This threat to narrative – understood as 'the ability to recount one's entire life'[23] – is, for Benjamin, directly related to the contemporary fragmentation of human experience, a situation evidenced in people's growing incapacity to communicate with, or listen to, one another. Our mass-media age has converted personal *communication* into a system of impersonal *communications* – a technological system in which experience becomes synonymous with information. If storytelling has now become a vanishing art, states Benjamin, the global dissemination of information, and the attendant necessity for immediate explanation, have played a crucial role:

Every morning brings us the news of the globe, and yet we are poor in noteworthy stories. This is because no event any longer comes to us without already being shot through with explanation. In other words, by now almost nothing that happens benefits storytelling; almost everything benefits information.[24]

Other more recent critics have offered perceptive commentaries on this postmodern crisis of narrative imagination. In *The*

Dismemberment of Orpheus: Toward a Postmodern Literature (1971), Ihab Hassan speaks of 'culture and consciousness, turning against themselves, yielding everywhere metaphors of inversion in anti-art'. One of the dominant accents of silence which persists in postmodern literature is, he observes, 'the negative echo of language, autodestructive, demonic, nihilist'. Postmodern writing 'burlesques the very mystery of art' and 'burns into the ash of parodic apocalypse'.[25] Frederic Jameson spells out some of these apocalyptic implications in a study entitled 'Postmodernism, or the Cultural Logic of Late Capitalism' (1984). The 'postmodern force field' opened up by what Jameson refers to as the 'schizophrenic writing' of Beckett, Sollers and other contemporary authors, is one where the narrative subject has lost its capacity to organize its past and future into coherent experience. The result is a 'practice of the randomly heterogeneous and fragmentary' – a practice which Jameson, following Derrida and the deconstructionist philosophers, calls *textuality* or *écriture*.

The collapse of narrative coherence is expressed at two basic levels: the *breakdown of the signifying chain* and the *breakdown of temporality*. Jameson gives the following shorthand account of the former breakdown:

Meaning on the new view is generated by the movement from Signifier to Signifier: what we generally call the Signified – the meaning or conceptual content of an utterance – is now rather to be seen as a meaning-effect, as that objective mirage of signification generated and projected by the relationship of Signifiers among each other. When that relationship breaks down, when the links of the signifying chain snap, then we have schizophrenia in the form of a rubble of distinct and unrelated signifiers.[26]

This collapse of coherent signification means not only the loss of the narrative ability to order the past, present and future of a sentence, or more generally of a text, but also the loss of our ability to unify the past, present and future of our own psychic or biographical experience. What we are then faced with is a 'schizophrenic fragmentation' of narrative – resulting in the typically postmodern phenomenon of a discontinuous present

/

divorced from both historical time and human subjectivity. As Jameson explains,

The breakdown of temporality suddenly releases this present of time from all the activities and the intentionalities that might focus it and make it a space of praxis; thereby isolated, that present suddenly engulfs the subject with undescribable vividness, a materiality of perception properly overwhelming, which effectively dramatizes the power of the material Signifier in isolation. This present of the world or material signifier comes before the subject with heightened intensity, bearing a mysterious charge of affect, here described in the negative terms of anxiety and loss of reality . . .[27]

The fragmentary character of postmodern writing typifies this kind of narrative disordering. The narrator feels helplessly exposed to a textual play in which each signifier or sentence borders on silence, threatening to lose contact with what precedes or follows it, and thus frustrating all narrative attempts to link the present with a remembered past or anticipated future. Jameson sees the Beckettian text as offering a powerful illustration of such a self-destructive narrative – 'where a primacy of the present sentence in time ruthlessly disintegrates the narrative fabric that attempts to reform around it'.[28]

But the question still remains as to whether we can legitimately speak of the end of narrative in any absolute or schismatic fashion. For does not even Beckett's breakdown of storytelling itself take the form of a story told and untold? Or as one of his own narrators puts it, is not his desire to bring the story to an end not 'itself a search for a story to begin'?[29] In short, does the deconstruction of narrative imagination, witnessed in both contemporary literature and philosophy, really mean the end of narrative in all its forms; or does it not, perhaps, also point to the possibility of other properly postmodern modes of narrative in however self-critical a guise?

It is just such a question which Paul Ricoeur addresses in the second volume of his monumental *Time and Narrative*, entitled *Fiction and Narrative* (1984). Noting the trend in contemporary writing towards a dissolution of narrative order, Ricoeur asks if we might not interpret this as an invitation to the reader to

actively engage with the text in order to recreate some new kind
of narrative sense, to recompose the text which the author has
decomposed. But in order to prevent the reader becoming
utterly frustrated in his efforts to rewrite the narrative for
himself, the author must have introduced into the text new
narrative codes: codes more subtle, complex and disguised than
those of traditional narrative, but still somehow *related* to the
latter – albeit in the sense of inversion or derision. The idea of an
absolute rupture with all forms of narrative expectancy, however,
would make the very activity of reading itself impossible.[30] The
innocent eye sees nothing, as Ricoeur reminds us. So that even
the anti-narratives of postmodern writing presuppose, on the
reader's behalf, some reference to the narrative paradigm that
is being negated or transformed.

Be that as it may, Ricoeur is prepared to admit that we may
well be moving in the direction of a culture which will attempt
to abolish all traces of narrative imagination, and by implication
all reference to the historical past or future. This is not an
impossibility. But if it is a possibility, it is one, Ricoeur suggests,
which threatens to destroy the very notion of human culture
itself. He leaves us with this poignant and defiant plea:

Maybe we are, in fact, the witnesses – or the artisans – of a certain
death, that of the art of narrating, from which proceeds the death of
storytelling in all its forms. . . . Nothing actually precludes the possibility that the cumulative experience which, at least in the cultural zone
of the West, offered an identifiable historical style, should today be
stricken with death. . . . Nothing excludes the possibility that the metamorphosis of narrative plot should somewhere confront a limit beyond
which we could no longer acknowledge the formal principle of temporal
configuration (between past, present and future) which makes narrated
history into a unified and complete story. And yet . . . and yet. Maybe
it is necessary, *in spite of everything*, to continue to have confidence in
the need for concordance which still structures the expectancies of
today's readers, to continue to believe that new forms of narrative,
which we are not yet in a position to identify, are already in the process
of being born, forms which would testify that the narrative function is
capable of metamorphosis without actually dying. For we have no idea

of what a culture could be in which one no longer knew what it means to *narrate*.[31]

Perhaps the survival, despite all the odds, of some kind of narrative imagination in the postmodern age is as important as its erosion. Is Ricoeur's hope against hope not also echoed in the resolution of Beckett's own unnamable narrator –

You must say words, as long as there are any, until they find me, until they say me . . . perhaps they have carried me to the threshold of my story, before the door that opens on my story, that would surprise me, if it opens, never know, in the silence you don't know, you must go on, I can't go on, I'll go on.[32]

3 *Ginger and Fred* (Fellini)

If contemporary literature has so keenly registered the crisis of imagination in our age of mass communications, how much more likely is this to be the case with contemporary cinema – a

Still from Fellini's 'Ginger and Fred'

medium which is, after all, an integral part of this communications technology. Film is, of course, confronted with an added
dilemma. For the decline of the individual imaginative subject
appears to be an almost inevitable casualty of film itself, i.e. as
a vehicle of mechanically reproduced and retransmitted images.
Whence the circular problem of how such a mass medium as
cinema can hope to put its own mass media culture into question.
Here we find the problem of the camera turning back on the
camera, reflecting its own imaging process; the problem of
cinema's self-exposure which has so preoccupied contemporary
film-makers, from Fellini and Altman to Resnais and Godard.[33]

Fellini's *Ginger and Fred* (1985) is a brilliant cinematic indictment of the postmodern Civilization of the Image. Once again,
as in much contemporary philosophy and literature, we witness
the paradigm of mimetic parody – and the attendant paradox of
attempting to deconstruct parody by means of parody. Fellini
presents us with a film which mockingly portrays the pseudo-
world of TV consumerism. He tells the story of two ageing
variety artists, Ginger and Fred, who are trying to make a come-
back by reviving their good-old-days tapdance routine for a
popular Television Spectacular. The Variety Show in question
features Ginger and Fred as the 'genuine article' – that is, as an
authentic *live* TV representation of Yesterday's *original* Dance
Hall presentation. But as their stage names betray, this 'authentic' partnership of Ginger and Fred is itself no more than an
'imitation' of the 'truly authentic' Hollywood stars – Ginger
Rogers and Fred Astaire. And the *mise-en-abîme* process does
not stop here. It is extended further (in fact indefinitely) by our
awareness, as spectators of Fellini's film, that Fred Astair and
Ginger Rogers were, in their films of the thirties, themselves
purporting to re-enact on the Hollywood Silver Screen a 'live'
theatrical dance act. But this supposedly live performance was
itself, of course, merely an illusion produced by their films . . .
and so on.

So what we have in Fellini's *Ginger and Fred*, as in Mallarmé's
Mimique, is a play of perpetual allusion: a series of multiple
imitations without any real original. Ginger and Fred never
actually existed. They are pseudonymous performers whose very

performance makes reality imitate the image. A major distinction, however, between Mallarmé's interrogation of *mimesis* and Fellini's is that the latter focuses not on a literary-theatrical production of images but on the filmic reproduction and retransmission of images to millions of viewers. The main aim of Fellini's film is to demythologize the pseudo-world of the television image. But he is aware that this demythologization runs the risk of being mistaken – by many viewers of his film – as a mere *duplication* of the mythology. 'I wouldn't be surprised if the public fail to fully recognize the ironic, parodic and critical dimensions of my film', admits Fellini rather ruefully in an interview in *Le Monde*. 'What I represent is so close to the truth, and at the same time so far short of the totally absurd and degrading truth it represents, that it is possible, after all, that the viewers of *Ginger and Fred* will simply see it as a documentary, a reportage of what they see everyday on TV!'[34] Indeed Fellini's very use of the term 'truth' to designate the actual *falsehood* of the mass-consumption TV culture he seeks to expose, epitomizes the vicious circle of postmodern parody.

Aware of this problem, Fellini has gone to great lengths to prevent such a confounding of imitation and reality, of artifice and truth. He deploys numerous 'distancing' devices in *Ginger and Fred* to counter the viewers' conditioned tendency to confuse the *means* of representation (e.g. his own film) with *what* is represented (e.g. the pseudo-world of consumerist television). These devices include: the replacement of linear 'realist' narrative with a fragmented montage technique which aims to resist the spectator's habit of passively identifying with the events portrayed; the use of a stylized babble or media-speak to underline the *artificiality* of the TV 'show'; recurring shots of background mirrors – in the dressing rooms, make-up parlours, rehearsal centres and even on the TV stage-floor itself – which remind us that what we are witnessing is itself a mere replay of surface images. Indeed, Fellini even goes so far as to parody the whole Star System generated by the culture of the Silver Screen, choosing two typical 'Fellini stars' for the roles of Ginger and Fred – Giuletta Massina (who played in *Nights of Cabiria, La Strada* and *Julietta of the Spirits*) and Marcello Mastroianni (who played in *La Dolce Vita*, *8½* and *The City of Women*). By so doing, Fellini seems to be acknowledging the fact that even his own films have become part of the contemporary cult of the celluloid image. So that any attempt by him to parody this cult must logically include some element of self-parody.

The principal target of Fellini's film remains, however, the mass-media tendency to fabricate models of pseudo-existence for a servile public. This tendency leads to the erosion of the distinction between being and appearance, between what *is* and what *is not*. 'We want to *be* what we see on television, to inhabit the houses we see there, to consume the commodities TV publicity imposes on us', remarks Fellini. Consumer television brings about a situation where 'our greatest desire is to *resemble* someone or something in a kind of collective homogenization, thereby forgetting our own identity.'[35]

Ginger and Fred sets out to expose this homogenizing process. The film is punctuated by the image of a giant transmission spire, extending into the sky like a latter-day tower of Babel. The numerous scenes of the variety artists preparing and performing their acts for the TV Show are ominously dwarfed by this ever-revolving electronic beam of light: a seemingly all-seeing eye which in fact sees nothing at all but blindly relays identical pre-recorded images to millions of identical pre-tuned television screens. This mechanical eye which towers over the recording studio is only matched in inexpressiveness by the permanent smile on the TV compère supervising the order of pseudo-events within the studio. There would seem to be no escape. And even when Fred and Ginger remove their masks and make-up after the show and return to their 'real' lives once again – Ginger to her domestic simplicity and Fred to his alcoholic consolation – the camera wheels back to the night sky lit only by the omnipresent transmission beam, relentlessly broadcasting its images of unreality to every corner of society. It is this invasion of reality by prefabricated falsehood which *Ginger and Fred* so vehemently denounces. Fellini himself offers this account of his film's iconoclastic intentions:

The film tries to transmit several signals about this phenomenon. The antenna which sweeps the sky is for me a symbol of an extraordinary scientific discovery which has made possible formidable technical advances and engendered an immense logistical organization . . . but that all too often serves to propagate inauthentic and derived images which wallow in an atmosphere of obligatory festivity, a celebration of emptiness, nothingness, the void. Commercial television puts everything into the same sack of advertising, sing-song and hype. So that even the most horrible tragedy, the most disturbing reality, can be made to seem acceptable. A disproportion occurs where images are always only images, nothing but images. Reality, tragedy, life, cease to have any existence beyond the little screen on which they appear. And hence we come to expect no more of ourselves than the reaction of *spectators*, all desire for reflection and even feeling being annihilated.[36]

This kind of television culture, Fellini concludes, is mutilating our capacity for solitude and violating our most intimate and secret spaces. 'Imprisoned by its invasive rituals, we stare at a luminous box which spews forth thousands of events which cancel each other out in a vertiginous spiral.'[37]

Fellini's critique is directed particularly against the commercialized media networks which increasingly dominate Western popular culture and install what he calls a Dictatorship of Insignificance. While habitually associated with the American multi-channel system, the reign of consumerist TV images has now been extended to most parts of the globe. Indeed, the pervasive spread of the commercial media was specifically noted by the UNESCO Report on Communications of 1980, a document which alerts us to the dangers of a rapidly expanding communications industry dominated by 'supranational technology and non-accountable powers'.[38] Saul Bellow, the Nobel prize-winning author, has echoed these sentiments in a series of impassioned attacks on the new multi-national television culture. Bellow claims that an expanding empire of mindless 'light and noise' is now threatening the very basis of Western civilization as we have known it.[39] There is, he says, a disturbing neglect of the 'real furniture of the human soul' witnessed, for example, in sensationalized TV presentations which render the viewer 'immune to reality even as cataclysms occur before our eyes'.

This desensitizing of human experience is compounded by the erosion of narrative coherence and continuity caused by the fragmentary nature of TV production and consumption. (Bellow cites recent statistical reports which show that the majority of American children have become so used to 'channel-switching' at the press of a remote-control button that they rarely watch a single programme from beginning to end.) The resulting diminution of the human attention span exacerbates the general movement of our postmodern culture towards a disjointed consciousness and poses a genuine threat to the very notion of human liberty. The task of the contemporary artist, Bellow retorts, is to try to 'disinter reality from the trash'.

Fellini would no doubt concur with the tenor of such remarks. But the problem remains of how to effectively communicate this message to the public at large. As already noted, Fellini is aware of the difficulties involved in trying to critically unmask a mass media culture by means of a mass medium such as cinema. For in order to convey the disjunctive effects of this culture the film-maker is almost invariably compelled to employ its methods. Thus Fellini finds himself caught in a mirror-play of parody which threatens to swallow up all reference to reality. The real world becomes indistinguishable from the imitational one. And when, for example, the characters of *Ginger and Fred* finally leave the TV centre and make their way back to the city streets through which they first arrived, they still remain immersed in a pseudo-world of advertising slogans and clichés. Indeed, the train station where Ginger and Fred part company in the closing shot, actually displays a giant TV screen incessantly spewing forth images. Even the outer world has become a worked-over version of the televisual text – an ever-expanding web (*textum*) in which the spider and the fly have become one and the same. But how many viewers of Fellini's film actually register this built-in irony? Or indeed the further irony that as they themselves (the viewers) make their way out of the cinema onto the neon-signed, commercial-postered roads of city or town, they too are merely transiting from one mediatized text to another? There would seem to be no exit – no way of breaking through the multiple mirrors. Even the critical power of parody appears neutralized.

4 *Paris, Texas* (Wenders)

Much of postmodern cinema is caught up in a 'winner loses' logic. The more it strives to expose the world of pseudo-images by parodying those images, the more it seems to confirm the omnipotence of the very system it wishes to contest. The more striking the portrait of a totalizing system of false imitations, the more impotent the viewer feels. To the extent, therefore, that the film-maker *wins* by successfully representing an omnivorous system of mass media representation, to that same extent he *loses* – 'since the critical capacity of his work is thereby paralysed; and the impulses of negation and revolt, not to speak of those of social transformation, are increasingly perceived as vain and trivial in the face of the model itself'.[40]

This winner loses logic is a common feature of those contemporary films which attempt to demystify the mesmeric power of mass-produced images by means of such images. Apart from Fellini's *Ginger and Fred*, one might also cite here Pakula's *Network*, Eyre's *The Ploughman's Lunch*, Truffaut's *Day for Night* or the various film critiques of the American Dream as an alienated pseudo-image by directors such as Scorcese (*The King of Comedy*), Coppola (*One from the Heart*), Altman (*Nashville*) and Wenders (*The American Friend* and *Paris, Texas*). The problem confronting each of these directors is how to construct a parody which will not degenerate into pastiche. For with the growing threat to the individual imagination – and, by formal extension, to the very notion of a personal *style* – we find the emergence of a near global kind of media-language where the traditional ideas of a social, national or personal identity are voided of real content and reduced to the level of empty imitations. Frederic Jameson, one of the most perceptive commentators of this postmodern trend, describes the dilemma as follows:

Parody finds itself without a vocation; it has lived and that strange new

Scenes from Wenders' 'Paris, Texas'

thing pastiche slowly comes to take its place. Pastiche is, like parody, the imitation of a peculiar mask, speech in a dead language; but it is a neutral practice of such mimicry, without any of parody's ulterior motives, amputated of the satiric impulse, devoid of laughter and of any conviction that alongside the abnormal tongue you have momentarily borrowed, some healthy linguistic normality exists. Pastiche is thus blank parody . . . With the collapse of the high-modernist ideology of style – what is as unique and unmistakable as your own fingerprints – the producers of culture have nowhere to turn but to the . . . imitation of dead styles, speech through all the masks and voices stored up in the imaginary museum of a now global culture.[41]

This pervasiveness of pastiche is evidenced in the contemporary consumers' desire for a society transformed into sheer images of itself, into pure spectacle – a society where, in Guy Debord's phrase, the 'image has become the final form of commodity reification'.[42]

Wim Wenders' *Paris, Texas* (1984) describes the plight of imagination in the contemporary world of pastiche. The very title is a mock allusion to Paris, France: and as such it reflects the impossible quest of postmodern man for roots or origins in a society where everything has been reduced to imitation. Wenders' film explores the contemporary hankering for some authentic 'memory' unadulterated by the commodification of the American Dream.

Although Wenders is himself a German director, he believes that the loss of 'original memory' in today's American culture has become a generalized feature of the Western world as a whole. Through the spread of a commercial communications system, the interchangeable culture of Coca-Cola, Levi's Jeans and Burgerlands has penetrated to every corner of our globe. 'The Americans have colonized our unconscious', remarks Wenders, 'and recreated the so-called "free" world according to their own image.'[43] Wenders' choice of Texas as a location for his film is no doubt an allusion to the pseudo-society which has virtually become a multi-national model for our age, thanks in large part to such cult TV soap operas as *Dallas* or *Dynasty* which have now been transmitted in most countries in the world. Wenders' film, in short, is concerned with the plight of narrative imagination in a world turned Texan – a world of surfaces increasingly deprived of memory or self-reflection, where fantasy and reality have become so confused and the notion of self-identity so diluted that it no longer seems possible to tell one's story.[44]

Paris, Texas is, as Wenders informs us, constructed around the image of 'a man leaving the freeway and walking straight into the desert'.[45] Travis has, it would seem, abandoned the American Dream of the open highway leading to a promised land. He has also abandoned speech. Four years later, Travis returns from his desert purgatory, his dark night of the soul, mute and apparently empty. He refuses to speak his name or give his identity. And it is from this existential zero point that he will begin to retrace his narrative, to piece together the scattered fragments of his former existence. Wenders recounts Travis' quest to regain a sense of historical continuity, to become a true father to his lost son and a true son to his own dead father – by returning to a forgotten place called Paris, Texas where he himself was first conceived.

Travis has no memory of Paris, Texas. All he possesses is a faded photograph of a derelict patch of land left to him by his parents. And, likewise, the sole record Travis has of his own wife and child is an old photomat strip. Collected from the highway motel where he has been convalescing by his brother Walt (a successful billboard advertiser), Travis is brought back to Walt's home in Los Angeles. Here Travis' son, Hunter, is being fostered. Hunter's only memory of his father and mother – Travis and Jane, who walked out on him and on each other after a traumatic split-up four years previously – is that provided by a home movie. Starting from this movie within the movie, Wenders traces the gradual attempt made by father and son to *remember* each other, to reconstruct the family scene of *le temps perdu*.

This quest for recollection takes place against a typically postmodern landscape of urban fragmentation. Their first tentative encounters are made all the more vulnerable by being graphically framed by shots of amorphous cityscapes – criss-crossing fly-overs, multi-corporation office blocks and airport runways where screaming jets land and take off by the minute. But in spite of this incessant interference from the megapolis of noise and concrete, father and son slowly develop some kind of contact. As they come to know each other they become increasingly more aware of the missing link in their relationship. Jane, the mother, is still absent. And so leaving Los Angeles (and the foster parents) behind them, Travis and Hunter set off towards Texas in search of the *third person* of their holy trinity, the remaining member of the 'original' family.

The evasive figure of the lost mother dominates the quest structure of Wenders' film, just as it does in Pynchon's V. The mother is the archetypal symbol of 'origin' – the very concept of which is ostensibly threatened by the postmodern culture of substitution and imitation. The mother exemplifies historical memory. She represents the possibility of returning to the source, of retelling one's personal life history. But the quest is by no means a foregone conclusion. An ominous note is struck at one point on the journey when Travis is confronted by a Crazy Man shouting (as the script tells us) 'like a voice crying in the wilderness'. As he wanders across an overpass spanning a gigantic 16 lane freeway, Travis is assailed by these words from the crazy prophet of doom:

I make you this promise on my mother's head, or right here and now, standing on the very head of my mother, our Good Green Mother Earth, which anybody who wasn't born in a fuckin' sewer ought to know and understand to the very marrow of their bones. . . . There is nowhere, absolutely nowhere in this godforsaken valley . . . Not one square foot of that will be a safety zone. . . . You will all be extradicted to the land of no return. You'll be flying blind to nowhere. And if you think that's going to be fun, you've got another thing coming.[46]

The location chosen for this postmodern prophecy of doom is itself highly significant. Is not the serpentine network of inter-locking car lanes a typical postmodern involution of the modern American dream of the pioneering freeway leading to a promised land? The brief description entered in Wenders' own Director's script is telling: 'A baffling labyrinth of intertwining highways, overpasses, entrances and exits appears . . .'. After a prolonged search – with all the trappings of a parodic 'road' story à la Kerouac – Jane is finally located in the red-light underworld of Houston, Texas. The everyday reality of Jane's life is the very opposite of the 'idealized' mother. She works in a peep-show club where customers pay to see her act out their sexual fantasies in a basement booth panelled with one-way mirrors. The parallel with V.'s looking-glass boudoir is suggestive: Jane too serves as a fetishized object catering to voyeuristic desires. And she also resembles V. in her role as a fallen pentecostal angel hiding out in the depths of a postmodern metropolis. Moreover, there is a telling allusion to the sinister legacy of the American dream of freedom: the outside wall of the peep-show club features a faded mural of the Statue of Liberty brandishing her flame.

Travis rents out the fantasy booth and watches Jane behind the one-way screen. But they never *see* each other face to face – only through a glass darkly. They do, however, succeed in making contact through *words*. Refusing to pursue his relationship with Jane at the level of obsessional desire – i.e. the voyeuristic *imago* – Travis communicates with her by means of a telephone link. Turning aside from the see-through glass, Travis enables Jane to gradually identify him, and herself, in the story which he recounts of their past life together. And Jane eventually responds in kind by retelling and therefore remembering her own past. In this manner, they recover together the power of lost speech and lost memory. They endeavour to penetrate the false veneer of the mirror-image by narrating to each other the untold dimensions of their respective experiences for the first time. Travis and Jane are thus portrayed as latter-day versions of Orpheus and Eurydice who seek to escape the underground maze of pseudo-images in which they have been imprisoned by renouncing the voyeuristic medium of obsessional vision. They learn the art of mutual dis-possession, as it were, and reach toward a form of genuine communication, however brief, by abandoning the image in favour of the word. Their face to face is verbal, not visual. Its very condition of possibility is an unconditional postponement of vision. This renunciation of the image (as commodity possession) also entails a more general renunciation of the American Dream itself (as belief in a messianic origin and end). *Paris, Texas* refuses the traditional Hollywood tale of the family happily reunited after a long ordeal. And in a sort of parodic inversion of the Orpheus myth, it is Travis who must eventually vanish so that Jane can re-emerge into the light. Or to use the trinitarian metaphor, the father must forgo his rights of unifying possession and disappear so that the absent pentecostal mother can meet again with her son. The mirror-play of fetish images must dissolve so that language can reach through the looking glass to another kind of meaning.

But what kind of a meaning can this be? Now that Travis has told his true story, how is he to end it? Where does he go from here? Standing alone on a Houston sidewalk, surrounded on all sides by giant inter-reflecting glass highrises, Travis would seem devoid of destination. And the concluding shot of him smiling as he drives along an Interstate highway – past a neon-lit poster for Republic Bank sporting the slogan 'Together We Make It Happen' – offers no clear solution. Will he remain in some alienated no-man's-land? Will he return to the silence of the desert? Or seek solace in the aimless wandering of the highway leading nowhere? Wenders chooses to leave this question dismayingly unresolved.

Travis' narrative of origins is thus left suspended in mid air. He still retains his tattered photograph of the patch of land in Paris, Texas. But this ancestral memory cannot be recovered as a *literal* reality. It has ceased to be a geographical place where Travis, Jane and Hunter might recommence a life together. At best, the memory has become a kind of moral conscience, recalling a moment of past hope which must be acknowledged as *past*: a utopian recollection which cannot be realized in the postmodern world of commodified images, but which stands nonetheless – qua memory – as an indictment of the existing world, a testimony to how things might have been in another kind of world. Wenders himself seems to regard this testimonial power of the photograph as a critical counterpoint to the very medium of cinema itself. He writes:

I think that photography has remained much more intact as both form and act than has cinema. Everywhere in the world, we can still come across photographs which have a conscience and a morality of what they are about. There is a form and a style in this work whereas in cinema, style, form and the consciousness of action are vanishing more and more. Cinema has been profoundly affected and emptied by advertising and by television. But there is an ethic in the photograph in contrast to cinema which has become *catastrophic* in this regard. . . . The American dream presents itself as a nightmare through the images it produces.[47]

And we might also recall here the significance Wenders attaches to the word in *Paris, Texas*: Travis communicates with Jane through a telephone link and learns to play with Hunter through an intercom system. Indeed his parting message to Jane and Hunter is left in the form of a tape recorder. Face to face encounter is, curiously, made possible through the medium of the word.

So where does this leave Wenders himself as a film-maker? If it is true that *Paris, Texas* points to the non-cinematic media of the photograph and the narrated word as possible means of contesting the postmodern cult of the pseudo-image, it is equally true that this message is conveyed through the medium of cinema itself. And so we are back once again with the paradox of cinema trying to deconstruct itself from within, trying to combat the power of the cinematic image by means of cinematic images. And even if cinema itself were to be renounced in favour of the photograph or the word, it is by no means sure that one would discover a language of reality untainted by the civilization of the commodified image. Wenders' formal quest is, in the final analysis, quite as unresolved, and perhaps unresolvable, as Travis' own narrative quest.

The films of Fellini and Wenders are by no means isolated curiosities. They express, albeit in a heightened form, a fundamental crisis in contemporary cinema as a whole. Gilles Deleuze has argued in *L'Image-Movement, Cinema I* (1983) that this crisis is an integral dimension of post-Hollywood cinema, reflecting a wide variety of social, political, moral and aesthetic factors. These include, for Deleuze, the second world war and its consequences, the collapse of the American Dream in both its cultural and economic aspects, the growing consciousness of minority groups, the extraordinary inflation of images both in the external world of society and within people's heads, and the bankruptcy of the old Hollywood genres.[48] All of these factors have combined to erode the basic humanist belief that some universal situation could give rise to an action capable of transforming Western society. And such an erosion of faith in the power of human action has been reflected cinematically in the breakdown of what Deleuze calls the 'action-image' of traditional cinema. This has resulted in the search for a new kind of image – a 'reflexive-image' which self-consciously adverts to its own crisis of representation.

Much of postmodern cinema is characterized by the emergence of this new self-reflective image, one which manifests itself, according to Deleuze, in terms of the following traits.

(i) *The Dispersive Situation.* The image no longer possesses a single identifiable context of reference but relates to multiple interchangeable and often inexpressive personages or events.

(ii) *The Dissolution of Spatial and Temporal Continuity.* The connections between events lose their linear causal thread and become increasingly determined by chance and contingency – the episodes themselves surpassing the intentions of the characters who experience them.

(iii) *The Replacement of the Action Plot by an Open-ended anti-plot of Aimless Wandering.* The adventure genre loses its initiatory status and its 'realist' linkage to an historical sense of place, becoming instead a to-ing and fro-ing in undifferentiated cityscapes or underworlds (e.g. Fellini's TV studio and Wenders' peep-show booth could, in principle, be located anywhere in the postmodern universe).

(iv) *The Denunciation of Faceless Conspiracies.* There is a growing sense of unease about the invasion of human privacy and interiority by a communications system which reprocesses human experience in the form of electronically reproducible images: images which reduplicate reality, which in turn begins to reduplicate the images. (And this sense of media conspiracy is frequently accentuated by the use of the camera as a sort of an invisible third eye or anonymous monologue determining the rapport between the persons perceiving and the persons perceived.)

(v) *The Critique of the Rule of Cliché.* Postmodern society is increasingly portrayed as an artificial world woven together out of repeatable clichés and bereft of any real experience of historical praxis or coherence.

Deleuze regards this last characteristic as the most alarming. He offers this apocalyptic account of the omnipresent power of clichés:

They are floating and anonymous images which circulate in the external world, but also penetrate each person and constitute his internal world, so much so that each one of us possesses no more than the psychic clichés by means of which he thinks and feels, becoming himself a cliché amongst others in the world which surrounds him. Physical clichés of sight and sound and psychic clichés feed off each other. In order for people to survive in such a world it is necessary that this miserable world has infiltrated into their innermost consciousness, so that the inside is like the outside.[49]

This is exactly the kind of situation which Fellini's *Ginger and Fred*, or indeed Scorcese's *King of Comedy*, seeks to parody in the form of the television Variety Show which sucks its interchangeable performers and viewers into the same void of non-meaning. It is also the scenario evoked by Altman in *Nashville* where everything that happens on or off the stage – each 'live' event – is reduplicated in tape-recordings, visual reproductions and televized performances. Altman's film brilliantly captures an American society where everybody imitates everybody else, a pseudo-world of vicarious experience extending from popular culture to national politics. *Nashville* is a mock-heroic spoof of the whole Country and Western music industry as a multi-media mimicry of the 'authentic' cultures of the 'original' pioneers. And this mirrorland of pastiche – where each character becomes substitutable for the other since the very notion of 'identity' has been reduced to that of mere 'image' – itself serves as backdrop for a US Presidential Campaign, a media hype in which the faceless candidate, messianically promising to change society by changing the National Anthem into something everyone can sing, eventually becomes confused with a local pop idol called Barbara Jean (herself a mere manipulandum of the advertising industry).[50]

But is it possible to explode the falsehood of clichés by means of a parody which actually heightens their falseness? Does such a cinematic burlesque, even in the form of self-mockery, not run the risk of further contributing, despite itself, to the vertiginous proliferation of clichés? Or as Deleuze pertinently asks: 'How can cinema hope to denounce the sinister organization of clichés when it participates in their fabrication and propagation as much as TV or the mass circulation magazines?'[51] And there is, of course, an additional danger: that the critique of the commodified image may reach such apocalyptic proportions that it becomes a pure act of negation, exposing a void from which new pseudo-images automatically spring up. We would then be facing a situation where every image becomes a cliché, either because one demonstrates its falsehood or because one denounces its apparent omnipotence. But if such is the case, it is difficult to resist the conclusion that there does indeed exist 'a diffuse world conspiracy, comprising a generalized enslavement of minds which extends into any place whatsoever and propagates death everywhere'.[52]

Rather than subscribe to such a nihilistic conclusion, Deleuze calls for a 'mutation' in cinema capable of producing a totally new kind of image: a 'thinking image' (*image pensée et pensante*) which would disengage the imagination from the spiral of negative parody and relate it to an alternative project of positive political commitment.[53] This is also what Walter Benjamin seems to have had in mind in his essay, *The Work of Art in an Age of Mechanical Reproduction*, when he spoke of the capacity of film to produce certain 'shock effects' conducive to a 'heightened presence of mind'.[54] Benjamin was one of the first to warn against the tendency of technological mass-media to reduce the human imagination to such a point of 'self-alienation that it experiences its own destruction as an aesthetic pleasure of the first order'.[55] He was determined to resist this tendency. Adamant that there was to be no going back to the revered humanist aesthetic of an 'authentic' and unreproducible art work, Benjamin urged that the only effective way to combat the contemporary self-alienation of the imagination was to *politicize* it. Whether such a politicization of the postmodern imagination is actually possible is indeed a crucial question – one which we will be returning to in the general conclusion to this work.

5 Le Magasin de Ben (Vautier)

Le Magasin de Ben is now a permanent exhibit of the National Museum of Modern Art in the Beaubourg Centre, Paris. But it was not always so. When this work was first constructed in 1958

MUSÉE NATIONAL D'ART MODERNE, PARIS

Ben Vautier, 'Le Magasin de Ben'

it was located on a street in the city of Nice. Here it remained for several years as a *monument manifeste* of the avant-garde *Fluxus* movement whose central aim was to break down the traditional distinction between art and reality. This influential movement comprised many American and European artists who took their inspiration from the anti-art tendencies of Dada and Duchamp, producing a series of experimental forms in the sixties and seventies – most notably those of 'performance', 'the happening', 'the open work' and 'deconstruction' (e.g. the Support/Surface group).[56]

Ben Vautier was a leading member of the *Fluxus* movement, both as practitioner and theorist. His 'Shop' on display in the

Beaubourg Centre reflects this dual activity: it is at one and the same time a form of living sculpture and a critical comment on itself by means of self-mocking graffiti daubed all over the work – e.g. *'Je signe tout'*, *'L'art est ego'*, *'Le nouveau est toujours revolutionnaire'* or *'Il n'y a pas de mauvais gout'*. *Le Magasin de Ben* is the art image exposed as commodity. It is a small but human-scale junk shop full of discarded objects, from old post-cards and second-hand records to various bits of sidewalk bric-à-brac. Mixing together the traditionally separate media of painting, sculpture, writing and theatre performance (i.e. a performance in which the spectators browsing through the shop themselves become the actors), Ben subverts all conventional aesthetic divisions. The main purpose of this mixed-media exper-iment is to demystify art itself by blurring the sacrosanct bound-aries separating the real and the imaginary, the artist and the audience, the aesthetic object and everyday consumer item. Ben's iconoclastic work makes the point that *tout est art* – which is, of course, another way of saying that *rien n'est art*. *Le Magasin de Ben* is self-parody brought to its most ridiculous extreme, and intentionally so.

Can we, then, continue to speak here of a work of art? Are we not confronted rather with a pure hoax? How else describe this piece of anti-art originally situated on the real streets of a real city for passers-by to wander through, a work which violated the taboo of the untouchability of art, debunking the very essence of aesthetic distance and disinterestedness? Was not Ben's Shop originally intended as a send-up of the whole idea of the Museum as a place where sacred objects are eternally preserved from the fleeting character of everyday expenditure and consumption? Was it not presented as an open-access 'fluxus' where art and reality flowed through each other with carefree abandon? But if such was Vautier's original parodic intention, it would seem to have been negated by the transposition of the work from the street in Nice to the Museum of Modern Art in Paris. He appears to have undermined his initial project by allowing it to be put on display as a work of art. We may well wonder. And we are, one suspects, supposed to wonder.

When we first encounter *Le Magasin de Ben* in Beaubourg,

we are disoriented. What, we ask ourselves, is this pseudo-imitation of a real shop doing in a museum? Consulting the habitual 'art notice' beside the work, our puzzlement grows. For the notice duly informs us that this exhibit was not designed for a museum at all, but rather as a mockery of the whole idea of museum art. So that what we are witnessing is, in fact, a second-hand parody of an original parody – an imitation in Beaubourg of an imitation which initially existed in a real street. The basic distinction between art and reality remains radically undecidable.

Ben himself is quite aware of the circle of mimicry which his work sets up. To allow that *tout est art*, leads, by his own admisssion, to the postmodern conviction that art is no more than a 'mockery of itself' and that the 'artist is someone who prefers to be ridiculous rather than banal'.⁵⁷ Ben thus brings Duchamp's legacy of derision to its logical conclusion. He emulates the maestro of anti-art of whom it was said: 'His ready-mades counterfeit reality; his self-inventories fake art history; his cryptic masks, jokes and disguises impersonate human character . . . Yet his paradoxes take us to the heart of post-modern life.'⁵⁸

As we wander off, dismayed by the unresolvable enigma of *Le Magasin de Ben*, we may look for solace in the other works of postmodern art which surround it in Beaubourg. But we soon discover that Ben's work is no mere idiosyncrasy. It is part of a whole exhibition of works which reflect and reinforce the unde-cidable status of each other. On the same floor of the Beaubourg Centre – the fifth and highest floor, the postmodern summit of this museum of modern art – we are confronted with a multi-plicity of self-destructing objects: objects not made of traditional art materials like marble, bronze, wood, canvas or oil paint but of mass-produced synthetic materials such as plastic, metal, plexiglass, polystyrene, concrete, felt or neon waves. Indeed we realize that the collection of fetish-commodities displayed inside Ben's Shop is almost a miniature replica of those on display outside it! There is César's *Compressed Car* (1962) like a piece of discarded scrap from an urban wasteland. There is Naim June Paik's pile of TV sets endlessly repeating sequences of nonsynchronized images and provoking in us a sense of random discontinuity (as we try to assimilate all the different screens at once). There is Rauschenberg's ironically named *Oracle* (1965): a sound collage comprising battered pieces of mechanical junk each of which transmits a different long-wave radio signal. This medley of disjointed sounds and objects serves to repudliate the depersonalizing communications industry which so conditions contemporary experience. And crowning this postmodern dance of death, we have Andy Warhol's *Electric Chair* (1966). Warhol has been celebrated as the 'pope of pop art'. He has desacralized the aesthetic function by choosing both his forms and themes from the commonest mass-produced materials – Campbell's soup tins, Coca-Cola bottles, television commercials, seriographed photos from glossy magazines, and so on. *Electric Chair* exemplifies Warhol's pop-parodying of our anti-humanist culture. It reproduces an image of death utterly devoid of human presence. The electric chair is empty. There is no human executioner and no human victim executed. Just an anonymous machine: an allegory of man's inhumanity to man without the slightest sign of man.

All of these exhibits might be described as anti-humanist *allegories* as opposed to humanist *symbols*, to borrow Benjamin's useful distinction. The symbol carries an 'aura' which is to the world of objects what 'mystery' or 'depth' are to the world of human experience. The symbolic aura *humanizes* things and endows them with the 'power to look back'; it invites us to experience objects as unique, whole and original. Allegory, by contrast, may be said to typify the reproducible object; it represents a fragmented and impersonalized thing-world where the very idea of an autonomous image is meaningless. As a form of representation, voided of any living presence, allegory testifies to the numbness and flatness of a contemporary society where things are reduced to commodities and human experience to a series of disconnected sensations. Unlike the symbol which nourished humanist hopes of salvation in and through history, allegory 'lies like a frozen landscape before the eye of the beholder'. It offers an apocalyptic vision according to which 'history takes on meaning only in the stations of its agony and decay, the amount of meaning being in exact proportion to the presence of death and the power of decay'.[59]

The substitution of allegory for symbol in postmodernist art would seem to be a telling symptom of 'the increasing alienation of human beings who take inventories of their past as of lifeless merchandise'. The allegories of anti-art present us with an experience of *depthlessness* which accurately reflects the commodified nature of contemporary culture. But in thus reducing art to a random collection of empty objects, does anti-art not run the risk of augmenting the very cult of superficiality which it is ostensibly exposing? Citing the particular example of Warhol's images, Frederic Jameson identifies this critical dilemma in the following ideological terms:

Andy Warhol's work in fact turns centrally around commodification, and the great billboard images of the Coca-Cola bottle or the Campbell's Soup Can, which explicitly foreground the commodity fetishism of a transition to late capital, *ought* to be powerful and critical political statements. If they are not that, then one would want to begin to wonder a little more seriously about the possibilities of political or critical art in the postmodern period of late capital.[60]

One of the major difficulties here is, of course, the loss of critical distance. The limitless extension of commodified images would appear to leave no room for the human subject to take refuge, reflect and respond with an alternative mode of vision or action. The extent of this difficulty may be illustrated by returning to our Beaubourg example and asking the question: is it possible to escape from the world of parody and pastiche which the postmodern images of Ben Vautier, Andy Warhol and others present to us? If we look out of the windows of the Beaubourg museum, the first thing we see is an adjoining space full of popular performing artists – mimics, musicians, confidence-tricksters, magicians, mimes, acrobats, etc. Are we to consider this transitional space of 'live happenings' *outside* the museum as *more* or *less* 'real' than the anti-art images we have been contemplating *inside* the museum? And if we let our gaze travel further still, beyond the open square to the city of Paris itself, can we be certain that the commercial highrises of Montparnasse or La

Defense – which tower over this urban landscape of jumbled styles and sounds – are signs of a world any less contaminated by the commodity fetishism parodied by the postmodern works within Beaubourg? Was it not, moreover, precisely to confuse any decidable sense of inner and outer that the architects Piano and Rogers designed this museum in the form of an anti-museum: that is, a gallery with not walls but windows, an invertible space where inside and outside mirror each other in a kind of uncanny replication? By conspicuously exposing the mechanical trappings of pipes, wires, air extractors, elevators and iron girders on the *exterior* of the building (rather than concealing them in the interior), and by colouring them as they usually are on architects' plans, have not Piano and Rogers subverted the very distinction between an industrial and an aesthetic space, between factory and fantasy, between commodity and art? This would seem to suggest that the Beaubourg museum is itself no less an instance of post-modern deconstruction than the works which it houses on its fifth floor. Beaubourg is, as it were, *Le Magasin de Ben* writ large – another example of the aesthetic of parody which 'undercuts itself in anti-art or loses itself in life'.[61] A museum without walls.

Beaubourg might also be considered a parody of the high-tech functionalism of modernist architecture itself – a form of construction which mimics the aesthetic of *avant-garde* utopianism and thereby anticipates the emergence of a fully-fledged postmodern architecture. Typical examples of such postmodern buildings would be the TV AM Centre in London, the glass and granite AT + T headquarters in Manhatten, the Public Service Buildings in Portland, Oregon and the Bonaventura Hotel in LA (discussed in our Appendix). What characterizes such architecture is the abandonment of the high modernist emphasis on formal novelty – based on an aesthetic of the Great Leap Forward – in favour of a hybrid mixture of period styles. We find architectural motifs from various traditions being jumbled together in a random and parodic manner. Design becomes *collage*. As one of the most prominent exponents of postmodernist architecture, Robert Venturi, declared: 'creating the new means choosing from the old'. A sentiment echoed by Philip Johnson, designer of the AT+T building, when he proclaimed that 'we can no longer *not* know history'. But history is now understood, of course, not as a utopian advance towards the future, but as an interplay of diverse traditions: a diversity which postmodern architecture recycles in the guise of parodic visual quotations.

Whether such parody actually represents what one critic has called the 'general anaesthesia implicit in the development of our technological society',[62] or whether, on the contrary, it signals a subtle subversion of this very society from within, remains an open question.

6 The Palace of Living Arts

The contemporary tendency to equate image and commodity may be seen from another, and quite different angle, if we leave the Museum of Modern Art in Beaubourg and travel several thousand miles westward to the Palace of Living Arts in California. The contrast between these two kinds of postmodern museum are telling. Whereas Beaubourg offered us examples of

'The Palace of Living Arts'

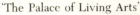

art becoming anti-art, the Palace of Living Arts offers us works of non-art, of pure artificiality, masquerading as art. Rather than exposing their own unreality as imitations, the exhibits in the Palace contrive to imitate art itself *as if it were reality*. Far from contesting the commodification of the image, therefore, this false museum celebrates it – and commercially exploits it. Here the pseudo-image reigns supreme. And without the slightest hint of irony. Parody, it appears, has begun to take itself literally.

The Palace of Living Arts is located, significantly, beside the Movieland Wax Museum in Buena Park in Los Angeles. At the entrance to the Palace stands a marble statue of Michael Angelo's *David*. An 'authentic' replica. Inside the museum we find three-dimensional 'life-size' reproductions of the famous masterpieces of Western art. But these imitations are, we are led to believe, *better* than the originals. They purport to reproduce the originals *as they really were* when the artists first created them. What we are being offered is a privileged eye-witness insight into the original composition of such works as Leonardo's *Mona Lisa*, Michael Angelo's *Pieta*, El Greco's *Cardinal Guevara*, Gainsborough's *Blue Boy* and, of course, the *Venus de Milo*. Beside each of these 'real-life' reconstructions we find a copy of the original works as they now appear in the Prado, the Tate, the Louvre, the Uffizi, etc. The purpose of such a comparative device is to convince the viewer that what he is witnessing here in California is not some cheap secondhand experience but an actual improvement on what is displayed in the European galleries themselves.

The general philosophy of the Palace of Living Arts, as Umberto Eco has observed, is not 'we give you the reproduction so that you will desire the original' but 'we give you the reproduction so that you will have no further need of the original'.[63] The sensational value of the imitations is further hyped-up by seemingly omniscient audio-visual recordings and voice-overs which helps us to 'relive', in the here and now of present-day California, the exact psychological and historical circumstances which the artist supposedly experienced as he produced his work. And lest we begin to think we are being served up some sort of multi-media artifice (which, of course, we are), there are inscriptions to remind us that these exhibits have been specially commissioned from professional artisans of the art-works' place of origin – e.g. Michael Angelo's *Pieta* is described as a 'genuine' copy fashioned by 'genuine' Florentine artisans. And, we are also discretely reminded, such commissions were at no inconsiderable expense!

But the crowning exhibit of the Palace's entire collection is, undoubtedly, the *Venus de Milo*. There we see her in all her pristine splendour, leaning gracefully against an Ionian column of a classical temple with *both* arms now intact and her life-like colouring and gestures fully restored! Just as the original model would have stood before the original classical artist. As the accompanying inscription boasts: 'Here is Venus de Milo brought to life as she was in the time when she posed for the unknown sculptor in Greece some two hundred years B.C.' And to highlight the claim that this reconstruction, made possible by the most advanced techniques of laser reproduction and holography, is far more 'real' than the art-work it imitates, we are also presented with a small but exact copy of the one-armed, lustreless and time-worn statue as it appears in the Louvre in Paris. Make no mistake about it, the Palace of Living Arts proclaims, the life-like reconstruction before your eyes is far more authentic than the classical original.

Only at one point does the illusionism of the Palace fall short. And that is in the reproduction of Van Eyck's *Portrait of the Arnolfinis*. Everything about this painting is realized in perfect three-dimensional imitation, with the exception of a single but highly significant detail: the convex mirror which Van Eyck had painted in the background of his picture, reflecting the Arnolfini couple from behind, is left blank. Unlike the original, the Palace's imitation shows a mirror which reflects nothing. This omission is not for technical reasons; it would be very simple to have reproduced the mirror-reflection with an illusionist expertise and exactness far surpassing Van Eyck's. The omission is more of a symbolic order, as Eco perceptively notes:

Confronted with an instance where art had consciously played with illusion and measured itself against the vanity of images through an image of an image, the industry of Absolute Falsehood did not dare attempt a copy, because to do so would have risked revealing its own lie.[64]

It is a short distance from this popular display of 'highbrow' imitations to the 'lowbrow' equivalents of the neighbouring Californian Disneyland (one of several located in the US). Most of the 'original' scenes and characters which Disneyland reproduces with hyper-realistic accuracy are, of course, the fictional inventions of Walt Disney's own films: Mickey Mouse, Donald Duck, Peter Pan, etc. But Disney's dream of a plastic fantasyland where the traditionally separated worlds of man, animal, nature and technology could be brought together in a miraculous synthesis, is perhaps best epitomized in his extraordinary invention of 'audioanimatronics'. Here Disney's lifelong ambition to fashion a form of simulation truer than truth, a form of imitation more lifelike than nature itself, would appear to be realized. By means of this ingenious technical device, Disney comes close to making the ancient myth of the Golem a literal reality. Eco offers the following detailed analysis of this amazing feat of imitation:

The technique of audioanimatronics was the pride of Walt Disney who had finally succeeded in breaking through the wall of the second dimension, of realizing not just a film, which is illusion, but a total theatre, and not with anthropomorphic animals but with human beings. It is true that Disney's automatons are masterpieces of electronics: each was conceived by studying the expressions of a real actor and then fabricating reduced models, that is by constructing absolutely precise skeletons of real computers in a human form and then covering them with an incredibly realistic 'flesh' and 'skin' made by a group of artisans. Each automaton obeys a programme which synchronizes the movements of mouth and eyes with words and sounds; each repeats again and again his preestablished role (a sentence, one or two gestures) and the visitor captivated and surprised by the succession of scenes and compelled to look at more than one at a time – to the left, to the right, in front of him etc. – never has time to turn around and realize that the automaton he has just seen is already repeating his eternal scenario. The technique of audioanimatronics is used in several different sections of Disneyland and even reanimates a collection of American Presidents . . . . Living humans would not do better, and would cost more, but what is most important is that they are not humans and that we know this. The pleasure of imitation, as the ancients already recognized, is fundamental to the human soul, but here, in addition to enjoying a perfect imitation, one takes pleasure in the persuasion that the imitation has reached its apogee and that now the reality will always be inferior.[65]

But Disney went further still. He pursued this persuasion to its literal conclusion in his EPCOT project (acronym for the Experimental Prototype Community of Tomorrow). EPCOT was actually constructed by Walter Elias Disney Enterprizes on reconverted Florida wasteland. Costing 900 million dollars, this science fiction utopia with controlled climate, waste-recycling apparatuses and disease eradication methods, represents a 'Madison Avenue ad-man's fantasy come true: two concentric circles of pavilions featuring the latest wares of Corporate America, displayed for visitors willing to pay to see advertising at its best.'[66] Even utopia, the promise of a perfect future, has become a fake.

The imitations of Disneyland and the Palace of Living Arts are symptomatic of the consumerist ideology of postmodern America. This ideology would have us believe that copies are more desirable than originals, that the function of images is to provide us with a model for living, that pseudo-reality is more consumable than reality; and that even if the ideals of the historical past or future cannot actually be made *flesh* in the here and now, they can at least be made *plastic*. Such an ideology dominates the new Society of Contrivance where the mass production and dissemination of images has become everyday business, extending from the public spheres of commerce and popular culture to the most private recesses of individual experience. Increasingly accustomed to live in a world of pseudo-events and pre-packaged fantasies, the consumer citizens begin to mistake the shadow for themselves. And even national and international politics would appear to have become a competition between promotional images: a phenomenon dramatically illustrated in the domination of political campaigns by television and advertising. The paradigm of interreflecting mirrors thus assumes a particular relevance for the whole communications culture which so pervasively informs contemporary American society. 'The images themselves become shadowy reflections of one another', as Daniel Boorstin accurately remarks. 'One interview comments on another, one television show spoofs another; novel, television show, radio program, movie, comic book, and the way we think of ourselves, all become merged into mutual reflections.'[67] In a society where the image has replaced the thing, there would seem to be no escaping the labyrinth of mirror-play. The language of commodified images spreads out to include everywhere and everything. After all, 'if the right "image" will elect a President or sell an automobile, a religion, a cigarette, or a suit of clothes, why can it not make America herself – or the American Way of Life – a salable commodity all over the earth?'[68]

The ideology of the pseudo-image is not confined to America, any more than Disneyland is confined to California. The cult of imitation and pastiche has now become an integral feature of Western society as a whole – and even indeed of Communist society. This is not simply because the commercial American culture of Coca-Cola and denim jeans is increasingly emulated by the young citizens of Communist countries. There is another and more particular sense in which the basic Communist ideology of the New Man often promotes a practice of empty imitation: what the Czech writer, Milan Kundera, calls 'totalitarian kitsch'. The Communist image of a superhuman worker-hero, whom all citizens are obliged to imitate, is no less artificial, Kundera suggests, than the American image of the perfectly commodified man (i.e. the ideal consumer). Both ideologies prefabricate anonymous types to which the man in the street is expected to mechanically conform. And the specifically Communist version of such a pseudo-model is epitomized, for example, in the cult of the Mass Parade. Here the real world of human failings and imperfections is glossed over by the collective image of identically smiling automatons. In *The Unbearable Lightness of Being*, Kundera provides us with this description of Communist kitsch:

As a group approached the reviewing stand, even the most blasé faces would beam with dazzling smiles, as if trying to prove they were properly joyful or, to be more precise, in proper *agreement*. Nor were they merely expressing political agreement with communism; no, theirs was an agreement with being as such . . . The unwritten, unsung motto of the parade was not 'Long Live Communism!' but 'Long Live Life!'. The power and cunning of communist politics lay in the fact that it had appropriated this slogan. For it was this idiotic tautology ('Long Live Life') which attracted people indifferent to the theses of communism to the communist parade.[69]

The ideology of imitation, shared in different ways by both Americanism and Communism, might be described accordingly as a cult of *life without death*. Whether as commodity or kitsch, the pseudo-image conceals the unpalatable realities of man's finite historical existence. But is this not the very opposite of the tendency to deconstruct the image which we identified as a central characteristic of postmodern philosophy and art – a tendency which might more accurately be defined as, if anything, a cult of *death without life?* Be that as it may, these two extremes of affirmativism and negativism – standing at opposite poles of postmodern culture – would appear to have this at least in common: both abolish the distinction between the imaginary and the real, the imitation and the original. And by so doing, both tendencies subscribe to the pervasive postmodern suspicion that we can no longer speak of a properly human imagination capable of transforming reality and discovering therein alternative possibilities of existence. Is it possible for postmodern man to establish a new modality of relation between imagination and reality? And one which does not simply appeal to a nostalgic return to a defunct humanism, but pushes postmodernism beyond its present aporias of parody and pastiche to another kind of cultural experience, more human even than that of the old humanism? This is the question we must address in our conclusion.

APPENDIX

Some additional remarks on postmodern art, architecture and music

1 Postmodern art

Apart from the examples of postmodern art already cited in our Introduction and present chapter, there are other parodic works which merit mention. The following is a summary inventory of some of the most striking instances to be found in the plastic arts: Marie Lippens' send-up of Rembrandt's revered seventeenth-century self-portrait suspended between the curved naked legs of a woman; Tano Festa's take-off of Michael Angelo's painting of Adam in the Sistine Chapel reproduced in a multiple photomat series; Raoul Hausmann's *ABCD, Portrait de l'Artiste* which parodies the classical genre of portraiture in the form of a waste-paper collage of printed dockets; Andy Warhol's involuted parody of Leonardo's Last Supper; Robert Ballagh's pop repro-ductions of Velasquez, David and Ingres. But besides such parodies of classical genres, one might also cite some of the postmodern parodies of contemporary consumer images: Roy Lichtenstein's reproductions of comic-strip characters; Claes Oldenburg's pseudo-imitations of hamburgers; and, of course, Andy Warhol's silk-screen and acrylic imitations of consumer commodities like Brillo boxes, soup tins, Coca-cola bottles, etc.

The parodic model also extends to mixed-media sculptures such as the following: Reinhard Mucha's metallic parody of baroque architecture, *Le Problème de la Figure et du Fond dans L'Architecture Baroque, pour Toi Seul il ne reste que la Tombe*; Richard Baquie's mock-heroic tribute to the humanist sculpture of the past, *Autrefois . . . . 1984*, a mixed-media assembly of

Below and right: 'Parodies' by
Robert Ballagh

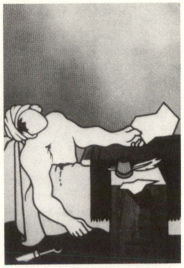

Below: Roy Lichtenstein, 'Good
Morning, Darling' and
Tom|Wesselman, 'Still Life
No. 33'

Below: Larry Rivers,
'Dutch Masters and Cigars'

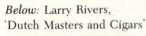

window, metal, ventilator, wind, and electronic lettering repeatedly announcing slogans such as 'words are no more than the
projection of your own seduction'; Martial Raysse's neon spoof
of the Statue of Liberty, *America, America* – itself perhaps an
indirect allusion to Robert Rauschenberg's pastiche of the Statue
of Liberty in his silk-screen Pop Icon, *Overdrive*. And we should
also mention, finally, Nam June Paik's video installation, *Arc
Double Face*, where the sacred architectural symbol of modern
France, the Arc de Triomphe, is disassembled and demystified
by means of a double-faced arch of piled video screens, each one
of which reproduces, in a repetitive and asynchronic sequence,
images of the Arc de Triomphe as it disintegrates. Paik it was
who declared that 'just as the technique of collage has replaced
oil painting, the cathode tube has replaced the canvas'. A pioneer
of the influential *Fluxus* movement, Paik has experimented with
a variety of new forms from Combine Paintings and multi-media
Concerts (*e.g. Hommage à John Cage* which blended the idioms
of music, theatre, video and computer technology) to Sound
Sculpture, Performance, Video and Environmental art (e.g. *TV
Bouddha*). One of the main objectives of Paik's *Plural Works*
has been the dismantling of the rapport between medium and
message. 'The message is *elsewhere*', Paik cryptically observes,
'neither in the "image" nor in the "subject" but in the interval,
in the rhythm and perpetual flux of chromatic energies and
sounds.' In his video installation, *Arc Double Face*, Paik
juxtaposes images drawn from publicity spots, private memory
and revamped documentaries to the point where it is impossible
to determine what is real and what artificial. As John Cage, the
postmodern American composer and inspirational figure for the
Fluxus movement, remarked: 'With Paik one always has the
impression that anything could happen, even dangerous things
at the physical level.' In short, Paik pushes the postmodern
parody of art to the threshold of self-destruction. The ex-centric
paradigm is arrestingly illustrated in his numerous celebrations
of the heterogeneous, the random, the unpredictable and the
ridiculous.

2 Postmodern architecture

Since the term postmodern came into common currency in architecture it is appropriate to add some further comments on this subject, merely alluded to hitherto. Charles Jencks and Paolo Portoghesi are two of the leading commentators on postmodern architecture. In his first major work on this theme, entitled *The Language of Post-Modern Architecture* (Academy editions, 1977), Jencks defines postmodernism as a 'radical eclecticism'. He explains his reasoning thus:

The present (post-modern) situation tolerates opposite approaches, and I hope that architecture doesn't prematurely crystallise around a single style and doctrinaire approach as it has so many times in this century. If there is a single direction I prefer, the reader will discover that it is is pluralistic: the idea that an architect must master several styles and codes of communication and vary these to suit the particular culture for which he is designing. I have called this 'adhocism' in the past, and I use the term 'radical eclecticism' here to give this approach a name . . . Modern architecture took every culture as its province, it claimed to be universal; and under the pressure of fashion, technology and specious argument, these claims have led to its indiscriminate practice around the world. It's rather as if world leaders took the inflated claims of Esperanto seriously and had this ahistorical, logical language spoken in every major city. We wouldn't be conversing with much pleasure, elegance or wit. . . . In short, its claims to universality should be exposed as ideological, and modern architecture should be quickly put in its semantic place – where it belongs with respect to other styles and approaches (p. 7).

In a subsequent work, *Current Architecture* (Academy Editions, 1982), Jencks offers a somewhat modified definition of the term postmodern. He sees it now less as a complete break with modernism than as a mixture or collage of modern and non-modern codes – e.g. vernacular, commercial, metaphorical, contextual, traditionalist and so on. The characteristic feature is defined accordingly as 'double coding' and its main motivation is described as an attempt to undermine the 'elitism inherent in modern architecture and the architectural profession' (p. 111).

While the term postmodern covered a wide variety of buildings it was sufficiently coherent to enable Paolo Portoghesi to group together seventy architects from round the world for a 1980 Venice Biennale exhibition. Portoghesi subsequently published an influential work entitled *Postmodern, The Architecture of the Post-Industrial Society* (Rizzoli, New York, 1983). Here he offers a useful set of clarifications. The postmodern arises, he argues, from a basic dissatisfaction with the logic of modernity which in the early decades of this century acquired the rigidity of a statute and whose main article was the annihilation of tradition – 'the obligation toward renewal, the theology of the new'. Portoghesi offers the following diagnosis:

This perverse guarantee of perpetual renewal has given modernity the appearance of an elusive shadow, difficult to contend with because of its readiness to assume ever-changing forms and strategies. But in the end, a sense of uneasiness upset even the certainties of the Modern: the discomfort of men of culture when evaluating its products. Sixty years comprise a man's life, and just as a man of this age looks back (and just as the others tend to judge him), the trial against the Modern has been outlined as a physiological necessity, as an unpostponable goal for the new generations, at least since 1968. Therefore, a trial against the Modern and its consequences, but not only this; the Postmodern is a rebellion originating in the realization that in the past sixty years everything has changed in the world of social relationships and production; that industry has undergone radical transformations, and the energy crisis has once more uncovered problems that had been thought to be solved for some time.

The statute of modernity had been custom-made for a society in which the revolution of information that has profoundly shaken all the structures of our world had not yet occurred. Before a Postmodern culture, there previously existed a 'postmodern condition,' the product of 'postindustrial' society. It was inevitable that sooner or later this creeping, underground revolution would end up changing the direction of artistic research. What was less foreseeable was that instead of developing in the futurist-mechanical sense, in the '2000' style, as many had imagined, art steered its course toward Ithaca. It made its way toward the recovery of certain aspects of tradition, and reopened the discussion, the impassible embankment erected by the avant-garde between present and past, and went back to mix the waters with creative results. This recovery of memory, after the forced amnesia of a half century, is manifest in customs, dress (folk, casual and the various revivals), in the mass diffusion of an interest in history and its products, in the ever vaster need for contemplative experiences and contact with nature that seemed antithetical to the civilization of machines. (p. 7)

Portoghesi goes on to argue that architecture was one of the first disciplines to confront the crisis of modernity and respond to the emerging desires of postmodern society. Directly related to everyday life, architecture had become a conspicuous symptom of the negative consequences of the modern project. Modern architecture betrayed its bankruptcy in the alienation of the modern city – 'the suburbs without quality, the urban environment devoid of collective values that has become an asphalt jungle and a dormitory; the loss of local character, of the connection with the place: the terrible homologation that has made the outskirts of the cities of the whole world similar to one another, and whose inhabitants have a hard time recognizing an identity of their own' (p. 7). Postmodern architecture, by contrast, seeks to resist the modern obsession with the new at all costs and to obviate the destructive consequences of this obsession on the spatial environment. The postmodern architects have discovered that the 'imitation of types' is more important than relentless innovation. And Portoghesi speaks accordingly of a 'new renaissance' being outlined, determined to 'recover certain aspects of the past, not to interrupt history but to arrest its paralysis' (p. 8). He concludes that as applied to architecture the term postmodern refers to a plurality of tendencies directed toward an escape from the crisis of the Modern Movement together with its premises of inevitable progress. Portoghesi writes:

Since modernity coincides in Western architectural culture with the progressive rigorous detachment from everything traditional, it should be pointed out that in the field of architecture, the postmodern means that explicit, conscious abolition of the dam carefully built around the pure language elaborated *in vitro* on the basis of the rationalist statute.

This language is put into contact again with the universe of the architectural debate, with the entire historical series of its past experiences, with no more distinctions between the periods before or after the first industrial revolution. With the barrier torn down, old and new waters have mixed together. The resulting product is before our eyes; paradoxical and ambiguous but vital, a preparatory moment of something different that can only be imagined: reintegration in architecture of a vast quantity of values, layers, semitones, which the homologation of the International Style had unpardonably dispersed. The return of architecture to the womb of its history has just begun. . . (p. II)

A third influential commentator on the rapport between architecture and postmodernism is Frederic Jameson. In his controversial study, 'Postmodernism or the Cultural Logic of Late Capitalism' (*NLR*, No. 145, 1984), he locates the phenomenon of postmodern architecture within its post-industrial socio-economic context. The main example he cites and analyses is the labyrinthine Bonaventura Hotel in downtown Los Angeles, designed by business magnate and architect John Portman. While this building is considered by Jencks as late modernist or 'transitional', Jameson sees it as a typically postmodern double blend of modern and non-modern codes, of architectural (academic) and popular (commercial) interests. Contrary to the modernist orientation towards functionalism and geometrical abstraction, the Bonaventura Hotel introduces a subversive sense of spatial disorientation. Mischievously displacing our normal experience of inside and outside, of vertical and horizontal, by means of mirror surfaces which reflect each other and a maze-like system of escalators, elevators and winding corridors, the hotel confounds our sense of direction; it invites us to wander aimlessly through the bars and boutiques of commercialized anonymous space. Jameson ventures this perceptive account:

Portman's *Bonaventura* is a popular building, visited by locals and tourists alike . . . With a certain number of other characteristic postmodern buildings, the *Bonaventura* aspires to being a total space, a complete world, a kind of miniature city (and I would want to add that to this new total space corresponds a new collective practice, a new

The Bonaventura Hotel

The Pompidou Centre

mode in which individuals move and congregate, something like the practice of a new and historically original kind of hyper-crowd) . . . It does not want to be a part of the city, but rather its equivalent and its replacement or substitute . . . whence the deliberate downplaying and reduction of the entrance function to its bare minimum . . . This diagnosis is to my mind confirmed by the great reflective glass skin of the *Bonaventura* (which) repels the city outside; a repulsion for which we have analogies in those reflector sunglasses which make it impossible for your interlocutor to see your own eyes and thereby achieve a certain aggressivity towards and power over the Other. In a similar way, the glass skin achieves a peculiar and placeless dissociation of the *Bonaventura* from its neighbourhood: it is not even an exterior, inasmuch as when you seek to look at the hotel's outer walls you cannot see the hotel itself, but only the distorted images of everything that surrounds it. (p. 82–3)

A similar experience of dislocation is to be had from *within* the building where seated in one of its revolving cocktail lounges, you are passively rotated about and offered a spectacle of the city itself, now transmuted into its own images by the glass windows through which you contemplate it. In the *Bonaventura*, people lose their sense of spatial control. And this is also evident from the curious observation that since the opening of the hotel in 1977, visitors have had great difficulty in locating any of the stores in the lobby; and even if they did find the appropriate boutique, they would be unlikely to be as lucky next time around.

This latest mutation in space – postmodern hyperspace – has finally succeeded in transcending the capacities of the individual human body to locate itself, to organize its immediate surroundings perceptually, and cognitively to map its position in a mappable external world. And this alarming disjunction point between the body and its built environment – which is to the initial bewilderment of the older modernism as the velocities of space craft are to those of the automobile – can itself stand as the symbol and analogue of that even sharper dilemma which is the incapacity of our minds, at least at present, to map the great global multinational and decentred communicational network in which we find ourselves caught as individual subjects. (p. 84)[70]

3 *Postmodernism and music*

Music has been conspicuously absent from our preceding analysis of postmodern culture. One reason for this is the apparent reluctance of most cultural commentators to apply the categories of postmodernism to this medium as they have done to others. In what follows we present some tentative remarks on what such an application might entail.

Some of the major traits of postmodernism are becoming increasingly evident in various movements of contemporary music. There is, for example, a notable tendency in certain quarters to confound the conventional distinction between classical and commercial music. Some practitioners of so-called 'serious' music are beginning to draw on compositional techniques made available by the pop industry, while a number of popular musicians have been known in recent years to parody and rearrange melodic quotations from the classical tradition. Let us take each of these trends in turn.

Since Schoenberg and the introduction of serial and atonal music, Stockhausen and Boulez (among others) appear to have brought the modernist movement of *avant-garde* music to a logical extreme. Alternative forms have been emerging which subvert the very basis of the classical/modernist heritage. John Cage's use of 'chance', 'randomness', 'silence' and even mixed-media devices, challenged all accredited norms of composition and, on occasion, replaced the very idea of a *composer* with that of the *performer* (for example, *Variations V*). The characteristics of compositional definition and structure were abandoned in favour of a performance without fixed parameters.

This preference for *randomness* (Cage and his disciples) over *structure* (Schoenberg) has been developed in various ways by the recent movement of 'West Coast Music'. Works by Steve Reich, Terry Riley, and John Adams tend to dispense with the traditional roles of composer and conductor altogether. Riley's *In C* is a case in point – a group of musicians improvising on a single key which is indefinitely repeated and reiterated. And Adams has experimented with similar modes of improvisation, occasionally 'quoting' some motif or other from a 'classical' composer (e.g. Debussy) which is then varied and rearranged in parodic fashion.

The availability of electronic recording techniques such as sound computers and sequencers have, of course, facilitated this process of musical *bricolage*. The German group, *Tangerine Dream*, which came to prominence in the late sixties, cleverly exploited the devices of tape manipulation, made available by the new technology, to produce a collage of real and artificial sounds. Such procedures have suggested alternatives to the modernist model of the compositional author as an individual imagination working from its own inner resources or 'genius'. Not surprisingly, the use of synthesisers and such like were roundly condemned by the adherents of classical music. Particularly suspect was the association with tendencies towards consumerism and automation prevalent in pop music (which commonly exploited electronic techniques of *mixage*, reduplication and reversibility). Indeed, the British Society of the Performing Arts actually considered banning the use of computer synthesisers in 'serious' music, fearing, among other things, the erosion of the traditional acoustic distinction between natural and instrumentally composed sound.

Despite such opposition, the blending of serious and commercial music has become more frequent in recent years. Apart from the California musicians already mentioned, the works of Tomita, Frank Zappa and Philip Glass also provide evidence of this trend. Mixed-media compositions are now almost a commonplace. And it is surely significant that records by Glass not only feature contributions from pop musicians but can be found as easily in the 'pop' section as the 'classical' section of record shops. The revered distinction between highbrow and lowbrow music, so jealously guarded by the modernist aesthetic, is being steadily eroded.*

Note: As Glass remarked during the *Arena* programme on his work (first broadcast by BBC in January 1987): 'art music is becoming pop music at the same time that pop music is becoming art music'. In the late sixties, Glass broke from the *avant-garde* mainstream of academic music, represented by Stockhausen and Boulez, and decided to incorporate a wide diversity of influences, ranging from Western pop techniques to the cyclical rhythms and repetitions of Asian

Certain features of postmodernism are equally identifiable in movements of contemporary pop. The practices of musical bricolage and parody are becoming the order of the day. Synthesisers are frequently used to scramble and reassemble motifs drawn from both classical and popular traditions (e.g. folk, rock and punk). This has led to a wide variety of parodic compositions. One finds canonical classical themes being converted into jazzed-up or jazzed-down versions – from hit-parade parodies of Bach by Walter Carlos to Serge Gainsbourg's irreverent pastiches of Mozart, Brahms and Chopin, to pop variations on Stravinsky by Zappa and Public Image Ltd.

But pop is also beginning to parody itself. David Bowie is an explicit but by no means isolated example of this. We have Hip Hop groups like Mantronics jumbling together musical styles from a whole diversity of movements – jazz, blues, rock, reggae, heavy metal, etc; Heaven 17 reviving Gary Glitter, Sandy Shaw and the Nolan Sisters; Prince aping Little Richard aping Chuck Berry; or indeed the later Beatles themselves experimenting in self-parody (their White Album released in the seventies, for example, uses electronic techniques to cut up and mix around various songs from their own previous albums). One even notes the emergence of groups which mimic the very idea of pop music itself – Public Image Ltd have produced a record entitled *Album* and a tape entitled *Cassette*! It seems that pop music is becoming increasingly an assortment of musical footnotes to itself.

If one may speak of a postmodern trend in music it would be one which not only erodes the distinction between serious and pop music but also breaks down, in certain instances, the very division between music and other media. Records are released simultaneously in video versions. Live performances become TV or radio performances. And one might even cite examples of musical *bricolage* being overlaid with textual *bricolage*, the latter frequently being drawn from postmodern works of literature and

---

and African traditions. Yet another mark of this departure from the mainstream of academic concert music was a tendency by musicians like Glass, Riley and Reich to draw from postmodern developments in other media, in particular the visual arts and literature.

philosophy. Thus we find a performing artist like Laurie Anderson mixing classical and pop instrumentation (e.g. electrified violin) to produce a commercialized version of Wagner or interpolating literary quotations from contemporary authors like Burroughs and Pynchon. Predictably, many critics and audiences of her mixed-media performances have had difficulty in identifying her work as either 'high art' or 'popular culture'. And, finally, one could mention the recordings of a group like Scritti Politti which parody the whole ideology of pop, both musically and lyrically, as a consumer narcissism (there is, for example, a playful mimicry of the Beatlemania phenomenon in their Rock-a-Boy-Blue number). And they have even gone so far as to rehearse explicit quotations from such postmodern critics as Lacan, Foucault and Derrida (e.g. 'I'm in love with a Jacques Derrida/Read a page and know what I need to/Take apart my baby's heart/I'm in love'). Here we witness a pop form putting itself into question and exulting in a play of unpredictable allusion. As a parody of both commercial music and highbrow discourse, Scritti Politti seems to be suggesting that there is no realm of contemporary culture exempt from the deconstructive turn. If Derrida can make it to the Top Ten then nothing seems impossible.

Whether such exercises in parody are symptomatic of a trapped mind which knows it can no longer create something new, or whether they represent an anti-elitist desire to democratize intellectual culture by making it available to a popular audience, remains to be seen. In the realm of music, as in other realms, postmodern culture may be read as either the Twilight of Great Art or as the clearance of a space where alternative modes of communication may emerge.

CONCLUSION

After Imagination?

'Imagination is the irrepressible revolutionist' (Wallace Stevens)

Where do we go from here? How may we hope to ever escape the endless self-parodying of postmodernism which announces the 'end' of everything but itself? And if postmodernism subverts the very opposition between the imaginary and the real, to the point where each dissolves into an empty imitation of the other, can we still speak of imagination at all? Does imagination itself not threaten to disappear with the disappearance of man? Is there life, for the human imagination, after deconstruction? Has the very notion of a postmodern imagination become a contradiction in terms?

There is, I think, a danger that the postmodern obsession with the demise of imagination may consolidate the growing conviction that human culture as we have known it – that is, as a creative project in which human beings have an ethical, artistic and political role to play – is now reaching its end. As we have seen in our last two chapters, there is increasing evidence to suggest that the death of imagination also implies the death of a philosophy of *truth* (along with the corresponding notions of interpretation, meaning, reference, narrative, history and value). Such apocalyptic implications are strikingly illustrated in a recent deconstructionist document entitled *After Truth: A Post-Modern Manifesto*, a text which usefully summarizes many of the points made by the contemporary critiques of imagination we have been examining. The following is a selection of some key passages from this representative, if somewhat alarmist, document:

We must learn to live after truth . . . In front of us is an abyss. We cannot 'know' what lies there because it is 'knowledge' that we leave behind . . . We tell a tale of nihilism in two stages: relativism and reflexivity. When we consider the status of our theories and our truth, we are led to relativism. Relativism, in turn, turns back on itself and disappears into the vicious spiral of reflexivity. Nothing is certain, not even this . . . This is no ordinary time. The modern age opened with the destruction of God and religion. It is ending with the threatened destruction of all coherent thought. The age was held on course by stories of progress and emancipation . . . But these stories are now exhausted. There are no new stories to replace them . . . The paradigm for constructing paradigms is now collapsing . . . We are entering a period of 'abnormal' thought . . . The only political ideals left are those of the cynical and the paranoid. Such disillusion has lurked in the wings of European culture for two centuries. Now it can command centre stage. We are paralyzed by the performance and we cannot leave the theatre. All the exits are blocked.[1]

Trapped as we are in this labyrinth of endless play, the only remaining strategy, the authors suggest, is one of *active nihilism*. But can such a programme of lucid disruption and disillusionment really serve as a guideline for meaningful thought or action? Is it possible for the human imagination to remain *human* once truth has been completely erased from the scenario of existence?

It is no doubt salutary to debunk the more naive aspects of the humanist imagination: e.g. its belief in the inevitability of historical progress and its almost messianic claims for the idealist subject. It is no bad thing that we cast a suspecting glance at the proverbial humanist vision of man as a 'free and sovereign artificer' determining his own nature 'without constraint from any barrier'.[2] But we should be wary of slipping from such healthy scepticism to denying the creative subject any role whatsoever in the shaping of history. Deconstruction too has its limits and must acknowledge them. So that while accepting that the 'humanist imagination' does indeed require decentering – in so far as it tends to sustain the untenable claim that the autonomous individual is the sole master and solitary centre of all meaning

– we must insist on the possibility, in the wake of deconstruction, of restoring some notion of a properly *human* imagination. Given the specific characteristics of postmodern culture, which daily confront us and which cannot be wished away, such a revised version of imagination will differ of necessity from its humanist predecessors. We cannot eschew this task of revision. For the alternative is to submit to the corrosive rhetoric of an apocalyptic pessimism which not only encourages feelings of paralysis but points, in the longer term, to the possible demise of humanity itself.

1 Towards an ethical imagination

To resist such an alarming view of things is an ethical responsibility. If the deconstruction of imagination admits of no *epistemological* limits (in so far as it undermines every attempt to establish a decidable relationship between image and reality), it must recognize *ethical* limits. We reach a point in the endless spiral of undecidability where each one of us is obliged to make an ethical decision, to say: *here I stand*. (Or, at the level of collective responsibility, *here we stand*). Here and now, in the face of the postmodern logic of interminable deferment and infinite regress, of floating signifiers and vanishing signifieds, here and now I face an *other* who demands of me an ethical response. This call of the other to be heard, and to be respected in his/her otherness, is irreducible to the parodic play of empty imitations. It breaks through the horizontal surface of mirror-images and, outfacing the void, reintroduces a dimension of depth. The face of the other resists assimilation to the dehumanising processes of commodity fetishism. Contesting the cult of imitation without origin, it presents us with an image which does indeed relate to something: the ethical existence of the other as an *other* – the inalienable right to be recognized as a particular person whose very *otherness* refuses to be reduced to a mimicry of *sameness*. Beyond the mask there is a face. Beyond the anonymous system, however all-encompassing it may appear, there is always what

Emmanuel Levinas has termed, the resistant ethical relation of the 'face to face'.[3]

We do not *know* what the 'face' *is*. Its epistemological status remains undecidable; but our inability to grasp the other on our terms, i.e. in our cognitive projects, does not prevent us from acknowledging, ethically, that we are being addressed here and now by another – a person with concrete needs – in and through the image of the face. An other in need makes the ethical demand upon me – 'where are you?' before I ask of the other the epistemological question – 'who are you?' And this ethical priority entails a correlative priority of praxis over theory. We are responsible for the suffering of the other before we know his or her credentials. Ethics has primacy over epistemology and ontology. Or to put it less technically, the good comes before the question of truth and being. At the most basic level of pre-reflective lived experience, the ethical face discloses a relationship to an other before knowledge and beyond being.

This does not of course mean that our response to the face which appeals to us in and through the image is *indiscriminate*. Ethical action does not mean uncritical action. On the contrary, it demands constant discernment. For quite clearly it is one thing to respond to the face of a dictator (e.g. Hitler) and another to respond to the face of a slave (e.g. a holocaust victim). In the former we discern an image of ruthless power; in the latter an image of powerlessness. Only in the second case is the ethical exigency unconditional. And such basic acts of discernment occur at an ethical level, long before we attempt to explain these distinctions in epistemological deductions, foundations or systems. When a naked face cries 'where are you?', we do not ask for identity papers. We reply, first and foremost, 'here I am'.

Even the 'terrorist' knows this. Hijacking the mass-media and holding its viewers to ransom, the 'terrorist' has learnt to exploit the ethical dimension of the image. He knows that the most effective way of securing his demands is to hide his own face and allow the terrorized face of the hostage to be relayed across the world's TV screens. Or else the 'terrorist' turns round, removes the mask, becomes a martyr, goes on hunger-strike, opts to suffer rather than do wrong, to endure violence rather than inflict it on others (as it may well have been inflicted on him). As Terence McSwiney, the Irish Republican hunger-striker remarked: 'The contest is not one of vengeance but of endurance. It is not those who can inflict the most but those who can suffer the most who will conquer.'

However controversial the progagandist use of the face may be, one thing is clear: it assumes the possibility of an ethical response to mass-media images. Even here the ethical power of the powerless manifests itself. Whatever our response to such images in practical or ideological terms, we are haunted by the destitute face of hostage or hunger-striker. But this primacy of the ethical response in no way dispenses us from the task of critical discrimination; it requires it. Without such critical discrimination our ethical response of empathy might be manipulated for unethical purposes. For the sake of others, we must always be discerning in our response to the other.

To respond to the ethical dimension of images does not mean turning one's back on the postmodern condition. There is no return ticket to the humanisms of yesterday – short of ignoring the present time in which we live. Nor would such a return be desirable. The humanist cult of autonomous subjectivity tended to exclude the other to the point where the self was ultimately defined as an act of pure negation (e.g. Sartre). A more fitting response to the postmodern dilemma is to radically reinterpret the role of imagination as a relationship between the self and the other. We may thus take stock of what deconstruction has to offer: a dual dismantling of imagination as i) a humanist cult of the transcendental self and ii) an onto-theological imitation of the imperialist other. Having thus demystified the excesses of the premodern and modern paradigms of imagination, we may be in a position to discover another kind of relation between self and other -- one more human than humanism and more faithful to otherness than onto-theology.

What we are calling for is an ethical reinterpretation of imagination capable of responding to the challenge of postmodernism. Debunking the conventional models of imagination as either a sovereign master or a mimetic servant of meaning, we find that our   inherited notions of self and other have become undecidable. But this moment of deconstructive critique is only the first step towards an ethical imagination.[4] We must go further. The deconstructive critique must itself be subjected to critique out of ethical respect for the other. Only by thus submitting deconstruction to ethics can we prevent it degenerating into an apocalyptic nihilism of endless mirror-play. The deconstruction of self and other as fetishized 'origins' must ultimately serve the emergence of an ethical relation between self and other.

But where are we to find the golden thread which leads beyond the deconstructive labyrinth of parody towards such an ethical relation? We find it in the face which haunts imagination: the ethical demand to imagine *otherwise*. This demand is the irrepressible residue of even those images of the other transmitted through our global communications network. The ethical imagination is responsible because it is first a response to the other. It is an imagination able to respond *here I am*, even in the midst of the euphoric frissons of apocalyptic mirror play. But this notion of ethical responsibility is in no way to be taken as a moralizing censorship of images as 'evil'. It does not endorse a puritanical disdain for the new technological media. On the contrary, an ethical imagination alert to both the liberating and incarcerating potentials of postmodern culture, would be one determined to use all available technologies to pursue its concern for the other. Are there not impressive examples of this? As when television reports of the Vietnam war actually managed to 'conscientize' a sufficient part of American public opinion to end the war? Or when Bob Geldof and the other rock musicians in the Live Aid for Africa Concert in 1985 demonstrated how a broadcast, motivated by TV images of Ethiopian famine victims and transmitted worldwide through the satellite channels of the mass-communications system, could succeed in soliciting an ethical response from millions of people.

While it is true that media images often banalize and anaesthetize our perceptions, they can also do the opposite – enlarge our imaginative horizons and extend our sympathies by putting us in contact with other people in other places. This expansive potential of the media image allows, furthermore, for the possibility of a *democratization* of knowledge and culture. Our mass-communications culture is radically altering the inherited notions of literacy. But the challenge is to use the media image to supplement, rather than supplant, the civilization of book and canvas with another civilization of communication where, as Josef Beuys put it, everyone has the chance to become an artist. The particular task of the ethical imagination in such a civilization of postmodern communications is to ensure that a democracy of images avoids superficiality and remains dialogical, i.e. attentive to the demands of the other.[5]

If deconstruction has committed an error it is, above all, its tendency to eclipse the ethical dimension. It sometimes forgets that the images of all signifying systems of play and parody, of *difference* and dissemination, of aporia and apocalypse, remain ultimately answerable to the concrete ethical exigency of the *face to face relation*. Behind and beyond the image a face resides: the face of the other who will never let the imagination be. Perhaps this is what Levinas had in mind when he spoke of the ethical role played by the other in a postmodern world which can no longer see beyond its own paralysis,

not because everything is permitted, and by means of technology, possible, but because everything has become indifferent. The unknown is immediately rendered familiar and the new habitual. There is nothing new under the sun. The crisis spoken of in Ecclesiastes is not due to sin but to *ennui*. Everything becomes absorbed, engulfed and immured in the Same. . . . Everywhere one suspects and denounces the machinations of spectacle, the transcendence of empty rhetoric, play. Vanity of vanities: the echo of our own voices, taken as a response to what few entreaties remain to us; everywhere fallen back onto our own feet, as after the ecstasies of a drug. Except the other who, in all this *ennui*, one cannot abandon.[6]

Despite the somewhat alarmist tone of this passage, the basic point is clear: we cannot subscribe to apocalyptic emptiness because we cannot renege on our responsibility to the other. Or to put it more simply – we cannot let imagination succumb to the vicious circles of pastiche because the other simply will not allow us. It is here in the everyday claim of the face to face relation that we discover the still small voice which bids us continue the search for an ethical imagination – even when it is being pronounced dead.

2 Towards a poetical imagination

A postmodern imagination responsive to the ethical dimension of things would be *critical*. But it would also be *poetical*. I use this term in the broad sense of 'inventive' making and creating carried by the word *poiesis*. If the ethical imagination is not to degenerate into censorious puritanism or nostalgic lamentation it must also give full expression to its *poetical* potential. The imagination, no matter how ethical, needs to play. Indeed one might even say that it needs to play *because* it is ethical – to ensure it is ethical in a liberating way, in a way which animates and enlarges our response to the other rather than cloistering us off in a dour moralism of resentment and recrimination.

From its earliest beginnings and throughout the various stages of its genealogical development, the western understanding of imagination has been marked by these two fundamental dimensions, the ethical and the poetical. The fortunes of each dimension, and of their mutual interrelationship, have shifted from one time to another. Whereas Platonic and Judeo-Christian teaching tended to give priority to the ethical, the modern philosophies of romanticism and existentialism almost invariably championed the poetical. Thus while Socrates banned the poet from his ideal theocentric republic, Shelley and Schiller, for example, hailed the poet as the unacknowledged legislator of mankind, declaring morality subordinate to art. But whatever the particular emphasis, the imagination in both its premodern and modern variations maintained some basic link between the claims of *ethos* and *poiesis*. This formative bond must be retained and explored in our postmodern culture.

Aware of a certain deconstructionist tendency to dismiss ethics as an anachronism (i.e. an ideological leftover of bourgeois humanism or of Western metaphysics generally), I have stressed the urgency of retrieving an ethical perspective for the post-modern imagination. But it is important not to weigh down one side of the balance in our efforts to redress the other. The postmodern imagination is as much in need of *poiesis* as of *ethos*. It needs to be able to laugh with the other as well as to suffer. And here is perhaps the place to concede that the deconstructionist habit of foregrounding the idiom of 'play' has, despite its frequent abuses and excesses, something very valuable to offer. We have, during the course of our preceding analyses, had numerous occasions to observe that the metaphor of play has enjoyed a privileged status in postmodern philosophies. We have seen how this was especially the case with Derrida, Lyotard, Lacan and Barthes. There is also an abundance of references to the motif of 'play' in contemporary art, ranging from the use of the chessgame metaphor by Beckett (*Endgame*) and Canetti (*Auto da Fe*) to the significant role played by the player/clown figure in the works of Böll (*The Clown*), Grass (*The Tin Drum*), Mann (*Mephisto*), Fellini (*Ginger and Fred*), Wenders (*Paris, Texas*), Herzog (*The Ballad of Bruno*) and Godard (*Pierrot le Fou*). And in recent years, the exponents of both Artificial Intelligence Research and the New Physics – e.g. Hofstadter, Prigogine – have been repeatedly stressing the pre-eminence of play and dance models as expressive of the essentially indeterminable character of matter. Suffice it to remark here that the predominance of the play paradigm is not simply reducible to an intellectual Parisian fashion, but corresponds, in some respect, to a general rediscovery of the *poiesis* dimension of our world.

If we have been inclined, in preceding chapters, to interpret the postmodern paradigm of play in its negative apocalyptic aspects it is perhaps important to affirm at this point some of its more positive implications. The ex-centric characteristics of the play paradigm may be construed as tokens of the poetical power of imagination to transcend the limits of egocentric, and indeed anthropocentric, consciousness – thereby exploring different possibilities of existence. Such 'possibilities' may well be deemed impossible at the level of the established reality: a point made by Lévi-Strauss in *Tristes Tropiques* when he defined play as a cathartic power to make what is impossible at the empirical level of existence possible at a symbolic level.[7] And it is assuredly this same capacity for imaginative play that Joyce celebrated in *Finnegans Wake* as the tendency of 'nighttime consciousness' to have 'two thinks at a time', to deploy itself freely and creatively 'between twosome twiminds'.

Here we are no doubt touching on the radical discovery of the *unconscious* which has so informed our contemporary culture. Psychoanalysis revealed the unconscious as a playground of images and symbols which defy the laws of formal logic. 'The alternative "either-or" cannot be expressed in the process of dreaming', noted Freud, 'Both of the alternatives are usually inserted in the text of the dream as though they were equally valid.'[8] This logic of the imaginary is one of *both/and* rather than *either/or*. It is inclusive and, by extension, tolerant: it allows opposites to stand, irreconcilables to co-exist, refusing to deny the claim of one for the sake of its contrary, to sacrifice the strange on the altar of self-identity. This unconscious discourse of imagination is most immediately obvious as a play of words – *double-entente, jeu de mots*, slips of the tongue (*parapraxis*) – or indeed any instance of language laughing at its own contradictions, refusing to take itself too seriously, having the humility to go on playing even when its consciously intended meaning is humiliated, its will to power exposed, its ego wounded or deflated. Such unconscious discourse has been aptly termed by Lacanians as 'the discourse of the Other'. And for this reason: it occurs when the controlling censorious ego is off-guard, taken by surprise, overtaken from behind by that *otherness* which precedes the sense of self and subverts the priorities of self-possession.

This language of the unconscious, expressed at the level of the imaginary and the symbolic, is the portal to poetry. Poetry is to be understood here in the extended sense of a play of *poiesis*; a creative letting go of the drive for possession, of the calculus of means and ends. It allows the rose – in the words of the mystic Silesius – to exist *without why*.[9] Poetics is the carnival of possibilities where everything is permitted, nothing censored. It is the willingness to imagine oneself in the other person's skin, to see things *as if* one were, momentarily at least, another, to experience how the other half lives. Is this not what occurs in drama or fiction, for example, when we are transported into another person's mind and body existing in another time and place in another culture and society? Then we experience the world as if we were Oedipus, Hamlet, Anna Karenina. But not just the world of heroes and heroines. The poetical imagination equally empowers us to identify with the forgotten or discarded persons of history. It invites excluded middles back into the fold, opens the door to prodigal sons and daughters, and refuses the condescending intolerance of the elite towards the preterite, the saved towards the damned. The poetical imagination opposes the apartheid logic of black and white.

The space of the Other, safeguarded by the ethical imagin-ation, by no means precludes the poetical imagination. On the contrary, it may be seen as its precondition. The Other which laughter brings into play, transgressing the security fences of self-centredness, is a catalyst for poetical imagining. Otherness is as essential to the life of *poiesis* as it is to that of *ethos*. In both cases it signals a call to abandon the priority of egological exist-ence for the sake of alternative modes of experience hitherto repressed or simply unimagined. Indeed without the poetical openness to the pluri-dimensionality of meaning, the ethical imagination might well shrink back into a cheerless moralizing, an authoritarian and fearful censorship. And, likewise, a poetical imagination entirely lacking in ethical sensibility all too easily slides into an irresponsible *je me'en foutisme*: an attitude where anything goes and everything is everything else because it is, in the final analysis, nothing at all. This is where the poetical readiness to tolerate the *undecidability* of play must be considered in relation to the ethical readiness to *decide* between different modes of response to the other (e.g. between those that transfigure and those that disfigure, those that care for the other in his/her otherness and those that do not).[10] And here, once again, we would stress that it is not a question of sacrificing the poetical to the ethical. It is rather a matter of ascertaining the mutually enhancing virtues of both aspects of imagination. Each is indispensable to the other.

Ethics and poetics are two different but complementary ways

in which imagination can open us to the otherness of the other. By deconstructing our pseudo-images of selfhood into a play of undecidable possibilities, the poetical imagination can bring us to the threshold of the other. It can shatter not only the chains of imposed reality, but also the *imagos* which enslave us in self-obsession, fixation and fear. So doing, it releases us into a play of desire for the other. In this way, the poetical imagination discloses the language of the unconscious as the desire of the other. And in its movement toward self-disposession and self-surpassing it may even offer what some might call a mystical or sublime intimation of alterity. But it cannot go further. Poetics cannot actually transcend the symbolic projects of my unconscious desire and *encounter* the other in his/her otherness. It is here that poetical imagination defers to its ethical counterpart. The face of the other, addressing me ethically here and now, cuts across the image-chain of desire and says 'come'. The image of the face is that which sets my desire for the other in motion in the first place. But it is the other disclosed through the image of the face which also bids me go *beyond* my desire and become responsible to and for the other. If a poetics of imagination is what keeps desire alive as an interminable play of possibility, it is an ethics of imagination which distinguishes between the desire which remains imprisoned in my subjective projects and the desire which responds to the otherness of the other's face (i.e. not the other that I envisage but the other that envisages me).

Finally, a poetical imagination attuned to the dilemmas of our postmodern condition, also needs to commit itself to the invention of an alternative *social* project. Such a project would seek to overcome both the humanist fallacy of wilful mastery (voluntarism) and the onto-theological fallacy of submissive obedience (quietism). What is more, it would directly confront the inflation of pseudo-images which paralyzes our contemporary social consciousness (consumerism). This kind of project might be engendered by a poetical imagination prepared to explore different possibilities of social existence. 'The possible's slow fuse', as Emily Dickinson wrote, 'is lit by the imagination.' Resisting the pervasive sense of social paralysis, the poetic imagination would nourish the conviction that things *can be changed*. The first and most effective step in this direction is to begin to *imagine* that the world as it is could be *otherwise*.

Such possibilities of socio-political invention are of course correlative, if by no means identical, with new possibilities of artistic invention. For art, as an open-access laboratory of imaginative exploration, is one of the most powerful reminders that history is never completed. As such, art can remain the most persuasive harbinger of a *poetics of the possible*.[11] But in order to realize this promise, it must continue to believe that a poetic imagination can play a liberating role in postmodern culture. The importance of such a rediscovery is dramatically underlined by Ihab Hassan in the conclusion to his study of postmodernism entitled *The Dismemberment of Orpheus* (1971). Postmodern art, he insists, must refuse to allow 'imagination to abandon its teleological sense: change is also dreams come true'. And such a refusal is itself inseparable from the hope that 'after self-parody, self-subversion and self-transcendence, after the pride and revulsion of anti-art will have gone their way, art may move toward a redeemed imagination'.[12] But such sentiments are no more than pious wishes unless we take full stock of the considerable obstacles which oppose the poetical task of imagination in our postmodern age. It is not enough to state *what might be done*. We also have to reckon with the practical factors which militate against us doing it.

3 Postmodernism and late capitalism

One of the most daunting obstacles is undoubtedly the economic one. The consumerization of the image does not spring from nowhere. It is symptomatic of an ideology of empty imitation intimately related to the dominant economic system of consumerism that has now achieved almost worldwide proportions.[13] Faced with such a global system, it may even seem futile to try to unmask its omnipresent effects; for to do so merely adds, some would argue, to the sense of its ineluctable power. The society of the pseudo-image becomes all the more imposing with our every effort to debunk it.[14] Even moral judgements about a new culture of superficiality and depthlessness are deemed increasingly inappropriate: there is a common feeling that the contemporary consumer is no mere manipulated victim but actually conspires with the whole production system of commercialized images. Daniel Boorstin makes this point in his book, *The Image: A Guide to Pseudo-Events in America*:

The fantastic growth of advertising and public relations together with everybody's increasing reliance on dealers in pseudo-events and images cannot – contrary to highbrow clichés – accurately be described as a growing superficiality. Rather these things express a world where the image, more interesting than its original, has itself become the original. . . . Advertising men, industrial designers and packaging engineers are not deceivers of the public. They are simply acolytes of the image. And so are we all. They elaborate the image, not only because the image sells, but also because the image is what people want to buy. . . . We are sold it and we buy it and enjoy it for its image and how we fit into the image. The language of images, then, is not circumlocution at all. It is the only simple way of describing what dominates our experience.[15]

Whereas liberal social commentators such as Boorstin tend to speak of this global phenomenon in terms of a general *Americanization* of contemporary existence, other more ideologically oriented critics call it by the more specific name of 'late capitalism' (Jameson, Eagleton) or 'the ideology of advanced industrial society' (Marcuse, Touraine). But the introduction of an ideological dimension, often from a radical or neo-Marxist perspective, does not by any means lead to a more optimistic assessment of contemporary culture.

In such works as *One-Dimensional Man* or *Eros and Civilization* (particularly its 1966 Preface), Herbert Marcuse warns of the erosion of criticism in a society increasingly devoid of any genuine *opposition*. The emergence of a mass advertising culture entails the association of merchandise with pseudo-images of the libidinous unconscious. The power system governing the new affluent society no longer even needs to justify its domination, so effective is its 'social engineering' of imagination, its ability to deliver fetish goods which satisfy its consumers. 'Like the unconscious, the destructive energy of which it so successfully represents', writes Marcuse, the commodity system is 'on this side of good and evil, and the principle of contradiction has no place in its logic'.[16] Advanced industrial society thus manages to contain all moves towards qualitative change. Its achievements appear so total as to stifle any critical rationale for transcending this society. Marcuse's overall verdict is pessimistic. He is even prompted to designate this system as insurmountable and totalitarian:

In this society, the productive apparatus tends to become totalitarian to the extent to which it determines not only the socially needed occupations, skills and attitudes, but also individual needs and aspirations. It thus obliterates the opposition between the private and public existence, between individual and social needs. Technology serves to institute new, more effective, and more pleasant forms of social control and social cohesion. The totalitarian tendency of these controls seems to assert itself in still another sense – by spreading to the less developed and even to the pre-industrial areas of the world, and by creating similarities in the development of capitalism and communism.[17]

The technology of commodity images is not a neutral process. It is inseparably bound up with a political ideology which appears to have infiltrated the contemporary world experience to the point of no return. Its project of domination has become so extensive, indeed, that the possibilities of imagining, not to mention enacting, alternative projects of social existence seem entirely remote – perhaps even non-existent. Hence Marcuse's despair:

As the project unfolds, it shapes the entire universe of discourse and action, intellectual and material culture. In the medium of technology, culture, politics and the economy merge into an omnipresent system which swallows up or repulses all alternatives. The productivity and growth potential of this system stabilize the society and contain technical progress within the framework of domination. Technological rationality has become political rationality.[18]

The fissures of despair, already evident in the writings of Boorstin and Marcuse in the sixties, have widened into a gaping abyss by the time the cultural commentators of the seventies and eighties take their soundings. In his formidable essay on 'Postmodernism, or the Cultural Logic of Late Capitalism' (1984), Frederic Jameson analyses some of the main signs of the apocalyptic nihilism identified as a hallmark of the postmodern crisis. 'The last few years', he writes,' have been marked by an inverted millenarianism, in which premonitions of the future . . . have been replaced by senses of the end of this or that (the end of ideology, art, or social class; the crisis of "Leninism", social democracy, or the welfare state etc., etc.): taken together all of these perhaps constitute what is increasingly called postmodernism.'[19] The postmodern turn is frequently predicated upon a radical break or *coupure* with the terminal expressions of modern humanist culture – e.g. existentialism in philosophy, the great *auteurs* genre in cinema, abstract expressionism in painting, or the 'modernist' poetry of Yeats, Eliot, Pound and their post-war disciples. What replaces these modern movements from the sixties onwards is a counter-culture of self-parodying forms. To our own selection of six such postmodern forms (examined in our last chapter), we may now add Jameson's own shorthand list:

Andy Warhol and pop art, but also photorealism, and beyond it, the 'new expressionism': the moment, in music, of John Cage, but also of the synthesis of classical and popular styles found in composers like Phil Glass and Terry Riley, and also punk and new wave rock; in film, Godard, post-Godard and experimental cinema and video, but also a whole new type of commercial film; Burroughs, Pynchon, or Ishmael Reed, on the one hand, and the French *nouveau roman* and its succession on the other, along with alarming new kinds of literary criticism, based on some new aesthetic of textuality or *écriture*.[20]

And architecture too, of course, bears witness to its own brand of *coupure*: the rise of a postmodern populism (as outlined for example in Robert Venturi's manifesto *Learning from Las Vegas*) which sets itself firmly against the high modernism of the International Style and its 'charismatic Masters', Walter Gropius, Le Corbusier and Mies Van der Rohe.

Thus, at all levels, postmodernism effaces the dividing line between High Culture and Mass Culture. It playfully embraces those very aspects of the Consumer Culture Industry which the critical ethos of modern humanism – from existentialism and the Frankfurt School to the American New Criticism – had repudiated. The one-dimensional wasteland of consumerist society so vehemently denounced by the Adornos, Marcuses or Bellows, provides postmodernism with its chosen materials of both form and content. 'The postmodernists', as Jameson explains, 'have been fascinated by this whole "degraded" land-scape of schlock and kitsch, of TV serials and Readers Digest culture, of advertising and motels, of the late show and the grade-B Hollywood film, of so-called paraliterature with its airport paperback categories of Gothic and Romance, the popular biography, the murder mystery and science-fiction or fantasy novel.'[21]

The postmodern celebration of mass-media culture is, to a significant degree, a symptom of today's multi-national capi-talism. It is not just one more style of fashion, but a 'cultural dominant' inextricably related to the socio-economic dominant of our time. Our society has now reached a point where aesthetic production has become integrated into commodity production generally.[22] And one of the most serious consequences of such a merger is the new facility of the established commercial culture to recuperate or neutralize the 'oppositional' power of art. Thus while much of modernist art and literature prided itself on its capacity to negate the established view of things – to *épater la bourgeoisie* – one finds that even the most offensive aspects of postmodernist parody or anti-art are easily assimilated by the official culture. Hence, for instance, Warhol's attempted exposure of the consumerism of media culture and its manipu-lative images of desire and nostalgia, became so revered by the consumer culture itself that, in the words of one critic, 'his work is no more subversive than a catering service and as such fits the age of Reagan nicely'.[23] Subversion yielded to sedation.

This is as true of Warhol's billboard series – now celebrated icons of consumer pop culture – as it is of Beuys' so-called 'artless' collages, which have become, despite the artist's anti-establishment stance, prime cultural assets of the German government and coveted exhibits of major international banks.

This convertibility-into-cash syndrome has given rise to a new fetishism of cultural objects. Late capitalism, with its tax-exemption laws for art patronage and its promotion of the investment market of the gallery-dealer system, has effectively demolished the radical intent of the 'art for 5 kopeks' manifesto of the *avant-garde*. The price spiral in art trading, as Robert Hughes sardonically observed, has led to a disconcerting paradox:

Works of art, once meant to stand apart from the realm of bourgeois luxury and display their flinty resistance to capitalist values, (are) now among the most eagerly sought and highly paid for. . . . Even the conventions of art appreciation become, in the face of a spiralling market, a dead language, analogous to advertising copy and producing the same kind of knee-jerk reverence in a brutalized culture of unfulfillable desire.[24]

The deconstructionist would probably want to avoid such talk of a 'cultural dominant' and its rapport with the 'ideological dominant' of late capitalism. He would tend to see such a political interpretation as another example of the old humanist/historicism which attempts to reduce the play of cultural *differences* to the overall simplicity of some Master Narrative. Jean-François Lyotard appears to advance this kind of argument in his study, *The Postmodern Condition: A Report on Knowledge* (1979). Lyotard does not dispute the fact that there is an intimate link between the demands of consumer capitalism and the kitsch nature of postmodern culture. Indeed, he offers a graphic account of this very complicity:

Eclecticism is the degree zero of contemporary general culture: one listens to reggae, watches a western, eats McDonald's food for lunch and local cuisine for dinner, wears Paris perfume in Tokyo and 'retro' clothes in Hong Kong; knowledge is a matter for TV games. It is easy to find a public for eclectic works. By becoming kitsch, art panders to the confusion which reigns. . . .[25]

But rather than resort to the *antimodern* solution (as he puts it) of moral or political denunciation, Lyotard prefers the *postmodern* solution offered by a new 'aesthetic of the sublime'. Such an aesthetic resists the temptation to reconcile the multiplicity of language games which prevail in our culture; it refuses to totalize them into 'a real unity'. The price to be paid for such totalization, Lyotard claims, is terror. We are counselled, accordingly, to abandon the humanist nostalgia for a whole picture or global narrative – which would seek to explain the *real* truth of our times. The business of the postmodernist, urges Lyotard, 'is not to supply reality but to invent allusions . . . which cannot be presented'. The only solution is to embrace the deconstructionist vow: 'Let us wage war on totality; let us be witnesses to the unpresentable; let us activate the differences and save the honour of the name.'[26]

The postmodern sublime is thus hailed as a privileged experience of heterogeneity, a limitless allusiveness which defies the rules of hermeneutic interpretation or reflective judgement. The resulting experience of the sublime conveys an intrinsic combination of pleasure and pain: the pleasure that what we witness exceeds presentation and the pain that this excess exposes the aesthetic inadequacy of 'imagination and sensibility'.[27]

But what, we may ask, does it mean when such supposedly 'sublime' works as Rauschenberg's *Oracle* or César's *Compression II* present us with a heap of mechanical wreckage which replicates the reflections of anonymous cityscapes with 'hallucinatory splendour'? What are we to make of the inanimate vacuity expressed by Warhol's soup cans or by Doug Bond's polyester figures which convey the fetishization of the human body as pure surface? How are we to respond to the sublimity of postmodern parodies where the debris of urban squalor and alienation is exhibited as a glossy mirage without depth or density? Or, finally, to cite what is considered by some as the very emblem of postmodern art, Lucas Samara's *Mirrored Room*: what is the distinction between sublime irrepresentability and consumer narcissism in a room just large enough to enter, with mirrors on every surface reflecting the viewer into an indefinitely expanding series of fragmented copies?[28] Is the postmodern aesthetic of the sublime not itself, and perhaps in spite of itself, a symptom of the 'cultural dominant' of our present technological world system?

While Jameson does not advert to the celebration of the sublime in the recent writings of Lyotard and the deconstructionists, he does attribute the term 'the hysterical sublime' to the general postmodern cult of excess and fragmentation. And he argues that the contemporary tendency to reduce the historical present to a mere collage of random forces (whose effectivity is both undecidable and unpresentable in terms of a global historical narrative), merely reinforces the ideology of 'depthlessness'. The cult of the hysterical sublime betrays the emergence of a 'new culture of the simulacrum . . . whose erosion of the link with history is itself a symptom of its complicity (intended or otherwise) with the new world space of late multinational Capital.'[29]

Unlike the romantic notions of the sublime outlined by Burke and Kant, the postmodern notion is not concerned with the experience of Nature or Transcendence (i.e. as powers incommensurable with human consciousness and inducing feelings in us of awe or terror). In the postmodern experience of the sublime, the unfathomable mysteries of Nature and God have been replaced by those of technology and mass communications. Now the sentiment of the sublime is one intimately linked with our sense of powerlessness before the faceless inhumanity of multinational Capital. Its very *unpresentability* is an expression of man's self-estrangement, his sense that history and society, or even art, have ceased to provide him with a meaningful model of understanding or action. The cult of the hysterical sublime thus feeds off the contemporary sense of helplessness – of being everywhere exposed to that enormous 'anti-natural power of dead human labour stored up in our machinery': an alienated power which turns back against us in unrecognizable shapes and paralyzes all projects of collective as well as individual praxis. Posturing as some mysterious sublimity, the technology of mass consumerism appears to exist timelessly in its own right. In short, one of the most sinister aspects of postmodernism has been, arguably, its failure to critically identify and analyse the intrinsic rapport between the dehumanizing power of this technology and the historical development of late capitalism.

Convinced of the necessity to remedy this postmodernist eclipse of historical reference, Jameson relates the various modern phases of cultural development to parallel stages in the socio-economic history of the West.[30] Following the model sketched by Mandel in *Late Capitalism*, he correlates nineteenth-century realism with the stage of market capitalism, modernism with the stage of monopoly capitalism, and postmodernism with the contemporary stage of late multinational capitalism. Whereas certain modernist movements – e.g. Malevich's and Meyerhold's constructivism, Marinetti's futurism, Le Corbusier's utopianism or Leger's socialist expressionism – continued to affirm the positive potential of mechanized industry for a Promethean reconstruction of human society, this no longer seems a viable option for postmodernism. The postmodern phase of consumerist culture bears witness to an unlimited expansion of capital – aided by the proliferation of the media, advertising and computer industries – into hitherto uncommodified areas of experience, e.g. the worlds of domestic privacy and even, as Marcuse noted, the unconscious itself.

This last postmodern phase corresponds to the fact that consumer capital deploys machines not just of *production* but, more and more frequently, of *reproduction*. The electronic media of TV and mass communications function by reproducing form on form rather than producing form from matter; they transmit audio-visual forms through the electrical forms of invisible waves, waves which articulate nothing as such but carry flattened image surfaces within themselves. And this perhaps explains why postmodern works, which seek to represent such *unpresentable* modes of reproduction, frequently induce in us the feeling of the *technological sublime*. For in so far as postmodern works increasingly resort to a play of surface mimesis in order to speak *about* their own process of reproduction (i.e. film, video, TV, print or sound recordings), they end up in a kind of self-parody – a form of self-deconstruction whose undecidable paradoxes leave us breathless and, as it were, totally mystified. Moreover, this experience is, as we have noted, by no means confined to art museums and literary texts. It is also powerfully evidenced in the postmodern architectural spaces which are growing up around us, spaces where 'the distorting and fragmenting reflection of one enormous glass surface to the other can be taken as paradigmatic of the central role of process and reproduction in postmodernist culture'.[31] Everywhere we look we find signs of the technological reproduction of the simulacrum.

4 Strategies of resistance

How then are we to combat this expansion of the technology of the simulacrum into both our inner and outer spaces? Where are we to find a place of critical distance where we may begin to imagine alternative projects of social existence capable of counteracting the paralysis which the 'technological sublime' induces in us? It is not sufficient to merely *know* that the technological colonization of images is a symptom of a globally computerized network of 'third stage' multinational capital. For a simple awareness of the ominous equation of culture and capital might just exacerbate the prevailing 'high tech paronoia'. The bald claim that contemporary existence is dominated in all its aspects by the omnivorous Logic of the Simulacrum may well serve to *consolidate* the power of late capitalism, rather than diminish it. An oppositional project of action is also needed. Knowledge must be converted into strategies of resistance.

So we are back with the double question: what is to be done and how is it to be done? The pessimistic conclusions of most postmodern commentators would incline one to the view that there is nothing to be done. Or that even if there were, there would be no way of doing it. A few thinkers have, however, come up with suggestions.

Marcuse for example suggests, in his later writing, that some refuge may be found if we can save art from anti-art and rediscover its 'aesthetic dimension' of formal distance and transcendence. In this way, art might serve as an antidote to the anti-humanism of contemporary culture.[32] Marcuse declines, however, to indicate how this retrieval of a lost aesthetic dimension could be translated into a project of ethical or social practice.

A quite different kind of strategy is outlined by Umberto Eco in *Faith in Fakes* (1985). He calls for 'cultural guerilla warfare'. There is, Eco says, no point in trying to expose some ideological conspiracy *behind* the new mass-media culture. This media network has become its own ideology. In other words, we can no longer speak of an identifiable message being transmitted through the airwaves. All we have is a series of random and conflicting meanings which cancel each other out, leaving us with nothing but a flux of surface images. Eco explains:

Regardless of what is said through the means of mass communication, when the recipient is surrounded by a medley of communications which simultaneously reach him through different channels, the nature of the information communicated has little importance. What counts is the progressive and uniform bombardment of information in which the different contents flatten out and lose their difference.[33]

Unlike the means of production which governed industrial society, the means of communication governing 'post-industrial' society (to use Daniel Bell's term) are no longer controllable by the will of the individual or indeed of the collective. And in the face of such a faceless communications system we are all of us, 'from the director of the CBS chain to the President of the United States, passing by Martin Heidegger and the most humble peasant of the Nile Delta, the new proletariat'.[34]

But Eco staunchly refuses, even in the light of this admission, to succumb to the postmodern drift toward paralysis and paranoia. He insists that some mode of resistance must be found. The first move is to eliminate false solutions. We must rule out the possibility of trying to take control of the global media network, for if this were achievable – which is by no means certain – it would merely result in a 'totalitarian' control of public opinion from above. Nor does any hope lie in the strategy of using one form of the media to criticize another (i.e. newspapers against cinema or cinema against TV and so on); for such a mirror-play of inter-media critiques is condemned to an infinite regress. Nor does the answer lie in a back-to-nature movement which seeks to opt out of postmodern society altogether, returning to the uncontaminated pasturelands of transcendental meditation and macrobiotic vegetarianism. For even such opting-out strategies are compelled to employ the means of techno-logical communication if they are to communicate their message (e.g. pop music, 'alternative' magazines, radio or television).

Concluding therefore that there is no possibility of redirecting the mass communications system from *within*, and no possibility of finding a way *out*, Eco recommends what he sees as the only remaining solution: a cultural guerilla campaign.

Those who wish to launch an effective resistance must abandon all vain attempts to change the media at the point of *transmission*. They must concentrate instead on the opposite end of the system – the point of *reception*. The new resisters will become, in Eco's words, 'provos of Critical Reception' committed to a 'door to door guerilla campaign' – a campaign which encourages each human recipient of our mass media culture to develop his own critical capacities for interpreting and discriminating between codes of communication. Eco sketches this blueprint for the semiological guerrilla movement:

The universe of technological communication would become traversed by guerilla groups of communication who would reintroduce a critical dimension into passive reception. The threat posed by a situation in which the *medium is the message* would henceforth be converted, in the face of the media and the message, into a return to individual resistance. To the anonymous divinity of Technological Communication our answer could be: 'Not Thy, but *our* will be done'.[35]

Eco's proposal thus assumes the form of an anarchistic individualism: a strategem where each victim of the mass media conspiracy says *no* to the system, interpreting the transmitted multiplicity of images in whichever way he chooses. But if this is for Eco the 'only solution for free human beings', it is one with serious shortcomings. By affirming the right of each media recipient to give his own meaning to the images and sounds which surround him, are we not in fact leaving the basic system of media consumerism intact? Are we not simply transforming mindless consumerism into mindful consumerism? The individual may well be free to *interpret* commodity images as he wishes; but he is not free actually to *produce* alternative kinds of images. Anything goes at the level of reception, while the system of transmission continues unchallenged. And it is not certain, furthermore, that such a liberty of critical consumption could provide any helpful equivalent in political action. Unless, perhaps, one wishes to advocate some form of armed guerilla resistance to the powers that be. (A prospect which Eco himself does not entertain.) But recent examples of such resistance movements in contemporary Western society – e.g. Baader-Meinhof, Action Directe or the Red Brigade – hardly inspire confidence. For quite apart from the carnage, such militant anarchist groups depend very largely on media coverage to communicate their oppositional views. Here again the message becomes one with the medium, a mass spectacle in its own right, another simulacrum in the Civilization of Images.

Yet another strategy of resistance to the contemporary paralysis of Western culture takes the form of a neo-marxist programme of dialectical materialism. Frederic Jameson, Louis Althusser and Terry Eagleton offer three recent versions of such a project. For reasons of economy, however, most of our remarks will be confined to the first of these. The neo-marxists are determined to combat the postmodern eclipse of critical opposition. This is reflected in Jameson's insistence, for example, that the *aesthetic* of postmodernism be related to an *historical* perspective where we can grasp its significance as the cultural dominant of late capitalism. But Jameson dismisses all ethical condemnations of postmodernism made in the name of a free human imagination. (A dismissal which would appear to apply as much to a humanist critique à la Marcuse as to an anarchist critique à la Eco.) What is to be deplored, he says, is not the abolition of the human subject as such, but the absence of a dialectical model able to situate this abolition in historical terms. The danger with postmodern culture in this regard is that its 'image addiction' serves to reduce historical reality to 'visual images, stereotypes or texts': a reductionism which effectively precludes 'any practical sense of the future and of the collective project, thereby abandoning the thinking of future change to fantasies of sheer catastrophe and inexplicable cataclysm'.[36] Jameson is adamant that this reductionist tendency should be understood not *ethically* but *dialectically* – as an inevitable part of the unfolding logic of late capitalism. Any attempt to comprehend it in terms of 'moral or moralizing judgments' is deemed a 'category mistake',[37] a fall-back to old value systems now defunct. 'The cultural critic and the moralist', writes Jameson, 'along with the rest of us, is now so deeply immersed in postmodernist space, so deeply suffused and infected by its new cultural categories, that the luxury of the old fashioned ideological critique, the indignant moral denunciation of the other, becomes unavailable.'[38]

Thus dismissing ethics as a sort of humanist anachronism, Jameson invokes a post-humanist (Althusserian) model of Marxist materialism – one capable of thinking the cultural evolution of late capitalism dialectically as *both* catastrophe *and* progress. But, we may ask, does this move away from a critical individualism to a dialectical collectivism provide us with a satisfactory answer? Does its implicit assertion that postmodernism is an historical inevitability not also in fact *augment* our sense of helplessness before the anonymous laws of the consumer society? Surely the total denial of a semi-independent cultural space, where a critical and poetical imagination could contest the dehumanization of humanity and project alternative possibilities of existence, condemns us once again to inertia?

Jameson is not unaware of this dilemma. But such is his commitment to a global dialectic of historical evolution and mutation that he seems unable to come up with any viable answer. He feels compelled to deny the option of critical distance in a society of the simulacrum where, by his own admission, the respective domains of culture and capital have become so inflated as to become co-extensive. The ability to establish some kind of distinction between the imaginary and the real – which the idea of critical distance presupposes – no longer appears possible in a culture which dissolves the 'real' into pseudo-images. The postmodern conflation of imagination and reality seems to rule out the existence of some alternative *topos* outside of the 'massive Being of capital'. We seem to be deprived of any such utopian breathing space from which to launch an effective critical assault. The potential for such distance is, says Jameson, annihilated by the omnipotent reign of postmodern superficiality: 'we are submerged in its henceforth filled and suffused volume to the point where our now post-modern bodies are . . . incapable of distanciation'.[39] In such a world, it would seem that nothing can avoid the fate of co-optation. Every effort to contest the system or create alternatives is condemned to failure before it begins. Even the countercultural experiments of local resistance and guerilla warfare, Jameson concedes, 'are all somehow secretly disarmed and reabsorbed by a system of which they themselves might well be considered a part, since they can achieve no distance from it'.[40]

His back to the wall, Jameson decides to make a dialectical virtue of necessity. He concludes that it is the very demoralizing condition of postmodern culture which actually constitutes its moment of truth. Reverting implicitly to the idea of the postmodernist sublime (which he had earlier criticized), Jameson declares that the world system of multinational capitalism confronts us with an 'unrepresentable totality', one which calls for a new science of 'cognitive mapping'. Such a science will take the form of a renovated version of dialectical materialism, a version capable of grasping the forms of postmodern parody as accurate descriptions of the present historical predicament of late capitalism. Paradoxical as it may seem, says Jameson, such parodic forms may be read as 'peculiar new forms of realism (or at least of the mimesis of reality) *at the same time* that they can equally well be analysed as so many attempts to distract and divert us from that reality or to disguise its contradictions and resolve them in the guise of various formal mystifications'.[41] And with a final flourish of dialectical daring, Jameson even suggests that the reign of a multinational collective space in which everyone and everything is implicated may itself be construed as the dialectical pre-condition for the elaboration of a new type of 'internationalism'.

But where, we may reply, is one to find the critical basis for such a science? And how can one continue to talk of 'realism' and 'reality' at all, if one grants the postmodern abolition of the distinction between the imaginary and the real? As mentioned, Jameson sought to ground his appeal for a new science of cognitive mapping on the anti-humanist model outlined by Althusser. And this implies the acceptance of an absolute break between the ideological notion of the *imaginaire* and the Marxist-scientific notion of *knowledge*. Thus refusing any recourse to a hermeneutic model of the human imagination with an interpretative 'point of view', Jameson appears to endorse the Althusserian view of a science capable of 'knowing' the totality of the world abstractly – even though this totality remains sublimely 'unrepresentable' for the human imagination as such. Not surprisingly, Jameson (like Althusser) remains vague about the precise contents of such theoretical knowledge. All we can be sure of is that such a science of mapping will start from the 'truth of postmodernism', i.e. the world space of multinational capital. But we cannot go further. We cannot say exactly what kind of positive socio-political form, if any, such a science will take: 'The political form of postmodernism, *if there is any*, will have as its vocation the invention and projection of a global cognitive mapping.'[42] To put it in plainer terms, the task of this new theory will be to invent a new theory!

It is hard to imagine any dialectical science, however postmodern, which could make sense of such tautologies. The postmodern logic of circular parody appears to have contaminated even the most masterly of postmodern commentators – Jameson himself. And perhaps he admits as much when he states, paradoxically, that the basic 'truth' of postmodernism to be expressed by the new science of mapping is that 'there are no true maps'.[43]

5 Beyond the labyrinth?

Are we to conclude then that every attempt to think through postmodernism is condemned to the postmodern disease of endless circularity? It is certainly unlikely that any amount of 'knowledge' about the falsehood of our experience is going to help us think or act in a more effective or liberating way. A form of pedagogy, however accurate and scientific, which does no more than explain the intricate mechanisms of our enslavement offers little consolation. It is not enough to provide a new cartography of our postmodern imprisonment. We also need to find ways within the labyrinth which lead *out* of it.

This is where we return to our appeal for an ethical-poetical imagination. Such an imagination could not be content with merely mapping the logic of postmodern culture. Taking full heed of such descriptions, it would also strive to i) open us to the concrete needs of the other in the postmodern here and now, and ii) explore how we might effectively engage in the transformation of our social existence. The ethical-poetical imagination refuses to wait around for 'the dialectics of development to work themselves out'. And it repudiates any cognitive model which dismisses morality, and by extension human rights and needs, as an ideological leftover from bygone days.[44]

This does not mean that we blithely conjure away postmodernism; nor that we revert to the humanist model of an anthropocentric imagination (i.e. one which wilfully negates reality and conjures up anti-worlds out of its own solitary subjectivity). The ethical-poetical imagination we are advancing accepts that there is much to be learned from the postmodern deconstruction of the humanist subject and its pretentions to mastery. Such a deconstruction may indeed prove, if we acknowledge its limits, to be a healthy *dispossession* of the ego-centric subject. But only on condition that we understand such dispossession as a *via negativa*, a purgation which is not an end in itself but a point of departure for something else. After the disappearance of the self-sufficient imagination, another kind must now reappear – an imagination schooled in the postmodern truth that the self cannot be 'centred' on itself; an imagination fully aware that meaning does not originate within the narrow chambers of its own subjectivity but emerges as a response to the *other*, as radical interdependence.

Several important consequences flow from this. The *alienation* of man in our one-dimensional society need not be taken as an unequivocal signal of the end of humanity. (Though it might well mean this if we refuse the ethical option altogether and submit to the impersonalizing sway of late capitalism). The phenomenon of postmodern alienation may also be construed, ethically, as a sign that man cannot tolerate the Logic of the Simulacrum without ceasing to be human. Passing through the dark night of undecidability, we eventually decide for a practice of imagination capable of responding to the postmodern call of the other reaching towards us from the mediatized image. On the far side of the self-reflecting looking glass, beyond the play of masks and mirrors, there are human beings who suffer and struggle, live and die, hope and despair. Even in those televisual images which transmit events from the furthest corners of our globe, we are being addressed, potentially at least, by living others: the Columbian girl buried up to her neck in the mud of avalanche, the emaciated skeleton of the Ethiopian famine victim, the gaze of hostage or hunger-striker, the running body of the Vietnamese infant covered in napalm, the tormented casualties of Afrikaner apartheid and all those oppressed faces of geo-political power games. Are not those of us who witness such images (as well as those who record and transmit them through the communications network) obliged to respond not just to surface reflections on a screen but to the call of human beings they communicate? Are we not bound to insist that moral conscience is much more than a symptom of some outdated humanist ideology?

A deconstructionist might object that there is no way of discriminating between images since the status of the image is undecidable – i.e. since one cannot determine a representational relationship between the image and its original. But epistemological undecidability does not necessitate ethical undecidability. Perhaps we have to renounce the traditional habit of establishing ethical judgements upon epistemological foundations. For even where epistemological distinctions no longer seem available, we are still compelled to make ethical distinctions. (This raises the question of an ethical hermeneutics touched on below.) Most of us would grant, for instance, and for ethical reasons, that there *is* a significant difference between the status of the following three images: 1) the face of the TV starlet in the commercial for a well known brand of soap; 2) the face of Marilyn Monroe in Warhol's serigraph; and 3) the face of the Vietnamese girl burnt by napalm on CBS news. While each of these images shares the same status as a technical reproduction of a mass communications system, they are different at an ethical level. The soap opera starlet speaks to us here not as another person but as a fetishized effigy of streamlined consumerist dreams. The Warhol image of Monroe, repeated fifty times, addresses us at yet another level – that of a multiple parody of the Hollywood *imago*; (but if this implies, arguably, an ethical dimension of critique in its mimicry of the vacuity of consumer images, it does not yet relate to an *other* who makes a positive ethical demand upon us). The third image of the napalmed girl, by contrast, features a face which cuts through the chain of empty simulacra and asks – 'where are you?'

Some people may be so desensitized by the mass media logic of pseudo-events and empty imitations that they do not respond to this appeal – either because their sensibility has become banalized to the point of being incapable of reacting at all; or else because the only reaction they are capable of is a sensational thrill at the shock quality of the image. But the image of the Vietnamese girl speaks to us even if we do not listen or respond. It demands moral outrage. It demands that we sit up and say, 'this must end'. In short, the ethical dimension of the demand is in no way diminished by the failure of many of us to respond ethically to this demand.

If interpreted ethically (rather than just epistemologically), the postmodern crisis and its attendant sense of impending catastrophe may be seen as a sort of protest against the inhumanity of our times. And perhaps the recent debunkings of the humanist claims for sovereign subjectivity may themselves be read as a veiled ethical demand for a new recognition of the irreducible alterity of the other. Viewed in this light, we would be in a position to say that after Virtue there is still the possibility of ethics, that after Man there is still the possibility of humanity – and more than a self-parodying post-man wandering about in an anonymous communications system devoid of real senders or addressees. But the ability to grasp such possibilities remains the task of an ethical-poetical imagination, an imagination radically de-centred in the sense of being opened to the demands of the other in the postmodern here and now.

The hermeneutic task

Such an imagination is not reducible to paradigms of *mimesis*, *production* or *parody*. It does, however, draw some basic truth from each of its historical configurations. It is prepared to learn from its own history, to listen to the lessons of its own stories.

From the *mimetic* paradigm of onto-theology it learns that imagination is always a response to the demands of an other existing beyond the self. From the *productive* paradigm of humanism it learns that it must never abdicate a personal responsibility for invention, decision and action. And from the *parodic* paradigm of its own postmodern age, it learns that we are living in a common Civilization of Images – a civilization which can bring each one of us into contact with each other even as it can threaten to obliterate the very 'realities' its images ostensibly 'depict'.

It is not because an image is *mimetic, productive* or *parodic* that it is good or bad. Its ethical status does not derive from its being sacramentalized by the icon maker, humanized by the romantic artist or technologized by the media producer. No image is either good or bad but interpretation makes it so. And we understand 'interpretation' here in the primary sense of a pre-reflective praxis, a way of reading the demand of the other by responding to it. We 'interpret' images in this respect in the same manner as an actor 'interprets' a role (i.e. as a mode of relating to others). The question of *theoretical* interpretation comes afterwards. It is at the secondary level of reflective interpretation of the primary interpretation of praxis that the epistemological problem of 'knowledge' arises. What is needed therefore is a critical hermeneutics capable of identifying the interests which motivate the interpretation of images in a given context. The aim of such a hermeneutic is to discriminate between a liberating and incarcerating use of images, between those that dis-close and those that close off our relation to the other, those that democratize culture and those that mystify it, those that communicate and those that manipulate.

This requires in turn that imagination undertakes a hermeneutic reading of its own genealogy: one which critically reassesses its own traditions, retells its own stories. Thus instead of conforming to the official censure of imagination in premodern thought, such a hermeneutic reading would brush this tradition against the grain, allowing repressed voices to speak out, neglected texts to get a hearing. So, for example, in tandem with the biblical condemnation of Adam's transgression, it might cite

the biblical affirmations of the 'good *yetser*' or of other creative
activities of play and dance – e.g. the *sophia* which plays like a
child before the face of the Father on the eve of Creation (*Prov.*
8,30); David and the House of Israel dancing before their Lord
(*Sam.*, 6:5, 21); or the popular doctrine of Christ as 'Lord of the
Dance', one who prefers the playful openness of infants to the
cunning calculations of Pharisees and Inquisitors. These Scriptural motifs of creative play are celebrated in the spiritual
writings of such diverse figures as St Jerome, Origen, Gregory
of Nyssa, Maximus the Confessor and certain mystical thinkers.[45]
And here, as well as in certain passages in the Talmud and
Kaballah, we find evidence of what might be described as a
counter-current to the official onto-theological tradition:
neglected movements which highlight the positive eschatological
role of imagination as the property of *homo ludens* co-creating a
Kingdom with a *deus ludens*.

In similar fashion, one might chose to read the Greek tradition
of imagination in a different light. One could, for instance,
contrast the punitive version of the Prometheus legend (as
reported by Plato and other classical commentators) with the
liberationist reading of the same legend, or also with the analogous legend of Hermes – the child god who first explored the
possibility of creative art by transforming an empty shell into a
musical instrument. As the legend goes, the boy Hermes
emerged from his cave one day to find a discarded tortoise shell
which he interpreted as a means of producing music and song,
once equipped with strings and accompanied by rhymed verse.
Whence Hermes' role as messenger of the gods and inventor of
human signs and symbols (lending his name indeed to the term
'hermeneutics' – the science of interpreting signs). It could be
argued accordingly that Hermes, the child of *poiesis* and play,
is as important an ingredient of Greek mythology as Prometheus,
the hero of crime and punishment. And it is perhaps useful to
recall here Plato's observation in the *Protagoras* (322c) that
Hermes was the one chosen by Zeus to supplement Prometheus'
gifts to man with the art of justice (*dikē*) and respect for the
other (*aidōs*). Finally, an alternative reading of the Greek
tradition would also lay greater emphasis on those marginal and

often ignored passages in Plato and his followers which make mention of the visionary and ecstatic power of images.[46]

Rather than construing the premodern and modern interpretations of imagination as *either/or* alternatives, our postmodern hermeneutic would seek ways of integrating them – combining the ethical emphasis of the former with the poetical emphasis of the latter. A new alliance would be forged where the hidden or officially neglected dimensions of each paradigm (premodern and modern) might converge and breathe new life into an ostensibly dying imagination. Moreover, the openness to alterity – exacted by both the ethical and poetical needs of imagination – may well signify a timely aptitude to also look beyond the narratives of Western culture. Then we might genuinely begin to appreciate what 'other', non-Western cultures have to offer. For it is certain that the Third World cultures of Africa, Asia and Latin-America provide us with *different* stories of imagination, with rich narratives hitherto unexplored and unimagined by Western civilization. Here again we are reminded that the poetico-ethical imagination we are advancing is above all an empathic imagination: versatile, open-minded, prepared to dialogue with what is not itself, with its other, to welcome the difference (*dia-legein*), to say even to its sworn adversary – *mon semblable, mon frère*.

The historical task

The kind of imagination required to meet the challenge of postmodernism is, then, fundamentally *historical*. It is one capable of envisioning what things might be like *after* postmodernism. And also, of course, what things were like *before* it. As such, it pursues the critical task of exploding the fetish of a timeless present which paralyzes contemporary culture. It reminds us that humanity has a duty, if it wishes to survive its threatened ending, to remember the past and to project a future. We cannot even begin to *know* what the postmodern present is unless we are first prepared to *imagine* what it has been and what it may become.

To abandon the imaginative quest for historical *depth* would be to surrender to the prevailing positivism which declares that things are the way they are and cannot be otherwise. And this would be tantamount to embracing the postmodern cult of 'euphoric surfaces' which dissolves the critical notions of authenticity, alienation and anxiety in a dazzling rain of 'discontinuous orgasmic instants'.[47] The gravest error of anti-historical postmodernism is to neglect the hermeneutic task of imaginative recollection and anticipation, to dismiss such a task as no more than a 'pathological itch to scratch surfaces for concealed depth'.[48] This renunciation of historical interpretation and change must be resisted.

The historical imagination seeks to transfigure the postmodern present by refiguring lost narratives and prefiguring future ones.[49] Moreover it feels *obliged* to interpret historically in this way; for it is aware that the project of freedom can easily degenerate into empty utopianism unless guided in some manner by the retrieval of past struggles for liberation. Hence the necessity for what Paul Ricoeur has called a 'depth hermeneutic' of historical imagination. Such a hermeneutic would be committed to the reinterpretation of our cultural memory. It would thus be in a position to counter the apocalyptic aporias of postmodernism by introducing an 'oppositional' perspective nourished by the recollection of the struggles for a just society reaching right back to the very beginnings of Western history – to the Greek search for the good life or the biblical stories of exodus and emancipation from bondage. Back indeed, to the foundational myths of Prometheus and Adam.

An ethically responsible imagination does not, of course, invoke tradition as some kind of Master Narrative to be reimposed on the present. It resists the authoritarian idea of a Narrative of narratives which totalizes historical experience and peremptorily reduces its diversity to a single, all-embracing plot. But it does insist on the need to record the formative narratives of the past as invaluable archives of human suffering, hope and action. In a sense, one might even say that the ethical critique of postmodernism *presupposes* the 'critical distance' afforded by the remembrance of past narratives. 'Critique is also a tradition', as Ricoeur has it.[50]

Any project for future alternatives to the paralysis of the present needs to remain mindful of the narratives of the past. The ethical imagination demands such an 'anticipatory memory' – in order to reread history as a seed-bed of *prefigured* possibilities now erased from our contemporary consciousness. The concrete struggle to transfigure our one-dimensional society cannot dispense with the hermeneutic services of such an historically attuned imagination. 'The authentic utopia', as Herbert Marcuse has stated, 'is grounded in recollection.' And this means that the *forgetfulness* of past sufferings and aspirations makes life more tolerable under a dehumanizing system. By contrast, the remembrance of things past may become a 'motive power in the struggle for changing the world': a reminder that the horizons of history are still open, that *other* modes of social and aesthetic experience are possible.[51] Viewed in this perspective, postmodernism may be reinterpreted as an opportunity to experiment with a radical pluralism which combines a wide variety of historical traditions and projects in a manner which answers the particular needs of each particular culture. A postmodern imagination, ethically and poetically attuned to the lost narratives of historical memory, may offer ways of breaking the stranglehold of the dominant modern ideology of progress – an ideology which has tended to reduce the multiplicity of historical experiences to a single totalizing doctrine.[52]

The narrative task

But if the narrative imagination recalls the forgotten 'others' of history, it equally calls for a reinterpretation of the notion of the 'self'. Postmodern philosophy, as we have seen, rejects the model of the humanist subject. Structuralism denounced it as an ideological illusion or surface play of unconscious signifiers. And some post-structuralists went further still in declaring the human self to be a 'desiring machine' which exults in schizophrenic disorder. One thus finds the self being portrayed as, for example, a 'dispersed decentred network of libidinal attachments, emptied of ethical substance and psychical interiority, the ephemeral function of this or that act of consumption, media experience, sexual relationship, trend or fashion'.[53]

An ethical imagination responsive to the demands of the other, refuses however to accept that the self is nothing but a heap of reified technique or commodified desire. The ethical imagination bids man to tell and retell the story of himself. And it does so not to shore up the illusion of self-sufficiency, but out of fidelity to the other. It is above all the *other* who demands that I remain responsible. For if there is no longer a self to abide by its promises, there is no ethical relation possible. Ethics, in other words, presupposes the existence of a certain *narrative identity*: a self which remembers its commitments to the other (both in its personal and collective history) and recalls that these commitments have *not yet* been fulfilled. This narrative self is not some permanently subsisting substance (*idem*). It is to be understood rather as a perpetually self-rectifying identity (*ipse*) which knows that its story, like that of the imagination which narrates it, is never complete. It is because it is inseparable from the activity of a poetical-critical imagination which sustains it, that the self's commitment to the other – the other who addresses me at each moment and asks me *who I am* and *where I stand* – is never exhausted.

The identity of the narrative self is, consequently, one that cannot be taken for granted. It must be ceaselessly reinterpreted by imagination. To reply to the question 'who?', is to tell one's story to the other. And the story is always one which narrates a relation to the other, a tale of creation and obligation that never comes to an end. This is why the model of narrative identity, in contrast to that of egological identity (permanent *sameness*), includes change and alteration within selfhood. Such a model constitutes the self as the reader and the writer of his own life. But it also casts each one of us as a narrator who never ceases to revise, reinterpret and clarify his own story – by relating himself in turn to the cathartic effects of those larger narratives, both historical and fictional, transmitted by our cultural memory. The notion of personal identity is thus opened up by the narrative imagination to include that of a *communal* identity. The self and the collective mutually constitute each other's identity by receiving each other's stories into their respective histories. Self-identity, in whatever sense, is always a 'tissue of narrated stories'.[54]

We would say, finally, that narrative identity is a *task* of imagination, not a *fait accompli*. And here the poetical and ethical aspects of this narrative task point to a political project. In telling its story to the other the imaginative self comes to recognize more clearly its *unlimited* responsibility to others. This responsibility extends beyond my personal history (and also beyond the secluded intimacy of an I-Thou dialogue) to include a collective history. But it does not derive from some abstract duty, some pious 'ought'. It is a responsibility solicited in each hour of the historical present by others who address and obsess me, reminding me that the self is never sufficient unto itself. Narrating itself to the other, the imagination realizes that it is forever in *crisis*; and that this very crisis of conscience is a revelatory symptom of its inability to reduce others to the representational form of any given image – be it *mimetic, productive* or *parodic*. This is why we feel bound to continue the search for a postmodern imagination, one willing to accept that whatever particular narrative it chooses or whatever image it constructs, there is always some dimension of otherness which transcends it. And, needless to say, this narrative quest for something always other entails radical possibilities of political praxis.[55]

The narrative relation of self to other – which imagination recollects from the historical past and projects into the historical future – is a story which cannot be brought to an end. It is a story irreducible to both the fiats of transcendental subjectivity and the globalizing Logic of the Simulacrum. We must go on telling it if we are to make the postmodern imagination *human* again. To abandon this story would be to condemn ourselves to the circles of empty imitation which predominate today, to renounce all hope of imagining alternative forms of cultural and political practice. It is here and now, in the very darkness of the postmodern labyrinth that we must begin again to listen to the story of imagination. For it is perhaps in its tale of the self relating to the other, that we will discover a golden thread which leads beyond the labyrinth.

Postlude

After imagination, is there not still imagination? Are there not
signs of life to be found even in the postmodern images of a
dying culture – Travis' enigmatic smile at the end of *Paris, Texas*
as he drives through the maze of billboarded, neon-lit freeways;
Ben Vautier's anti-art mimicries; Warhol's pop reproductions of
media stars; Beckett's moribund figures in *Imagination Dead
Imagine*, whose breathing almost imperceptibly mists the glass?
Disinherited of our certainties, deprived of any fixed point of
view, are we not being challenged by such images to open
ourselves to *other* ways of imagining? Is our bafflement at the
dismantling of any predictable relationship between image and
reality not itself an occasion to de-centre our self-possessed
knowledge in response to an otherness which surpasses us: a
sort of *kenosis* whereby our subjective security empties itself
out, dispossesses itself for the sake of something else? Might we
not surmise here an ethical summons lodged at the very heart
of our postmodern culture? And also a poetic summons: to see
that imagination continues to playfully create and recreate even
at the moment it is announcing its own disappearance?

Even when it can't go on, the postmodern imagination goes
on. A child making traces at the edge of the sea. Imagining
otherwise. Imagination's wake. Dying? Awaking?

Notes

Introduction: imagination now

1 H. Rosenberg, *Artworks and Packages*, Horizon Press, New York, 1969.
2 F. Jameson, 'Postmodernism and Consumer Society' in *Postmodern Culture*, ed. H. Foster, Pluto Press, 1985, pp. 111–26; and 'Postmodernism or the Cultural Logic of Late Capitalism' in *New Left Review*, No. 145, 1984, pp. 53–91.
3 A. Warhol, *From A to B and Back Again*, Cassell, London, 1975, quoted by M. Gibson in *Les Horizons du Possible*, ed. du Felin, Paris, 1984, p. 75.
4 I. Hassan, *The Dismemberment of Orpheus: Towards a Postmodern Literature*, Oxford University Press, 1971, p. 254.
5 E. H. Gombrich, *The Story of Art*, Phaidon, 1972, p. 119ff.
6 N. Kazantzakis, *Report to Greco*, Faber, 1973, pp. 500–5.
7 J. Walker, *Art Since Pop*, Thames and Hudson, 1975, p. 41.
8 J. Derrida, *La Carte Postale*, Flammarion, Paris, 1980, pp. 154–5. See Tom Dwyer's useful summary of Derrida's strategy in this work in 'Future Perfect', *St Stephens*, University College Dublin, vol. 4, no. I, 1986, pp. 25–6:

If there are no 'originals', then there are only 'reproductions'. If there are no love letters signifying a unique bond between sender and addressee ('destinataire'), then there are only postcards. So Derrida writes of 'Eros in the age of technical reproduction', parodying epistolary amours and paying homage to Benjamin at one stroke . . . The postal-philosophy, the certainty of inheritance and destination, undoes itself in the beginning. It stands for the assumption that writing is trivial and that what is important, the 'meaning', can be removed intact. Derrida points out the contradictions of a postal regime which believes that the idealism of meaning represents what is valuable in a text but betrays this dogma at its post-offices by fixing the postal rate by weight rather than according to the significance of the message that is to be transmitted. . . . The distinction between passive and active (traditionally 'reading' and 'writing') depends on the conviction that one knows the difference between transmission and reception, original and reproduction, letter and postcard, something which is hardly possible after Derrida's (deconstruction) . . . The postcard then makes simultaneous war on anticipated certainties and hierarchies which in the end depend on anticipation and retro-action. Derrida sees Heidegger's version of the Greek for 'truth' – *aletheia* – as a parcel that has to be opened and transmitted as in the children's party-game. The 'true' is what has been seen to be, what now is, and what ever will be. Derrida plays on this 'original Greek truth' which extends its presence across time, with his neologism 'ateleia' which speaks no longer of continual progressive revelation but makes a false god of the tele-era, the epoch of instant communication and of none.

In an essay entitled 'Ulysse grammophone: L'oui dire de Joyce' (in *Genèse de Babel: Joyce et la création*, CNRS, Paris, 1985, pp. 227–64), Derrida elaborates on his analysis of 'la babelisation du système postal dans *Finnegans Wake*' outlined in *La Carte Postale*.

9 In an essay entitled 'L'imagination dans le discours et dans l'action' in *Du texte à l'action: Essais d'herméneutique, II*, ed. Du Seuil, Paris, 1986, pp. 215–16, Paul Ricoeur gives this useful summary account of the problematic and equivocal nature of imagination in Western philosophy:

Far from clarifying this radical equivocity, the theories of imagination received from the philosophical tradition divide up in function of what seems to each paradigmatic in the spectrum of basic meanings. They thus have a tendency to, in each case, constitute univocal but rival theories of imagination. The space of theoretical variation can be oriented in terms of two opposite axes: on the side of the object, the axis of presence and absence; on the side of the subject, the axis of a fascinated or critical consciousness.

In terms of the first axis, the image corresponds to two extreme theories, illustrated respectively by Hume and by Sartre. At one pole of this first axis, the image relates to a perception of which it is merely the trace, in the sense of a weakened impression. Towards this pole of the image, taken as a week impression, gravitate all of the theories of the reproductive imagination. At the other extreme of the same axis, the image is essentially construed in function of absence, of what is other than present. The various versions of the productive imagination – portrait, dream, fiction – refer in different ways to this fundamental otherness.

But the productive imagination, and even the reproductive to the extent that it comprises the minimale initiative concerning the evocation of something absent, operates on a second axis according to whether the subject of imagination is capable or not of assuming a critical consciousness of the difference between the real and the imaginary. The theories of the image here divide up along an axis which is no longer noematic but noetic, and whose variations are regulated by degrees of belief. At one end of the axis, that of a non-critical consciousness, the image is confused with the real, mistaken for the real. This is the power of the lie or error denounced by Pascal; and it is also, *mutatis mutandis*, the *imaginatio* of Spinoza, contaminated by belief for as long as a contrary belief has not dislodged it from its primary position. At the other end of the axis, where the critical distance is fully conscious of itself, imagination is the very instrument of the critique of reality. The transcendental reduction of Husserl, as a neutralization of existence, is the most complete instance of this. The variations of meaning along this second axis are no less ample than the above. What after all could be in common between the *state of confusion* which characterizes that consciousness which unknown to itself takes for real that which for another consciousness is not real, and the *act of distinction* which, highly self-conscious, enables consciousness to posit something at a distance from the real and thus produce the alterity at the very heart of existence?

Such is the knot of aporias which is revealed by an overview of the ruins which today constitute the theory of imagination. Do these aporias themselves betray a fault in the philosophy of imagination or the structural feature of imagination itself which it would be the task of philosophy to take account of?

On this difficulty of defining the concept of imagination see also Mary Warnock, *Imagination*, Faber, 1976, p. 35; Iris Murdoch, 'Ethics and Imagination' in *The Irish Theological Quarterly*, vol. 52, 1986, p. 96; and Liberato Santoro, 'Aristotle and Contemporary Aesthetics' in *Diotima*, vol. 10, 1982, pp. 114–15.

10 Paul Ricoeur, *Temps et Récit III*, ed. du Seuil, Paris, 1985, pp. 355 ff.

11 Michel Foucault's notion of epistemic structures and ruptures is to be found in both *The Archaeology of Knowledge*, Pantheon, 1972 and *The Order of Things*, Pantheon, 1970. Foucault thinks of the 'episteme' of an age not so much as a universalist ideology or world view (*Weltanschauung*) but rather as a system of possible discourse underlying a body of conceptual knowledge and determining what statements and views predominate in that age (see Foucault, *Power/ Knowledge*, Pantheon, New York, 1980, p. 112. See also commentary by J. Rajchman, *Michel Foucault*, Columbia U.P., 1985, pp. 25f.). We use the term epistemic structure or paradigm in the broad sense of a configuration of knowledge, language and imagery which characterizes the dominant way in which imagination is viewed in a particular historical epoch. We also retain from Foucault

the genealogical notion of history as a plurality of mutations and discontinuities rather than a single continuum of some absolute spirit or material dialectic. The notion of 'paradigm shifts' has been proposed by Thomas Kuhn in *The Structure of Scientific Revolutions*, Chicago U.P., 1962. Our use of the idea of narrative paradigms is also much indebted to Paul Ricoeur's recent work on the role of narrative in time, history and fiction, cf. *Temps et Récit II*. Seuil, Paris, 1984, pp. 27–35 and *Du Texte à L'Action*, Seuil, Paris, 1986, p. 16:

What we call paradigms are types of emplotment resulting from the sedimentation of narrative practice itself. We touch here on a fundamental problem, that of the alternation between innovation and sedimentation. This phenomenon is constitutive of what one calls a tradition and is directly implicated in the historical character of narrative schematism. It is this interchange between innovation and sedimentation which makes the phenomenon of deviation possible. . . . One must understand that deviation is only possible on the basis of a traditional culture which creates in the reader expectancies which the artist takes pleasure in exciting or disappointing. This ironic rapport could not arise in a total paradigmatic emptiness . . . . It is only conceivable in terms of a regulated imagination.

12 F. Nietzsche, *Thus Spoke Zarathustra*, Penguin, 1961, pp. 142–4.
13 While the term 'postmodern' had been used in an occasional way, e.g. by the historian Arnold Toynbee in 1938 and by the literary critic Ihab Hassan in 1971 – it was in architectural theories of the mid seventies that it first achieved international recognition as a critical term. Charles Jencks was perhaps the most influential commentator of postmodern architecture. His first major study on the subject, *The Language of Postmodern Architecture* (Academy Editions, London) was published in 1977, and this was followed by a more comprehensive comparative study, *Current Architecture* (Academy Editions, London), in 1982. Here Jencks offered a useful definition of the term and a brief account of its genesis, p. 111:

Post-modern is a portmanteau concept covering several approaches to architecture which have evolved from Modernism. As this hybrid term suggests, its architects are still influenced by Modernism – in part because of their training and in part because of the impossibility of ignoring Modern methods of construction – and yet they have added other languages to it. A Post-Modern building is doubly coded – part Modern and part something else: vernacular, revivalist, local, commercial, metaphorical, or contextual. In several important instances it is also doubly coded in the sense that it seeks to speak on two levels at once: to a concerned minority of architects, an elite who recognize the subtle distinctions of a fast-changing language, and to the inhabitants, users, or passersby, who want only to understand and enjoy it. Thus one of the strong motivations of Post-Modernists is to break down the elitism inherent in Modern architecture and the architectural profession. Sometimes Post-Modernism is confused with Late-Modernism. Some architects practice both approaches, and there are also, inevitably, buildings which are transitional. . . .

The term Post-Modern has a complex genesis. It was used in a non-architectural context as early as 1938 by the English historian Arnold Toynbee, and applied to architecture by Joseph Hudnut in 1949, but its first use in the currently accepted sense was in my own articles of 1975. A year later, and quite independently, the architect Robert Stern (apparently influenced by Peter Eisenman) and the critic Paul Goldberger were using the term in the United States. By 1977 the usage had become popular (for example, Douglas Davis was asked by his editor to put it in the title of his book *Artculture: Essays in the Post-Modern*, although, characteristically, the term is not defined, nor even used). The same may be said of C. Ray Smith's book *Supermannerism: New Attitudes in Post-Modern Architecture* (1977) in which the term appeared in the subtitle only because it had become fashionable. Because of this loose usage I attempted in 1978 a definition to distinguish Post-Modern from Late-Modern architecture and to focus on the positive notion of double coding instead of historicist imagery alone (which was the major American definition). The two usages, European and American, were somewhat different although both schools of thought focused on the important work and theories of Robert Venturi and Charles Moore. They differed, and still do, over the emphasis placed on urbanism, participation, ornament, and image: Americans stress the latter two aspects, Europeans the former two. But as the term is an umbrella covering a variety of schools, this division should not be overstressed. There was a wide enough general agreement for a large exhibition on the subject, the 1980 Venice Biennale organized by Paolo Portoghesi. There, seventy architects from around the world, who have sharp differences among themselves, were loosely grouped under the banner Post-Modern. Both the heterogeneity and commonality of current Post-Modern work should be kept in mind.

For further comments on postmodernism and architecture see our conclusion to section 5 of chapter eight and also our Appendix to chapter eight.

14 J-F. Lyotard, 'Une Note sur le *Post*' in *Le Postmoderne*, Galilée, Paris, 1986, p. 125.

15 J-F. Lyotard, 'A Conversation' in *Flash Art*, no. 921, 1985, pp. 32–5 and also *Le Postmoderne*, p. 51:

Another way to bereave the universal emancipation promised by modernity would be to 'work through', in the Freudian sense, not only the loss of this object, but also the loss of the subject to whom this horizon was promised.

This would not only mean that we acknowledge our finitude, but the elaboration of the status of 'we', the question of the subject. . . . Such an elaboration can only lead, I believe, to the abandonment of, first, the linguistic structure of communication (I/you/him) which, consciously or otherwise, the moderns accredited as an ontological and political model.

16 J-F. Lyotard, 'A Conversation' in *Flash Art*, p. 33. See also Lyotard's introduction to *Le Différend*, ed. de Minuit, 1983, p. 11.

17 Robert Hughes, *The Shock of the New: Art and the Century of Change*, BBC Publications, 1980, p. 11.

18 Ibid., p. 375,

19 Ibid., pp. 385, 400.

20 J-F. Lyotard, 'A Conversation', *Flash Art*, p. 34.

21 J–F. Lyotard, ibid. pp. 34–5; 'Missive sur L'histoire universelle' in *Le Postmoderne*, pp. 45–63.

22 E. Lévinas, *Colloque De Cérisy Autour de Lévinas*, Paris, 1987; and 'Ethique et Philosophie Première' in *Phréatique*, no. 39, Paris, 1986, p. 127.

23 J-F. Lyotard, Interview in *Libération*, 21 June, 1986, p. 36; and *Le Postmoderne*, pp. 52–4.

24 Martin Heidegger, *Letter on Humanism* in *Phenomenology and Existentialism*, eds R. Zaner and D. Ihde, Capricorn Books, N.Y., 1973, p. 168.

25 M. Heidegger, *The Origin of the Work of Art* in *Poetry, Language, Thought*, trans. A. Hofstadter, Harper & Row, N.Y., 1971, pp. 73, 76. Heidegger's critique of the humanist subject is primarily aimed at the apotheosis of the human consciousness as that which reduces Being to a mere representation or image (*Bild*). This occurred with the rise of modern idealism and romanticism, Heidegger argues in 'The Age of the World View' (*Holzwege*, 1950) – 'The world's becoming an image is one and the same occurrence as man's becoming a subject in the midst of what is' (p. 85). And he goes on to explain how the more the human subject asserts himself as the centre of the universe, the more the universe is transformed into an anthropomorphic image: 'The more extensively and thoroughly the world is available as something conquered . . . then the more subjectively, that is assertively, the subject rises up, and the more irresistibly reflection on the world, theory of the world, turns into a theory of man, into anthropology. It is no wonder that humanism is in the ascendant only where the world becomes an image' (p. 86).

26 Quoted by K. Soper, *Humanism and Anti-Humanism*. Hutchinson,

1986, p. 10. I am much indebted to Soper's lucid and wide-ranging analysis for my own discussion of this subject.

27 J-F. Lyotard, 'A Conversation' in *Flash Art*, p. 33.

28 See in particular Lévi-Strauss's concluding chapter 'History and Dialectics' in *The Savage Mind*, Chicago U.P., 1966; Foucault's Foreword to the English edition of *Les Mots et les Choses*, Gallimard, Paris, 1966 (translated into English as *The Order of Things*, Vintage, New York, 1973); Althusser's 'Ideology and Ideological State Apparatuses' in *Lenin and Philosophy and other Essays*, NLB, 1971; Barthes, 'The Death of the Author' in *Image-Music-Text*, Fontana, 1977; Derrida, 'The Ends of Man' in *Margins of Philosophy*, University of Chicago Press, 1983. Another significant voice in the polyphonous critique of humanism is that of Paul Ricoeur. Ricoeur's hermeneutic stance offers a different inflection from the structuralist/deconstructionist movement in that it posits a mediational role between and beyond the extreme humanism of modern idealism and the radical anti-humanism of the postmodernists. In his concluding section of *Main Trends in Philosophy* (Holmes and Meier Publishers, N.Y., 1979), entitled 'Man and the Foundation of Humanism', Ricoeur notes that 'humanism has no choice but to recognize that it is un-"founded" (*sans fondement*) – as a wager, or as a cry' (p. 372). And he adds that 'while contemporary philosophy of every school is at one in its ethical demands – as recorded in the Universal Declaration of Human Rights – it splinters into conflicting tendencies in its ultimate views of humanism. Philosophers do not agree amongst themselves when it comes to their conclusions about the final liberation of man' (p. 392). In short, as Ricoeur sees it, the present humanist controversy is a 'conflict of interpretations' between those romantic humanists who wish, in the face of the contemporary crisis, to preserve man at the centre of the universe and those radical anti-humanists who support, for example, the Lacanian plea in *Ecrits* (1966, p. 282) that the subject be 'dethroned, no longer centred on consciousness of self' or Lévi-Strauss' claim in *La Pensée Sauvage* (1962, p. 326) that 'the ultimate goal of the human sciences is not to constitute but to dissolve man'. Ricoeur's own dialogical hermeneutics proposes a way beyond the polarized extremes of the idealist *subject*, on the one hand, and the structuralist *system* on the other:

The idea that man understands himself only by interpreting the signs of his humanity hidden in literatures and cultures calls for no less radical a transformation of the concept of subject as of that of cultural text. For one thing, the indirect understanding of one-self implied by the hermeneutic act rejects the intuitionism of a philosophy founded on the *cogito*, with its claim to constitute itself in self-sufficiency and consistency, and attests the dependence of its meaning on the meaning of what it understands outside itself. For another thing, comprehension of a text does not end with discovering the codes that make up its structures but with revealing the image of the world, the mode of being, towards which it points. But this revelation is in turn only the counterpart of the dethroning of the subject who takes the roundabout route via the world of signs in order to understand himself. Thus the hermeneutic circle marks the simultaneous abandonment of the notions of system and of subject(*Main Trends*, p. 369).

In this respect, Ricoeur would tend to support the Heideggerean critique of humanism: 'What he "dismantles" (*deconstruit*) is obviously not respect for man as the most valuable of beings but the metaphysics of the subject on which some thinkers would have this ethics of respect hinge (p. 362). We will be returning to this crucial question in the conclusion to this work.

29 J. Derrida, 'The Ends of Man'.
30 See Peter Fuller, *Aesthetics after Modernism*, Writers and Readers Press, 1983, p. 28.
31 H. Foster, Preface to *Postmodern Culture*, Pluto Press, 1985, pp. xii–xiii.
32 R. Kearney, *Poétique du Possible*, Beauchesne, Paris, 1984.

Chapter one: the Hebraic imagination

1 *Encyclopaedia Judaica*, vol. 8, MacMillan, 1971, p. 1318. For other definitions of the *yetser* see: *The Interpreters Dictionary of the Bible*, Abington Press, New York, 1962, p. 685: 'The Hebrew word *yetser* for which the RSV retains the translation 'imagination' in two places (*Gen.* 6:5; 8:21) does indeed seem to mean the power of forming mental images, but presumably also as a prelude to action, and in three of the five instances of the KJV obviously a bad action. In only two passages (I *Chr.* 28:9 and 29:18) does the English word have a good, or at least a neutral, sense. Here, as in *Deut.* 31:21, the RSV translates "purposes" or "plans". In the later rabbinic view the word *yetser* was taken to mean "impulse" and the "good impulse" and the "bad impulse" were elements in the human personality.' See also Frank Porter, 'The Yeçer Hara' in *Biblical and Semitic Studies*, Scribner, New York, 1901, p. 109. Other useful definitions of this enigmatic term are to be found in *A Hebrew and English Lexicon of the Old Testament*, Oxford, Clarendon Press, 1907, p. 427; G. Cohen Stuart, *The Struggle in Man between Good and Evil. An*

inquiry into the Origin of the Rabbinic concept of Yetser Hara,
Uitgevermaatschappij, F. H. Kok, Kampen, 1984; M. Buber,
'Imagination and Impulse' in *Good and Evil*, Scribner, New York,
1952; G. Moore, 'The Origin of Sin' in *Judaism*, vols 1, 111, ch. 3.

2 See M. Buber, *Good and Evil*, pp. 90–97, and E. Fromm, *You Shall be as Gods: A Radical Interpretation of the Old Testament*, Fawcett, 1966, pp. 125 ff.

3 E. Fromm, *You Shall be as Gods*, p. 126.

4 M. Buber, *Good and Evil*, p. 70.

5 Ibid., 75–7.

6 Ibid., p. 80.

7 Ibid., pp. 91–2.

8 See, for example, J-P. Sartre, *Being and Nothingness*, Philosophical Library, New York, 1956.

9 M. Buber, *Good and Evil*, p. 92.

10 For similar rabbinic condemnations of the evil *yetser* see *Lev. R.*, 91 and *Bera Choth*, 60b.

11 For an analysis of this and other rabbinic interpretations of the *yetser* see S. Schecter, 'The Evil Yetser: The Source of Rebellion' in *Aspects of Rabbinic Theology*, Schocken, New York, 1961, pp. 242 ff.

12 Quoted and analysed by F. Porter, 'The Yetser Hara: A Study of the Jewish Doctrine of Sin', p. 103.

13 Quoted Schecter, 'The Evil Yetser: The Source of Rebellion', p. 258.

14 Quoted Porter, 'The Yetser Hara', p. 113.

15 S. Freud, *Moses and Monotheism*, Vintage, New York, 1939, p. 144.

16 *Ibid.*, p. 152. On Freud's knowledge of Jewish literature, and particularly the rapport between libidinal *eros* and the Talmudic notion of sexual desire, *daath*, see David Bakan, *Sigmund Freud and Jewish Mysticism*, Beacon Press, Boston, 1975, especially the chapters on 'Sexuality' (33) and the 'Interpretation of Dreams'(29).

17 Quoted Porter, 'The Yetser Hara', p. 103.

18 Ibid., p. 109.

19 M. Buber, *Good and Evil*, 130–1, 142.

20 M. Schecter, 'The Evil Yetser', pp. 250–1.

21 F. Porter, 'The Yetser Hara', p. 116.

22 Ibid., pp. 122–3.

23 E. Fromm, *You Shall be as Gods*, p. 142.

24 Ibid., pp. 133, 135.

25 And he adds: 'Man must choose between the basic alternatives of life and death. In the verse, "See I have set before you this day life and good, death and evil" (*Deut.* 30:15), life is equated with good,

and death with evil . . . Life is the highest norm for man; God is alive and man is alive; the fundamental choice for man is that between growth and decay.' Ibid., pp. 141–2. See also p. 125: 'The Bible leaves no doubt that it does not consider man either good or evil, but endowed with both tendencies'; and p. 127: 'The prophets . . . teach that there is nothing inherently evil in man's nature that would prevent him from choosing the good which is in him as a potentiality, just as is the evil. If it is true that the "evil drive" is possible only after man has emerged from the original unity with nature and has acquired self-awareness and imagination, it follows that only man can sin, can regress, can lose himself. In the Jewish view man is born with the capacity to sin, but he can return, find himself, and redeem himself by his own effort. . . . The Talmud summed up this view thus: "If God created the evil inclinations, he also created the Torah as its antidote" (*Baba Batra*, 16a).'

26 See, for example, Cain's accusation in the Midrash that God is responsible for the murder of Abel: 'Master of the World, if I have killed him, it is Thou who hast created in me the evil *yetser*' (*Exodus. R.* 46); or again 'It is revealed and known to Thee that it is the evil *yetser* that incites us' (*SE.* 63a); or 'Israel said: Master of the world . . . even when we sin and make Thee angry, be not removed from us, for we are the clay and Thou are the Potter' (*Jer.* 18:6).

27 M. Buber, *Good and Evil*, pp. 93–7.

28 H. Arendt, *The Human Condition*, University of Chicago Press, 1958, p. 75.

29 H. Arendt, *The Life of the Mind*, vol. 11, *Willing*, Secker and Warburg, 1978, p. 18.

30 P. Ricoeur, *The Symbolism of Evil*, Beacon Press, Boston, 1967, pp. 130–1. See D. Ihde's useful summary of Ricoeur's reading of the Adamic myth in *Hermeneutic Phenomenology*, Northwestern U.P., Evaston, 1971, p. 120–1: 'The Adamic or anthropological myth, according to Ricoeur's interpretation . . . situates the origin of evil not prior to man but in the bad use of freedom by man himself. . . . The biblical God is holy and innocent, and biblical man is finite and innocent. Creation begins as an essential good at both the divine and human poles. Moreover, man, although he is the "first man", "relates the origin of evil to an *ancestor* of the human race as it is now whose condition is homogeneous with ours" ' (*SE*, p. 233). It is this characteristic which makes the Adamic myth properly anthropological. The plot is the movement from a primordial innocence to an existential deviation. Man deviates from his

originally good destination through an act of will. . . . By accepting a temptation Adam initiates evil, which then becomes the condition of all men through our actual history. Evil is *historical*, not structural. The first reading of the Adamic myth announces what Ricoeur calls the ethical vision of the world in radical form. Evil originates in an act of will – the subject is responsible for and takes upon himself radical evil as *bad will*. God remains innocent; man, through his deviation, corrupts the universe. In its biblical setting, this myth sees evil as a historical end. Deliverance is *eschatological*. Biblical history becomes the history of rectification and the hope for deliverance. And although there are a series of modifications and variants, the "return" to innocence is to be through a human figure. The People or the Remnant are to be delivered through a Messiah or the Son of Man. The myth sees deliverance as a restoration of condemned freedom to its uncondemned state.'

31 Quoted G. Scholem, *On the Kabbalah and its Symbolism*, Schocken, New York, 1952, p. 178.

32 This etymological play between the terms for creation (*yetsirah*) and imagination (*yetser*) is to be found in several Talmudic and Kabbalistic passages, e.g. the Talmudic comparison between the human thoughts created by the *yetser* and the clay fashioned by the Potter. See Porter, 'The Yetser Hara', pp. 141, 144. The *Book of Creation (Sefer Yetsira)* is a mystical body of interpretations composed mainly between the third and sixth centuries and alluding to an older text referred to frequently in the Talmud. It consists mainly of a rabbinic treatise on cosmology which exerted a wide influence on Kabbalistic thinking. An anonymous work, it is considered to be one of the first Hebraic texts of systematic reflection. See Rabbi Hayyim de Volozhyn, *L'Ame de la Vie*, Verdier, Paris, 1986, p. 363, Note 42.

33 G. Scholem; *On the Kabbalah*, p. 176.

34 Ibid.

35 Ibid. For further parallels between Jewish and Christian interpretations of the rapport between divine and human creation see N. Williams, *Ideas of the Fall and of Original Sin*, Toronto, 1927, particularly chapter 2, 'The Adam Story and The Evil Imagination'; P. Ricoeur, *The Symbolism of Evil*, p. 131; and also our Appendix to this chapter on 'The Image of God Debate'.

36 G. Scholem, *On the Kabbalah*, pp. 197–8. In his novel, *Joseph and His Brothers*, English translation, Knopf, New York, 1974,

pp. 438–9, Thomas Mann offers a fascinating account of the creation of the *Golem* in terms of an implied analogy with aesthetic creation.
37 G. Scholem, 'The Golem of Prague and the Golem of Rehovot' in *The Messianic Idea of Judaism*, Schocken, New York, 1971, p. 335.
38 Ibid., pp. 336–7.
39 Ibid., pp. 337, 340.
40 Ibid., p. 337.
41 Ibid., p. 337.
42 Ibid., p. 338.
43 Ibid., p. 340.
44 G. Scholem, *On the Kabbalah and its Symbolism*, p. 178.

Chapter one   *Appendix:* The 'Image of God' debate

1 *The Interpreter's Dictionary of the Bible*, p. 682.
2 I am indebted to Bernard Dupuy, the French biblical scholar and exegete, for these references to the Hebrew play of words.
3 For an extended account of Maimonides' commentary on *demuth* see Appendix to our third chapter, 'The Medieval Imagination'.
4 Rabbi Hayyim, *L'Ame de la Vie (Nefesh Hahayyim)*, p. 281.
5 *The Interpreter's Dictionary of the Bible*, p. 684.
6 Ibid., p. 684.
7 Rabbi Hayyim, *L'Ame de la Vie*, pp. 35, 58–9. For an interesting commentary on the rapport between Jacob's ladder and the creative spirit of the *shekinah* see C. Smith, 'The Symbol of *Shekinah*' in *European Judaism*, vol. 85, pp. 44–5.
8 Rabbi Hayyim, *L'Ame de la Vie*, p. 43.
9 Ibid., pp. 46–7.
10 Ibid., p. 62.
11 Ibid., pp. 322, 364.
12 Ibid., pp. 10–11.
13 Ibid., p. 13.
14 Ibid., pp. 19–21.
15 Ibid., p. 35.
16 Ibid., p. 36.
17 Ibid., p. 39.
18 Ibid., pp. 40–1. As Isaiah puts it: 'It is your faults which create a separation between you and your God' (*Is.* 59,2).
19 E. Levinas, *Préface* to Rabbi Hayyim's *L'Ame de la Vie*, p. xiii.
20 Ibid., p. ix.
21 Ibid., p. x. See also Levinas' more extensive and detailed discussion

of these themes in 'A l'Image de Dieu' in *L'Au-delà du Verset: Lectures et Discours Talmudiques*, ed. Minuit, 1982, pp. 182–200.

22 *The Interpreter's Dictionary of the Bible*, p. 684.

23 Ibid., p. 685.

24 F. Porter, 'The Yetser Hara', pp. 136–7.

25 *The Interpreter's Dictionary of the Bible*, p. 685.

26 For useful commentaries on Augustine's concepts of the *Imago Dei* and imagination generally see T. Van Bavel's *Répertoire Bibliographique de St. Augustin*, Nijhoff, 1963, pp. 3464–3502, 4414–4428, 4431, 3298, 3311; Olivier du Roy, *L'intelligence de la Foi selon St. Augustin*, Etudes Augustiniennes, Paris, 1966, pp. 45–6, 204–5, 264–6, 434–5, 437; E. Gilson, *The Christian Philosophy of St. Augustine*, Gollancz, London, 1961, pp. 211–12, 276–7, 151–2, 217–24.

27 *Sifre Deut.* 32. See G. F. Moore's commentary on this theme in 'The Origin of Sin', p. 485 and also the *Encyclopaedia Judaica*, p. 1318: 'As a personification of the permanent dualism of the choice between good and evil, the rabbinic notion of the two inclinations shifts this dualism from a metaphysical to a more psychological level' – i.e. two tendencies in man rather than two cosmic principles.

28 R. Bultmann, *Theology of the New Testament*, vol. I, SCM, London, 1952, section 25.

29 Ibid., section 37–8. See also my doctoral thesis, *L'Eschaton et L'Etre: Approche du Possible*, University of Paris X, 1980, pp. 347–350.

30 Nicholas of Cusa (Cusanus), *Trialogus de Possest* in *A Concise Introduction to the Philosophy of Nicholas of Cusa* by J. Hopkins, University of Minnesota Press, 1980. Cusanus' reinterpretation of the 'Image of God' debate in terms of the category of 'actualized-possibility' differs from the mainstream Christian philosophies which gave primacy to the notions of substance and being (*esse*). Augustine, for example, identifies the Yahweh of Exodus 3:13 with *esse* and Aquinas speaks of God in terms of the *ipsum esse subsitens*. See J. Caputo, *Heidegger and Aquinas*, Fordham University Press, 1982.

31 Cusanus, *Trialogus de Possest*, pp. 120–1.

32 Ibid., p. 69.

33 Ibid., p. 79.

34 Ibid., p. 91.

35 Ibid., p. 93.

36 Ibid., p. 99.

37 Ibid., pp. 101–3.

38 Eriugena, *Periphyseon* (III, 678c). Cusanus recommended his

students to study Eriugena's work, written in the ninth century and condemned as heresy in 1210 and 1225 as it was considered to be in breach of the mainstream realist tradition of medieval and scholastic thought. See Dermot Moran, *Nature and Mind in the Philosophy of Eriugena*, Cambridge U.P. 1988, Chapter I. It is also curious how Eriugena's view of creation as a 'ladder' parallels that of the Jewish mystical and Talmudic commentaries on Jacob's ladder. As Moran puts it: 'Eriugena wants to safeguard the human ability to have direct access to the divine, and to in fact become divine. He argues that there is no intermediary between the human being and God, even though humans are placed half way down the ladder of being nevertheless they also transcend and contain the entire ladder of being in themselves, and as a kind of transcendent non-being are able to merge with God. God reveals himself directly to man in theophanies, and mankind is able to have direct vision of God.'

39 Cusanus, *Trialogus de Possest*, p. 103.
40 Ibid., p. 105.
41 See R. Kugelman, 'The First Letter to the Corinthians' in *The Jerome Biblical Commentary*, Geoffrey Chapman, London, 1969, vol. 2, p. 271. See also on this theme *Traduction Oecuménique de la Bible*, ed. du Cerf, Paris, 1981, p. 518.
42 Cusanus, *Trialogus de Possest*, p. 113.
43 Ibid., p. 113.
44 Ibid., p. 113, 115.
45 Ibid., p. 133. Despite the overriding Christian emphasis of Cusanus' account, one might note certain analogies with the Jewish tradition of interpretation. One such example is the author's fascination with the holy power of certain letters as a mode of 'symbolic viewing'. Cusanus observes for instance that the letter 'e' is to the term *possest* what the divine Creator is to the world (p. 133). This reflection is reminiscent of the Kabbalistic speculations on the letters of the holy alphabet of creation, where the Hebrew letter 'e' or Aleph plays a central role. It was, we remember, the removal of the letter 'e' from the 'emeth' inscription on the forehead of Jeremiah's *golem* that transformed the holy phrase 'God lives' into its opposite 'God is dead'. In another of his treatises entitled *Iconae*, Cusanus elaborates on the sacred role which symbols and images can play in leading us to God. He equates, as did the Kabbalah and Jewish mysticism, the power of creation with the power of creative letters: '*Sic Deus, cuius loqui est creare, simul omnia et singula creat. Et cum verbum Dei sit Deus, ideo Deus in omnibus et singulis est creaturis.*' (p. 133).

46 Cusanus, *Trialogus de Possest*, p. 139.
47 Ibid., p. 149.
48 Ibid., p. 151.
49 Ibid., p. 151.

Chapter two: The Hellenic imagination

1 N. Frye, *The Anatomy of Criticism*, Atheneum, New York, 1969, p. 334.
2 D. Donoghue, *Thieves of Fire*, Faber, London, 1973, p. 26. See also p. 61: 'But there came a day when men felt a desire to rise above their station, distinguishing themselves from animals and the things of earth. . . . The fire which Prometheus stole was the means by which men demanded a new destiny, and took on the guilt of achieving it. Fire enabled them to move from nature to culture, but it made culture a dangerous possession: it made tragedy probable. The Promethean fire was not originally intended for man, it was part of a divine order of things and it has always retained, in its stolen history, traces of an outraged origin. It is not fanciful to think that man by receiving the stolen fire made himself an "abomination", a freak of nature, to be added to the list of freaks execrated in Leviticus. We have found the stolen fire identified with reason and knowledge, but it is probably better to identify it with the symbolic imagination: we have not grown so accustomed to the creative power of imagination as to think it common, in the nature of the human case, like knowledge or reason. We think imagination a wonderful power, unpredictable and diverse, and we are satisfied to call it divine and to ascribe to it an early association with transgression. A Promethean says of it that it is the most precious part of man, perhaps the only precious part, the only respect in which man's claim to superior character is tenable.'
3 It is important to note from the outset that our modern notion of 'creativity' – stemming largely from the romantic-idealist aesthetic of subjectivity – is not the same as that found in biblical and Greek cultures. The Hebrew term *yetsirah* referred to the act of shaping, forming or moulding things with a view to a specific purpose or plan, as when Yahweh created man from dust or the potter formed his clay. The Greek term *poiesis*, for its part, referred to the act of a craftsman who makes things as much for everyday use as for artistic use. Neither carry the specifically romantic sense of a subjective mind creating an unreal or ideal world out of its own interior

resources – a properly modern idea which we will be analysing in chapters 4, 5 and 6.

4 C. Kerenyi, *Prometheus; Archetypal Image of Human Existence*, Thames and Hudson, London, 1963, p. 70.

5 D. Donoghue, *Thieves of Fire*, p. 34.

6 This formulation is from Kenneth Burke, *The Philosophy of Literary Forms*, Louisiana State University Press, 1969, pp. 59–60. See D. Donoghue, *Thieves of Fire*, p. 44.

7 One should not overlook, however, the important distinction between the Judeo-Christian notion of the creation of the world *ex nihilo (berath)* and the Platonic demiurge's rearrangement of already existing matter in the *Timaeus*. Plato tells us that the demiurge's motive for creation was to frame the world from disordered and inharmonious matter, as a unique copy of a unique, perfect and eternal model. Since the 'framer of the universe' was 'good and therefore without envy, he wished all things to be as like him as possible' (*Timaeus*, 29). The creation could only be one – i.e. not repeated or doubled – since the divine pattern upon which it was modelled was 'one': 'For god's purpose was to use as his model the highest and most completely perfect of intelligible things, and so he created a single visible living being, containing within itself all living beings of the same natural order' (*Tim.* 30–31). There was only one created universe accordingly, 'for that which comprises all intelligible beings cannot have a *double*. . . . Since it is manufactured according to its pattern' (*Tim.* 31). Plato and the Greeks did not share the biblical view that man's creative power might somehow be used to participate in or complete God's original creation. There was no talk of a 'second creation' or an eschatological Kingdom.

8 See Jacques Derrida's discussion of the Platonic notion of imaging and imitating in *Dissemination*. Athlone Press, 1981, particularly the sections entitled 'Plato's Pharmacy' and 'The Double Session'.

9 N. Frye, *The Anatomy of Criticism*, pp. 41–2.

10 See René Girard's perceptive account of the double character of the sacrificial scapegoat as villified demon and deified hero in *Les Choses Cachées depuis la Foundation du Monde*, Grasset, Paris, 1978, chapters I–IV. Denis Donoghue has noted how this ambivalent status of the Promethean/Adamic scapegoat is a recurring feature of European literature: 'Prometheus' double nature is always acknowledged; as by Coleridge who said that he was the Redeemer and the Devil jumbled together' (*Thieves of Fire*, p. 37). Milton also made much of this theme in *Paradise Lost* where Adam's theft of forbidden

knowledge is compared to Prometheus' theft of fire (*Thieves of Fire*, pp. 35–39).

11 N. Frye, *The Anatomy of Criticism*, p. 207.

12 Ibid., p. 207. One should be wary, however, of equating the status of Adam and Prometheus in any absolute sense. Prometheus is actually divine, a Titan, whereas Adam, although in close relation to God in Eden, is radically separate from God as a created being. Adam is the 'first man' and it is his attempt *qua* man to attain divine knowledge that precipitates the fall.

13 D. Donoghue, *Thieves of Fire*, p. 54.

14 P. Ricoeur, *The Symbolism of Evil*, p. 224.

15 Ibid., pp. 224–5: 'there is, then, guilt on the part of Prometheus, guilt which is overshadowed by that of Zeus in consequence of the torment to which he is subjected by him and which in turn overshadows that of Zeus in consequence of the secret with which he threatens him. . . . It was this guilt that Aeschylus wished to express by the Titanic nature of Prometheus. Freedom has its roots in the chaotic depths of being; it is a moment in the Titanomachy. Prometheus calls unceasingly upon Gaia, symbol and epitome of the chthonic powers; from the beginning he summons ether, winds, springs, earth, and sun to bear witness; his defiance is in keeping with the gigantic character of mountains and waves. In his freedom, elementary wrath looms up . . . Prometheus bound bears witness . . . to the deep-seated complicity of the wrath of God and the wrath of man, of the wicked god and Titanic freedom. . . . It seems to me, then, that this *hybris* of innocence, if I may call it so, this violence that makes Prometheus a guilty victim, throws light retrospectively on the original theme of the myth, the theme of the theft of fire. . . . The tragedy of Prometheus begins with the unjust suffering. Nevertheless, by a retrograde motion, it makes contact with the original germ of the drama: the theft was a benefaction, but the benefaction was a theft. Prometheus was initially a guilty innocent.'

16 Ibid., p. 224. This notion of the fall of Zeus marks a crucial difference from the status of the biblical Creator God, Yahweh, who is not directly implicated in the fall of man. Zeus, unlike Yahweh, is not above the events of the world as dictated by Fate. Hence in the *Iliad* we find Zeus bemoaning the collapse of Troy. Zeus, like the other gods, the Titans and mankind generally, is subject to Fate.

17 Ibid., p. 230.

18 For an illuminating commentary on the 'myths of phantasy' related

in the Greek legends of Dionysus, Narcissus and Orpheus see Herbert Marcuse, *Eros and Civilisation*, Beacon Press, Boston, 1974, pp. 165–7. On the Orpheus myth see Ihab Hassan, *The Dismemberment of Orpheus*, Oxford University Press, 1971. On the Dedalus myth see *Mythologie Générale*, Larousse.

19 Aeschylus, *Antigone*, pp. 582–625. See Ricoeur, *The Symbolism of Evil*, p. 226.

20 P. Ricoeur, *The Symbolism of Evil*, p. 226. One should also note the existence of another reading of Aeschylus, for example the *Oresteia*, as enacting some sort of progress from a primitive retributivism embodied by the Furies, to a more cooperative order inaugurated by Athena, a progression mirrored elsewhere in Greek tragedy in the movement from the chthonic deities to the gods of Olympus, darkness to light, primitivism to civilization. In the light of such a reading, Prometheus' eventual rehabilitation could be seen as symbolizing a belief in the possibility of advancement rather than a mere regression or condemnation to an evil fate.

21 For an analysis of the pre-Socratic treatment of images and imagination see M. W. Bundy, *The Theory of Imagination in Classical and Medieval Thought*, Illinois University Studies in Language and Literature, Urbana, Illinois, vol. XII, 1927, chapter I, pp. 13–18; F. M. Cornford, *From Religion to Philosophy*, Harvester Press, 1980, pp. 158, 109, 250–1; and J. Burnett, *Early Greek Philosophy*, London, 1908, pp. 228–32.

22 M. W. Bundy, *The Theory of Imagination*, p. 18.

23 These two Greek terms, *phantasia* and *eikasia*, used by Plato to denote the imaging function are by no means synonymous. *Eikasia*, from the same root as *eikona* or image, plays an entirely passive, unreflective and receptive role which Plato associates with the lowest faculty of the soul in his 'Simile of the Divided Line' in the *Republic*, *Phantasia*, by contrast, can on occasion play a more positive and active mimetic role in providing a sort of ladder up which the soul may ascend, aided and guided by reason, towards a contemplation of the Forms. We shall be returning to this point later in our discussion. Despite their differences, however, both *eikasia* and *phantasia* serve a mimetic or imitational function.

24 In conjunction with Plato's discussion of the Promethean 'art of making' in the *Protagoras* one might also consider Aeschylus' mention of the *technai* in the Chrous of *Prometheus* (477 ff).

25 The suggestion that man possesses a 'portion' of divinity, a 'kinship' with the gods, by virtue of 'the common resemblance between man's

arts and those of the gods' is to be found in Léon Robin's French edition of the text in *Platon: Oeuvres Complètes*, Pléiade, Paris, 1940, note 50, p. 1252. And one might usefully compare this Platonic allusion to man's 'portion' of the divine art of making with the rabbinic notion of Jacob's 'portion' (*hebel*) in the divine plan of the Creator in *Deut.* 32:9, discussed in our Appendix to chapter 1.

26 For a detailed analysis of the Platonic equation of imagination and imitation see J. P. Vernant, 'Image et Apparence dans la Théorie Platonicienne de la Mimésis' in *Journal de Psychologie*, 2, April-June, 1975, pp. 133–160.

27 On this opposition between the public word of the *polis* and the private world of fantasy, see H. Arendt, *The Human Condition*, University of Chicago Press, 1958.

28 J. Derrida, *Dissemination*, p. 167.

29 Ibid., p. 92.

30 Ibid., p. 93. Derrida is speaking here of the imitational practice of writing rather than imagination proper, but the same principles of mimetic detour and representation apply in both cases.

31 Ibid., pp. 97–115.

32 M. W. Bundy, *The Theory of Imagination*, pp. 37–8.

33 M. W. Bundy, *The Theory of Imagination*, p. 23. See also J-P. Vernant, 'Image et Apparence', pp. 142, 155.

34 J-P. Vernant, 'Image et Apparence', pp. 156–7.

35 See H-G. Gadamer's analysis of this passage of Plato's *Cratylus* in *Wahrheit und Methode*, Tübingen, 1960, pp. 360–84. See also Bundy, *The Theory of Imagination*, pp. 18ff.

36 In *Timaeus*, 71b, Plato speaks of certain images of the mind which 'make the part of the soul that lives in the region of the liver cheerful and gentle, and able to spend the night quietly in divination and dreams, as reason and understanding are beyond it. For our makers remembered that their father had ordered them to make mortal creatures as perfect as possible, and so did their best even with this base part of us and gave it the power of prophecy so that it might have some apprehension of truth. And clear enough evidence that god gave this power to man's irrational part is to be found in our incapacity for inspired and true prophecy when in our right minds; we only achieve it when the power of our understanding is inhibited in sleep, or when we are in an abnormal condition owing to disease or divine inspiration.' It is also worth noting the paradoxical connection between 'holy madness' and imagination admitted by Plato in the *Phraedrus* (244) and the *Apol.* (22b) where he speaks of a divine

frenzy of vision from which come *ta magista to agathon*. See M. W. Bundy's lucid commentary on this Platonic notion of divinely inspired images, *The Theory of Imagination*, pp. 41–2.

37 *Timaeus*, 71b–72a: 'It is the function of someone in his right mind to construe what is remembered of utterances made in dream or waking by those who have the gift of prophecy and divine inspiration, and to give a rational interpretation of their visions, saying what good or evil they portend and for whom, whether future, past or present. It is not the business of any man, so long as he is in an abnormal state, to interpret his own visions and utterances; there is truth in the old saying that only a sane man can attend to his own concerns and know himself. Hence the custom of setting up spokesmen to pronounce judgements on inspired prophecies.' Our translation of Plato's *Timaeus* are from the Penguin Classics edition, 1965, pp. 97–8.

38 See P. Ricoeur's analysis of Aristotle's notion of *mimēsis* in the *Poetics* in *Time and Narrative*, vol. I, University of Chicago Press, 1984, pp. 31–52. See also H. Osborne's useful summary in 'The Concept of Mimesis' in *Aesthetics and Art Theory*, Dutton, 1970, pp. 74–8.

39 In particular the *De Anima*. There are, of course, certain passages in the *Poetics* where Aristotle does imply that there is a creative imagination at work, e.g. in chapter 9 where he attributes the superior value of tragedy over history to its ability to produce paradigms and archetypes and thereby generate possible worlds which exemplify the links between the necessary and the plausible in human actions; or in chapter 17 where he speaks of the poet's active and constructive participation in his own creations.

40 Aristotle, *De Anima*, 427b: 'Imagination is different from both perception and thought; imagination does not occur without perception and without imagination there can be no belief.' Moreover, while imagination is generally unreliable if taken on its own, it can serve the interests of truth if made subservient to perception or knowledge which are true, *De Anima*, 428a. Thus while imagination depends on perception, they are not identical. Sensation is a necessary but not a sufficient condition for imagination, as indeed for all mental activity.

41 For a more detailed account of these aspects of Aristotle's treatment of imagination see M. W. Bundy, *The Theory of Imagination*, pp. 19–26; and C. Castoriadis, 'La Découverte de l'imagination', *Libre*, Paris, 1978, pp. 150–90.

42 M. W. Bundy, *The Theory of Imagination*, p. 22. See, for example,

De Anima 427b, 21–4, where Aristotle declares that 'in imagination we are like spectators looking at something dreadful or encouraging in a picture (*graphē*)'.

43 On Aristotle's treatment of active imagining, see 'La Découverte de l'imagination', pp. 177–99. For Aristotle rational thought and moral behaviour involve deliberation; deliberation involves the contemplation of possible future outcomes, and that involves imagination. This brings out a distinction between the faculty of imaging which can be more or less passive (as in dreams for instance) and that of active imagination: the deliberate contemplation by imagination of possible outcomes which Aristotle believes is a necessary condition of rational action and of moral behaviour (*De Anima*, 431b). Aristotle goes on to argue that when imagination moves it doesn't move without desire. Action requires both a mental picturing of possible outcomes and a desire to realize one of those outcomes and avoid others (*De Anima*. 433a–433b).

44 See Aristotle's analysis of the 'active intellect' or *nous poiĕtikos* in book III of *De Anima*. This theory of the *nous poiĕtikos* gave rise to a series of mystical interpretations of the creative power of the mind and even led some commentators, for example Averroes, to argue for one 'active intellect' of God in which human minds participated: the 'unfallen part of the mind'.

45 B. Croce, *Aesthetic*, Farrar, New York, 1972, p. 170.

Chapter three: the medieval imagination

1 As explained in our Preface we have chosen to forego discussion of the contribution made by the Arabic commentators. Averroes and Avicenna, to the medieval synthesis of Greek (Aristotelian/Platonic) ontology and biblically-inspired theology. Discussion of the Arabic/ Islamic sources, as well as other more peripheral ones, would have meant extending our analysis beyond the *dominant mainstream* of medieval thought: a mainstream which remained, for a number of complex historico-political-religious reasons, largely conditioned by the conflation of Graeco-Roman and Judeo-Christian modes of thinking.

2 E. Gilson, *Le Thomisme*, Paris, 1942, p. 120. See also F. Copleston's useful account of 'Christian Thought in the Ancient World' in *A History of Medieval Philosophy*, Methuen, 1972, pp. 19 ff. On Heidegger's definition of 'onto-theology' see, for example, his *Identity and Difference*, Harper, New York, 1969, pp. 42–75. See

also Paul Ricoeur's useful deployment of this term in *La Mal*, Labour Fides, Geneva, 1986, pp. 24–6.

3 F. Copleston, 'Christian Thought', pp. 19, 25.

4 Plotinus, *Enneads*, 5, 5, trans. K. Guthrie, Alpine, New York, 1918, p. 551.

5 *Select Works of Porphyry*, trans. T. Taylor, London, 1823, p. 223.

6 *Proclus*, trans. T. Taylor, London, 1823, Vol. 2, p. 140. See also M. W. Bundy, *The Theory of Imagination in Classical and Medieval Thought*, . pp. 142–3; and C. Ramnoux, 'Les Modes d'expression du Philosopher d'apres Proclus' in *Savoir, Faire, Esperer*, Brussels, 1976, pp. 332–7, where the author identifies a more positive reading of images in Porphyry as a means of expressing truths in symbolic form.

7 Augustine, *De Genesi ad Litteram* in *Patrol. Lat.* 34, 458. See also M. W. Bundy's commentary on this passage, *The Theory of Imagination*, p. 168.

8 In this respect Augustine's treatment of imagination also bears the mark, on occasion, of Aristotelian psychology. This influence probably derives from his familiarity with the theories of the classical rhetoricians as well as from neo-Platonists like Porphyry who synthesized elements of Plato and Aristotle. Thus in the *De Trinitate*, Augustine distinguishes between i) the *external* activity of imagination which receives material sensations or impressions, and ii) its *internal* capacity to rearrange these images in the form of mental representations which may 'assist reasoning'. In one of his letters, Augustine seems to invoke an Aristotelian notion of *mimesis* to account for the complex work of mentally recombining our representational images before the 'inner eye' (*acies animi*) of the soul: 'I remember only a single sun for in fact I only perceived one sun in reality; but if I wished I could represent two or three suns. . . . So also, while I remember the size of the sun as I actually perceived it, I am able to picture it as greater or smaller according as I wish' (Epistola, VIII, 3). In this and other texts, Augustine appears to endorse a psychological account of imagination as a mental ability to rearrange the simple images passively derived from experience in terms of new complex images. This would certainly seem to be the import of the following passage from the *De Trinitate* (11, 10): 'I cannot have any memory of a bird with four feet for I have never seen such a thing, but I may easily imagine such a bird by adding to the winged form that I have seen, the form of a quadraped that I have also seen.' These select citations should suffice to demonstrate

how Augustine reformulates three principal characteristics of the classical treatment of the image i) as an impression of memory; (ii) as a mental representation of the soul; and iii) as a mediation between our empirical and rational experience.

9 On Augustine's notion of the *imago dei*, see our note 26 to the Appendix of chapter 1.

10 Richard of St Victor, *De Unione Corporis et Spiritus* in *Patrol. Lat.*, 177. 285. See M. W. Bundy's analysis of this passage, *The Theory of Imagination*, pp. 170–5.

11 Ibid.

12 F. Copleston, 'Christian Thought', p. 98.

13 Ibid., p. 99.

14 Ibid., p. 99.

15 All quotations are from *St Bonaventura Opera Omnia*, Op. Collegii S. Bonaventura, Florence, 10, Vols. For useful commentaries on Bonaventure's theory of imagination see E. Gilson, *The Philosophy of Bonaventure*, Paterson N.J., 1965, and E. Spargo, *The Category of the Aesthetic in the philosophy of St. Bonaventure*, N.Y., 1954.

16 Bonaventure commentaries on the commandments are in *De Decem Praeceptis Collatio II*, in *Opera Omnia*, 5, 514, 22–24. I am indebted to Joseph Bottum of Boston College for much of this material on Bonaventure.

17 See Pico della Mirandola's useful account of the medieval denunciations of the demonic imagination, *De Imaginatione*, trans. H. Caplan, Yale University Press, 1930, pp. 85 ff. The medieval notion of the demonic imagination was derived not only from the biblical account of the idolatrous use of images but also from the classical philosophical concept, frequently found in the Stoics, of a *phantasia proterva*. For other accounts of the complex nature of the medieval approach to images see P. Dronke, *Fabula: Exploration into the Uses of Myth in Medieval Platonism*, Leiden, Brill, 1974; M. D. Chenu, *Nature, Man and Society in the Twelfth Century*, Chicago U.P., 1968; and E. Curtius, *European Literature and the Latin Middle Ages*, Routledge and Kegan Paul, 1953.

18 Aquinas, *Summa Theologiae*, London, 1925, 4. 87–8. See also F. Copleston. *Aquinas*, Pelican, London, 1955, p. 179.

19 *Summa Theologiae*, 1, 78, 4.

20 F. Copleston, *Aquinas*, p. 48.

21 *Summa Theologiae*, 4. 179; 5. 112.

22 Ibid., 2. 53.

23 Ibid., 5, 147.

24 J. Le Goff, *L'Imagination Médiévale*, Gallimard, Paris, 1986; and E. Gombrich, *Ideal and Idols: Essays on Values in History and in Art*, Oxford, Phaidon, 1979.

25 E. Gombrich, *The Story of Art*, Phaidon, London, 1972, p. 95: 'On one thing nearly all early Christians were agreed: there must be no statues in the House of God. Statues were too much like those graven images and heathen idols that were condemned in the Bible. To place a figure of God, or of one of His saints, on the altar seemed altogether out of question. For how would the poor pagans who had just been converted to the new faith grasp the difference between their old beliefs and the new message, if they saw such statues in churches? They might too easily have thought that such a statue really "represents" God, just as a statue by Pheidias was thought to represent Zeus. Thus they might have found it even more difficult to grasp the message of the one Almighty and Invisible God, in whose semblance we are made.'

26 See M. P. Hederman, 'Cinema and the Icon' in *The Crane Bag*, Dublin, vol. 8, no. 2, 1984, p. 92; and also L. Bouyer, *Vérite des Icônes*, Criterion, 1985, pp. 7, 10.

27 E. Gombrich, *The Story of Art*, p. 97.

28 M. P. Hederman, 'Cinema and the Icon', p. 94.

29 Ibid., p. 95; see also Bouyer, *Vérite des Icônes*, p. 16.

30 M. P. Hederman, 'Cinema and the Icon', p. 95. Hederman sums up the theological presuppositions of the iconography debate in these vivid terms: 'In the Roman Church the emphasis on the relationship between the Father and the Son had a restricting and monopolizing effect on the way in which the mystery of the Trinity was expressed. This was connected also to the desire within the Roman Church to establish the fact that it alone possessed the full and unique access to the divine life. Such fears and preoccupations inevitably led to a downgrading of the free and universal charism of the Holy Spirit and an emphasizing of the authoritative function of the Papacy and the Magisterium as the guaranteed source and hall-mark of grace. Paternalism was the overriding culture and religious mould of this time. Everything in the history and the make-up of the medieval Roman Church contributed to this cultural bias in favour of a centralized, authoritarian, uniform, ordered and paternal-istic organization. The Trinity was understood in similar terms. The Father was the absolute and ultimate source of all; the Son was a totally obedient and yet equal person. Only the Son could reveal

the *image* of the Father and the autonomous inspirational power of the Holy Spirit in this regard was looked upon with suspicion.'

31 F. Zeri, *Renaissance et Pseudo-Renaissance*, Rivages, Paris, 1986.
32 E. Gombrich, *The Story of Art*, p. 12.
33 R. Hinks, *Caravaggio*, London, 1963.
34 William Blake also made the comment that 'the reason Milton wrote in fetters when he wrote of angels and God, and at liberty when he wrote of devils in Hell, is because he was a true poet and of the devils party without knowing it'.
35 M. P. Hederman, 'Cinema and the Icon', p. 93. On this influence of the official Raphaelesque aesthetic on religious art see also, P. Pye, 'Religious Art: the Extile and the Mainstream' in *The Crane Bag*, vol. 7, no. 2, 1983, pp. 85–6.
36 E. Gilson, *Elements in Christian Philosophy*, Mentor, New York, 1960, p. 120.
37 J. le Goff, *L'Imaginaire Mediévale*.

Chapter three *Appendix 1:* The onto-theological notion of being as production

1 M. Heidegger, *Basic Problems of Phenomenology*, trans. A. Hofstadter, Indiana U.P., 1982, p. 100. See the excellent and illuminating commentary by J. Caputo in his chapter on 'Heidegger's Critique of Scholasticism' in *Heidegger and Aquinas*, Fordham U.P., 1982, pp. 72–4, 88.
2 See J. Caputo, 'Heidegger's Critique of Scholasticism', pp. 73–4.
3 M. Heidegger, *Nietzsche*. vol. II, *The End of Philosophy*, trans. J. Stambaugh, Harper and Row, 1973, p. 12.
4 J. Caputo, 'Heidegger's Critique of Scholasticism', p. 89.
5 Ibid., p. 90.
6 M. Heidegger, *Nietzsche*, vol. II, p. 19.

Chapter three *Appendix 2:* Philoxenes of Mabboug

1 Philoxènes, *Letter To Patricius*, 106; quoted G. Lardreau, *Discours philosophique at discours spirituel, autour de la philosophie de Philoxènes de Mabboug*, ed. du Seuil, Paris, 1985, p. 125. In what follows we are greatly indebted to Lardreau's work and especially the section entitled 'La hâte à representer: Critique de l'imagination', pp. 125–33.
2 Lardreau, *Discours philosophique et discours spirituel*, p. 126.

3 Ibid., p. 126–7.
4 Ibid., p. 127.
5 Philoxenes, *Memre contre Habib*, III, 306; quoted in A. de Halleux, *Philoxènes de Mabboug*, p. 429 and Lardreau, *Discours philosophique et discours spirituel*, p. 133.

Chapter three   *Appendix 3:* Maimonides

1 M. Maimonides, *The Guide of the Perplexed*, trans. S. Pines, Chicago, 1963, p. 23.
2 Ibid., pp. 22, 30–1
3 Ibid., p. 337.
4 Ibid., p. 173.
5 Ibid., p. 335.
6 Ibid. (Vol. III), p. 61.
7 Ibid., p. 337.

Chapter four: The transcendental imagination

1 The imagination's potential for creative immediacy was not, of course, entirely ignored by premodern philosophies. But where acknowledged it was almost invariably condemned. This condemnation dated back to the origins of Western thought. It was reflected in the influential legacy of the rebellious deeds of imagination as narrated in the foundational myths of both biblical and Greek culture. Adam's sin was to have sought to become 'like god' by acquiring the imaginative knowledge of good and evil. And Prometheus' crime was to have given men direct access to the fire of the gods thus enabling them to become creators of their own world. In each of these mythic narratives, the rebels of imagination were severely punished by the gods for trying to usurp their powers and emulate their ways. But once man had received the stolen fire, he could not return it or ignore it. Imagination was an inalienable part of his inheritance.

While some traditional philosophies recommended the maximum curtailment of imagination, others – as we saw – allowed it a minimal 'mimetic' role. At most, man might conform to truth i) by renouncing the temptation to create value *immediately* and ii) by faithfully reproducing it as *mediated* through the order of reality ordained by God – that is, through the world of nature and of a divinely-ordained society (e.g. Plato's Republic or the structures of Medieval Christendom). This explains why, at an epistemological level, classical and medieval philosophies tended to consign imagination to a merely transitional position between reason and perception. Its function was generally restricted to that of transmitting mimetic images of reality to the purifying citadel of reason.

But imagination was not always content with such a subservient role. It frequently contrived to overreach its assigned limits. Whereas *perception* received truth as mediated through out natural experience, and whereas *reason* received truth as mediated through the objective laws of morality, religion and philosophical speculation, *imagination* threatened to cast aside all such modes of orthodox mediation and proceed immediately to the origin of truth itself – and, worse still, to mistake this origin for itself. As an active creative power which presumed to produce truth from within itself, imagination was outlawed by premodern philosophy.

2 Regarding the influence of such occult movements on the German idealists and romantics, see E. Benz, *Les Sources Occultes de la Philosophie Romantique Allemande*, Vrin, Paris, 1968; M. H. Abrams, *Natural Supernaturalism: Tradition and Revolution in Romantic Literature*, New York, 1973; F. Yates, *Giordano Bruno and the Hermetic Tradition*, New York, 1969; A. Viatte, *Les Sources Occultes du Romantisme: Illuminisme-Théosophie 1770–1820*, Paris, 1979; R. Brown, *The Later Philosophy of Schelling: The Influence of Boehme on the Works of 1809–1815*, Cranebury, New Jersey, 1977; G. Hanratty, 'Hegel and the Gnostic Tradition' in *Philosophical Studies*, vol. 30, 1984. Although Kant himself was extremely dismissive of mystical thinkers, whom he lambasted as *Schwärmerei*, the general movement of German idealism was deeply influenced by the occult philosophies which granted a central role to imagination. Kant's revision of his theory of imagination in the second edition to the *Critique of Pure Reason* may have had something to do with his rationalist antipathy towards the enthusiastic claims for imagination made by the hermetic tradition.

3 Kant, *Critique of Pure Reason*, trans. N. Smith, London, 1964. Our reading of Kant's theory of transcendental imagination is much indebted to M. Heidegger's work *Kant and the Problem of Metaphysics*, Indiana University Press, 1962, and particularly the section 'transcendental Imagination as the Root of both Stems', pp. 144–8.

4 M. Heidegger, *Kants These über das Sein*, Frankfurt-on-Main, 1962.

Kant makes a similar point in his *Unique Proof for the Existence of God* when he writes that 'existence is in no sense a predicate or determination of any object whatsoever. . . . The concept of *positing* is perfectly simple and identical with that of being in general'. In *Kant and the Problem of Metaphysics*, Heidegger explicitly relates Kant's 'Copernican Revolution' in our understanding of being to his discovery of the transcendental imagination as the source of human knowledge.

5 See C-G Dubois, *L'Imaginaire de la Renaissance*, P. U. F., 1985.

6 R. Klein, 'L'imagination comme vêtement de l'âme chez Marsile Ficin et Giordano Bruno' in *La Forme et l'Intelligible*, Gallimard, 1970, p. 88.

7 It has been argued, however, that Bruno did exert a significant influence on the later movement of German idealism in the eighteenth and nineteenth centuries – particularly on Schelling and Hegel. See F. Yates, *Giordano Bruno*.

8 J. Starobinski, 'Jalons pur une Histoire de l'Imagination' in *La Relation Critique*, Gallimard, 1970, p. 186. See also the sources cited in note 2 above.

9 See M. Heidegger, *Being and Time*, trans. Macquarrie and Robinson, Blackwell, Oxford, 1973, section 44 and also 'Nietzsche's Word: God is Dead' in *The Question concerning Technology*, trans. Lovitt, Harper, 1977, pp. 53–115. In these texts, Heidegger defines the Cartesian character of modern metaphysics as a reduction of being to the subjective acts of *cogitatio, certitudo, institia*. This position is epitomized in Leibniz's formula: '*Iustitia nihil aliud est quam ordo seu perfectio circa mentes.*'

10 For contemporary commentaries on Descartes' negative assessment of imagination see J-P Sartre, *Imagination*, Alcan, 1936 and M. Merleau-Ponty, *L'oeil et l'esprit*, Gallimard, 1964, pp. 36–60.

11 Quoted by B. Willey, *Seventeenth Century Background*, Pelican, London, 1972, p. 85.

12 Spinoza, *On the Improvement of the Understanding*, Dover Books, 1955, p. 19.

13 See S. Hampshire on this relation between imagination and temporal illusion in his *Spinoza*, Penguin, 1951, pp. 173–5, 195.

14 Sartre, *L'imagination*, chapter 2.

15 Leibniz, *New Essays in Human Understanding*, in *Philosophical Writings*, Dent, 1973, p. 152.

16 B. Croce, *Aesthetic*, Noonday Press, New York, 1972, p. 185.

17 Ibid., p. 204.

18 B. Willey, *Seventeenth Century Background*, pp. 262–3. Willey also has a useful account of the Cambridge Platonists' treatment of imagination, e.g. John Smith who wrote: 'Our imaginative powers . . . breathe a gross dew upon the pure glass of our understanding and so sully and desmear it, that we cannot see the image of divinity sincerely in it.'

19 W. Blake, *Selected Poems*, Penguin, p. 128; W. B. Yeats' 'Explorations in *Collected Poems of W. B. Yeats*, McMillan, 1957. In another poem entitled 'Fragments', Yeats links Locke's mechanistic philosophy with the ravages of the industrial revolution, which he sees as a second 'fall': 'Locke sank into a swoon/the garden died/ God took the spinning-jenny/out of his side'. See also J. Engell, *The Creative Imagination: Enlightenment to Romanticism*, Harvard University Press.

20 R. Sokolowski, 'Fiction and Illusion in David Hume's philosophy' in *The Modern Schoolman*, XLV, 1963, pp. 200–3.

21 Hume, *A Treatise of Human Nature*, Oxford, 1888 (1976). See also M. H. Abrams, *The Mirror and the Lamp*. Oxford University Press, 1971, p. 164.

22 Hume, *A Treatise*, p. 266.

23 Ibid., p. 260.

24 Ibid., p. 358.

25 See Sartre's critique of Hume's 'illusion of immanence' in *L'Imagination*, chapter 2.

26 G. Deleuze, 'Le pouvoir de l'imagination dans la morale et dans la conscience' in *Empirisme et Subjectivité*, P.U.F., 1973, pp. 41–71.

27 Hume, *A Treatise*, p. 121.

28 Ibid., pp. 267–8.

29 There are three main meanings of 'transcendental' in Kant. First, as in the term 'transcendental imagination' it means that imagination serves as an *a priori* condition of knowledge, as opposed to the *a posteriori* or empirical sources of knowledge. Second, the term 'transcendental' is opposed in Kant to 'formal' (e.g. as two different kinds of logic). And third, at the level of expression, Kant speaks of a transcendental use of the categories.

30 Kant, *Critique of Pure Reason*, p. 24.

31 Ibid., p. 144.

32 Ibid., p. 146.

33 Ibid., p. 147.

34 H. Marcuse, *Eros and Civilization*, Beacon, Boston, 1955, p. 174.
35 Kant, *Critique of Judgement*, trans. J. C. Meredith, Oxford U.P., 1952, p. 244.
36 Ibid., p. 89. My analysis here owes much to M. Warnock's lucid commentary, 'Imagination and Creative Art: Hume, Kant and Schelling' in *Imagination*, Faber, 1976, pp. 43–69 and to H. Marcuse's interpretation of Kant's theory of imagination in the *Critique of Judgement* in Chapter 9 of *Eros and Civilisation*, pp. 172–80.
37 Kant, *Critique of Judgement*, p. 240.
38 Ibid., p. 314.
39 M. Warnock, p. 49.
40 Ibid., pp. 49–51.
41 Ibid., pp. 54–55.
42 Kant, *Critique of Judgement*, p. 245.
43 M. Warnock, *Imagination*, Faber and Faber, 1976, p. 56. The author offers the following useful example, pp. 56–7:

> In the contemplation of beauty the imagination is free and takes pleasure in its sense of freedom, just because it can so easily form an image. The pleasure is a pleasure in doing something which one can do. It is rather as one might learn how to play a certain kind of ornamentation in a piece of keyboard music, and take pleasure in one's ability to produce the required kind of ornament. The sound would give one pleasure but so would one's own ability to produce the sound in the right way and at the right time. Similarly the imagination, in grasping a thing as beautiful, can easily grasp the rule or design *in* the thing before it, and frame pictures or presentations of the form of the thing, creating its own rule as it goes along. In the contemplation of the sublime, on the other hand, the imagination is brought to a full stop, and can go no further. All it has to work on is the form of the thing before it which suggests certain *ideas*. But no further images can be produced to render these ideas concrete or familiar. We cannot, hearing a great exposition in a Beethoven sonata (to continue with the keyboard analogy), discover any rule by which we can go on in this way for ourselves.

44 Kant, *Critique of Judgement*, p. 246.
45 Warnock, p. 58.
46 Kant, *Critique of Judgement*, p. 314.
47 Warnock, p. 63.
48 Heidegger, *Kant and the Problem of Metaphysics*, note, p. 144.
49 Fichte, *The Vocation of Man*, trans. W. Smith, Open Court, 1965, p. 141.
50 Quoted C. Castoriadis, *L'Institution Imaginaire de la Société*, ed. du Seuil, Paris, 1975, pp. 204–5. See also Fichte, *The Vocation of*

Man, pp. 140–1. For a useful and concise commentary on Fichte's development of Kant's theory of the transcendental imagination, see R. Kroner, *Von Kant bis Hegel*, Tübingen, 1961, vol. I, pp. 476–86.

51 Schelling, *Sämtliche Werke*, Stuttgart, 1885, III, pp. 349 ff. See also R. Kroner, *Von Kant bis Hegel*; M H Abrams, *The Mirror and the Lamp*, pp. 120 ff; and G. Marcel, *Coleridge and Schelling*, ed. Aubier-Montaigne, Paris, 1951, pp. 61–3. On the interaction between German and British philosophies of imagination see J. Engell, *The Creative Imagination*, Heidegger provides a perceptive account of Schelling's attempts to dismantle the dualistic hierarchies of traditional onto-theology in his *Schelling Abhandlung über das Wesen der Menschlichen Freiheit*, Tübingen, 1971.

52 Schelling, *Werke*, X, p. 192. See Abrams, *The Mirror and the Lamp*, p. 210.

53 See Warnock, *Imagination*, p. 68.

54 Ibid., p. 64.

55 Abrams, *The Mirror and the Lamp*, pp. 150 ff; G. Marcel, *Coleridge and Schelling*, pp. 61–3, 166–8, 188–9, 235–7; G. Orsini, *Coleridge and German Idealism*, S. Illinois U.P., 1969.

56 From Coleridge's Notebooks, *Ars Poetica*, quoted by M. Warnock, in *Imagination*, p. 92. In certain passages of the *Biographia Literaria*, Coleridge does acknowledge a certain debt to Schelling and the German idealists.

57 Coleridge, *Biographia Literaria*, XIII.

58 Ibid., pp. 176–8. Quoted and compared to an analogous passage in Schelling's *System of Transcendental Idealism* in G. Marcel's appendix to his *Coleridge et Schelling*, p. 260.

59 Our reading is at variance with the standard commentaries on this passage. See for example, Warnock, *Imagination*, p. 91: 'How far did Coleridge go with Schelling and Kant? It may be said that he is not completely committed, at least in this passage, to idealism; for the work of actual creation is ascribed to the deity, while the human imagination is a repetition in human terms of this divine activity.' J. Derrida has argued in 'Economimesis' (in *Mimesis: desarticulations*, ed. Philosophie en Gref, Paris) that even the Kantian theory of the productive imagination is itself a mimetic activity, pp. 62, 67, 73. For example, p. 62:

Mimesis occurs not only in the reproductive acts, as is self-evident, but also in the free and pure productivity of imagination. The latter only deploys the primitive power of its inventivity in *Listening* to nature, its dictation, its edict. . . . Genius raises the liberty of play and the pure productivity of imagination to its highest point. It provides the rules, or at least the examples, but it has its rules dictated to it by nature: so much so that the very distinction between free art and mercenary art, with all the apparatus of hierarchical subordination which it commands, reproduces nature in its act of production, and so only breaks with *mimesis*, as the imitation of what is, in order to become one with the free unfolding and refolding of *physis*.

60 The Coleridgean model would be something like this: i) primary imagination (anterior to secondary imagination and to fancy); ii) secondary imagination (posterior to primary imagination but superior); iii) fancy (posterior to both primary and secondary imagination and inferior to both).

61 One needs to make a distinction here between the first and second generation of English romantics. Shelley, Hazlitt and Keats all speak of the imagination's power of 'sympathy', of freeing one from the 'Bastille' of one's own egoism and consequently as a heightened form of utilitarian benevolence (à la Godwin). They regarded Wordsworth's version as the 'egotistical sublime', i.e. a form of imagination which was, like the Kantian transcendental self, too 'monadic' and lacking a socio-political dimension.

62 Nerval was largely responsible for introducing German idealism and romanticism into France. Baudelaire, for example, referred to imagination as the 'queen of the faculties'.

63 Schiller, *On the Aesthetic Education of Man* (first published in 1795), trans. E. Wilkins and L. Willoughby, Clarendon Press, 1967.

64 See W. Desmond's clear exposition of Hegel's distinction between the 'mimetic' and 'productive' uses of art in *Art and the Absolute: A Study of Hegel's Aesthetics*, SUNY, 1986, especially chapter I on 'Art, Imitation and Creation'.

65 W. Stevens, *The Necessary Angel, Essays on Reality and Imagination*, Faber, 1942, pp. 150–1.

66 D. Donoghue, *Thieves of Fire*, pp. 77–9.

67 J. Starobinski, 'Jalons pur une Histoire de l'Imagination', pp. 187–9.

Chapter four   *Appendix:* Heidegger's interpretation of the Kantian imagination

1 M. Heidegger, *Kant and the Problem of Metaphysics*, trans. J. Churchill, Indiana U.P., 1962, p. 177.

2 Ibid., p. 177.

3 Ibid., p. 140.

4 Ibid., p. 138.
5 Ibid., p. 149. See also M. Heidegger, *Kant and the Problem of Metaphysics*, p. 149.
6 M. Heidegger, *Kant and the Problem of Metaphysics*, p. 135.
7 Ibid., p. 135.
8 Kant, *The Critique of Pure Reason*, p. 112.
9 M. Heidegger, *Kant and the Problem of Metaphysics*.
10 Kant, *The Critique of Pure Reason*, p. 143.
11 M. Heidegger, *Kant and the Problem of Metaphysics*, pp. 248–9.
12 See C. Schrag, 'Heidegger and Cassirer on Kant' in *Kant Studien*, vol. 58, 1967, p. 92.
13 M. Heidegger, *Kant and the Problem of Metaphysics*, p. 180.
14 Ibid., p. 192.
15 Ibid., pp. 162–6. Here Heidegger discusses the central role played by the imagination in practical reason.

Chapter five: The existentialist imagination I – Kierkegaard and Nietzsche

1 H. Marcuse, 'The Affirmative Character of Culture' in *Negations*, Beacon Press, Boston, 1968, p. 95.
2 Ibid., pp. 96–7.
3 Ibid., p. 98.
4 Kant, *Idee zu einer allgemeinen Geschlichte in Weltbürgerlicher Absicht* in *Werke IV*, Berlin, p. 153.
5 H. Marcuse, 'Philosophy and Critical Theory' in *Negations*, pp. 150–1.
6 J-P. Sartre, *Existentialism and Humanism*, Metheun, 1948.
7 S. Kierkegaard, *Eithor/Or*, Anchor Books, New York, 1959.
8 For a lucid and systematic outline of these three dialectical phases, see Kierkegaard's *Stages on Life's Way*, Schocken Books, New York, 1967.
9 Kierkegaard's description of Abraham's existential crisis of faith is in *Fear and Trembling*, Princeton University Press, 1941.
10 One even observes the curious situation where Kierkegaard uses the essentially *aesthetic* strategy of pseudonyms (i.e. fictional authors) when he is ostensibly presenting an *ethical* or *religious* viewpoint. Kierkegaard did write a work called *The Point of View for my Work as an Author* (Harper, 1962) in which he intended to disclose the true reasons and motivations behind his various pseudonyms. But it is significant that this work was withheld from

publication by Kierkegaard during his own lifetime. And while Kierkegaard did put his signature to a number of 'devotional' works there is no guarantee that these works represent the 'truth' of Kierkegaard's overall philosophy.

11 Kierkegaard, *Sickness unto Death*, Anchor Books, New York, 1954, p. 83. The transcendental and dialectical idealists embrace a form of abstract speculation which ignores the irreducibly paradoxical nature of the rapport between the finite and the infinite. As such, they seek to turn their backs on the 'offense' contained in the paradox of the Christian Incarnation: 'Speculation naturally had the notion that it "comprehended" the God-Man – this one can easily comprehend, for speculation in speculating about the God-Man leaves out temporal existence, contemporaneousness and reality' (Ibid., p. 83).

12 Kierkegaard, *Training in Christianity*, Princeton University Press, 1967, p. 102.

13 Ibid., p. 85. In *Sickness unto Death*, p. 248, Kierkegaard also describes imagination as a power which falsely overcomes the 'offense' of the God-Man paradox by 'dreaming' that God and Man are one.

14 Kierkegaard, *Training in Christianity*, p. 184.

15 Ibid., p. 184.

16 Kierkegaard, *Journals and Papers*, ed. Hong, Indiana U.P., I, p. 749. In man's desperate attempt to become one with himself there is, notes Kierkegaard, 'an interplay of finitude and infinitude, of the divine and the human, of freedom and necessity'.

17 Kierkegaard, *Training in Christianity*, p. 186.

18 Ibid., p. 185.

19 Ibid., pp. 190–1. Anti-Climacus, the pseudonymous author of this work, refers to the Greek youth, Themistocles, who yearned day and night to resemble his ideal, 'until he himself became as great a conqueror as the man (i.e. Miltiades) whose renown had made him sleepless'.

20 Ibid., p. 186.

21 Ibid., p. 187.

22 Ibid., pp. 188–9.

23 *Kierkegaard's Journals* (Dru edition), entry 936.

24 Kierkegaard, *Either/or*, p. 288. Kierkegaard clearly has his relationship with Regina in mind here. In this work as in *Repetition* (both dedicated to Regina), the author deals with the principle of hope; indeed *Repetition* was originally written under the pseudonym of Victorius de Bona Speranza. In both these works Kierkegaard is

reflecting on how hope led him to the 'wondrous' (*admirari*) Regina, and to the painful disappointment which he declares he can never forget. The 'nil admirari' maxim is shrouded in an aura of irony and equivocation. It expresses at once the wisdom of a man experienced in life's hardship, and the stoical condescension of the aesthete.

25 See the opening paragraphs of *Sickness unto Death*, where Kierkegaard criticizes the Hegelian dialectic of the self; and also *The Concept of Dread*, Princeton University Press, 1944, pp. 41–99. Kierkegaard's description in these texts of the human efforts to synthesize the negative and positive poles of his self into one spirit is clearly derived from Hegel's discussion of the dialectic of self-consciousness in the *Phenomenology of Mind* (trans. J. Baillie, New York 1967) and particularly the sections on the master/slave struggle and stoicism. See for example, pp. 243–5: 'The freedom of self-consciousness (self-identity) is indifferent towards natural existence, and has therefore to let this matter go and remain free. The reflection is thus duplicated. This freedom takes only pure thought of its truth and thus lacks the concrete filling of life. . . . It has gone back into itself. . . . It has no freedom in itself.'

26 *Kierkegaard's Journals*, entry 967.

27 Kierkegaard, *Sickness unto Death*, p. 202.

28 Kierkegaard, Journal Entry III, A 1. (*Journals and Papers*, Vol. II, 1587).

29 Kierkegaard, *Sickness unto Death*, p. 248.

30 Ibid., p. 251.

31 Ibid., p. 251.

32 Kierkegaard, *Training in Christianity*, p. 84.

33 Ibid., p. 207. See also ibid., p. 109: 'Thy kingdom was not of this world and is not; this world is not the abode of thy church. . . . If it imagines that it is to triumph here in the world . . . then it has perished, then it has confounded itself with the world.' And again, ibid., p. 205: 'The triumphant church conceives truth falsely not as way but as goal, as result, as what might be called a surplus, a dividend.' Kierkegaard categorically rejects the idea of a Christian community or congregation in history as an 'impatient anticipation of eternity': 'congregation has not its abiding place in time, but only in eternity . . . for everyone is and must remain an individual before God'.

34 Ibid., p. 206. Also pp. 216–18. For a more elaborate analysis of this theme see my article, 'Kierkegaard's Concept of the God-Man', in *Kierkegaardiana*, vol. XIII, Copenhagen, 1984, pp. 105–22.

35 F. Nietzsche, *The Gay Science*, Vintage Books, 1974, pp. 181–2.

36 Nietzsche, *The Genealogy of Morals*, Anchor Books, 1956, pp. 147ff.

37 M. Heidegger, *Nietzsche* (4 vols), Harper and Row, 1979–. See also Heidegger's illuminating essay 'The Word of Nietzsche: *God is Dead*' in *The Question concerning Technology and other Essays*, Harper and Row, 1977, pp. 53–155.

38 Nietzsche, *The Will to Power*, Weidenfeld and Nicolson, 1968, para. 424.

39 Nietzsche, *The Genealogy of Morals*.

40 Nietzsche, *The Will to Power*, books 12 and 14.

41 Ibid., para 452.

42 Nietzsche, *The Gay Science*, para. 374. See Mary Warnock's essay, 'Nietzsche's Conception of Truth' in *Nietzsche, Imagery and Thought*, ed. M. Pasley, Methuen, 1978, pp. 64–83.

43 Nietzsche, *The Will to Power*, book 8.

44 Cited and analysed by P. Pütz, 'Nietzsche: Art and Intellectual Inquiry' in *Nietzsche, Imagery and Thought*, p. 4.

45 P. Pütz, 'Nietzsche', p. 10.

46 See Heidegger's perceptive commentary on this passage in his *Nietzsche I.* entitled *The Will to Power as Art*, section 24.

47 See René Girard's suggestion in *Mensonge Romantique et Vérité Romanesque*, Grasset, Paris, 1961, pp. 307–8 that the existentialist turn represents not so much the end of romanticism as the emergence of a deviant or pessimistic romanticism. In such an existentialist romanticism, the self is still the source of deification but as a *néant* rather than a *being*, as a *negation* rather than a *creation*.

Chapter six: The existentialist imagination II – Sartre

1 See G. Lukács' critique of existentialism in 'The Ideology of Modernism' in *The Meaning of Contemporary Realism*, Merlin Press, 1962; and R. Girard, *Mensonge Romantique et Vérité Romanesque*, Grasset, 1961.

2 A. Camus, 1955 Preface to the English translation edition of *The Myth of Sisyphus*, Vintage Books, New York, 1955, p. V.

3 See especially the section of The *Myth of Sisyphus*, pp. 49–68, entitled 'The Absurd Man', which begins with a quotation from Dostoyevsky's *Possessed*. See also R. Girard's contrasting interpretation of Dostoyevsky as a critic of romantic humanism and nihilism in *Mensonge Romantique et Vérité Romanesque*, pp. 286–7 and p. 313.

4 Camus, *The Myth of Sisyphus*, p. 68.

5 Ibid., p. 69.

6 Ibid., (1955 Preface).

7 Ibid., pp. 86–7.

8 Ibid., p. 87.

9 Ibid., p. 91.

10 M. Heidegger, *Kant and the Problem of Metaphysics*, pp. 207–8.

11 Ibid., p. 222.

12 Ibid., p. 238.

13 For a polemical but well documented account of the influence of Heidegger's anti-humanism on contemporary French philosophy (Foucault, Derrida, Lacan, etc.) see L. Ferry and P. Raynaud, *La Pensée 68: Essai sur l'Anti-humanisme Contemporain*, Gallimard, Paris, 1985.

14 J-P. Sartre, *Imagination: A Psychological Critique*, University of Michigan Press, 1962. Sartre's primary critique here is directed against what he calls the 'illusion of immanence' which characterizes the empiricist accounts of the image as a quasi-material deposit in the mind (e.g. Hume).

15 E. Husserl, *Ideas*, Collier, New York, 1962, pp. 200–1. For a more elaborate account of Husserl's theory of the imaginary, see my *Poétique du Possible*, pp. 59–66.

16 Sartre, *Imagination*, p. 143.

17 Sartre, *The Psychology of Imagination*, Citadel Press, New York, 1972, p. 1.

18 Ibid., pp. 26–7.

19 Ibid., p. 18.

20 Ibid., p. 138.

21 Ibid., p. 16.

22 Ibid., pp. 12–13.

23 Ibid., p. 129

24 Ibid., p. 120.

25 See J. Feel, *Emotion in the Thought of Sartre*, Columbia University Press, p. 42.

26 Sartre, *The Psychology of Imagination*, pp. 22–6.

27 Ibid., pp. 231, 250.

28 Ibid., p. 18. Sartre also shows by means of a phenomenological description how the imagining of a cube differs from its perception and its conceptual understanding. The percept is a progressive series of different real presentations: to perceive a cube is to present it 'gradually' and 'exactly' from all its sides. Conceptual understanding offers us a single and simultaneous grasp of the cube: we conceive

the cube as a *whole*, in all its dimensions, 'simultaneously' and 'exactly'. The image, while simultaneous like conception and presentative like perception, differs from both in that it fails to provide an 'exact' apprehension of the *real* object intended, it remains a *quasi-apprehension* of the cube. On this point, Sartre's existential account differs from Husserl's essentialist one which maintained that the image was that which when freely varied could yield exact and essential knowledge of the object.

29 Ibid., pp. 167ff. See also on this theme the following commentaries, R. Goldthorpe, 'Sartre's Theory of Imagination' in *The Journal of the British Society of Phenomenology*, vol. IV, no. 2, 1973; R. Grimsley, 'Sartre and the Phenomenology of Imagination' in *JBSP*, vol. III, no. 25, 1966; A. Greenway, 'Imaginal Knowing' in *JBSP*, vol. V, no. I, 1974; G. Todes, 'A Comparative Phenomenology of Perception and Imagination' in *Journal of Existentialism*, vol. VII, no. 25, 1966; and E. Kaelin, *An Existentialist Aesthetic*, University of Wisconsin Press, Madison, 1962.

30 Sartre, *The Psychology of Imagination*, p. 18. Also p. 210: 'If I posit Peter as he might be at this moment in Berlin . . . I grasp nothing, that is, I posit nothingness.' Sartre elaborates further on this enigmatic claim on pp. 165–261.

31 Ibid., p. 13.

32 Ibid., pp. 171–2.

33 Ibid., p. 40. Sartre also relates this phenomenon of 'possession' through imagination to the pivotal role played by witchdoctors and other impersonators in the ritual dances and customs of primitive tribes.

34 Ibid., p. 32.

35 Sartre, *Situations IV*, Gallimard, Paris, 1952, pp. 371–2.

36 Sartre, *The Psychology of Imagination*, p. 177.

37 Ibid., Section IV.

38 Ibid., p. 179.

39 Ibid., p. 205.

40 Ibid., p. 205.

41 Ibid., p. 212.

42 Ibid., p. 212.

43 For commentaries on this rapport between Sartre's theory of imagination and his literary writings see T. Flynn, 'The Role of the Image in Sartre's Aesthetic' in *Journal of Aesthetics and Art Criticism*, Vol. 33, 1974; E. Kaelin, *An Existentialist Aesthetic*; A. Bauer, *Sartre*

and the Artist, University of Chicago Press, 1963; M. Greene, 'Sartre on Imagination' in *JBSP*, vol. IV, no. 2, 1973.

44 Sartre, *The Psychology of Imagination*, pp. 259–60.

45 Ibid., p. 273.

46 Ibid., p. 273.

47 Ibid., p. 270. Sartre posits two stages of imaginative negation. The first which enables us to distance ourselves from things so as to intend the world as a meaningful totality: this primary stage is, it seems, operative in all acts of consciousness. The second which proceeds to project imaginary objects by means of a second negation of the world initially constituted in its totality: this stage is specific to imagination as a *sui generis* act of consciousness which differs from perception – it constructs a properly 'fictional' world by nullifying the world initially posited by consciousness. While the first act of negating imagination 'constitutes' the world in the manner of a transcendental synthesis *à la Kant* – a world which prior to consciousness merely existed as an undifferentiated and unsynthesized manifold; the second act of negating imagination goes on to 'isolate' a properly 'imaginary' object, intended by this second negation, as something beyond the real world, as something unreal and out of reach (p. 263).

48 Ibid., p. 271.

49 Ibid., p. 273.

50 Ibid., p. 255.

51 Ibid., p. 281.

52 Ibid., p. 282.

53 Sartre, *Being and Nothingness*, Philosophical Library, New York, 1956, p. 615. See also our commentary on this theme in Sartre's philosophy in *Modern Movements in European Philosophy*, Manchester University Press, 1986, chapter 3.

54 Sartre, *The Psychology of Imagination*, p. 272. The 'nihilistic' character of Sartre's conclusion to *Being and Nothingness* is expressed in phrases such as this, p. 620: 'the *ens causa sui* remains as the lacked, the indication of an impossible vertical surpassing which by its non-existence conditions the flat movement of consciousness'.

55 Sartre, *Being and Nothingness*, p. 96. See our more detailed study of Sartre's notion of 'possibility' as a project of the imagination in our *Poétique du Possible*, pp. 34–55, 117–35.

56 Sartre, *Being and Nothingness*, p. 93. Sartre adds that 'ontologically it amounts to the same thing to say that value and possibility exist

as external limits of a lack of being which can only exist as a lack of being (the *pour-soi*) – or that the upsurge of freedom determines its possibility and thereby circumscribes its value' (p. 565).

57 Ibid., p. 102.

58 Ibid., p. 98.

59 Ibid., p. 94: 'Nothing makes value exist – unless it is the freedom which by the same stroke makes me myself exist – and also within the limits of concrete facticity – since as the foundation of its nothingness, the for-itself cannot be the foundation of its being.'

60 Ibid., p. 96.

61 Sartre, *Existentialism and Humanism*, Methuen, 1948.

62 For a more comprehensive analysis of this distinction between authenticity and sincerity see our chapter on Sartre in *Modern Movements in European Philosophy*, and L. Trilling, *Sincerity and Authenticity*, Oxford U.P., 1974.

63 Sartre, *Existentialism and Humanism*.

64 R. Girard compares Dostoyevsky's nightmare vision with the contemporary cult of existentialist individualism in *Mensonge Romantique et Vérité Romanesque*, p. 315 ff.

65 Sartre, *Literature and Existentialism*, Citadel Press, 1972, p. 18.

66 Ibid., p. 15.

67 Ibid., p. 19.

68 Ibid., p. 23.

69 Ibid., p. 24.

70 Ibid., p. 24.

71 Ibid., p. 49.

72 Ibid., p. 53.

73 Ibid., p. 158.

74 Ibid., p. 159.

75 Ibid., p. 62;

76 R. Girard, *Mensonge Romantique et Vérité Romanesque*, p. 292.

77 Ibid., p. 294.

78 Ibid., p. 300.

79 Sartre, *Literature and Existentialism*, p. 159.

80 It was perhaps with such dialectical reversals in mind that Heidegger observed in *Letter on Humanism* that Sartre ultimately remained locked within a system of metaphysical oppositions.

81 See our more extensive analysis of the Sartrean dialectic of sadism and masochism in *Modern Movements in European Philosophy*, pp. 63–8.

Chapter seven: The parodic imagination

1 Conference held in the Pompidou Centre, Beaubourg, Paris, 23 January 1986, entitled *Sur La Place de l'Intellectuel Aujourd'hui*. See *Le Matin*, Paris, 25 January 1986.

2 D. Boorstin, *The Image: A Guide to Pseudo-Events in America*, Harper, New York, 1961, p. 36.

3 Cited and analysed by I. Hassan, *The Dismemberment of Orpheus: Towards a Post-Modern Literature*, Oxford U.P., 1971, pp. 256, 184–6.

4 Cited by M. Gibson, *Les Horizons du Possible* éd. du Felin, 1984, p. 212. Gibson also offers some perceptive analyses of Duchamp's anti-art works, e.g. 'The Woman and Chocolate Machine'.

5 A. Warhol, *From A to B and Back Again: The Philosophy of Andy Warhol*, Cassell, London, p. 7. Analysed by Gibson, *Les Horizons du Possible* pp. 73–5. The Irish artist, Bobby Ballagh, also offers interesting examples of the postmodern tendency towards imitation, parody, pastiche and self-exposure of the consumerist pseudo-world which informs the contemporary consciousness. For illustrations and analysis of Ballagh's work see C. Carty, *Robert Ballagh*, Magill, Dublin, 1986.

6 J. Derrida, *Spurs*, University of Chicago Press, 1978, p. 53.

7 H. Lawson, *Reflexivity: The Post-Modern Predicament*, Hutchinson, London, 1985, p. 115.

8 J. Lacan, 'The Function and Field of Speech and Language in Psychoanalysis' in *Ecrits: A Selection*, Tavistock, 1977, pp. 30–114. See also my chapter on Lacan in *Modern Movements in European Philosophy*, pp. 268–82.

9 Rimbaud, 'Lettre au Voyant' in *Completed Works and Selected Letters*, ed. W. Fowlie, University of Chicago Press, 1966, p. 307.

10 Lacan, 'The Agency of the Letter in the Unconscious' in *Ecrits*, p. 146ff.

11 Lacan, 'The Function and Field of Speech and Language in Psychoanalysis'.

12 Lacan, *Séminaire II*, ed. du Seuil, Paris, 1978, p. 87.

13 Ibid., p. 286.

14 Cited and analysed by Ferry and Reynaut in 'L'Anti-humanisme Lacanien' in *La Pensée 68*, pp. 251–8.

14a Lacan explores the feminist dimension of the Freudian critique of 'man' as a self-possessed narcissistic subject (phallus) in *Le Séminaire Encore*, ed. Seuil, Paris, 1975. See also the psychoanalytic critiques of the masculinist subject by feminists like Hélène Cixious, Luce Irigaray and Julia Kristeva.

15 Quoted F. Jameson, 'Postmodernism or the Cultural Logic of Late Capitalism', p. 90. Althusser's model is no doubt an allusion to Marx's famous statement about the inverted relation of the real (history) and the imaginary (ideology) in *The German Ideology* (International Publishers, New York, 1970): 'in all ideology men and their circumstances appear upside down as in a *camera obscura*'.

16 See our chapter on Althusser in *Modern Movements in European Philosophy*, p. 313.

17 Althusser, 'Philosophy as a Revolutionary Weapon' in *Lenin and Philosophy and Other Essays*, NLB, 1971.

18 Althusser, 'Ideology and Ideological State Apparatus' in *Lenin and Philosophy and Other Essays*. For a critical discussion of this theme see our *Modern Movements in European Philosophy*, p. 305.

19 Althusser, 'Freud and Lacan' in *Lenin and Philosophy and Other Essays*.

20 Ibid.

21 Althusser, 'A letter on Art in reply to André Daspré' in *Lenin and Philosophy*: 'to answer most of the questions posed for us by the existence and specific nature of art, we are forced to produce an adequate (scientific) *knowledge* of the processes which produce the "aesthetic effect" of a work of art . . . Like all knowledge, the knowledge of art presupposes a preliminary *rupture* with the language of *ideological spontaneity* and the constitution of a body of scientific concepts to replace it. If it is a matter of *knowing* art, it is absolutely essential to begin with '*rigorous reflection on the basic concepts of Marxism*': there is no other way.' See also our *Modern Movements in European Philosophy*, pp. 312–13.

22 Bourdieu, *Le Sens Practique*, ed. de Minuit, Paris, 1980, p. 70:

To convert the constructions used by science into transcendent entities in order to justify the structured and reasoned ensembles which are produced by the accumulation of innumerable historical actions, is to reduce history to a 'process without subject' and to merely replace the 'creative subject' of subjectivism with an automaton subordinated to the dead laws of a history of nature. This emanational vision, which makes Structure, Capital or the Mode of Production into an entelechy unfolding in a process of autorealization, reduces the agents of history to the role of structural 'supports' and reduces their actions to simple epiphenomenal manifestations of the power of the Structure to develope itself according to its own laws and to determine or overdetermine other structures.

23 Cited and analysed by Ferry and Reynaut, *La Pensée 68*, p. 211 (note).

24 Althusser, *For Marx*, Pantheon, 1972.

25 M. Foucault, Forward to the English edition of the *Order of Things*, Vintage, 1973, p. XIV.

26 Ibid., p. XIV.

27 Ibid., p. 243.

28 Ibid., p. 243.

29 Ibid., p. XXIII.

30 Ibid., p. XXIII.

31 Ibid., p. XXIII.

32 Ibid., p. 387.

33 Ibid., p. XVI.

34 Ibid., p. XVIII.

35 'Borges and the World of Fiction: An Interview with Borges by S. Heaney and R. Kearney' in *The Crane Bag*, Dublin, 1982, vol. 6, no. 2, 1982, p. 78.

36 M. Foucault, *This is not a Pipe*, Trans. and Intro. by J. Harkness, University of California Press, 1983, p. 10. See also p. 58 on the question of Magritte's painting as parody.

37 Ibid., pp. 53–4.

38 Ibid., p. 54. See also Foucault's interesting comments on Warhol in 'Theatricum Philosophicum' reprinted in *Language, Counter-Memory, Practice*, Cornell U.P., New York, 1977.

39 Foucault, *Madness and Civilization*, Tavistock, 1967, pp. 288–89.

40 Barthes acknowledges an explicit debt to Lacan and to Althusser in 'Change the Object: Mythology Today' in *Image-Music-Text*, Fontana, 1977, pp. 165–9.

41 Barthes, *Mythologies*, Paladin, 1973, p. 11.

42 As Lévi-Strauss remarked in *Tristes Tropiques* (Atheneum, New York, 1971), the logic of the imaginary is to be understood as 'the fantasy production of a society seeking passionately to give symbolic expression to the institutions it *might* have had in reality' had the socio-political conditions of that society been more conducive to the resolution of its problems. But since the remedy was lacking at the practical level of social action, the society begins 'to dream them, to project them into the imaginary'.

43 Barthes, *Mythologies*, p. 12.

44 Ibid., p. 159.

45 Ibid., p. 157–8.

46 Ibid., p. 158.

47 Barthes, 'The Death of the Author' in *Image-Music-Text*, Fontana, 1977, p. 142.

48 Barthes, *Writing Degree Zero*, Cape, 1967.

49 Barthes, 'The Death of the Author', p. 143.

50 Ibid., p. 145.

51 Ibid., p. 148.

52 Ibid., p. 146.

53 Ibid., pp. 146–7.

54 Ibid., p. 147.

55 Barthes, 'The Photographic Message' in *Image-Music-Text*, p. 31.

56 Barthes, 'The Third Meaning' in *Image-Music-Text*, p. 55.

57 Ibid., p. 63.

58 Ibid., p. 64.

59 Ibid., p. 63.

60 Ibid., p. 66.

61 Barthes, 'Change the Object Itself: Mythology Today' in *Image-Music-Text*, p. 169. Barthes goes on to imply that the whole of Western history is involved in an ideology which is essentially mythological, p. 167: 'no longer only the narrow sphere of French society but beyond that, historically and geographically, the whole of Western civilization (Graeco-Judeo-Islamo-Christian) unified under the one theology (Essence, Monotheism) and identified by the regime of meaning it practices – from Plato to *France-Dimanche*.'

62 Barthes, 'Inaugural Lecture at the Collège de France' 1977, published in English in *The Oxford Literary Review*, vol. 4, no. 1, 1979.

63 J. Derrida, 'The Ends of Man' in *Margins of Philosophy*, University of Chicago Press, 1983.

64 Derrida, 'Plato's Pharmacy' in *Dissemination*, Athlone Press, 1981, p. 168.

65 Derrida, 'The Double Session' in *Dissemination*, p. 187.

66 Ibid., p. 188.

67 Ibid., p. 191.

68 Ibid., p. 194,

69 Ibid., p. 194.

70 Ibid., p. 192. Derrida explores this argument at more length in his discussion of Kant's theory of the productive imagination in 'Economimesis', pp. 62, 67, 73–4.

71 Derrida, 'The Double Session', p. 193.

72 Ibid., p. 195.

73 Ibid., p. 198.

74 Ibid., p. 210.
75 Ibid., p. 223: 'Mallarmé *reads*. He writes while reading; while reading the text written by the Mime, who himself reads in order to write. He reads for example the *Pierrot Posthume* so as to write with his gestures a mimic that owes that book nothing, since he reads the mimic he thus creates in order to write after the fact the booklet that Mallarmé is reading.'
76 Ibid., p. 206.
77 Ibid., p. 206.
78 Ibid., p. 208.
79 Ibid., p. 207.
80 Ibid., p. 220.
81 Ibid., p. 211.
82 Ibid., p. 219.
83 Ibid., p. 223.
84 Derrida, 'The Attending Discourse' in *Dissemination*, p. 325.
85 See Ferry and Reynaud's commentary on Derrida's *Glas* in *La Pensée 68*, pp. 193–4.
86 Derrida, 'The Attending Discourse', p. 324.
87 Derrida, 'Differance' in *Speech and Phenomena*, Northwestern U.P., 1973, p. 130.
88 Derrida, 'A Letter to a Japanese Friend' in *Derrida and Difference*, eds D. Wood and R. Bernasconi, Parousia Press, 1985, p. 6,
89 Derrida, 'D'un ton apocalyptique adopté naguère en philosophie' in *Les Fins de L'Homme*, eds P. Lacoue-Labarthe et J-L. Nancy, Galilée, Paris, 1981, p. 474. The English translations are my own. An English version of this essay has appeared in *Semeia* 23, 1982, pp 63–97, by J. Leavey. There is also an illuminating commentary on this text by J. Caputo entitled 'Heidegger and Derrida: Cold Hermeneutics' in *JBSP*, vol. 17; no. 3, 1986, pp. 252–74, where the author gives a quasi-mystical reading of Derrida's notion of 'apocalypse without apocalypse'.
90 Derrida, *ibid.*, pp. 476–7.

Chapter seven   *Appendix:* A note on Postmodernism and computer science

1 D. Hofstadter, *Gödel, Escher, Bach*, Vintage, New York, 1980, p. 296.
2 Quoted Hofstadter, ibid., p. 299.
3 Ibid., p. 308.

4 J-F. Lyotard, interview in *Libération*, p. 36. On the rapport between postmodern thought and computer science see also Anthony Wilden, *System and Structure*, Tavistock, 1977, and Gregory Ulmer, *Applied Grammatology*, Johns Hopkins U.P., 1985.

Chapter eight. Postmodern culture: Apocalypse now?

1 S. Sontag, 'The Aesthetic of Silence' in *Styles of Radical Will*, Farrar, Strauss and Giroux, New York, p. 4.

2 T. Tanner, *Thomas Pynchon*, Methuen, 1982, pp. 40–56. Tanner argues that by parodying the quest paradigm of the bourgeois novel, Pynchon offers a typical example of the postmodern rejection of the narrative genre. Our analysis below owes much to Tanner's commentary.

3 See D. Albright on Pynchon's *V.* in *Representation and the Imagination*, The University of Chicago Press, 1981, p. 153.

4 Tanner, *Thomas Pynchon*, p. 42.

5 Ibid., p. 44.

6 Pynchon, *V.*, Penguin, 1966, pp. 404–5.

7 Ibid., p. 406.

8 Quoted and commented on by W. Benjamin, 'The Work of Art in the Age of Mechanical Reproduction' in *Illuminations*, Fontanta, p. 243.

9 See Tanner, p. 55: 'The old myths no longer work. . . . They no longer serve significantly to frame or scaffold the contemporary world. . . . In their place we have temporary and transitory improvizations using the ephemeral detritus of the modern street. The privileged hierarchies of significance and interpretation of the past must be abandoned and we must look to the overlooked areas of the contemporary world for new sources of meaning – and perhaps new gifts of tongues. When all the old 'scaffolds' are down, perhaps – *perhaps* – something new and regenerative may appear'. See also P. Coates' reading of Pynchon's fiction as a form of radical subversion in 'Unfinished Business: Thomas Pynchon and the Quest for Revolution' in *New Left Review*, no. 160, 1986, pp. 122–8. Coates argues that one of Pynchon's main concerns is to parody the circuitry of the 'messageless communications of modern technology' in the form of multi-faceted works which could be likened to the silicon chip. The wastage of the consumerist media society is also exemplified in Pynchon's portrayal of characters as refuse/waste who refuse the system which has discarded them. Pynchon's own refusal to provide conclusive solutions or endings to his novels has, arguably, a radical

potential. In *The Crying of Lot 49*, Pynchon tells us that 'Oedipa wondered whether, at the end of this (if it were supposed to end) she too might be left with only compiled memories of clues, announcements, intimations, but never the central truth itself.' Coates offers this reading of what he sees as the revolutionary significance of Pynchon's denial of a decidable ending: 'And so one has the ending that is no ending, that rehearses the title of the book ("Oedipa settled back, to await the crying of Lot 49"), places the whole book in the future . . . and so inaugurates the eternal, infernal recurrence of the events it relates. . . . This ending projects one beyond the terms of the book by indicating the degree to which silence (the inarticulate of the dispossessed?) is more important and potent than language. The text cannot speak the Other: to do so would be to co-opt it, to destroy it by bringing it to the light. If the Other of the book is the world, the Other of speech is action – the revolution we will have to make if we are ever to break out of the revolving cycle of the book's recurrence. (As it heads towards a revelation and revolution that never materializes – since it has not yet occurred in reality – the book takes on the shape of a door that turns into a revolving door: a door it is very hard to go through, as it turns one back from one's goal to consider the grounds of one's failure to reach that goal) . . . the text becomes a code without a message (like the empty television set with which it began): an injunction to complete unfinished business' (Coates, 'Unfinished Business,' p. 128).

10 See D. Baird, *Samuel Beckett, A Biography*, Cape, 1978.
11 S. Beckett, 'Recent Irish Poetry' in *The Bookman*, 1934, no. 86.
12 Beckett, *Proust*, Grave Press, New York, 1931, p. 4.
13 Ibid., p. 50.
14 Ibid., p. 56.
15 'Dialogues with George Duthuit' in *Transitions*, no. 5, Paris, 1949, reprinted in *Samuel Beckett: A Collection of Critical Essays*, ed. M. Esslin, Prentice-Hall, New York, 1965.
16 Beckett, *Imagination Dead Imagine*, Calder, London, 1965, pp. 12–13.
17 See D. Albright, *Representation and Imagination*, Chicago U.P., 1945, p. 164.
18 Beckett, *Imagination Dead Imagine*, p. 7.
19 Ibid., p. 14.
20 Ibid., p. 8.
21 Beckett, 'The Unnameable' in *Three Novels*, Grove Press, New York, 1965. Beckett does not give up. He continues to write fictions

which go in search of reality, to struggle with words towards the revelation of silence, to strive for glimpses of that 'mystical experience' which as he put it in his *Proust* essay, 'is at once *imaginative* and *empirical*, real without being merely actual, ideal without being merely abstract, the ideal real, the essential, the extratemporal' (pp. 55–6). This commitment to the impossible possibility of a redeemed imagination which might reveal the mystery of being and open onto the other, is never abandoned. As the narrator of 'The Unnameable' concludes, even if the narrative journey towards meaning is no longer feasible, he will go on nonetheless.

22 Beckett in Interview with T. Driver in *Columbia University Forum*, 1961.
23 W. Benjamin, 'The Storyteller' in *Illuminations*, Fontana, 1973, p. 108; and also 'The Work of Art in the Age of Mechanical Reproduction' in *Illuminations*, pp. 219–55.
24 Benjamin, 'The Storyteller', p. 89.
25 I. Hassan, *The Dismemberment of Orpheus: Towards a Postmodern Literature*, Oxford U.P., 1971, p. 248.
26 F. Jameson, 'Postmodernism, or the Cultural Logic of Late Capitalism', p. 72.
27 Ibid., p. 73.
28 Ibid., pp. 72–3.
29 Beckett, 'The Unnameable'.
30 F. Ricoeur, *Temps et Récit*, vol. II, *La Configuration dans la récit de Fiction*, ed. du Seuil, Paris, 1984, pp. 42–3.
31 Ibid., p. 48.
32 Beckett, *The Unnameable*.
33 See Jeremy Madden-Simpson, *The No Word Image*, Easons, Dublin, 1987; *Cinema and Semiotics*, Screen Reader 2, London, 1981; and *Godard on Godard*, ed. J. Narboni and T. Milne, Secker and Warburg, London, 1972.
34 F. Fellini, Interview in *La Monde*, Jan. 21, 1986.
35 Ibid.
36 Ibid.
37 Ibid. See also J. Wyver, A. McRobbie and J.-F. Lyotard, 'TV and Postmodernism' in *ICA Documents*, 4, 1986; U.Eco, 'A Guide to the Neo Television of the 80's', *Framework*, 25, 1984; and the articles by L. Grossberg and J. Roberts in *Postmodern Screen*, vol. 28, no. 2, 1987.
38 See the MacBride Report of the UNESCO International Commission for the Study of Communication Problems, established

in 1977 and completed and published in 1980. There is a useful summary and analysis of this report by R. Pine in *The Media and Popular Culture* (*The Crane Bag*, Dublin, vol. 8, No. 2, 1984). Fellini's critique of the multi-national TV culture is primarily directed at the media magnate, Silvio Berlusconi, who not only monopolizes Italian television but also owns France's fifth channel. Indeed when the latter channel was peremptorily launched in February, 1986 (as an undisguised political perk before the March 1986 elections in France), a front page article in *Le Monde* (21 February 1986) talked about the advent of 'A New Age of Television', marking a definitive 'swing into the Civilisation of images and its corollary, the liberty of choice'. The multiplication of televisual options was hailed as a 'change in nature'. Fellini takes a different view.

39 See S. Bellow's contribution to the BBC programme, *Voices* in March 1986 and his lecture on 'the Role of the Writer in Contemporary Culture' given at Trinity College, Dublin, September, 1985.

40 F. Jameson, 'Postmodernism or the Cultural Logic of Late Capitalism', p. 56.

41 Ibid., p. 65.

42 Ibid., p. 66, from G. Debord, *La Société du Spectacle*, ed. Champ Libre, Paris, 1967.

43 Quoted by D. Hounam in his review article on *Paris, Texas, In Dublin*, no. 214, 1984, pp. 10–11.

44 See J. Hillman's vivid and iconoclastic account of this Texan consumerist society in *Interviews*, Harper and Row, 1983, pp. 127–8.

45 See D. Hounan, *Paris, Texas*.

46 *Paris, Texas* (Shooting Script and stills), Road Movies, Berlin, 1984, pp. 45–55.

47 W. Wenders, 'Arrêt sur Image' in *Le Monde*, Paris, April, 27–28, 1986.

48 G. Deleuze, *L'Image-Movement, Cinéma I*, éd. de Minuit, Paris, 1983, p. 278.

49 Ibid., p. 281.

50 This typically postmodern theme of substitutability is humorously exploited by Altman. The people of Nashville love Barbara Jean in exactly the same way as they love Haven Hamilton, Connie White, Bill, Tom, Mary or Jimmy Brown, in exactly the same way as they love screen stars Julie Christie, Elliot Gould (who appear as themselves in the film) or presidential candidates J. F. Kennedy and Hal Philip Walker. Love is thus engulfed in a logic of simulacra:

the persons loved become mirror-images of each other in an endless
fetishistic play. The hovering presidential prophet of a new era,
Hal Philip Walker, is the ultimate representative of the fetishized
replacement: he never actually appears in person but dominates
the film by virtue of his 'image', an image of presence in absence
professionally prefabricated and prerecorded by his election agents
and transmitted to the public through the mass media techniques
of the Nashville entertainment and advertising industry. This absent
fetishized signifier of the President sets a whole series of replacem-
ent-transfers in motion: Tom replaces Mary with Opal with Martha
with Linnea. Mary replaces Bill with Tom with Bill again. Mrs
Hamilton replaces J. F. Kennedy with Bobby Kennedy with Haven
Hamilton. Martha replaces Bud Hamilton with the soldier with the
miracle-working easy rider with another easy rider, Tom. Opal-
from-the-BBC replaces anybody with anybody else who will talk
into her microphone and croon for Britain about the soul of America.
While on the TV screens which serve as a sort of omnipresent
multiple backdrop to the action of the film, a documentary on empty
yellow buses replaces a Catholic service which replaces a Hot Gospel
service which replaces a Baptist service which in turn replaces
a country and western concert. Everything becomes the same as
everything else in this consumerist dreamland of empty imitations
and substitutions. And it is no accident that Barbara Jean's protector-
soldier and assasin-enemy sit beside each other at her concerts
gazing vacantly at her vacant expression. Altman demonstrates how
in the Nashville of consumerist pastiche we no longer know who is
manipulating who. We are left with a circle of endless substitution:
the crowd manipulated by the singers manipulated by the religious
evangelists manipulated by the political evangelists manipulated by
the media manipulated by. . . .

51 Deleuze, *l'Image-Movement, Cinéma I*, p. 283.
52 Ibid., p. 288.
53 Ibid., pp. 284, 290. Deleuze develops this conclusion in his second
    volume, *Cinema 2. L'Image-Temps*, ed. de Minuit, Paris, 1985.
    Here the author explores the notion of an *image-cristal* in certain
    contemporary film-makers such as Herzog, Tarkovsky and Losey
    who use images of 'mirrors' in a reflective-speculative rather than
    merely reflective-mimetic manner. This allows for a certain critical
    function in the film as it *reflects itself from within*. The film within
    the film strategy allows us to confront and reflect upon the actual
    process of film itself – which Deleuze identifies as the link between
    money, cinematic production and temporality. The *image-cristal*

serves as an *image-temps* which discloses an 'abyss of time' (p. 105) where our normal linear perspective is duplicated, inverted, reversed or exploded into a multiplicity of facettes. The *image-cristal* of the film uses 'mirrors' to expose the power of falsehood or fakery (*les puissances du faux*, pp. 165–202). Here cinema abandons the idea of representing an independent object and thereby renders the relationship between the real and the imaginary indiscernable (p. 171). The *image-action* thus becomes an *image-pensante* which confronts us with something that is *unthinkable*: the problematic rapport between the imaginary and the real, subject and object, the eye of the characters, of the camera and of the spectators. Much of postmodern cinema, although Deleuze does not employ the term, might thus be seen as a challenge to represent not the world but the way in which we come to represent and believe in a world: 'Il faut que le cinéma filme, non pas le monde, mais la croyance au monde, en deçá ou au-delá de nos mots' (p. 224). And Deleuze sees this new aesthetic of a 'thinking image' in contemporary cinema as containing within itself an 'ethical' dimension, a critical distance from the natural world so that we may critically commit ourselves to a different way of believing in the world (p. 225). Deleuze cites the work of Godard and Resnais as examples of such a critical 'thinking-image'. By confronting the viewer with i) a logic of visual paradoxes ii) the impossibility of totalizing images and iii) a rupture between the viewer and the world, Godard and Resnais explore the possibilities of a critical cinema which may also be a politically and ethically committed cinema. (See J. Greish's excellent analysis of Deleuze's work on cinema, 'Le Temps Bifurqué. La refiguration du temps par le récit et l'image-temps du cinéma' in *Revue des Sciences Philosophiques et Théologiques*, July, 1986, no. 70, pp. 429–35). Besides the examples already cited, one might also add to Deleuze's inventory of 'thinking-images' the films of Peter Greenaway, and particularly *ZOO* and *Draughtman's Contract*: here film becomes theory, the characteristic obsession with realist symmetry, order, coherence and narrative being continually frustrated by the abitrary functioning of images and signs, and by the doubling and parodying of normal modes of temporal perception. For further analysis of postmodernist trends in cinema see *Deconstructing Difference/ Screen*, vol. 28, no. 1, 1987, and *Postmodern Screen*, vol. 28, no. 2, 1987.

54 W. Benjamin, 'The Work of Art in the Age of Mechanical Reproduction', p. 240.

55 Ibid., p. 244.

56 See the Pompidou Centre's *Fiches de Consultation'* on *Ben* and *Abstraction/Deconstruction.*

57 Quoted by M. Gibson in *Les Horizons du Possible*, pp. 80–1.

58 I. Hassan, *The Dismemberment of Orpheus*, p. 258.

59 W. Benjamin, *Schriften I*, pp. 461, 488–90. Cited F. Jameson, *Marxism and Form*, Princeton U.P., 1971, pp. 73–7. Benjamin sees a connection between the use of allegory in contemporary art and the medieval and baroque art which was equally preoccupied with images of death and absence and decay. Both the medieval and postmodern cultures share a certain sense of impending apocalypse reflected in a preference for allegory over symbol. Umberto Eco takes up this idea in an essay entitled 'The Return of the Middle Ages' in *Faith in Fakes*, Secker and Warburg, London, 1986, pp. 59–86. He argues that while the Middle Ages was dominated by the realization that the Pax Romana which had held Christian Europe together as a single cultural-political empire was beginning to collapse, the postmodern age is dominated by an analogous conviction that the Pax Americana of liberal humanist man is on the threshold of disintegration. Collective insecurity is the key term which binds the two cultures. For just as the medieval world believed itself to be on the verge of collapse as the first millennium expired, our postmodern era is also haunted by apocalyptic fears of the ending of the second millennium: 'The recurrent themes of atomic and ecological catastrophe suffice to indicate vigorous apocalyptic currents' (p. 79).

60 Jameson, 'Postmodernism, or the Cultural Logic of Late Capitalism', p. 60.

61 Hassan, *The Dismemberment of Orpheus*, p. 248.

62 P. Fuller, *Aesthetics after Modernism*, Writers and Readers, London, 1983, p. 40.

63 Eco, *Faith in Fakes*, p. 19. (the translations of this text are my own).

64 Ibid., pp. 20–1.

65 Ibid., p. 46.

66 Quoted S. Schoenbaum in his review of R. Schickel's *The Disney Version*, Pavilion/Michael Joseph, 1986, in *TLS*, July 11, 1986, p. 758.

67 D. Boorstin, *The Image: A Guide to Pseudo-Events in America*, Harper, 1961, p. 258.

68 Ibid., p. 182.

69 M. Kundera, *The Unbearable Lightness of Being*, trans. M. H. Heim, Harper and Row, New York, 1984, p. 249. See also R. Nich-

oll's commentary 'On Kundera's *The Unbearable Lightness of Being*' in *Eidos*, vol. IV, no. I, 1985, pp. 103–19.

70 For further discussion on postmodernism and architecture see K. Frampton, D. Porphyrios and J.-F. Lyotard in *ICA Documents*, 4, 1986.

Conclusion: after imagination?

1 *After Truth: A Post-modern Manifesto*, published by the 2nd of January Group, Inventions Press, London, 1986.

2 The phrase is from the Renaissance humanist, Pico della Mirandola, quoted by K. Soper, *Humanism and Anti-Humanism*, p. 14.

3 E. Levinas, *Totality and Infinity*, Duquesne U.P., Pittsburgh, 1969. See our development of this theme in 'Ethics and the Postmodern Imagination' in *Thought*, Fordham University, New York, 1987. The Czech philosopher Jan Patŏcka also analyses the role of ethics in contemporary mass-media society in 'Les Fondements Spirituels de la vie Contemporaine' in *Etudes Phénoménologiques*, no. 1, 1985, pp. 72, 78–80. We understand the term 'ethics' here in the broad sense of a personal and social responsibility to others. This should not be confused with the more limited sense of 'morality' as a dogmatic system of abstract 'oughts'. It is also important to stress that in the ethical phrase 'here I stand', a 'we' is always implicated in the 'I' and a 'there' in the 'here'. We are not advocating an individualist moralism of sentimental relations: what Levinas rightly dismisses as an *égoisme à deux*. The ethical statement 'I stand' surpasses the epistemological statement 'I think', in that it *includes* the 'other' as its indispensable precondition (whereas the *cogito* does not). In contrast to the *cogito* which excludes all otherness in its primary gesture of self-foundation, the 'I stand' is to be understood in the sense of 'I stand up for and in for the other' – i.e. as an ethical obligation to safeguard the other, even to the point of substituting oneself for the other. Far from affirming the priority of the self over the other, the 'here I stand' actually deposes the pretence of self-sufficiency – acknowledging that my ethical identity as an 'I' derives from the call of the other ('where are you?'). The I does not precede the other – founding itself first and then going on to found the other (as the modern epistemology of the *cogito* and transcendental ego argued). In this light, one might argue that when the deconstructionist asks 'who is this I?' it may well – perhaps unbenownst to itself – serve the ethical purpose of de-centering the epistemological

subject as self-position, thereby opening it to an awareness of its debt and duty to the other-than-self. Here we might recall the original sense of *ethos* as *dis-position*. The face-to-face is a relation of disposition rather than of position. It is not a matter of two self-constituted subjects entering into a rapport of mutual presence. On the contrary, the face-to-face entails an ethical proximity of self to other which undercuts the comfortable notion of a co-presence. It transcends the exclusiveness of I-Thou intimacies. This ethical relation also diffuses our natural tendency to acquire a *total know-ledge* (i.e. as expressed in the traditional categories of presence: *logos, adaequatio, actus purus*, correspondence, representation, position, appropriation, etc.). The face-to-face can never be a complete or closed relation. The face of the other is always irreducible to my relation to it, or my representation of it. It dis-possesses me, decentres me, and by extension, dis-poses me to be an ethical subject-in-process (in Kristeva's sense) – a self always imbricated in a narrative temporality wherein its difference from itself, and the difference between itself and the other as face, is essential. We shall be returning to this point in our discussion of the 'narrative self' in the final section of this conclusion. Suffice it to say here that the face is never seen as such – that is, as a presence to be represented and thus appropriated by me as a knowing-positing-founding subject. The alterity of the face remains irreducible to both the presence-representation dialectic and the subject-object dichotomy of modern epistemology. As such, it institutes an historical ethical imagining wherein the 'I' is always obliged to project beyond its *imagos* of self-identity in the wake of an other who perpetually transcends such *imagos*. It is clear, finally, that this notion of the ethical subject as a dis-position before the face of the other is radically social and political in its implications (see note 55 of this conclusion). For a defence of deconstruction against charges of being anti-ethical, see R. Bernasconi 'Deconstruction and the possibility of Ethics' in *Deconstruction and Philosophy*, ed. J. Sallis, Chicago University Press, 1987, pp. 122–39.

4 This point is made by E. Levinas, for example, in 'Un Dieu Homme?', *Levinas: Exercises de la Patience*, no. 1, Obsidiane, 1980, p. 74; 'the contemporary anti-humanism which denies the primacy of being enjoyed by the person taken as an end in itself has perhaps opened a space for the (ethical) notion of subjectivity as substitution . . . the infinite patience and passion of the self whereby being empties itself of its *own* being'. In *Otherwise than Being or Beyond*

Essence, Nijhoff, The Hague, 1981, Levinas makes a similar point when he states that 'humanism must be denounced only when it is not sufficiently human'. It should also be pointed out that many of the 'anti-humanist' thinkers have acknowledged an ethical motivation to their deconstruction or dismantling of the humanist subject, e.g. Lacan, Foucault, Derrida, Barthes, Lyotard and Nancy. Although their critique of humanism has frequently been interpreted as a renunciation of ethical concern, most of these thinkers have gone to considerable pains to argue that this is not the case. The question remains however as to how a post-humanist ethics is to be justified, if at all. My suggestion in this conclusion is that the work of E. Levinas offers one of the most cogent efforts to establish the indispensability of ethics in a post-humanist culture.

5 The idea of a dialogical imagination has been suggestively explored by the modern Russian critic, Mikhail Bakhtin. Bakhtin champions the prospect of a popular-democratic culture typified by what he calls 'carnivalesque freedom'. 'Carnival is not seen by the people', he writes. 'They *live* in it and *everyone* lives in it, because by its definition it involves all of the people.' To participate in the carnival of democratized culture is to realize that our self-identity is not a given certainty but is always beholden to others. 'Dialogism' is for Bakhtin an ethical aspect of communication where the popular subverts the ruling ideology whose end is exploitation and control. The clown and fools of the carnivalesque imagination use the popular-democratic idioms of laughter and deflation to demystify the rigid status quo. They exult in the multi-faceted nature of discourse – *heteroglossia* – flaunting the uniformity of standardized language. Bakhtin's celebration of the democratizing potential of genuine popular culture is also evident in his claim that the life of imagination is to be found 'outside the artist's study . . . in the open spaces of public squares, streets, cities and villages'. The dialogical imagination is an agent of the poetics of the possible: it nourishes a culture of popular laughter which subjects the dominant ideology to a 'comic operation of dismemberment' and 'delivers the object into the fearless hands of the investigative experiment. . . ' See Bakhtin's *The Dialogical Imagination* (Austin, 1981) and Ken Hirschkop, 'Bakhtin, Discourse and Democracy' in *New Left Review*, no. 160, 1986,

6 E. Levinas, 'Idéologie et Idéalisme' in *De Dieu qui Vient à l'Idée*, Vrin, Paris, 1982, p. 31.

7 C. Lévi-Strauss, *Tristes Tropiques*, Atheneum, New York, 1971. On this theme see our note 42 to chapter 7.

8 S. Freud, *The Interpretation of Dreams*, Penguin, New York, 1976.
9 Heidegger makes much of this example in his analysis of poetry (e.g. *Der Satz vom Grund*, 1957). One might also mention here Keats' notion of 'negative capability' which he defined as an imaginative-poetic readiness to 'experience mystery, uncertainty and doubt without the irritable reaching after fact and reason'.
10 See our hermeneutic analysis of the distinction between ethical transfiguration and disfiguration in *Poétique du Possible*, especially chapters 7–10.
11 Ibid., pp. 174–99.
12 I. Hassan, *The Dismemberment of Orpheus*, p. 258. See also R. Hughes' defence of certain aspects of the modernist heritage against the excesses of postmodernism in *The Shock of the New*, p. 409: 'The signs of that constriction are everywhere today – in the small ambitions of art, in its lack of any effort towards spirituality, in its sense of career rather than vocation, in its frequently bland occupation with semantics at the expense of the deeper passions of the creative self. Perhaps the great energies of modernism are still latent in our culture, like Ulysses' bow in the house of Penelope; but nobody seems able to string and draw it. Yet the work still speaks to us, in all its voices, and will continue to do so. Art discovers its true social use, not on the ideological plane, but by opening the passage from feeling to meaning – not for everyone, since that would be impossible, but for those who want to try. This impulse seems to be immortal. Certainly it has existed from the origins of human society, and despite the appalling commercialization of the art world, its flight into corporate ethics and strategies, and its gradual evacuation of spirit, it exists today.'
13 See, for example, D. Boorstin, *The Image: A Guide to Pseudo-Events in America*, and A. Touraine, *The Post-Industrial Society*, Random House, New York, 1971, especially the chapter entitled 'Tomorrow's Social History; Classes, Conflicts and Culture in the Programmed Society'.
14 Boorstin, *The Image*, p. 194.
15 Ibid., p. 206.
16 H. Marcuse, 1966 Preface to *Eros and Civilization*, Beacon Press, Boston, 1966.
17 Marcuse, *One Dimensional Man: Studies in the Ideology of Advanced Industrial Society*, Beacon Press, Boston, 1964, p. XVI.
18 Ibid., p. XVI

19 F. Jameson, 'Postmodernism or the Cultural Logic of Late Capitalism', p. 53.

20 Ibid., p. 54.

21 Ibid., p. 55.

22 Ibid., p. 56.

23 Robert Hughes, 'Andy Warhol: 1928–1987', in *Time Magazine*, March 9, 1987, p. 90.

24 R. Hughes, *The Shock of the New*, p. 384. Hughes elaborates on some of the reasons for this commercialization of art in our contemporary consumerist culture, pp. 390–2: 'The American tax laws, in their benevolence towards the visual arts, have created the largest and most powerful institutional-framework that living art has ever enjoyed within its own culture . . . and so destroyed the *outsider* status of what used to be the vanguard. . . . Art would conquer the provincialism of America, smooth its frontier brutality, refine its shellback materialism, and take the raw edges off new capital. The idea of social improvement through art struck a responsive chord in the American rich, who proceeded to pour millions upon millions of dollars into the construction and endowment of museums and the getting of collections that would eventually fill them. . . . In so doing they set in motion a formidable system of cultural patronage. . . . Until then, the words "museum" and "modern art" had seemed, to most people, incompatible. "Museums are just a lot of lies". Picasso had said. "Work for life", Rodchenko exhorted his Constructivist comrades, "and not for palaces, temples, cemeteries and museums!". . . . From now on, modernism would tend to seem noble and exemplary rather than tense and problematic. The *avant-garde* no longer needed to fight the Academy; it was the Academy.'

25 J-F. Lyotard, *The Postmodern Condition: A Report on Knowledge*, Manchester U.P., 1979, p. 76.

26 Ibid., p. 82.

27 Ibid., p. 81. See also Lyotard, 'Presenting the Unpresentable: The Sublime' in *Artform*, no. 20, 1982, pp. 64–9. One might also note here the interest in the 'sublime' shown by other deconstructionist thinkers, e.g. Derrida in 'Economimesis', and J-L. Nancy, 'L'Affront Sublime' in *Poétique* nos. 30–34, 1984–85. On Foucault's interest in the sublime see J. Rajchman, *Michel Foucault*, pp. 17–22.

28 R. Hughes, *The Shock of the New*, p. 398.

29 F. Jameson, 'Postmodernism', p. 58. For a more positive interpretation of the social and economic implications of postmodern culture

see *Postmodernism and Politics*, ed. J. Arac, Manchester, U.P., 1956.

30 Ibid., p. 77.

31 Ibid., p. 79.

32 Marcuse, *The Aesthetic Dimension*, Beacon Press, Boston, 1978.

33 U. Eco, 'Towards a Semiological Guerilla Warfare' in *Faith in Fakes*, p. 136.

34 Ibid., p. 141.

35 Ibid., p. 144.

36 Jameson, 'Postmodernism', p. 85.

37 Ibid., p. 85.

38 Ibid., p. 86.

39 Ibid., p. 87.

40 Ibid., p. 87. See also R. Hughes, *The Shock of the New*, p. 394: 'The work of art no longer had a silence in which its resources could develop. It had to bear the stress of immediate consumption'.

41 Jameson, 'Postmodernism', p. 88.

42 Ibid., p. 92.

43 Ibid., p. 90.

44 See D. Latimer's critique of Jameson's position in 'Jameson and Postmodernism' in *New Left Review*, no. 148, 1984, p. 127. Michel Foucault explicitly acknowledged this problem in his later writings and began to explore the possibility of a new 'ethic of subjectivity' in our postmodern age. See J. Rajchman, *Michel Foucault*, pp. 36–8. Lacan was also preoccupied with the role of 'ethics' in psychoanalysis in *Le Séminaire VII, L'Ethique de la Psychanalyse* ed. du Seuil, Paris, 1986.

45 See our analysis of these commentaries in *Poétique du Possible*, pp. 267–72.

46 See in particular the Platonic references to ecstatic images and holy madness in *The Timaeus* and *The Phaedrus*, eexamined in the third section of our second chapter. Perhaps it is with a similar scruple in mind that Umberto Eco sets out in *The Name of the Rose* to rediscover the spirit of the hypothetically lost book of Aristotle's *Poetics*, that is, the book of laughter, the *comedy* without which the *tragedy* remains incomplete. The poetical imagination is mindful that the emblem of drama has two faces, gaiety and anguish.

47 D. Latimer, 'Jameson and Postmodernism', p. 121.

48 T. Eagleton, 'Capitalism, Modernism and Postmodernism' in *New Left Review*, no. 152, 1985, p. 70.

49 See our outline of a philosophy of figuration in *Poétique du Possible*.

50 P. Ricoeur, 'Hermeneutics and the Critique of Ideology' in *Hermeneutics and the Human Sciences*, Cambridge U.P., 1981, p. 100. Ricoeur adds: 'I would even say that it plunges into the most impressive tradition, that of liberating acts, of the Exodus and the Resurrection. Perhaps there would be no more interest in emancipation, no more anticipation of freedom, if the Exodus and Resurrection were effaced from the memory of mankind. . . .'

51 Marcuse, *The Aesthetic Dimension*, p. 73. The phrase from Horkheimer and Adorno is taken from their *Dialectic of Enlightenment*, Herder, New York, 1972, p. 230.

52 Charles Jencks makes this point in relation to postmodern architecture in *The Language of Post-Modern Architecture*, Academy Editions, London, 1977, p. 7.

53 See Eagleton, 'Capitalism, Modernism and Postmodernism', p. 71. He would seem to have Deleuze, Guattari and Barthes especially in mind. Eagleton outlines the following critique of the postmodernist rejection of an ethical or political subject, p. 70:

> For postmodernism there cannot be a rational discourse of ethical or political value, for values are not the kind of thing which can be in the world in the first place. . . . The dispersed, schizoid subject is nothing to be alarmed about after all: nothing could be more normative in late-capitalist experience. . . . There is really nothing left to struggle against, other than those inherited illusions (law, ethics, class struggle, the oedipus complex) which prevent us from seeing things as they are. . . . Postmodernism commits the apocalyptic error of believing that the discrediting of a particular representational epistemology is the death of truth itself, just as it sometimes mistakes the disintegration of certain traditional ideologies of the subject for the subject's final disappearance.

54 P. Ricoeur, *Temps et Récit III: Le Temps Raconté*, éd. du Seuil, Paris, 1985. Our exposition of narrative identity is indebted to Ricoeur's illuminating discussion of this theme, pp. 354-7.

55 The political implications of our project for a postmodern imagination are important. As we noted in our discussion of the ethical imagination above, the postmodern project requires a new relationship between theory and praxis. And this means that an 'imagining otherwise' entails, at the socio-political level, an 'acting otherwise'. It would be a mistake therefore to assume that the emphasis in our conclusion on the ethical/poetical dimensions of the postmodern imagination represents an eclipse of the political. On the contrary, the postmodern project we are advocating, marks a radical challenge to the conventional models of political power as 'sovereignty' – i.e.

centralized nation-states and geo-political blocks. A postmodern politics, compatible with the ethical-poetical imagination we are proposing, would be one of radical decentralization – one which fosters difference, plurality and otherness. It would resist what critics like Foucault, Lyotard and Kristeva denounce as the 'totalizing' tendency of political power. This would involve a movement from the centre to the periphery – or indeed a dismantling of this very dichotomy – a movement beyond the hegemonic nationalisms of 'nation-states' and the multi-nationalisms of military-industrial alliances, towards a *regional pluralism* in all societies. Such a postmodern movement, as the later Foucault realized, may well begin with particular commitments to 'local struggles', e.g. unemployment, anti-nuclear protest, environmental and energy campaigns, minority and women's rights, anti-discrimination protests, economic decentralization programmes and so on. Renouncing the temptation to propagate a New Universal Theory to resolve the global crisis of contemporary society, a postmodern politics would seek to pluralize and differentiate the activity of resistance. In this sense it would seek to distance itself from the 'ethnocentrism' of most modern ideologies of change emanating from the West. The king's head needs to be cut off in political theory, as Foucault remarks (*Power/ Knowledge*, Pantheon, New York, 1980, p. 121). The challenge is to go beyond the fetish of power as centralizing sovereignty, and its attendant notion of 'global theory', in favour of a 'local' struggle and criticism. This in turn entails an 'insurrection of subjugated knowledges' disqualified from the hierarchy of the established scientific knowledges. Such localization and differentiation of criticism should not, argues Foucault, be taken to mean that its qualities are those of an 'obtuse, naive or primitive empiricism', nor a 'soggy eclecticism' that opportunistically laps up any and every kind of theoretical approach; nor does it mean a 'self-imposed asceticism' that would degenerate into the worst kind of theoretical impoverishment. What the local character of criticism implies is, rather, a 'non-centralized kind of theoretical production . . . whose validity is not dependent on the approval of the established regimes of thought' (*ibid.* p. 81). This in turn requires that the postmodern intellectual ceases to view him/herself as a 'master of truth', as a *salvator mundi* who will redeem the world by fiat, by an act of inspired genius or will. Postmodern politics requires 'specific' rather than 'global' intellectuals. As Foucault puts it, 'A new mode of the connection between theory and practice has been established. Intellectuals have got used to working, not in the modality of the "universal" and the "exemplary" . . . but within specific sectors, at the precise points where their own conditions of life or work situate them (housing, the hospital, the asylum, the laboratory, the university, family and sexual relations). This has undoubtedly given them a much more immediate and concrete awareness of struggles. They have met here with problems which are specific. . .' (*ibid.* p. 126). And one might add to this list the equally 'specific' problems of apartheid, famine, third-world struggles, etc., which, while not necessarily being immediately part of our lived environment, are nontheless made part of our imaginative environment by means of communications technology and media. All this points towards an alternative kind of political theory and praxis – regional, differential, committed to concrete circumstances. We are not, of course, endorsing some kind of spontaneous or adhoc anarchism. The notion of 'regional struggles' is always predicated upon an 'historical knowledge of struggles', a genealogy which brings together the specialized areas of erudition with the disqualified areas of popular knowledge. As Foucault notes: 'What emerges out of this is something one might call a genealogy, or rather a multiplicity of genealogical researches, a painstaking rediscovery of struggles together with the rude memory of their conflicts. And these genealogies . . . could not even have been attempted except on one condition, namely that the tyranny of globalizing discourses with their hierarchy and all their privileges of a theoretical avant-garde was eliminated. Let us give the term *genealogy* to the union of erudite knowledge and local memories which allows us to establish a historical knowledge of struggles and to make use of this knowledge tactically today.' And what this requires is that we attend to discontinuous, localized and often illegitimized knowledges and practices 'against the claims of a unitary body of theory which would filter, hierarchise and order them in the name of . . . some arbitrary idea of what constitutes a science' (*ibid.* p. 83). The project of localized resistance and praxis has been developed by a number of postmodern theorists. Lyotard, in his debates with Habermas and in his correspondences in *Le Postmoderne* (Gallillee, 1987), defends postmodernism against the charge of neo-conservative nihilism and argues for the political recognition that 'Grand Theory' has had its day and that we now all belong to minorities of resistance. This point is also addressed by Hal Foster in his introduction to *Postmodern Culture* (Pluto, 1985): here he distinguishes between radical and conservative postmodernism, promoting the former as a 'critique which destructures the order of representations in order to reinscribe them'. This he describes as a 'postmodernism of resistance' which arises as a 'counter-practice not only to the official culture of modernism but also to the "false normativity" of a reactionary postmodernism . . . it seeks to question rather than exploit cultural codes, to explore rather than conceal social and political affiliations' (*ibid.* p. xii). A postmodern politics of differential/local struggle has also received much input from recent developments in Continental feminism – in particular the post-structuralist thinking of Julia Kristeva, Helène Cixious and Luce Iragaray, which champions the feminine as an historical subject-in-process, as a differentiation and dissemination of desire for other-ness. A new generation of critical commentators has emerged in recent times in support of a postmodern politics of decentralized practice and revolt. We might mention here the work of Gregory Ulmer whose *Applied Grammatology* (Johns Hopkins U.P., 1985) argues for a 'postmodernized pedagogy' in our era of communications technology; Thomas Docherty who campaigns for a 'chrono-political criticism . . . able to forge a future through the interpretative parodying of historical narrative' (*After Theory*, Blackwells, 1988); Jonathan Arac who provides a discriminating overview of the debate in *Postmodernism and Politics* (Manchester U.P., 1986); and David Tracy who outlines a 'postmodern hermeneutic of resistance and hope' in *Plurality and Ambiguity* (Harper and Row, 1987). One might also mention here our own modest attempts to adumbrate and apply such a postmodern hermeneutic in an effort to retrieve 'subjugated knowledges' by brushing the official readings of Irish colonial history against the grain – e.g. *Transitions: Narratives in Modern Irish Culture* (Wolfhound/Manchester U.P., 1987); *The Irish Mind: Exploring Intellectual Traditions* (Wolfhound/Humanities Press, 1984); *The Crane Bag Book of Irish Studies* (vols 1 and 2, Wolfhound Press, 1982/1987); 'Myth and Motherland' in *Ireland's Field Day* (Hutchinson, 1985); and 'Postmodern Ireland' in *The Clash of Ideas* (Gill and McMillan, 1988).

In summary we might say that a postmodern politics of local resistance would be (1) *post-centrist* (a regionalized mode of praxis informed by the decentralizing and pluralizing potential of the new communications technology and transcending the rigid frontiers of nation-states and geo-political blocks); (2) *post-patriarchal* (a femi-nist-allied praxis attentive to the hitherto suppressed dimensions of alterity, difference, marginality); (3) *post-egological* (a communalist praxis surpassing the confines of narcissistic individualism and its extension as *egoismes à deux*); (4) *post-logocentric* (a practice of 'double-coding' which enables us to have 'two thinks at a time', in Joyce's phrase – that is, to enter into dialogue with what is different and other, to welcome the difference (*dia-legein*) by exploding the fetish of a totalitarian Grand Theory and by opening ourselves to history as a 'bringer of plurabilities').

Names Index